HENRY BRANDON:
KING OF THE BOGEYMEN

The Vicious Villain of Vintage Cinema

By Bill Cassara & Richard S. Greene

Henry Brandon: King of the Bogeymen
© 2018. Bill Cassara & Richard S. Greene. All rights reserved.

All illustrations are copyright of their respective owners, and are also reproduced here in the spirit of publicity. Whilst we have made every effort to acknowledge specific credits whenever possible, we apologize for any omissions, and will undertake every effort to make any appropriate changes in future editions of this book if necessary.

No part of this book may be reproduced in any form or by any means, electronic, mechanical, digital, photocopying or recording, except for the inclusion in a review, without permission in writing from the publisher.

Published in the USA by:
BearManor Media
P O Box 71426
Albany, Georgia 31708
www.bearmanormedia.com

Printed in the United States of America
ISBN   978-1-62933-335-9 (paperback)

Book design and layout by Darlene Swanson • www.van-garde.com

Contents

	Acknowledgements xi
	Foreword by Stan Taffel xiii
Introduction	The Actor of a Hundred Personas xvii
Chapter 1:	House Lights Down/Curtain Up 1
Chapter 2:	An Actor's Life for Me - *The Drunkard*. 7
Chapter 3:	Three Iconic Roles: *Babes in Toyland* 21
Chapter 4:	Three Iconic Roles: *Drums of Fu Manchu* 45
Chapter 5:	Three Iconic Roles: *The Searchers*. 63
Chapter 6:	*Edge of Darkness* 73
Chapter 7:	Short Subjects & Other Appearances – *Our Gang Follies of 1938, Carnival in Paris, Ghost Treasure, Peter Pan,* Old Time Radio shows 85
Chapter 8:	Comedies – *Big Brown Eyes, Half a Sinner, The Paleface, Harem Girl, Scared Stiff, The Caddy, Knock on Wood, Casanova's Big Night* 101
Chapter 9:	Serials – *Jungle Jim, Secret Agent X-9, Buck Rogers* 119

Chapter 10:   Westerns – *Wells Fargo, Marshall of Mesa City, Ranger and the Lady, Bad Man of Deadwood, Under Texas Skies, Hurricane Smith (1941), Old Los Angeles, Cattle Drive, Wagons West, Pony Express, War Arrow, Comanche, Hell's Crossroads, Two Rode Together, Mission to Glory: A True Story*. 143

Chapter 11:   A Pictures – *Trail of the Lonesome Pine, Garden of Allah, Conquest, I Met My Love Again, Three Comrades, Last Train From Madrid, Spawn of the North, Beau Geste, Nurse Edith Cavell, Shepard of the Hills, Northwest Outpost, Joan of Arc, The Fighting O'Flynn, Vera Cruz, Bandido!, Ten Commandments, Life, Loves and Adventures of Omar Khayyam, The Buccaneer, Auntie Mame, The Big Fisherman* 181

Chapter 12:   B Pictures – *The Preview Murder Mystery, Killer At Large, Black Legion, I Promise To Pay, Island Captives, West Bound Limited, The Last Warning, Pirates of the Skies, Conspiracy, Ski Patrol, Doomed to Die, Dark Streets of Cairo, Son of Monte Cristo, Underground, Two in a Taxi, Night in New Orleans, Canon City, Hollow Triumph, Scarlet Angel* 215

Chapter 13:   Sci-Fi, Jungle Thrillers, Swashbucklers & Other Potboilers – *The Corsican Brothers, Wake of the Red Witch, Tarzan's Magic Fountain, Tarzan and the She Devil, Golden Horde, Flame of Araby/Lady Godiva of Coventry, Hurricane Smith (1952), War of the Worlds, Land Unknown, Raiders of the Seven Seas, Captain Sindbad*. 251

Chapter 14:   Z Pictures – *Okefenokee, Search for the Evil One, Gentle Savage, Manhandlers, Assault on Precinct 13, Hollywood Knight/Hard Knocks, Wizards of the Lost Kingdom II*. 281

Chapter 15:   When the North Wind Blows. 301

Chapter 16:	Television – Covers nearly sixty of Henry Brandon's small screen roles	311
Chapter 17:	Film Fandom/Sons of the Desert	387
Chapter 18:	Final Curtain	423
Chapter 19:	Epilogue: Evelyn Brandon and Henry Richard Brandon	449
Chapter 20:	Stage Synopsis/Theater Credits—Covers nearly ninety acting roles	451
	Bibliography	475

Appendices:

1. The Films of Henry Brandon 478
2. Author's Selection of Top 12 Henry Brandon Film Roles 493
3. Television Appearances of Henry Brandon 503

Signed "A memento from the dear dead days beyond recall." Collection of Richard Finegan.

"A movie star? No, I am an actor"

~ Henry Brandon

This book is dedicated to my wife Michelle, my belle

Bill Cassara:

For Patty

Rick Greene:

Acknowledgements

THE AUTHORS WISH TO thank the many people who helped this project become a reality; none more so than Native American Lisa "Little Wolf" Ballantyne, who dreamed an encounter with Henry Brandon that inspired her to organize the Facebook page "For the Love of Henry." Not stopping at that, she encouraged a testimonial in book form to celebrate the man. She was able to inspire and rekindle a long dormant energy for the authors to pursue this project. Along the way new discoveries were made identifying Henry's many film and television roles, and especially theater performances. Much of this information would not be available even a few years ago; and if it were not captured, like lightning in a bottle, it would never have been picked up in this form in the future.

There were many film buffs, friends of Henry and members of the "Sons of the Desert" who generously offered artifacts, recollections, film and photos of Henry. Special recognition goes to Paul E. Gierucki who does such a wonderful job at film preservation, he took time out from his many commitments to find and send on old videotapes of Sons' conventions past that featured Henry. Much appreciation also goes to author Irv Hyatt, who was right there at the beginning to encourage us and make available his treasures. We are especially grateful to the incomparable Rich Finegan who unselfishly contributed many photos (with revealing anecdotes from Henry) and trade paper write-ups that help make this book complete.

Special thanks go to: Jeff Abraham, Richard W. Bann, Jerry Beck, Elliot

Becker, Carla Bollinger, Aureo Branao, Rick Brandon, Jack Bridges, Michael Buckhoff, Frank Cali, Bill Cappello, John Carpenter, Walter Chacon, "Cliff-in-the-Balcony," Gary Cohen, John Duff, Becky Kane, Rob Falcone, John Field, Richard Finegan, Paul E. Gierucki, G.D. Hamann, Dave Lord Heath, Gloria C. Mattos Hughes, Irv Hyatt, Del Kempster, Katharine Lhota, Bill & Denise Major, Leonard Maltin, Bill Mandel, Marcus Maier, Dean McKeown, Gary McNerney, Kevin Mulligan, Ben Ohmart, Marcia Opal, Kit Parker, Brian Pinkerton, Jack Roth, Lou Sabini, Bob Saland, Gali Sanchez, Nick Santa Maria, Bob Satterfield, Randy Skredtvedt, Eric Shultz, Christopher Snowden, John Soister, Patrick Springer, Eric Stedman, Stan Taffel, Tracy Tolzmann, Ron Turk, The Walt Disney Studios, Ed Watz, David Webb, James Wiley II and Triston Yonce who all helped and encouraged this project.

Recognition also goes to the esteemed Edward (Ned) Comstock of the Doheny Library of the University of Southern California for making available the payroll records of the Hal Roach Studios and Pressbook Collections.

A big "tip-o-the derby" to author Craig Calman, whose influence is felt throughout these pages via his keen editorial eye. Craig is the author of *100 Years of Brodies with Hal Roach* (also published by BearManor Media).

The authors wish to single out our respective wives: Michelle Benton Cassara and Patty Greene who allowed us to dedicate our time and efforts to this wonderful project, they are highly supportive. A special tip of the hat goes to Rick Brandon, the son of Henry who provided some of his personal family photographs with insights.

Last but not least, the authors wish to express our sincere gratitude to our friend and scholar, Stan Taffel for writing the foreword to this book. Mr. Taffel is a renowned film collector, archivist and esteemed President of the Cinecon Motion Picture Festival of Los Angeles. Stan continues his involvement as Grand Sheik of the Hollywood Party Tent.

Foreword

*"…And from now on, you and I are
going to be very close friends"*

THOSE WERE MY PARTING words to Henry Brandon, the man who originally delivered them in his portrayal of the evil antagonist, Silas Barnaby from the now iconic motion picture classic, *Babes in Toyland*. This occurred after an entertaining dinner at a New York City restaurant in January of 1990. My interpretation of this short piece of dialogue poked innocent fun of the moment in the Hal Roach-produced film just after charges against Stan Laurel and Oliver Hardy have been dropped and Barnaby offers an olive branch to the would-be wrongdoers. He chuckled and I thought to myself, "I made Henry Brandon laugh."

By the time of our get together, I had long been schooled in his extraordinary, decades-long career that, in addition to motion pictures, encompassed theater, radio and television. The plight of a "working" actor is very different than one might expect. Often more than not, an actor doesn't know where or when his next job is going to happen, if at all. Henry knew this and was more than prepared for his life's journey that led from part to part in every medium for a period that lasted over *seven* decades and garnered some 200 big and small screen credits.

A gift for dialect, an expressive face and physical agility, Henry Brandon rose to every challenge he faced and gave us some of the most brilliantly portrayed character-actor performances of the 20th century. While he may not have been an "over the title" film star, his support of some of the heavyweights in the industry made every film he appeared in all the better for it.

How different John Wayne's performance might have been had Henry not been there, cast as the tribal leader, Scar, who snatched Natalie Wood away and massacred her family in *The Searchers*. As Fu Manchu, his diabolical tactics kept audiences coming back week after week to their neighborhood theaters for each exciting serial chapter.

Throughout his long career, many of his screen appearances often went uncredited. From Laurel and Hardy to Mel Brooks, for Henry it was about the work and everyone wanted to work with him. Whether the part had lines or not, he could play *anything* from an Indian to a General, from a Doctor to a Henchman. There was no challenge too great and no part too small.

He relished in reminiscing. At the dinner we attended, he spoke about the people he worked with and the parts he enjoyed most. As a young actor, his advice to me was sage and informative. "Audition and *keep* auditioning," he told me. "Treat each audition like a part and give it *more* than all that you've got."

He happily posed for a photo which is a treasured possession of mine. Unlike any other photo I've taken with a celebrity, instead of looking at the camera, Henry put his arm on my shoulder and looked at me as if he was glad to have shared his professional experiences with a newer member of the acting fraternity. In effect, he took the role of "supporting player" in that photograph, making me the star. Extraordinary!

When we said our farewells, it was hopeful that we would meet again and have more time to share stories about his career. Alas, it was not to be. Three weeks, later, Henry passed away. The actor I feared as a small child when he tormented the village of Toyland and later grew to revere as one of the truly gifted performers in the profession, now brought me to tears. No more tales about his life and times, never to hear about his beginnings in Berlin, coming to Hollywood and working through the decades. There was more to this story, more yet to be told. I thought that this amazing life would evaporate into the atmosphere.

That is, until now.

Bill Cassara and Rick Greene have given us the full, untold Brandon story, filing in the gaps that a hundred dinners could never have accomplished. Through these pages, Henry Brandon the man and artist *returns* to add dimension and substance. Bill and Rick now provide a tremendous gift to Henry's fans and to the entertainment industry. It is in these precious pages that we can begin to understand the true versatile measure of this man; a gentle fellow who commanded a strong presence in unparalleled performances. The most incredible life of a professional and respected thespian who, in his later years experienced the respect and love of grateful fans that appreciated all he gave to them through his craft.

And now I can thankfully complete that unfulfilled hope and have that 'one more dinner' with him in these pages. Like Claude Rains, Walter Brennan and William Demarest and all the legendary character players of long ago, may this work put Henry Brandon properly in his rightful place as one of the best and most versatile actors that ever labored before a camera.

And may you get to know Henry so well through this book that by the final paragraph, you too will feel that from now on, you and he are going to be *very* close friends.

Stan Taffel
Los Angeles, California

Babes in Toyland dual portrait. Collection of Richard W. Bann

INTRODUCTION
"The Actor of a Hundred Personas"

WHY A BOOK ABOUT Henry Brandon?

King of The Bogeymen is not a "films of Henry Brandon" tome nor is it a traditional biography. While it weaves elements of both of those film-book methods to tell the Brandon story, the authors take a decidedly more personal approach to capturing his career between these pages.

For one thing, both Bill Cassara and Rick Greene were friends of Henry Brandon. Great friends with robust relationships over a ten-year period in which our paths intersected again and again, thanks to dozens of events of The Sons of the Desert, the international Laurel & Hardy organization. Both of us were privileged to develop personal friendships with Henry that resulted in a closeness that can be likened to that of family. We traveled domestically and internationally together, visited Henry's Hollywood home, attended countless meetings, banquets and conventions, exchanged holiday cards and took the stage together. Both Bill and Rick considered Henry to be a dear, treasured friend… and the feelings were reciprocated.

That makes *Henry Brandon King of the Bogeymen* something far more intimate than *The Films of Henry Brandon*. This is, at its core, an affectionate tribute to the man we loved to hate, a detailed look at an incredible life and long career. It has been an honor to write his story and a revelation as we've watched his performances and come to some extraordinary conclusions about the depth and variety of his considerable talents.

While Henry is best remembered as a vicious villain of vintage cinema and television, thanks to his stage training and prodigious acting chops, he could play just about anything. Over his five decade career, he appeared in over one hundred motion pictures, one hundred television programs and dozens of stage productions. While we can only imagine what his early theatrical performances were like, the evidence on film and kinescope remains to paint the portrait of a cinematic chameleon.

His theater training came in very handy but Henry Brandon quickly realized that acting on film was quite different than acting in front of an audience on the stage. While Henry could – and often did – play his roles "over the top" (especially later in his career) he more often underplayed for the camera. This allowed him to display subtle character touches in both motion pictures and on television that made him fascinating to watch. These touches were not just to draw attention to his characterization, but they were often in service *to* that characterization. There are examples of this throughout the book. One might call them "scene stealing" touches. And one might be correct!

When we compare and contrast the acting styles of Henry Brandon with that of his villainous contemporaries like George Zucco, Lionel Atwill, Henry Daniell and Peter Lorre, a fascinating portrait emerges. As readers of this book are about to discover, Henry Brandon may not be *The Man of A Thousand Faces*, but he was most certainly *The Actor of A Hundred Personas*. He played young and old, brilliant and dull, wealthy and destitute, leaders and followers. Henry could assume the characteristics of any race as he portrayed Caucasian and men of color, American, British, German, Russian, Asian, Hispanic, Arab and Polish. Brandon was cowboy and Indian, hero and villain, hillbilly and pirate. He could disappear into any kind of man from any age and any strata of society.

Though Henry played Native Americans and just about every ethnic character, he knew that actors of color deserved those chances. He championed ethnic actors to portray their own race as you will read in these pages.

Henry was not a product of the "studio system," he was never signed to a long term contract and groomed for future greatness in the "star" tradition of Hollywood. Henry was a free-lancer, (a "free-agent" in modern vernacular). He built up his reputation as a versatile, dependable actor with a chameleon-like cloak. He was an actor "at will" which enabled him to conquer film, stage and the medium of television in a career that spanned over fifty-five years.

We believe Brandon's acting talent enabled him to craft a multitude of screen personas and is the key reason he isn't as well-remembered as his "bad guy" contemporaries. For Henry, it was the part, always the part, never the player.

1986 Sons of the Desert Convention *Babes in Toyland* sketch. L-R Tony Hawes, Henry, Joe Rooney, Tracy Tolzmann. Photo by Marcia Opal.

CHAPTER ONE
House Lights Down/Curtain Up

'TWAS OF A GLORIOUS Tuesday evening on that July 29, 1986, where four hundred members of the Sons of the Desert were enjoying the final night of celebration at the Laurel and Hardy bi-annual convention in Valley Forge, Pennsylvania. It was the fifth international conclave and the host, "Tent" (Philadelphia's Two-Tars) was putting on one heck of a show.

The Sons of the Desert is an international society whose mission is to celebrate the lives, careers and films of Stan Laurel (1890-1965) and Oliver Hardy (1892-1957). Unfortunately Stan and Ollie had long since passed on, but there were still dignitaries present as special guests who were revered by the members. Dr. John McCabe, the founder and "Exhausted Ruler" of the loosely structured organization, was present, as was Stan's daughter, Lois Laurel Hawes. Other notables who worked for the Hal Roach Studios included: Dorothy "Little Echo" DeBorba, Thomas Benton Roberts, Virginia Karns, Felix Knight, and the subject of this book, Henry Brandon, who created the role of "Barnaby" in the Laurel & Hardy holiday classic, *Babes in Toyland*.*

There were already four days of mirth and merriment, but the build-up and climax for the members at large culminated with the last scheduled event: A *Babes in Toyland* themed costume banquet at the Sheraton Valley Forge Hotel. To augment the decorations, Grand Sheik Roger Gordon and

---

* Oftentimes referred to as the re-released title, *March of the Wooden Soldiers*

his committee had built a remarkable set reconstructing the film version of the famous children's story. There were balloons of all colors of the rainbow, and a town square that featured a giant shoe that the storybook little old woman lived in. A police station, candy-cane props, cops, soldiers, and dozens of kids dressed in period costumes. The multicolored lights and music added to the ambience of a festive fair.

The Sons were the audience *and* the participants, and they all came dressed in costumes, which added to the authenticity of "Mother Goose Land." There was the town crier in old English garb, a butcher, baker, and candlestick maker, Simple Simon and the pie man, Little Jack Horner, a coachman, a cobbler, Jack and Jill, the quite contrary Mary, Peter Piper, the Three Little Pigs and even Little Bo Peep. There were also giant alphabet blocks; one spelling out "Toyland" and another set spelling out "RAT" in reference to the Barnaby character in Laurel & Hardy's version.

Preceding the festivities was a cocktail reception: "Barnaby's Mixer at the Well." All was swell when the man of the hour, Henry Brandon, made his entrance dressed and made up as "Barnaby," exactly fifty two years after the original filming of *Babes*, (as it was often affectionately referred to). Henry came to life revisiting his film portrayal as Silas Barnaby, he was a living legend and most Sons were simply in awe of him. For this party, he remained in character as he talked and posed for pictures with the appreciative aficionados, insulting and harassing them, trying to get his mortgage money from *anyone!*

The entertainment for the night included the soundtrack of the film, *Babes in Toyland,* with familiar music selections from the Victor Herbert/ Glen MacDonough operetta. It was topped by a real marching band that was all decked out and playing Laurel and Hardy's theme, *The Cuckoo Song*.

What the Sons didn't know was that earlier in the day there was a last-minute rehearsal to put together a skit as a surprise to the conventioneers. The idea was to stage a reenactment of "The Wedding Scene" from the film in which Stannie Dum and Ollie Dee *fake* Bo Peep's marriage to Barnaby. In the scene, Stannie is wearing a wedding dress and veil in place of Bo Peep to trick

Barnaby. After they are pronounced husband and wife, Ollie says, "and now you can kiss the bride." Ollie pulls back the veil to reveal it was Stannie instead of Bo Peep. Barnaby is fooled by the scheme and storms off; Ollie breaks the news that Stannie is now married to Barnaby, Stan's character breaks out into the most hilarious "cry" of his career. It came in stages: disbelief, a sorrowful plea, and then he notices the ring on his finger and was too much to bear. Poor Stannie burst out in despair and tears flowed down his cheeks.

Barnaby reborn in 1986. Photo by Marcia Opal.

For the convention, Henry Brandon cooked up this surprise to reenact the wedding scene. It was a tall order it seemed; there was Henry directing the action, Tony Hawes (Stan Laurel's son-in-law) would deliver the lines as the minister. Tracy Tolzmann, the Grand Sheik of the Blockheads Tent (and a dead ringer for the "Ollie" character) was handpicked for his role. His voice and mannerisms perfectly imitated suited Oliver Dee.

There was some tension beforehand that there wasn't a conventioneer among the crowd who could possibly impersonate Stan Laurel in this bit. A reasonable facsimile – *Two Tars* member Joe Rooney - was recruited although he was the only member of the quartet with no real theatrical experience.

For the reenactment to work, Joe in the scene recreation had to at least create the illusion he was Stannie Dum of Toyland. This was, after all, a discerning audience of Laurel and Hardy buffs who knew the film's every nuance. It was also the movie that kicked off Henry Brandon's cinema career and one in which he had very personal feelings about. After a few run-throughs, Stannie's wailings were not convincing enough. In director mode, Henry *motivated* the amateur actor by telling him, "Listen, you'll have to *sleep* with that old son-of-a-bitch, **now cry!**"

The banquet was in progress and the house lights were turned low. A light was focused on a male figure to start off the festivities; it was Felix Knight, who played Tom-Tom in the original film. He sang accompanied by a simple piano, sounding great, if a bit nervous. He was soon joined by a surprise guest; it was Virginia Karns who played Mother Goose in the same film, harmonizing as if they'd rehearsed for weeks – which they hadn't. It was later disclosed by Henry Brandon that Felix hadn't sang in public for fifteen years. The song drove many conventioneers to hushed tones and weeping of nostalgia. Member Becky Kane recalled, "I don't think there was a dry eye in the house when Virginia Karnes spontaneously got up from her table, walked over to Felix at the microphone and finished the song with him – hitting that high note as if it were a breeze!"

The main program featured children from a local theater troupe miming the story of *Babes in Toyland* to clips from the original soundtrack. Then it was time for the capper, the "Wedding Scene" reenactment that no one knew was going to take place. The players took their places under a frame of giant wooden blocks as they spoke their lines; it was enchanting to hear Henry Brandon's distinct voice as Barnaby.

There was some unexpected improvisation when Henry's Barnaby went off script as he was trying to slide the wedding ring onto Stannie's finger. He faced the crowd in mock astonishment and said, "What a fat, *hairy* finger it is, perhaps from milking sheep!" With that, the veil was removed and Ollie's line was; "and now, to kiss the bride" (revealing Stannie's smiling face). The boys laughed at their cleverness at outwitting old Barnaby. They chimed in; "Big bait catches big rat!" Barnaby stormed off as in the movie by saying, "The king shall hear of this" (to a massive round of applause).

The final moments were wrapping up, as Ollie divulged that Stannie would have to stay with Barnaby, "You're married to him now." The tears flowed as he cried; the audience erupting in laughter and applause, then a full-blown standing ovation. This unique recreation of a beloved sequence from *Babes in Toyland* by three of the Hal Roach Studios stars who made the original was THE highlight of this 1986 convention, one that would be discussed and recalled for decades to come.

The curtain call was a moment of personal triumph for Henry Brandon. He stood there, soaking in the applause, glistening with sweat, his false nose beginning to droop. This was HIS stage in front of HIS fans, and he took full control, directing the bows, introducing his fellow performers and delivering a heartfelt thank you to the audience. Henry had come full circle, portraying one final time the plum role given him by legendary producer Hal Roach back in 1934, for the members of a film society who clearly adored him.

Brothers Hugo & Henry Brandon in 1989. Photo by Becky Kane.

CHAPTER TWO
An Actor's Life for Me

Heinrich Kleinbach was delivered on June 8, 1912 in Berlin, Germany. He was the son of Hugo R. and Hildagard, his two siblings were Hugo O. and Maria. His brother and sister were born three and two years ahead of Henry respectively. Hugo was a merchant and world traveler with roots in the southern German city of Heilbronn.

Almost immediately after their third child was born, the Kleinbachs embarked on a new life immigrating to America, travelling first to Antwerp in Belgium where they boarded the "Kroonland" vessel. It must have been a concerning voyage for all because the Titanic had sunk in the North Atlantic Ocean just a few months earlier in April. Hildagard carried baby Heinrich when they arrived at Ellis Island outside of New York City on October 22, 1912. A brief hospital stay was ordered for the thirty year-old mother and her young son. They were soon released to travel to their final destination of Los Angeles.

The family decided to Americanize Heinrich's first name to Henry. It wasn't until 1936 he changed his surname professionally to "Brandon," a derivative of his mother's maiden name, "Brandonburg."

With the aid of sponsors, the Kleinbachs made their way across the country and settled in Los Angeles. The 1914 City Directory census showed the family living at 2380 West 30th St. Mr. Kleinbach was gainfully employed as a bookkeeper for Guarantee & Trust Co. By the 1920 federal census, he had been promoted to auditor of the same company.

Young Henry was enrolled in kindergarten early, at just four years old and the result was he was slightly older than the other children in his elementary school classes which caused some shyness and feelings of isolation. In a 1987 interview with *Starlog Magazine*, Henry remembered, "I had a wonderful Spanish teacher, a brilliant woman and she asked me to go out for the school plays, hoping she might bring me out of myself." Henry did so and the seeds for a career were planted right there.

The neighborhood where the Kleinbach's lived was comprised of mostly sturdy working class workers with a network of dusty alleyways connecting the homes. The two brothers had to learn to fight; one time they were beaten up by a couple of kids who were stronger than them and scrapping became a common theme for Henry through the years.

By 1923 the family moved to 746 Cavanaugh Road in the Township of Glendale, California, northeast of Los Angeles next to Burbank. It was just a few miles away from the high school of choice for their children; Benjamin Franklin High School. According to the 1928 Franklin Almanac, Henry was a member of the Senior Glee Club, Orpheus Club, Spanish Club, Stamp Club, Rooters' Club, an usher, and a member of the track team.

The most important acclaim in Henry's high school achievements was his involvement in the Drama Club, building on his grade school play experiences. He starred in the role of *Marriage of Nannette*, a comic opera performed in three acts. The cheers, the adrenalin hike and accolades were intoxicating for him. This was the genesis of Henry's future profession; the make-up, the scenery, the spotlights, the applause… a ham was born.

Back at home, Hugo Sr. had secured an important position as vice-president for the same title insurance company he had been working for. He had climbed the ladder of success and business was booming by June of 1928. Mr. Kleinbach knew he had a prodigy for a son; he wanted Henry to get the best college education money could buy.

For a talented young man like Henry, there were many institutions of higher learning at his beckoning. The prestigious private college, Stanford

University "The Harvard of the West" was his first choice and he was accepted there in June 1928. Henry's college major was political science*, and it is with conjecture that businessman Mr. Kleinbach wanted his son to pursue a career in law after graduate school. Henry was a natural in academics while also participating in the drama department. San Francisco, the cultural center of California was only 35 miles to the north.

Henry grew up fluent in the German language and his parents instilled in him a European appreciation of the arts. Listening to classical music, reading Shakespeare and attending professional entertainment became a consuming passion for him. Combined with his stimulating and challenging classes, Henry became not only a cultured young man but socially adept in all situations.

The Alpha Sigma Phi Fraternity, off site from the campus, welcomed Henry as a freshman pledge. This was a very prestigious development. Henry participated in each annual photo session and was labeled as part of the future "Class of 1932."

Henry had an interest in old cars and helped fix them mechanically. One photo in the 1929 Stanford yearbook shows him with three of his mates. A popular hangout for the college crowd was Dinah's Shack in Palo Alto where they featured a full chicken dinner with all the trimmings for Sunday diners for 25 cents. Evening meals were tastefully accompanied by a professional harpist.

For a college hi-jinx, Henry later recalled he was driven to the nearby city of San Jose where he willingly lost his virginity at the "red light district." The enticing but abrupt words from his lady of the evening; "well…hop on" never left his memory.†

Henry enjoyed a solid year at the university and was beginning his sophomore year in 1929 when the stock market collapsed in October. This had a huge impact especially on Stanford students. Luckily, Henry had the full dedication

---

* Stanford Quad Yearbook 1929-1931

† Henry Brandon conversation with co-author Cassara Dec. 1984

of his family to continue his burgeoning education. It also helped that Mr. Kleinbach was vice-president of a trust company during this crisis. What creditors could not pay were absorbed by the banks and later resold to the highest bidder. Henry stayed in school to complete his sophomore year of 1930.

The school thinned out a bit as some students had to go home to help with the family business or seek their own living, it looked like Henry was going to make the family proud and complete his education.

Henry was now a junior on campus by the time the 1931 classes commenced. On May 7, 1931 the *San Francisco Chronicle* wrote up a play announcement:

> Stanford Group will do *Dance of Death*. Henry Kleinbach was an esteemed part of the Germanic department of Stanford University that presented *Dance of Death* completely in German. Dr. Kurt F. Reinhardt, associate professor of the Germanic language, directed the play at the Little Theatre on campus.

Henry continued his stage work at the Stanford Theatre in a well-known farce: *The Inspector General* performed on July 13, 1931. Henry Kleinbach was mentioned only by name in a small write-up in the *San Francisco Chronicle*. The reviewer pointed out that the play had been "popular in Slavic, Scandinavian and Germanic lands for nearly a century."*

Then on the very day the *Chronicle* review was published, an earth shattering event occurred that affected Henry for the rest of his life. A local newspaper broke the news: **"Girl Killed in Palo Alto Crash."**

> Betty Hartsuk, 17, was killed last night on the highway a mile south of Palo Alto when the car in which she was riding overturned and pinned her beneath it following a collision with another car.†

---

* Most Americans are only familiar with this farcical tale from the color film starring Danny Kaye (1949).
† *San Mateo Times* July 14, 1931

Betty was a Palo Alto high school graduate. Also in the car were Betty's sister Mildred, Henry and a fellow Stanford student, Kenneth A. White, who hailed from Glendale. The Oakland newspaper elaborated that Mildred and Henry Kleinbach suffered no injuries.

Henry's friend, the ill-fated Betty Hardsuk

In the days before seat belts, even a minor automobile collision could be serious. The car was travelling on the California State Highway 101 (referred to as the El Camino Real) so speed could have been a factor. If the car overturned it is likely the rest of the occupants were thrown out.

It is not clear from newspaper reports who was driving the car; Betty was listed as a passenger. There were no accounts on the cause of the accident or if the unnamed driver was impaired.

At the very least, Henry was severely impacted in this life-changing tragedy. He had to quit school and return to live with his parents in Glendale. These were the darkest days of the Depression and money was reprioritized in the Kleinbach clan.

When Henry returned to Southern California, there were many advantages for the fledging thespian. His circle of theatre friends embraced his company & stage experience and there were stock acting opportunities at the local theatres. One of the most prestigious was the Pasadena Playhouse.

This jewel of a theatre – well on its way to becoming a local and then national institution was built in the Spanish Colonial Revival style and was located at 39 South El Molino, one city over from the family's Glendale base. The 686 seating capacity served the community well and drew many famous playwrights since its opening in 1925. Henry no doubt saw many plays there during his high school years, further cementing his desires to act on stage and fueling an internal debate between heart and mind. Making things more complicated, Henry revealed in an interview that, "my father was violently opposed to my acting."*

Henry rapidly realized his goal when he became part of the ensemble of supporting character actors at the Pasadena Playhouse. For the record, Henry performed in the popular stage play *Berkeley Square* from January 7-14, 1932.

The fantasy play had a time-travel theme and told the story of an Englishman who was transported back to London after the American Revolution to meet his own ancestors – a kind-of "Back to the Future" without the DeLorean or the Flux Capacitor. The actual "Berkeley Square" is a town square in Mayfair in the West End of London, in the City of Westminster. It was originally laid out in the mid-18th century.

Henry next appeared at the Pasadena Playhouse for the stage production of *Peter Gynt,* from July 26 to August 6, 1932. He had a part in this play about a Norwegian farm lad who wasted his time in a life based on avoidance of commitments. His day dreaming, boasting and brawling led him to many misadventures until he took stock of himself.

The young actor was well accepted by the players of the Pasadena Playhouse and he was making a name for himself, if not in the public eye,

---

* *New Orleans Times* Oct. 5, 1980

then amongst his peers. There was a little start up group of actors who fancied performing a melodrama at the Theatre Mart in Los Angeles. The play was called *The Drunkard* and it proved to be a cornerstone of Henry's career.

The Theatre Mart was a unique building for the arts created in 1925 and located at 605 North Juanita (one block east of Vermont one block south of Melrose). It was made up of a society of thespians dedicated to performing in the style of old English Musical Halls, but definitely not brash American vaudeville.

A call went out to a couple of producers from the Monterey peninsula up north; Preston Shobe and Galt Bell, who were staging plays at the Forest Theatre in Carmel. They were summoned to set up shop at the Theatre Mart.

A choice had to be made about what to produce; it had to be something that would draw an audience of course. Purchasing or renting a published script would be cost prohibitive, so a decision, a grand artistic and economic decision was made to dust off an original play produced by the one and only P.T. Barnum back in 1843. It was called, *The Drunkard*, and fortunately the play was never published and thus there was no rental fee.

Whether Barnum was the alleged originator of the catch-phrase "there's a sucker born every minute" is true or not, one thing was solid, he was a great showman who knew how to keep an audience's attention.

Could the creaky old play still be a draw? This melodrama featured a temperance theme where the characters were well defined as "good" or "bad." There was a young male character that had high moral virtues but was tempted by demon alcohol, the very scourge of youth. The virginal female lead was a standard cliché even then, but one that could be played for fun in this interactive, wildly theatrical setting. The audience participated in cheering when goodness prevailed, and the crowd relished booing the despicable villain character, Squire Cribbs.

**Henry Brandon as Squire Cribbs in The Drunkard.
Collection of Henry Brandon.**

With Bell directing, the cast was handpicked; Ruth Marion was the pure-of-heart heroine "Mary," and Samuel Ethridge took the "Edward Middleton" title role of the young man afflicted by liquor addiction. One of the troopers was Henry Kleinbach and he was ideal for the part of the play's scoundrel, the unscrupulous lawyer who tried to trick the drunkard of his money and property.

The show was built around the tall and lean Kleinbach, with his booming diction and confident manner, who quickly came to realize that Cribbs was the plum part of the whole drama. To transform his scalawag character; he would don make-up that included long, thick burnsides and highlighted eyebrows; an Edwardian top-hat; a frock coat and pristine white gloves. With this costume, Henry transcended himself to an old man character easily.

To help with the illusion, Henry performed in a crooked bent back position and his unsteady gait was aided by a thick cane. He also used this walking stick to gesture at certain words and also to tap the tall bottle of alcohol on the bar, beckoning the poor drunkard to drink. "It's very *good whiskey*," he would say. Somewhat surprising is Henry did not resort to the cliché of wearing a false handlebar mustache. Without the hindrance, Henry could better display animated facial expressions and indulge in his theatrically rich, commanding acting style.

The grand opening for *The Drunkard* was July 6, 1933. The theater's 330 seats were packed at one dollar each. The walls were decorated with posters from the Barnum era, buffet food was devoured, beer overflowed onto the peanut shelled floor, and the air was thick with the tang of merriment. The actors who had been rehearsing for weeks were slightly on edge with anticipation. Would their opening night audience embrace the over-the-top theatrics and join in the fun or merely sit there, unmoved and silent? Finally, the curtains were pulled exposing a brightly colored backdrop that announced the title:

The Drunkard; or, The Fallen Saved
(A Moral & Domestic Drama in Five Acts)

Tongue-in-cheek humor, mugging and heckling from the audience was the norm – and encouraged. The innocent heroine elicited sighs, the valiant hero produced cheers and the heartless, dastardly villain provoked boos and hisses. The piano player was part of the experience off-stage, emphasizing each movement with the proper lightness on the keys or emphatic, dramatic pounding.

The audience was just as much part of the show as were the actors. Henry sharpened his skills by rolling with the heckling from the crowd. The cast was rehearsed to act in a straight forward manner in order to stay true to the play. Anything burlesqued would hinder the actors, and let's face it, the play was corny enough. That is not to say that when someone got off a good taunt, an ad-lib from Henry would further engage the audience.

A memorable ad-lib from the audience came from the one, the only Groucho Marx one night. It was during the tenement scene when poor Ruth Marion, widowed by her drunken husband had just tucked her "chee-ild" in for the night. Suddenly there was a loud knock at the door, as Cribbs sought entrance – simulating the "knock" with a bent, thick oak walking stick. Miss Marion's line was, "I wonder who that can be?" Groucho piped: "A man with a wooden leg."* It brought the house down."

The ending, of course, featured a victory over the devil's villainy and the triumph of temperance: the abstinence of alcohol. This was heavily applauded, in mock appreciation by the crowd. Good was triumphant! Love conquered all! And the villain-- that scene-stealing, scenery-chewing villain – was vanquished!

The olio segment followed the play and everyone in the cast (breaking character) participated in song. The audience boisterously and more often drunkenly sang along with songs from the Gilded Age such as: "*In the Good Old Summertime, There's a Tavern in the Town, Down by the Old Mill Stream* and *The Curse of an Aching Heart.*"

The Drunkard was an immediate success and perfect for the Depression Era. Reminiscing about the achievements of the play many years later, Henry pointed out that one of the main reasons was because they were one of the first theatres to serve beer. In an interview with Producer Galt Bell, he explained:

> It was and is very much in key with the spirit of the day, the return to favor of bicycles, the good old days of cheer." He also said, "The show would not be anything without beer—it is served free along with pretzels, sandwiches and coffee.†

---

*   *Hollywood Citizen News* Dec. 4, 1933

†   *State* (Columbia, South Carolina) December 27, 1936

[9]   W.C. Fields used "The Drunkard" theme as a play-within-a-play in his feature film, *The Old Fashioned Way*

Illustration of Brandon as Squire Cribbs from Feg Murray's Seein' Stars syndicated newspaper column. Collection of Tony Hawes.

Despite the Volstead Act that was constitutionally in place since 1919, Los Angeles was a very "wet" town especially as sentiments against the prohibition of liquor were openly challenged. The fact that most of the crowd was pleasantly sloshed made it even more fun to cheer for the temperance theme of the play. It was a big joke cheering on the morals of sobriety while imbibing freely.

The Theatre Mart was considered a social club and attracted people in show business every night. Henry recalled that Cecil B. DeMille came and was spotted by the actors behind the curtain. In a later interview, Henry revealed, "It became a running joke, 'Hey, Cecil B. DeMille is in the audience.'"

Other notables who came were Boris Karloff, John McCormack, Billie Burke, Mary Pickford, John Barrymore and even W.C. Fields[*] who allegedly frequented the show some 30 times.[†] Fields would bring a bottle of whiskey with him to the show for his friend Jeffery Williams who was also in the play. The bottle was left on a table that said, "Take liberally-Dr. Fields D.T."[‡]

Director Bell said in an interview:

> One reason for 'The Drunkards' popularity is it affords a place for movie celebrities to relax. They come regularly, join in the singing and sometimes even take part in the entertainment. One notable evening Will Rogers and Fred Stone went up on the little stage after the drama's final curtain and reenacted skits, songs and dances they had made famous years ago.[§]

The Drunkard was a Los Angeles smash, but no one expected it to remain so after the first few weeks. A show business phenomenon, the crowd wouldn't let them change the bill. No one could possibly anticipate the show's triumph; it ran consecutively every evening for nearly three decades, until October 17, 1959. After 9,477 performances it finally closed.

Henry Kleinbach tasted the fruit of his notoriety and stayed with the troupe for the first 30 months; however Hollywood was scouting out this young talent and would soon call on him.

---

[*] Fields hired the cast for their established roles and he took the main character: Squire Cribbs as his own vehicle complete with a whip. Henry was the technical advisor.

[†] *Daily Mirror* July 19, 2008 by Larry Harnisch

[‡] Henry Brandon as told to Gary Cohen on KGO radio in 1983

[§] *State (Columbia, South Carolina)* December 27, 1936

Actor Prizes Villain Role in "Drunkard"

> Henry Kleinbach, member of the cast, is beginning to believe it pays to be bad. As Squire Cribbs, villain extraordinaire, in the old Barnum tear-ringer, Kleinbach is the scoundrel who holds the mortgage on the old homestead, etc. But he's receiving more fan mail and attention than any other male in the cast. Most of his fans are of the feminine sex, too. The actor refuses point blank to give up the part to anyone else.[*]

The *Los Angeles Times* reported Henry "continues to live up to his title of 'Schnitzelbank expert' by leading the audience in the singing of this favorite old song."[†] As of July 23rd Henry had been performing in "The Drunkard" for fifty-six weeks. His photo, an image as Lawyer Cribbs made the paper.

> As Henry Brandon quickly learned, the villain's machinations are what drove the plot and gave audiences someone to root *against*. Playing the "bad guy" was, frankly, more fun than being the hero and a good actor could really sink his chops into such roles, adding flavor and theatrics to make a truly memorable desperado. The 'larger-than-life' the villain, the more the public remembered and reviled the part. An emotional chord was struck as young Kleinbach came to realize that a career could be carved out with such skills in his acting bag of tricks.

What follows are the five acts and olio that comprised *The Drunkard* as performed in the Theatre Mart by Henry Brandon and his fellow thespians throughout the 1930's:

---

* *Los Angeles Times* February 14, 1934
† *Los Angeles Times* July 23, 1934

The Drunkard
Time –1843 Place—New York State

ACT I
Scene 1. *Interior of rural cottage*—"Go forth, my dear, as a dove from the ark of old."

Scene 2. *A lonely road in a wood*—"I fear this is the gentleman I seek."

Scene 3. *Same*—"She knows too much for my happiness."

Scene 4. *The cottage*—"Hail, Happy Pair!"

ACT II
Scene 1. The Barroom, Drunk, fighting. Shame! Agony!"

Scene 2. *The Wood*—"He is lost!"

Scene 3. *The Cottage*—"Oh, what a question for a doting wife."

ACT III
Scene 1. BROADWAY!!! "Take back your base brief."

Scene 2. *Wretched garret in New York*—"Help! Mercy!"

ACT IV
Scene 1. *A miserable shed*

Scene 2. *The Wood*—"A villain. I have lived—a villain let me die!"

ACT V
Scene 1. *The Cottage*—"Where is my redeemed one?"

Scene 2. *Same*—"Home sweet Home."

CHAPTER THREE
Three Iconic Roles – *Babes in Toyland*

As we reflect back on the long motion picture career of Henry Brandon, one thing becomes immediately apparent. Of all the wildly varied parts he portrayed on screen, three of these roles stand apart from the rest as iconic Brandon - as career-defining moments, as pop culture touchstones - which makes them quite worthy of intense examination in this and the two following stand-alone chapters.

Brandon was never one of those celebrated silver screen character actors, the ones who got nominated for Best Supporting Actor Academy Awards, the Claude Rains or Thomas Mitchell or George Sanders types. He was a working man's character actor, a B-Picture performer better categorized as one of the 'bad guys' along with fine players like Lionel Atwill, Henry Daniell and George Zucco. Atwill, Daniell and Zucco built entire careers playing and replaying the same basic persona – which doesn't detract from their skills, they were all consummate actors who were *very* good at their jobs. But unlike his contemporary screen scoundrels, Henry Brandon's strength – or one of them – lay in his versatility.

At the Roach Studios makeup department with Jack Casey.

If you read through many of the classic movie blogs on the internet these days and come across posts about Henry Brandon, one commonality is shock and surprise to learn that the same man who portrayed Silas Barnaby in *Babes in Toyland* is the same actor who was Chief Scar in *The Searchers*. Henry's talents crossed over nationality, ethnicity and skin color.

Aided by the skills of costumers, hair dressers and make-up professionals, he was able to lose himself in a wide variety of characters – lead criminals and henchmen, murderers and victims, good guys and bad guys, heroes and villains, starring roles and bit parts – and rising above these hundred or so movie characters, like sweet cream to the surface, are three iconic roles.

Early Barnaby test makeup. Collection of Richard W. Bann

Most actors are lucky to land one iconic role, much less three of them. It will become apparent that Henry's greatest strength – the acting chops that define this versatility – is also his greatest weakness, the very thing that prevented him from becoming a movie star. None other than the Duke himself, John Wayne, crystalizes the problem in an offhand comment during the filming of *The Searchers*, as we will soon see.

Coming at the very beginning and the mid-point of his film and television careers are these three quintessential Brandon performances. Silas Barnaby in *Babes in Toyland*, Doctor Fu Manchu in *The Drums of Fu Manchu* and Scar in *The Searchers* are Henry Brandon's ultimate screen moments, the three roles spanning from 1934 to 1955, all defining and redefining who he was and who he continues to be.

Babes in Toyland

It was one of those glorious evenings at the Theatre Mart prior to a performance of *The Drunkard*, when someone peaked out from behind the set and alerted the other actors; "Hal Roach is in the audience." It might have seemed like just another movie producer in attendance, but it wasn't.

Everyone knew of Hal Roach it seemed, he was the ruler of a film comedy empire. He had dethroned Mack Sennett as the new King of Comedy with his stable of stars: Stan Laurel & Oliver Hardy, Charley Chase, Thelma Todd & Patsy Kelly, the Our Gang kids, and scores of unique and talented stock players including Billy Gilbert, James Finlayson, and Billy Bletcher. Roach had previously furthered the careers of Harold Lloyd, Will Rogers, Max Davidson, Edgar Kennedy, Harry Langdon and ZaSu Pitts.

What no one could have possibly known that night was that Roach was scouting for his new feature production for Laurel and Hardy. The film was *Babes in Toyland* and for comedy contrast; Roach was on the lookout for a comic heavy to play the villain.

Hal Roach had bought the rights to film *Babes in Toyland*, an original operetta that was showcased on Broadway in 1903. Many revivals since that time kept the play vivid in the consciousness of the many who saw the stage production. In 1915 there was even an exhibit at the San Francisco/Panama Exhibition that featured the Mother Goose characters and wooden soldiers so evident in the play. It was called, *Babes in Toyland Grows Up*.

It was thought that bringing this nostalgic showcase to celluloid with the original music would be a knock-out, especially with Laurel and Hardy in starring roles. Bringing *Babes* to film would pose many logistical hurdles to overcome. The original play featured the characters of "Alan" and "Jane" in the hands of their miserly "Uncle Barnaby," who is desirous of securing their fortune. "The children run away and have adventures in the sea, through the "Kingdom of Spiders," and find themselves in "Toyland-little girl and boy land." As the lyrics go: "While you dwell within it, you are ever happy then."

Roach wrote a rudimentary script and envisioned all of his actors participating. He penciled in Stan Laurel as "Simple Simon" and Oliver Hardy as the "Pie Man." Mother Goose characters would abound and the Our Gang kids would augment the footage. Charley Chase could sing at least one of the songs made so popular, and even Thelma Todd and Patsy Kelly were announced for the cast.* Despite the talent in house, Roach recognized he would have to hire additional professional actors.

One of the first decisions was to scrap the characters of Alan and Jane for new characters. It was all the better to eliminate the stagey three acts as originally performed. Also nixed were "Uncle Barnaby's" two henchmen: Gonzorgo and Roderigo. Instead, Barnaby would be in league with an insidious army of dark-haired bogeymen.

Production started at the Roach Studios as early as January 1934, but it was mostly prep work. There remained many delays before a consensus on a script and directors were decided. The number one consideration for the Barnaby part was Roach's decision alone; it was his studio after all.

Roach no doubt considered every character actor in Hollywood for the plum role of Barnaby. It is undocumented exactly when Roach decided to take in the show at the Theatre Mart to watch *The Drunkard*. What is clear is Roach was bowled over by the performance of Henry Kleinbach in his Lawyer Cribbs role. This is that Roach wanted for his Barnaby part; an over-the-top melodramatic villain.

Henry elaborated:

---

* *Los Angeles Times* June 13, 1934

Mr. Roach came to see the show on a Saturday, and Monday I was in his office. I walked in and he said, "You're not the old son of a bitch I saw on the stage!" and I said, "Yes I am." He was fooled by my makeup. He said, "My God, I don't know what we're going to do with you." He hired four makeup men. They weren't as advanced as they are today. He finally found a wonderful old guy, an Irishman named Jim Collins who was head of makeup at Paramount for years. Jim used all sorts of wonderful things he used when he worked with Lon Chaney.[*]

Henry was outfitted with spectacles and a "chin piece" complete with goat whiskers and a wig that looked like a mane. It won Henry the job. According to payroll records of the Hal Roach Studios, Henry's first week of work was on August 7th, 1934. He was paid $200.00 that first week of pay.

The first day on the set I was very much in awe of Laurel & Hardy. We had a five or six page scene to shoot. Mr. Laurel had what we now call "go-fers," four or five of them. They were old vaudevillian friends of his whom he had coaxed Mr. Roach into hiring. I guess a lot of actors who have to get buoyed up for a scene, some of them use pills, some booze, Laurel used his "go-fers."[†] They would tell jokes, he would tell jokes, they would die laughing no matter what he said, and by the time he got in front of the camera he was up here (gesturing over his head), in the air. So after about half an hour of this, I thought, my God, picture making is easy, you just sit around and tell jokes! Then Stan said, "Well, let's think about his scene." He had the script and he said, "Look

---

[*] Q&A period with Sons 1986

[†] Henry was explaining the current vernacular for actors who "go fer this and go fer that." Henry also referred to them as "stooges."

Babe, I'll do this, and then let's cut this line. Henry, when he does that, why, you do this and so on.

So I very stupidly said, "Aren't we going to rehearse?" And Stan replied, "Do you want to *spoil* it?" In later years Henry would delight his audiences by repeating that story. He would also elaborate how beautiful the sets were and how richly the structures were crafted and painted.

It really was a huge undertaking by the "Lot of Fun." The set was enormous, 250 feet by 500 feet. It contained a faux "schoolhouse built of books, pencils and ink bottles; a picket fence of candy canes, Noah's Ark and a police station."* Henry often remarked to his fans in the 1980's that "*Babes* should have been shot in color."

While filming was done during the day, Henry continued his regular duties performing at the Theatre Mart. Tension was mounting between Roach and Laurel and it started when Roach presented his script before production; Laurel mocked his boss. Then when Roach assigned Raymond McCarey, a distinguished comedy director to the helm with a fresh script, dissention broke out.

Henry of course was given the script and recalled, "It was beautiful, a fairytale." He described the politics that were going on during production:

> I got to the studio early on as they were preparing and met the man who was to direct the picture. He was a young man; he couldn't have been more than thirty. His name was Ray McCarey. He was Leo McCarey's younger brother. We got to talking and comparing notes; what we thought about the part and it was wonderful because you don't get those chances very often in Pictures.
>
> We developed a wonderful relationship. He said, "Look, they

---

* *San Bernardino Sun* August 19, 1934

don't really have a designer here, I'm just wondering what sort of costume you might have." I said, "I have a friend at the Pasadena Playhouse where I got most of my training, Corliss McGee. Do you want me to ask him to make some sketches?" He said, "Would you do that?" And Corliss made some wonderful sketches which were what I ended up with. The elongated hat, long shoes with the large buckles, the jabot, the long coat, everything. He didn't get a nickel for that, he did it out of friendship, but we were on that basis. I hadn't been there for about a week, when I knocked on Ray's door. They said he was "no longer" on the picture. I was shocked.*

McCarey took Henry into his confidence, after the fact, on what happened that fateful day; while McCarey was in Roach's office, he explained to Henry, "Mr. Roach was sitting with his head in his hands, and Stan was there. I was explaining how he wanted to play a certain scene. "Apparently McCarey "accidently" struck Charlie Rogers in the face and in McCarey's own words; "sent him ass over tea kettles."

The result was, Roach told McCarey he would have to "divide the picture with Rogers and Gus Meins." McCarey promptly quit. Rogers wound up directing Laurel and Hardy while Meins directed all the other scenes.

Henry described Rogers as "one of Stan's 'go-fers." Even with Stan's choice of directors in place, there was still friction between him and Roach. Henry said the two would battle it out in the office, but never on the set. Then on August 14, 1934 Stan hurt his leg running in on a scene, according to Randy Skretvedt's definitive tome: "Laurel and Hardy the Magic Behind the Movies," that moment was described in detail:

> Stan was shooting a scene with Babe and Henry Brandon. He was supposed to run in as the scene began. As Rogers yelled,

---

* Henry Brandon interview

"Action," Stan tripped and fell from a raised platform, and tore some ligaments in his right leg He was rushed to Culver City Emergency Hospital, where his leg was put in a cast.

Stan needed time off to recover so the crew shot around him. On August 18, 1934 production temporarily stopped. Amazingly, Henry was still performing in *The Drunkard* during the evenings and thought he would be able to catch up on his sleep.*

One of Henry's favorite stories to tell before an appreciative audience was the night he was arrested. He fully elaborated about his arrest on a broadcast of *Talk of the Town* show on Simmons Cable in Long Beach:

> Stan had an accident on the set. They called it "an act of God." Hal Roach sent us all home without salary for at least a week.†
> I went out to celebrate and ended up at a bar on Hollywood Boulevard called The Brass Rail with a couple of my buddies from *The Drunkard*. We weren't feeling any pain so we went over to try and pick up a couple of girls. The waiters told us to go back to our seats and it got worse and worse. Finally, the manager/bouncer from *The Drunkard* (George Ratterman) picked up a waiter and slugged him. Then Larry Grenier held the waiter while George punched him a few times, then I waded in. Finally, I hit one waiter and he threw a sugar bowl at me, which hit me right on the nose and broke it. Then the cops came and hauled us off to the hoosegow. We made headlines!

---

* "Laurel and Hardy The Magic Behind the Movies" by Randy Skretvedt

† Henry's recollection contradicts the facts. He was fully paid during the shutdown according to the Hal Roach Studios payroll ledger now held by the University of Southern California Cinematic Arts Library

Barnaby and his Bogeymen. Collection of Richard W. Bann

Henry retold this story to a banquet crowd of the Midnight Patrol Tent[*] some 53 years later. He said the fight was on and the cops were called, then Henry paused for dramatic timing and said, "I hate the fuzz." Apparently the nice policeman used his sap stick to break up the fight and hauled everyone off. Henry explained when filming continued, his nose was in a completely different position.

The *Los Angeles Times* had a slightly different account of the events: **PLAY VILLAIN ARRESTED-Henry Kleinbach of *The Drunkard* Fame Seized with Three Others in Street Fight:**

> For fifty-nine weeks that stirring melodrama, *The Drunkard*, has played before capacity audiences in the little auditorium of the Theatre Mart, and for fifty-nine weeks the audiences roundly hissed the villain, who in real life is Henry Kleinbach, 22 years of age of 746 Cavanaugh Road.

---

[*] Sons of the Desert-The Laurel and Hardy appreciation society "tent" in Monterey, California in 1987

Maybe this constant hissing finally got the better of Kleinbach, or maybe he was rehearsing a part for a new play, or maybe he wasn't doing anything at all, but in any event he and three others were arrested yesterday on charges of drunkenness following a battle which police reported started in a restaurant at 6321 Hollywood Boulevard and ended in the street in front of the place.

Those said to have been in the fight with Kleinbach are George Ratterman, a theater manager, Bert Morris, actor, and Lawrence Grenier, actor. They pled not guilty in which their trial was set for next Thursday. The four were arrested by Officer Bates who said he found them with their clothing torn to shreds, but still battling vigorously. Unable to quiet them alone, Bates called for assistance and an employee of the café aided him.*

On August 23, 1934 Henry and Bert Morris were acquitted of charges of being drunk in public. Two of the other arrestees did not appear in court and a bench warrant was issued to them.

The morning that Brandon returned to the studio, everybody came out of their offices and cheered him. Everyone, that is, except Hal Roach, who walked up and said, "Not funny. No more barroom brawls."†

Since production still hadn't started up for *Babes*, Henry went right back to work acting at night. An article from *The Los Angeles Times* August 19, 1934:

Kleinbach Gives His Formula for Not Going Stale:

A friend asked Henry Kleinbach, while he was preparing to go on as the villain in *The Drunkard*, "How do you keep from going stale in the part of Squire Cribbs?"

"Well," said Kleinbach who has essayed the role over 400 consec-

---

* *Los Angeles Times* August 18, 1934
† "Laurel and Hardy The Magic Behind the Movies," by Randy Skretvedt

utive times, "as for going stale on a part from a long tenure, I have a formula for that. When the part seems to become ridiculous, as nearly any part is apt to do after you've played it for months, I am aware before I go on stage, that this audience has never seen this before. If one can remember that what he is doing is new to his audience, it doesn't seem too hopelessly stale to him."

As Henry's Barnaby character once said to Alfalfa in *Our Gang Follies of 1938*, "Let me open the door of fame for you." It seems that the metaphor could also describe Henry's ascent in the business at a young age. Adulation, notoriety, and receiving plum roles certainly impressed his father. Henry's dad who was so opposed to his son's acting "made a complete about face once he saw the checks coming in."* Henry remarked that his father was "all for his career" afterwards.

When filming resumed on "Babes," the cameras were capturing some of the most magical scenes ever materialized. There was Old Barnaby slinking around like a weasel to Laurel's Stannie Dum[b] and Hardy's Ollie Dee"†

Henry utilized all his melodramatic physical bag of tricks. There were frequent close-ups of his cunning, sadistic face. None so vivid as the first framed image of him in the storybook beginning introducing his character. Barnaby even received his own identifying sinister theme music when he entered a scene.

The movie took place in the mythical Toyland, where all the Mother Goose characters came to life. Laurel and Hardy fit perfectly in this fairytale setting, the innocence of their well-defined character's splendidly co-exist in this never land.

Barnaby held the deed to the old brown shoe and imposed himself to the old woman who lived in it. Under the guise to "show his deep respect" to her daughter (Little Bo-Peep), Barnaby demands his money. Mrs. Peep could

---

* *New Orleans Times* Oct. 5, 1980

† Based on characters "Tweedle Dee and Tweedle Dum" from Lewis Carroll's "Alice in Wonderland"

not come up with her mortgage payment on time, so naturally Barnaby offers his slimy self to marry Bo Peep "as a compromise."

Sixty-eight year old Barnaby is infatuated with Bo-peep. He explains when he comes across her tending her sheep. "Good morning my pretty little buttercup; I bring you a bouquet, a fragrant token of my deep devotion."

As Bo-Peep diplomatically excuses herself, Barnaby blocks her way with his cane. "Nay," he protested. "I have long admired you…gazed with wonder at your sweet and maidenly virtue…marveled at your tender loveliness. In short, I'm asking you to become my wife." He coaxes her by putting his hand on her shoulder. "I'm a very rich man, my dear…think carefully child, lest I resort to other means and that would be an ugly way to win a pretty wife."

Florence Roberts as Mother Peep, Charlotte Henry as Bo Peep and Henry Brandon as Barnaby in *Babes in Toyland.* **Collection of Rick Greene.**

Bo Peep boldly spits out the cutting words: "I wouldn't marry you if you were young, which you can't be…if you were honest, which you never were… and if you were about to die tomorrow, which is too much to hope for!"

The die is cast in this dramatic plot development. Mother Peep confides in her two roomers, Stannie and Ollie who sincerely offer to come up with the money, but don't. While leaving late for work at the toy factory, they run into Barnaby while Stan demonstrates his dexterity with the "pee wee game." We see the first interaction with Barnaby and the boys in this scene. As his hat is knocked off as a result of an errant batted pee wee, the old man menacingly approaches the two innocents.

Behind the scenes of *Babes in Toyland*, the cast with co-director Gus Meins. Collection of Rick Greene.

Barnaby retaliates by emphatically breaking Stannie's stick over his knee. Then, in an extraordinary close-up, we see the dirt under-the-nails of his fingers taking hold of Ollie's toothbrush mustache. He yanks some of the hairs off and sprinkles them to the ground. We hear Ollie's patented cry of pain as Barnaby hobbles off. "A crooked man with a crooked walk, crooked through and through."

Stan and Ollie's feeble attempts at borrowing money from the Toymaker not only fail; their bumbling destroys part of the workshop, upending Santa Claus into a drum. Santa is not amused when he was checking the progress of his "order of 600 one-foot high toy soldiers." Stannie got the order all wrong and created 100 six-foot high soldiers, they are instantly dismissed by the furious Toymaker. Because of this setback, the boys reluctantly drag their feet back to the giant shoe trying to get their courage to break the bad news to the Widow Peep.

Meanwhile, that skinflint Barnaby is expecting his funds and enters the really big shoe. He is scolded by the old woman, "Mr. Barnaby, when you enter my house, I'll trouble you to knock." Not discouraged, Barnaby says, "Your house, my dear lady? Did you say *your* house? Not until this little debt has been paid."

Little Bo Peep speaks up, "Momsy what does this mean?" An angry Barnaby replies, "It means my dear, that unless this mortgage is paid, you will all be thrown out into the streets. Of course we could *compromise*."

Barnaby incongruously offers himself again to Bo-Peep, this time addressing her mother. "Should your daughter reconsider my generous offer to become my wife, we could forget this little matter, and it could be her wedding present."

As we see Stannie and Ollie approach the home, she announces to Barnaby that he can "make out the receipt," only the boys can't deliver. As the lecherous old man announces that he will be foreclosing on the home, Stan pantomimes to Ollie to grab the mortgage papers from Barnaby's exposed pocket. We hear a loud *snap* and an Ollie howl of pain (the papers serve as the bait to a large rat trap device). Barnaby addresses Ollie with his infamous line: "Big bait catches big rat."

The next entanglement with the three main subjects is almost inconceivable, but perfect in the world of Laurel and Hardy. The big idea is similar in principle to the "Trojan Horse" strategy; gaining entry inside of Barnaby's dwelling for nefarious purposes. Stannie dons a mask and personally delivers a giant box tied ribbon to Barnaby's front door. The guise is to allow Ollie, who is inside the oversized box, to enter the house and steal the mortgage. Simple.

Barnaby is at once perturbed and asks, "Who is it at this time of the night?" Stan wins his trust by offering an early Christmas present and beckons him to open the door. The suspicious Barnaby asks, "Christmas present in the middle of July?" Stannie unprepared for this question seemingly ad-libs, "We always do our Christmas shopping early. It's from me and Ollie" (Pantomimes pointing inside the box).

Not suspicious, Barnaby opens the door to his lair and the box is delivered with a note: "Merry Christmas To: Mr. Barnaby From: Ollie Dee and Stannie Dum." Barnaby sincerely remarks, "Well, that's very nice of you." The ruse is soon discovered, exposing the embarrassed occupant. As Barnaby smiles sadistically, Ollie self- consciously gives us his patented "camera stare" and finger fiddles with the boarders of the box. Fade out.

For all their efforts, in the next scene we see Stannie and Ollie in the stockade. The King issued a Royal Proclamation whereas the two were found "guilty of burglary!" They are sentenced to be "dunked and exiled to Bogeyland forever." Bogeyland is the never-to-be-talked-about place in a child's mind and as we learn, it is Barnaby's personal domain as "King of the Bogeymen."

Meanwhile back at the ducking pond, the whole of Toyland is witnessing the miscarriage of justice that is Ollie Dee being dunked in the pond. His pathetic cries and near drowning moves Bo Peep greatly. She resigns herself to approach the poolside where the evil Barnaby is laughing with sadistic pleasure over Ollie's fate. Even Ol' King Cole laughs boisterously with his oversized stomach.*

Amidst the commotion of Ollie drowning and Stan crying, she addresses the old man. "All right, Mr. Barnaby—I consent." That kicks the scoundrel into

---

* According to Randy Skretvedt's book "Laurel & Hardy-The Magic Behind the Movies," the actor who played King Cole actually ruptured his stomach muscles after "laughing for two days straight."

action. He says, "With your Majesty's permission—I wish to withdraw my charges." King Cole responds with an enthusiastic, "Withdrawn they shall be."

Barnaby strikes while the iron is hot and a revolting, dramatic development ensues. "Friends of Toyland—I want you all to meet…the future Mrs. Barnaby!" The charges are dismissed for Stannie and Ollie and they are free to go. Barnaby approaches them to offer: "From now on—you and I are going to be very close friends." Not if Laurel and Hardy have anything to do with it.

The scene changes to Barnaby's house, he tells his small servant to "run over and tell the bride that all is ready and her lover is waiting." This puts forth the vulgar "Wedding of Barnaby to Bo Peep" in motion. Best man Ollie escorts the shy bride hiding beneath her veil in the proper place. Her dejected boyfriend, Tom-Tom watches through the window as are most of the townspeople. Barnaby senses his forth coming moment and beckons the minister, "come, come, Judge—let's waste no time."

As the minister recites the vows, a resigned female voice under the veil repeats the vows. With every step, Barnaby smiles with glee at the prospect of his conquest. He slips the ring on the bride's finger. The minister announces that they are now "Man and Wife." The bride is overcome with her crying.

Barnaby starts to lift the veil and announces, "And now, to kiss the bride." Ollie objects, "Haven't you forgotten something?" Barnaby, in an overly gracious moment remembers. "Oh, yes, the mortgage: my wedding present."

Ollie surveys the legal document, determines its authenticity and promptly tears it in half. With that, Ollie pulls back the bride's veil and announces: "Now, you may kiss the bride." It was Stannie all along in that dress. Barnaby recoils in shocked outrage; his face tells it all.

Barnaby belts out: "What is the meaning of this?" Ollie with a slight revenge factor, repeats what Barnaby said to him earlier: "Big bait catches big rat." As Barnaby stomps out the door, he promises: "The King shall hear of this!"

All of Toyland celebrates; there is Victor Herbert music, dancing, and we see most of the Mother Goose characters come out. It's truly a wonderful moment for all and the film conceivably could have ended at this point, but Barnaby has plans for revenge.

As the camera fades in we see Barnaby's reflection in the mirror. He is outraged: "Tricked, cheated, laughed at in the streets. The fools, so they think they can out-whit Barnaby, eh? Ha! I'll show them. There must be a way."

At that moment Barnaby's manservant (who was mopping the floor), inadvertently hits Barnaby in the face with the swab. Barnaby kicks the servant to the floor and yells at him: "Idiot, dolt, imbecile, *pig!*" Then a devilish idea comes forth.

The sinister Barnaby decides to pig-nap one of the three little pigs with an apple as bait. He explains his devious plan to his servant (to frame Tom-Tom with the evidence of the remnants) and asks, "Do you know the penalty for Pig-napping? Banishment to Bogeyland" He laughs diabolically at his cleverness.

The next scenes are mostly in pantomime as Barnaby sets out to steal a pig. Set to the music of Walt Disney's *Three Little Pigs*, we see the villain acting much like Disney's "Big Bad Wolf." As he unsuccessfully goes through the progress of each of their homes (even blowing one over) and getting bit, hit with a hammer and socked in the jaw in the process. Henry Brandon's Barnaby character reacts to each futile attempt until he manages to bag the one named Little Elmer, and carries him home.

Barnaby instructs his servant to take the "evidence" and place it inside of Tom-Tom's house, explaining: "That will prove that he not only stole the pig, but that he also ground him into sausage. And now, Little Elmer…we shall see."

The plan works. Tom-Tom is arrested and according to the King's Proclamation: "Has been found guilty of Pig napping, he will be immediately banished to Bogeyland by his Majesty, King Cole." A somber Stannie reflects; "Poor Tom-Tom, I'm glad we didn't have to go to Bogeyland." Then he asks the "worldly" Ollie what it is.

Ollie bravely explains to his curiousness friend, "Oh it's a terrible place.

Once you go there you never come back. When the Bogeymen get you, they eat you alive." He describes them as "half-man and half animal, with great big ears and a great big mouth and hair all over their bodies."

As the soldiers prepare to take Bo-Peep's love interest away, she defends this circumstantial evidence to the King. Barnaby interjects: "Why not let the law take its course, Your Majesty?"

Stannie and Ollie "smell a rat" and that it's Barnaby's doing. They rescue Little Elmer from Barnaby's house, but not in time to save Tom-Tom, as he has since been taken by raft- through an alligator-infested moat surrounding the village and thrown onto a riverbank.

Bo-Peep continues to protest to the King until Barnaby chides her, "Wasting your affection on a common pig-napper." Prompting Bo-Peep to say, "Tom-Tom is innocent and you know it, I hate you I hate you."

We then hear Ollie off camera yelling, "Just a minute." He enters the scene and places the very alive pig on a stool. "Mister Majesty, We found little Elmer in Barnaby's cellar." As Barnaby runs away, the King announces "I'll give fifty thousand guineas for the capture of that scoundrel, dead or alive." The crowd gives chase but the scallywag slips through.

The perky Bo-Peep uses the same raft the executioners used to transport her beau and arrives somewhere in Bogeyland. As she searches we see Barnaby go over the side of a water-well and disappear down below. Stannie and Ollie think they have trapped him and beckon him to come up, but to no avail. Barnaby had used a secret back entrance to escape into his own dark kingdom.

As Tom-Tom and Bo Peep find each other, Barnaby catches up to them and engages in a fist fight with his rival. We hear Barnaby's distinct scream as he falls over the edge to below. Losing the fight, he summons his Bogeymen to the charge by thumping a club against the cave wall. It works: hairy monsters jump down into the scene from all angles as he laughs triumphantly.

As this is going on, Stannie and Ollie finally figure Barnaby is not going to be up from the well. With great trepidation they are able to reach the bottom and follow his footsteps into the dark cavernous caves of Bogeyland.

The boys follow the screams to find all the principals, Ollie grabs Barnaby and announces, "Just a minute, Mr. Barnaby, you're going back with us and..." His sentence is unfinished as the monsters surround them. Ollie screams, "Ohhhh, the Bogeymen," as Stan lets out a hysterical, panicked cry.

The innocents out run their pursuers to the bottom of the well and ascend the stepping rocks to safety. Barnaby sees this and with blood thirsty revenge says, "They've escaped me, but I'll get them if I have to destroy the whole of Toyland." He directs his army "To the rafts."

Back at Toyland the streets are filled with reveling citizens. All the characters give Stannie and Ollie a hero's welcome for rescuing Tom-Tom and Bo-Peep. Being the only ones to ever return from Bogeyland, the King wants to hear the details and asks, "Did you catch Barnaby?" Ollie replies, "No sir. He was running so fast, we couldn't catch him." Stannie chimed in with, "He was scared to death, wasn't he?"

As this scene unfolds, the audience sees Barnaby on a raft filled with teams of Bogeymen. Barnaby has his arms crossed defiantly in a pose reminiscent of the famous painting of "Washington Crossing the Delaware." They are heading to the Toyland gates.

Ollie is still boasting about their exploits, describing what the Bogeymen look like. At that moment we see the hideous monsters come over the wall and overpower the gateman to enter Toyland. The townspeople see this, shriek and run to their homes for safety. Stannie and Ollie think it was their descriptions that scared everyone off, so they take turns beckoning them back. "Come back, there's nothing to be scared of, you're not scared now, they're not half as bad as they look."

Just then we hear the distinctive Barnaby voice, "There they are!" The boys yell in fright as Barnaby commands his army to "Follow me." As Bogeymen pour through the gates, the dramatic music intensifies.

Barnaby knows what he wants; he goes straight for the old shoe where the object of his affection is hiding with her family and Tom-Tom.

Simultaneously, Stannie and Ollie run to the warehouse and spot a box of darts. The sign reads: "4 Gross Steel Point Darts," just the thing to throw at the infiltrating hairy enemy.

The Bogeymen are in the process of overrunning Toyland and they indiscriminately take those sleeping in their beds and carry them off. That is, until they are hit with darts. We hear their yelps of pain and see them fall. As Bogeymen confront Stannie and Ollie, the boys throw handfuls of darts at the enemies' chests to fend them off.

Ollie triumphantly announces, "We'll fix those Bogeymen!" They continue the attack on the monsters, this time Ollie tees them up and Stannie bats them further into the advancing Bogeymen. Stannie's dexterity is in full swing as he easily hits his intended targets.

Bogeymen are by now on top of and climbing into the old brown shoe. One is reaching through the window trying to pull Bo-Peep. Each advancing monster is hit by a well-placed dart. Mickey Mouse helps by climbing into his zeppelin and flying over the battle scene dropping torpedoes. Explosions are heard, further throwing the clash into chaos.

The battle intensifies when a dart that is intended for Barnaby just misses his face and sticks into the window frame of the Old Shoe. Bogeymen are now carrying their victims off. These scenes terrified Depression-era children in the mid 1930's as well as Baby Boomer children when the film was on television later in the 1950's and '60's and still retain their power to induce delightful shivers in the 21st Century.

Barnaby, sensing a victory laughs as he makes his way through Toyland. Back at the warehouse, the boys are continuing their frontal attack. Stannie stops and says, "Say, you know what? Let's load it into the canon." As they do, Bogeymen confront a group of children in bed. They scream as they are carried away.

Barnaby starts to reroute when he is tripped by a rope held taut by the pigs. One of them bonks their would-be-pignapper over the brain with a balloon, stunning him for a moment.

As Stannie looks around for more darts, he stops and gazes at the one hundred, 6-ft. high wooden soldier army standing in military formation. Stannie points to them and casually remarks, "The wooden soldiers." Ollie and Stannie run to them and activate each one by pushing the button on the back. They then open the warehouse doors and lead them into the battle zone.

The music bursts into Victor Herbert's "March of the Toys" as the soldiers march out, the boys shake hands at their proud moment and march in place. The solders instinctively advance with fixed bayonets.

Bedlam is occurring in the town square; Barnaby is now carrying the screaming Bo-Peep. They both stop and react to the sight of the soldiers. One of them shoots a cannon at Barnaby. The projectile (is it a roll of toilet paper?) hits the intended target in the chest.

Soldiers are pushing Bogeymen against the trees; one of them gets his head stepped on by the soldiers. Children are squealing in delight as they hug the solders around the neck and away from danger. One little boy holds onto a soldier's leg until he is out of danger.

As Barnaby tries to exit from the soldiers' path, giant alphabet blocks fall down in an avalanche over the villain. They spell out: "R-A-T." The rest of the soldiers put the Bogeymen into retreat toward the open gate; they fall into the alligator habitat and we hear snapping and hissing, the Bogeymen are overwhelmed.

Since the cannon was already loaded with darts, Ollie suggests: "Let's give them a parting shot." Stannie lights the fuse as Ollie shuts his eyes. The cannon suddenly changes direction and it is Ollie who is hit with the darts, all over his backside. As Ollie howls in pain, Stannie cries and the townspeople laugh for joy as the music ends simultaneously with a fade out. The end title is shown in the form of turning the last page of a book. "And they lived happily ever afterwards."

The original script had a different finish as divulged in a newspaper article before release: "Barnaby has planned to rid the community of Tom-Tom by tying him to a rocket, but at the last minute he himself is sent soaring aloft. The rocket explodes and the twinkling lights spelled out the ending."*

Henry wrapped up his final week of work on November 3, 1934.† The total sum paid out for his film acting was $1,563.00.‡ He was paid by the hour.

Hal Roach had offered the City of Los Angeles the sturdy sets of the Toyland buildings as a gift to the city, hopefully to be housed in Griffith Park. The City did not act on this generous offer.

Henry Brandon divulged that "every character actor in Hollywood wanted to kill me for getting the Barnaby part. What they didn't realize was I was run all through the lot, they would have been exhausted."

Henry Brandon told a group of Laurel and Hardy fans in 1987§ that the constant friction between Roach and Laurel (demonstrated by his gesturing of his two fists coming together) allowed the give and take chemistry to make the film that is now considered a classic comic-fantasy and family holiday tradition.

---

*   *San Bernardino County Sun* August 19, 1934
†   Hal Roach payroll ledger
‡   Ibid
§   Midnight Patrol Tent banquet in Monterey, California

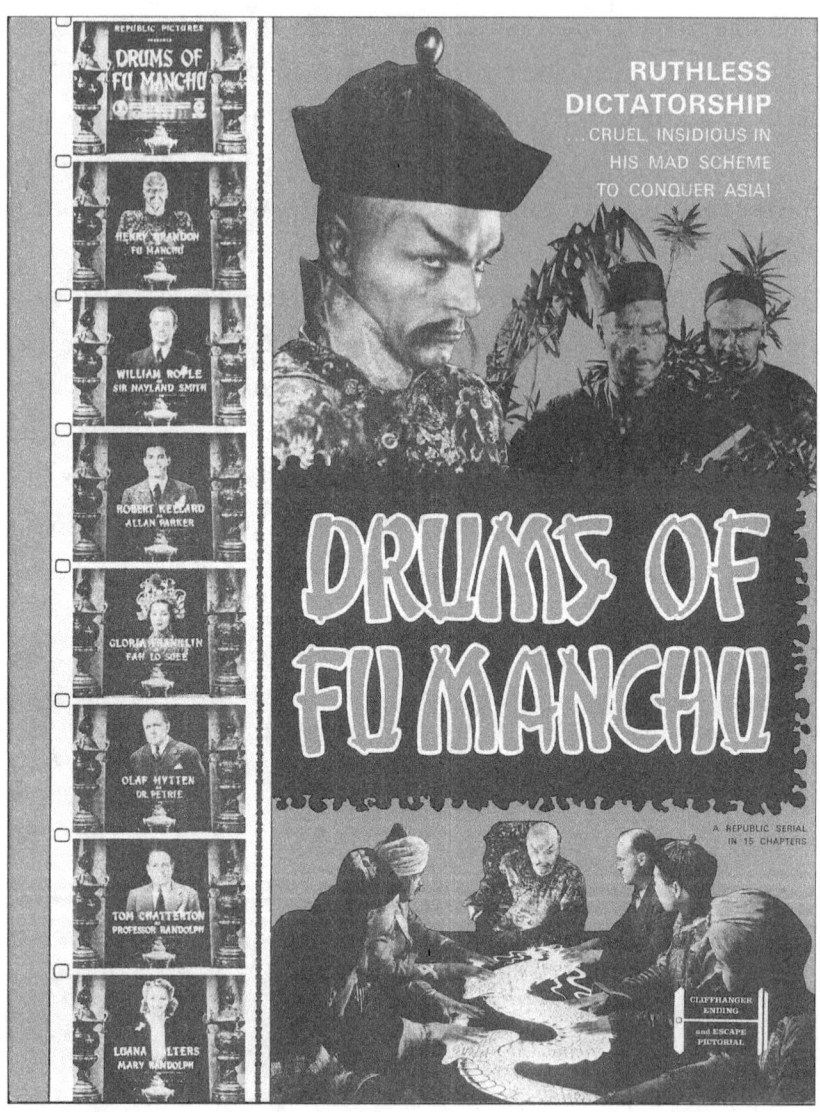

Drums of Fu Manchu serial fan publication by Jack Mathis in the early '70's. Collection of Rick Greene.

CHAPTER FOUR
Three Iconic Roles II - *Drums of Fu Manchu*

HENRY BRANDON WAS NO stranger to cliffhangers, portraying the lead villain/lead henchman roles in three serials for Universal Studios in the late 1930's virtually back to back. He played The Cobra in *Jungle Jim*, Blackstone in *Secret Agent X-9* and Captain Laska in *Buck Rogers* before landing his last and greatest serial part, the evil and insidious title character in Republic Studio's *Drums of Fu Manchu*. Not only one of the greatest serials ever made, *Drums* offers the definitive silver screen interpretation of Fu Manchu making it one of Henry Brandon's essential iconic performances.

Fu Manchu was created in a series of pulpy thrillers by the great Sax Rohmer (the pen name of Arthur Henry Ward) beginning with *The Mystery of Fu Manchu* (also known as *The Insidious Dr. Fu Manchu*) and continuing in a total of fourteen novels from 1913 until his death in 1959. The first few novels are written very much in the style of the Sherlock Holmes stories, with daring Sir Dennis Nayland Smith assisted by his dear friend and biographer, Dr. Petrie. These are the most effective of the Fu Manchu stories, as later entries have Dr. Petrie as a supporting character but the tales aren't told by him.

Fu Manchu had starred in several silent serial adaptations and notably portrayed by Boris Karloff in MGM's *The Mask of Fu Manchu* from 1932. Karloff looks terrific and does an admirable job as the bad Doctor but he's still miscast as that Karloff voice just doesn't fit this most ultimate of thriller villains and every time he talks, it's jarring.

In December of 1939, when *Drums of Fu Manchu* went into production by Republic Pictures, there were currently nine Fu Manchu novels out and the very latest was *The Drums of Fu Manchu*. (Note that the novel has 'The' in the title but the film drops it). However, the fifteen-chapter serial (the longest of Henry Brandon's four serials) is NOT an adaptation of that specific novel, but "Suggested by the stories of Sax Rohmer" as an opening title explains. The plot is a synthesis of ALL of the exploits but really borrows more from the earlier Karloff film than from the books.

Drums of Fu Manchu was in production longer than ANY Republic serial, showing the care that was taken to bring this important property to life. At the center of it all was Henry's compelling, larger-than-life performance as the evil but noble Fu Manchu in one of the most important roles of his entire career – a role he makes the most of.

Eric Stedman, who produced a restored edition of *Drums of Fu Manchu* for DVD in 2012 from 35mm film elements, summed it up perfectly in his introduction for that release. "Henry Brandon's Fu Manchu is second only to Charles Middleton's Ming the Merciless (from the *Flash Gordon* serials) as the finest serial villain that audiences love to hate."

In a 1972 interview with Henry Brandon for an issue of "Those Enduring Matinee Idols", he explains how he landed the role of Fu Manchu:

> They sent for me when they were (planning to do) a Zorro serial (*Zorro's Fighting Legion*). I went in and they were sitting there, about six of them, producers and directors. They always had two directors, one man couldn't do it all – they would alternate. They looked me over for about two or three minutes, asked a few questions. Suddenly, they all said "That's it! He's right!" And I walked out and said to myself, "I'm going to play a hero, finally, after all those villains!" I went home and called my agent and he

said, "You're not getting that one. They cast you in the following serial." That's how I got it... by going in to see about playing a nice guy!

Rohmer's initial vivid description of Fu Manchu was used for the design of the Republic serial character rather than the disappointing MGM-Karloff model. He wrote, "Imagine a person, tall, lean and feline, high-shouldered with a brow like Shakespeare and a face like Satan, a close-shaven skull and long, magnetic eyes of the true cat-green. Invest him with all the cruel cunning of an entire Eastern race, accumulated in one giant intellect, with all the resources of science past and present, with all the resources, if you will, of a wealthy government – which, however, has already denied all knowledge of his existence. Imagine that awful being, and you have a mental picture of Dr. Fu Manchu, the Yellow Peril incarnate in one man."

Chapter One is entitled "Fu Manchu Strikes" and begins with an introductory title card, "From the pages of fiction steps the most sinister figure of all time — FU MANCHU! Schooled in the ancient mysteries of the Orient he is as modern as Tomorrow! Ruthless, ageless, holding himself above human law, he embarks upon his most stupendous crime — the conquest of Asia! And with him comes the thunder of his summons of death — The Drums of Fu Manchu!"

Beneath these chilling opening titles, we get our first glimpse of Henry Brandon as Fu Manchu walking directly toward the camera, looking with undisguised menace right into OUR eyes as we hear the first inkling of those pulse-quickening drums. Drums that will soon signal each of the coming fourteen cliffhangers. From these wildly effective opening moments, it is clear that we are in for something special as the stage is expertly set for danger, thrills, torture and mayhem! Just what Saturday afternoons were made for.

The story proper begins on a rainy and dark downtown Los Angeles street as Sir Dennis Nayland Smith (William Royle) of Scotland Yard summons a cab, taking care that he isn't followed. He arrives at the office of his old friend, Dr. Petrie and before he can knock, an attempt is made on his life by a fanged dacoit named Loki – one of Fu Manchu's murderous obedient zombies. Each dacoit has a 'Y' shaped scar on his forehead, the result of Fu Manchu's operation on the frontal lobe of his brain! The jagged knife misses its mark as Smith and Petrie reunite and we learn that Dr. Fu Manchu isn't dead in Burma as Smith previously believed – he is back in California with the Si Fan, his evil organization. This is right out of the opening pages of the first Fu Manchu story and it is thrilling, melodramatic stuff.

Cut to a gong that rings itself. Fu Manchu enters. Henry employs a gliding walk that is quite unnerving. The Si Fan is seated around a long table in a dark room. They all rise and bow as their Master enters and Fu Manchu takes his place at the head of the table. Henry Brandon is wearing an excellent bald cap and has thin arching eyebrows and a very thin and long black mustache. He wears an ornate collarless robe and it truly feels as though the Devil himself has entered the room. Brandon has NEVER been more menacing or threatening on screen. And right here is the template for every James Bond villain yet to come – Dr. No, Goldfinger, Blofeld – they all have their genesis in Brandon's screen incarnation of Dr. Fu Manchu.

"I have summoned you here because events of grave importance have come to pass. I have promised that the sacred scepter will appear during this, the holy year." Fu Manchu, appearing with the scepter of Genghis Khan, will unite all the tribes of Asia against the West in full revolt. The scepter is hidden in the tomb of Khan, the location of which is revealed on three Mongolian scrolls – and we have our MacGuffin.

Dr. James Parker, an eminent archeologist, has one of the scrolls, explains Fu Manchu. "I move against Dr. Parker… tonight!" he intones as a gong sounds and the camera zooms in close on his feline features. This striking, dramatic introduction to Fu Manchu, whom we will spend quite a bit of time with over fifteen chapters, presents a screen villain unlike ANY we've ever seen before. He's calm and confident, in full control of his emotions. Henry uses a slightly high-pitched, foreign voice – almost a monotone – that commands your attention. Impressively, he sounds NOTHING like Henry Brandon! This clearly is the role of a lifetime.

A newspaper headline tells us that Fu has been successful, that Dr. Parker has disappeared and he is '**BELIEVED TO BE A VICTIM OF FU MANCHU**.' Parker's son Allan (Robert Kellard) seeks out assistance from Nayland Smith and Dr. Petrie, who gladly help this young American hero of the story. A Walter Winchell-type reporter has a scoop and is about to reveal – on the air – the location of the kidnapped Dr. Parker. We hear, for the first time loud and clear, those throbbing, deafening drums, and the reporter drops dead in mid-sentence. Smith, Petrie and young Parker rush to the radio station to find he's been murdered with a gelatinous poison dart that disintegrates! This will be no ordinary bang-bang car chase mystery criminal serial

Professor Edward Randolph (Tom Chatterton) has a clue as to the location of Dr. Parker's scroll which means he will become Fu Manchu's next victim. Allan Parker arrives with Petrie and Smith, as do six murderous dacoits. Fu Manchu's dark beautiful daughter Fah Lo Suee (Gloria Franklin) arrives secreted in a mummy case, to command the dacoits and kidnap Randolph. Quite the melee transpires as drums sound, knives fly, knockout gas is used and pandemonium reigns. Randolph is taken during the confusion and becomes a prisoner, along with Dr. Parker, of Fu Manchu.

When neither man will reveal the location of an ancient plaque that holds a clue to the whereabouts of the tomb, Fu Manchu tells them, "I must resort to sterner methods!" He explains, in a deliciously twisted way, about the "Seven Gates to Paradise," a torture apparatus of his own devising.

A body is strapped into a reclining box with seven compartments. Fu tells them, "The first gate is opened and some of my small hungry friends are permitted to join my guests." We see the shadow of some squirming ravenous rats. "I have had guests who have successfully passed three of the gates, but not one has ever come through the fourth!"

The Insidious Dr. Fu Manchu. Collection of Rick Greene.

Fu seems to use mental telepathy to tell his main fanged dacoit which of the two men to put into the device. It is Randolph who goes in, but he implores Dr. Parker not to reveal anything about the plaque. Just as Fu Manchu is about the open the first gate; Parker cracks and reveals the plaque is coming via train in the care of Randolph's pretty daughter Mary. Fu leaves to arrange for some harm to come to that train; Allan Parker arrives with Smith and some muscle to free his Dad and Randolph.

The first chapter is an exciting plot-packed three-reeler and is pretty violent, with a high body count. There are enough thrills and set-pieces in this initial thirty minutes than you'd normally have in any three chapters of a traditional serial; we haven't even come to the cliffhanger yet.

Fah Lo Suee arranges for Mary's train to collide with another train and secretes a dacoit on board to steal the plaque. Allan arrives via a ladder lowered from a bi-plane and as the drums begin to throb louder and faster, the trains collide in a fiery crash! All this and we still have fourteen serial chapters to go.

Cy Feuer contributes a masterful music score that incorporates the drums of Fu Manchu as an aural cue for thrills and excitement and it is VERY effective. However, it is never clear whether the drums are a musical cue for the audience or if the characters are supposed to also be hearing them, as sometimes they react to the noise and sometimes they don't. And where exactly the music is *coming* from remain one of many mysteries of Fu Manchu.

The second chapter is called "The Monster" for good reason. Allan and Mary defeat the dacoit and jump from the train before the collision. They are safe, although untold dozens must have been killed in the massive crash.

Fu punishes the dacoit who failed to retrieve the needed scroll, which is secreted inside the plaque, by springing a trap door and dropping him into a large tank with giant octopus! As soon as we see this, it becomes clear how THIS chapter is going to end.

Allan Parker finds the hidden scroll inside a secret compartment within the plaque Mary had, which Smith identifies as a 3rd Dynasty Mongolian papyrus that must be translated by an expert [Funny how Nayland knows at a glance that it is a 3rd Dynasty Mongolian papyrus but can't translate it]. They head to meet Dr. Humphrey at the museum for that purpose, but Fah Lo Suee gets there first and, via a drugged cigarette, has the helpless historian under Fu Manchu's control.

When Smith and Parker arrive with the scroll, Humphrey gets it and sneaks away to join Fu Manchu. Allan sees him leaving out of a window, takes a spectacular dive from the second story and hides beneath the car to arrive at Fu's secret hideaway. By this second chapter, it is wildly apparent that *Drums of Fu Manchu's* thrilling leaps, fights and stunts are leagues better than anything we've seen in Brandon's three Universal serials. No one was more adept at action sequences than the stuntmen and directors at Republic Studios.

Allan Parker has his first face-to-face encounter with Fu Manchu as he bursts into the Doctor's lair at gunpoint to reclaim the scroll. The master criminal, however, easily drops him through the trap door into the awaiting tentacles of his monster octopus as the drums pound away!

In all the sequences we've seen with Fu Manchu thus far, Henry Brandon has been in darkened and semi-darkened rooms with a diffused spotlight hitting just his face or eyes, emphasizing his eerie evilness. The oriental makeup is top rate. In fact, co-author Greene borrowed Henry's VHS copy of *Drums of Fu Manchu* in 1986 to watch the rare chapter-play for the first time and asked Brandon if his head had been shaved for the role. "Good Lord, no" Henry told him, "It was a bald cap. But a *very* good one! It fooled you!"

When asked about the make-up for Fu Manchu in the 1972 interview for "Those Enduring Matinee Idols" Henry elaborated, "The make up for Fu Manchu was a very, very difficult job. The gateman, the make-up man and I were the first ones on the lot. We got there about 4:30 in the morning. (The bald cap is) a complete rubber cap. It's something like rubber, and that has to be put on very carefully. If he didn't have me scrunch up my forehead, the cap would buckle during the day. It was designed by the greatest make-up man they ever had in Hollywood, Morris Sidermann. He invented all this rubber-type stuff they're using now."

The third chapter is called *"Ransom in the Sky"* and reveals Smith and Petrie's timely arrival to rescue Allan from the octopus death pit. As they drill the creature with bullets and pull Parker from the inky waters, Fu Manchu escapes through a back exit without the scroll. Dr. Humphrey sufficiently revives and translates it, but Fu still has a telepathic connection with him.

The criminal instructs his pawn (who hears drums that no one else does) to direct Allan and Mary into a trap at the museum.

Fu Manchu and his nemesis Nayland Smith (William Royle). Collection of Rick Greene.

When they arrive, they are attacked by dacoits, who manage to kidnap Mary. Fu offers to exchange her for the Dalai scroll, and Allan asks Nayland Smith if this is another trick. "One never knows, but Fu Manchu *will* keep his word!" Fu himself arrives to conduct this 'distasteful bargain.' Smith and Parker agree, and as Allan leaves with his enemy, Fu gloats, "Thank you, Gentlemen, for a very pleasant interview!" Brandon's delivery has just the right amount of snark.

They arrive at a deserted field and take off in a small plane. Mary, confined in the back, breaks the fuel line causing gasoline to escape. Fu Manchu reclaims the parachutes that Mary and Allan were to use, going back on the bargain due to Mary's treachery. He explains, "May I remind you that among my people honor is a sacred thing and those who defile it can expect no mercy!" As he exits the aeroplane doorway, leaving our heroes on a doomed plummeting plane, he says "Happy landing." The drums sound again and the chapter ends as the plane crashes.

The Pendulum of Doom opens with Mary and Allan surviving the crash and reunited with their comrades. Fu does some reuniting himself by assembling the Si-Fan again to inform them that he has the second scroll that will lead them to Khan's scepter and he will now embark on obtaining the third and final scroll, which is in the possession of a Dr. Chang.

The forces of both good and evil converge on Dr. Chang's offices and Fu Manchu arrives first. He improvises another torture device to compel Change to reveal the location of the Kardac Segment, which offers a clue to the third scroll. Again Sir Dennis and Allan arrive, do battle with dacoits and save Dr. Chang before Fu Manchu gets the information he needs. An eccentric collector possesses the Kardac Segment and this reveal is overheard by a dacoit on the ledge. Smith wounds the dacoit, who makes it back to his master's new headquarters but dies before he can report to Fu Manchu. No matter, because Fu captures Mr. Parker and is evidently a big fan of Edgar Allen Poe since he straps poor Allan into a pendulum device. The blade descends lower and lower, the drums roar and Fu Manchu urges Parker to reveal the identity of the collector who owns the Kardac Segment! A diabolical cliffhanger that leads into Chapter Five and *The House of Terror*.

Nayland Smith, of course, rescues Allan Parker from the razor-sharp pendulum. The plot takes them to a museum that uses wax figures, several of which are replaced by patient dacoits. This chapter features Dwight Frye as Professor Anderson, a minor role but further adding to the horror pedigree of *Drums* by having the co-star of *Dracula* and *Frankenstein* on hand. As the drums sound again, the dacoits attack Parker and Anderson. Frye acquits himself admirably in the melee, which is a red herring aimed at drawing Fu Manchu away from the real location of the Kardac Segment. Nayland Smith implores eccentric collector Ezra Howard to give him the Kardac Segment at his haunted-looking home during a raging thunderstorm. Fu Manchu wasn't fooled by the museum detour and is on hand to lead the attack and obtain the Segment. Curiously, his dacoits are soaked, but Fu Manchu doesn't appear to be wet at all. Interesting supernatural touches like these help *Drums of Fu Manchu* to stand apart from other serials, Republic or otherwise.

Manchu father and daughter, Fu and Fah (Henry Brandon and Gloria Franklin). Collection of Rick Greene.

In Chapter Six, *Death Dials a Number*, Fu Manchu obtains the Kardac Segment but not before a dacoit drops it and it makes a perfect impression in the fresh mud! This allows Nayland Smith to make a perfect plaster impression of it, giving both sides the information contained on the surface. It reveals that the Segment itself fits into a larger piece located in Asia which will finally reveal the location of the Tomb.

Fu captures Allan Parker and Henry Brandon gets a bit of break in this chapter since he makes a copy of Allan's face to impersonate him and leave the country. Brandon does voice-over duties but sits most of the short out as Robert Kellard plays both the real and the false Allan Parker. Kellard does a fine job playing Fu as Allan, capturing both Brandon's smug, superior look and his commanding walk.

Vengeance of the Si-Fan is the middle chapter of *Drums of Fu Manchu* and as such, takes the serial in a different and welcome direction. After six chapters of bouncing around Los Angeles, our little cast of characters all converge upon Asia for the back half, seeking out the scepter of Genghis Kahn. Arriving in Branapuhr, Allan Parker (the real one as Fu has disposed of his false Parker face) is able to infiltrate a meeting of the Si Fan disguised in a long, black hooded robe. Fu Manchu brings them the Kardac Segment and reveals that the larger piece it fits into is an idol located in the ancient Temple of the Blind Dragon which reveals the location of the Tomb. Before Fu reveals the modern name of the Temple, he is told Allan Parker is among them. In a tense and suspenseful sequence, Allan manages to pull a gun and attempt to escape, not knowing he's backing into two dacoits holding huge curved swords ready to decapitate him. Doesn't he hear those drums?!

Onward to Chapter Eight, *Danger Trail*, in which once again Nayland Smith rescues Parker by gunning down the two sword-wielding titans before they can separate Allan's head from his shoulders. The Si-Fan scatter and everyone heads to The Temple of the Sun with their Kardac Segments. Allan and Nayland Smith head out first on a dangerous trek across India (really the Iverson Ranch in Chatsworth, California) because Fu has sent word to the natives of the various tribes to attack the jeep when sighted. The chapter ends with the first such successful attack as the jeep goes over a cliff!

Chapter Nine is called *The Crystal of Death* and shows Allan and Nayland jumping to safety before their jeep plummets over a cliff and explodes. Mary, Petrie and Randolph soon arrive in a second jeep and they proceed to the Temple… but not before Fu Manchu captures both Mary and Allan. She is put under Fu Manchu's hypnotic power and Allan is tied to two huge trees to be torn apart! When Fu takes his leave of Parker to head to the Temple of the Sun, Allan asks for a drink of water. Fu Manchu cruelly pours the water on the ground near Allan's head with an evil little snicker. Brandon here shows a touch of nasty emotion that is deliciously effective.

At the Temple of the Sun, Smith's plaster Kardac Segments fits in place, but doesn't cause the idol to 'speak' as the prophecy proclaims. Fu Manchu arrives and tricks the Priest of Kardac by placing his authentic Segment into the idol and having Fah Lo Suee speak for the Goddess of the Sun… and orders a sacrifice. Fu has one handy… the hypnotized Mary, who is placed in the path of a kind of laser beam device created by mirrors and an ancient crystal. The deadly beam slowly creeps along, exploding little solid bronze statues on its path toward Mary's prone body. Here Henry Brandon allows Fu a moment of startling wide-eyed glee as his normally emotionless villain shows more and more emotion as we get close to the serial's impending climax.

Chapter Ten has the escaped-from-his-death-trap Allan Parker arriving in the nick of time to shoot out the mirror fueling the laser ray. Fu's treachery is revealed and just as the Priest orders his capture, he hurls gas bombs and escapes from the Temple.

Fu Manchu heads to Dragon Gorge with Loki and a few dacoits to gain entrance to the Tomb. In broad daylight and outdoors among the Iverson Ranch boulders, Fu Manchu isn't as terrifying as he was in the dark and sinister early chapters, but he is still quite formidable. Interestingly, Brandon recalled in 1987 for *Starlog Magazine:*

> Every once in a while when we were outdoors, in and out of cars and climbing up mountains and things, I would completely lose the character and the accent. Both Jack (English) and Bill Whitney would notice it and tell me I was losing it. I just didn't *feel* like Fu Manchu out in the open; it didn't feel right.

Fu Manchu arrives first at the hidden entrance, quickly followed by Allan and Sir Dennis, both of them avoiding the ancient spear gun trap that

Indiana Jones would have loved. Inside the tomb, Fu mentally summons his deadly drums, the loud vibrations of which cause sharp stalactites to fall down onto our heroes. There is a striking Lugosi-esque close-up of Henry Brandon's heavy-lidded eyes as he harnesses some supernatural power to summon the drums. Ten chapters in, and *Drums of Fu Manchu* still has some surprises up its ornamental sleeve.

Finally, our cast enters *The Tomb of Genghis Khan* in Chapter Eleven after a battered and bruised Smith and Parker capture Fu Manchu. A lever in the wall releases an iron door and Allan enters first and locates the scepter. But the tomb door slams shut and deadly gas is released from the floor! Allan slumps down and against a wall panel that slides open and allows him to escape certain death. Steven Spielberg and George Lucas most definitely saw *Drums of Fu Manchu* as a massive influence on their *Raiders of the Lost Ark* some forty years later.

Allan and Smith take Fu Manchu and the prized sacred scepter back to The Temple of the Sun while Parker then goes back to the Fort for soldiers to escort them. Even held captive in the hands of his enemies, Fu doesn't seem particularly concerned. And for good reason – he is soon rescued and released by faithful fanged Loki.

Fu Manchu regains the scepter and heads out to dynamite Allan Parker in his jeep. But Allan has been captured by Fah Lo Suee, who doesn't know that her father is free. They head *back* to the Temple so she can trade Parker for Fu Manchu in a prisoner exchange, unaware that they are heading into a dynamite trap! The massive explosion at Fu Manchu's hand is this chapter's climax.

Chapter Twelve means we will soon be in the home stretch of this long but wildly entertaining journey. Allan survives the car crash and hides while Fu Manchu is horrified to find his daughter's body in the twisted mangled car. He calls out her name twice in gut-wrenching sorrow, lifting her limp body in his arms. Even the insidious Dr. Fu Manchu is not infallible. Allan hides in the trailer behind the truck as the villains drive back to the Fu Manchu base camp. Fah Lo Suee never returns for the remaining chapters, so one can presume she was killed in this explosion at her father's hand. After Fu disappears into a tent with his daughter still in his arms, Allan fights off two dacoits as he escapes in the truck in a thrilling sequence.

As Parker gathers up his comrades at the Temple to make the dangerous journey back to the Fort with the scepter, Fu Manchu orders the tribesmen to set death traps all along the route. Their orders are to capture or to kill Parker and his party and bring the scepter to Fu Manchu. The heroes drive without lights, pistols ready, on the dangerous road. This won't be an easy task. Dozens of men with rifles fire on the speeding car in the darkness and they somehow make it through this gauntlet of hot lead to the final ambush spot. They pull off the road so Nayland and Allan can scout this last barrier on a ridge – and see an army of Fu's troops approaching on horseback. Allan Parker pushes a massive flaming signal fire down onto the hordes in a spectacular sequence but is attacked by a lone tribesman and they topple down into the flaming inferno below.

Chapter Thirteen is called *The Devil's Tattoo* and shows us that Mr. Parker avoided falling into those flames and that they can easily proceed with the scepter past the last ambush to the waiting gates of Fort Branapuhr. They need to get the relic into the hands of the local High Llama, who will use it to quell the uprising and return peace to Asia. Fu Manchu intercepts the message that brings the High Llama's emissary to the Fort to retrieve the scepter and bring it to him. Fu easily captures the emissary and his delegation. The master criminal makes himself up with a full beard and Cossack outfit to enter the Fort and reclaim the scepter. Professor Randolph and Allan Parker are both fooled by Fu Manchu's make-up and voice acting but he is asked to wait for an armed delegation; this definitely does not fit into his plans. Fu Manchu nabs the ornate case containing the scepter and steals a car to escape with it. However, as Randolph was examining the scepter in another room, Fu has only the case.

He isn't dissuaded so easily and attacks again that very night, sending three skilled infiltrators who use a cloudy acid to eat away at the safe and nab the scepter. These last few penultimate chapters involve the scepter changing hands back and forth until Fu Manchu finally has it, but is bottlenecked in town by the troops watching all roads.

In Chapter Fourteen, they at last manage to capture the entire Si-Fan criminal organization as the net around Fu Manchu closes in. Using the power of the scepter, Fu gains the allegiance of a local tribe who helps to capture Sir Dennis. Again, the craftsmen at Republic Studios continue to impress with exciting tracking shots of the pursuit and capture on horseback. The final cliffhanger of the serial is a pip! Fu Manchu's plan is to operate on Nayland Smith and turn him into a dacoit. He uses chloroform to knock him out, and picks up a scalpel while Loki grins, his fangs glistening in the candlelight, his jagged forehead scar seeming to pulse. Fu, leaning forward with the scalpel, intones "Sir Nayland Smith… dacoit slave of Fu Manchu," while the drums pound for one last cliffhanger.

The final chapter of *Drums of Fu Manchu* is called *Revolt*. This long, thrilling journey is about to reach its feverish climax. For a final chapter switcheroo, it is Allan who saves Nayland Smith, blustering in just as the sinister doctor is about to begin the dacoit operation. Fu Manchu summons the local tribes to assert his control. He projects the image of the scepter into the night sky like the Bat Signal, inciting the superstitious tribesmen to attack. The hills are alive with angry tribesmen and all seems lost. Allan goes to extinguish that searchlight. One well-placed bullet does the trick.

As the confused tribesmen lower their arms, Fu escapes via automobile and Allan jumps onto the roof of the speeding car. For the first time in fifteen chapters, Fu Manchu soils his hands by having to do actual battle with an enemy, engaging in a fist fight in a careening car with Allan Parker, still seeking vengeance for his father's death. Out of control, the car goes over a cliff and Allan is injured, but alive.

In a very unusual move for a film from Hollywood's Golden Age, the villain not only lives, but gets away unpunished for his litany of crimes. Fu Manchu returns to the empty, quiet tomb of Genghis Khan, apologizing for his failure. Yet he melodramatically vows, "…there will dawn another day… a day of reckoning, when the forces of Fu Manchu will sweep on to victory. This I pledge you!"

Fu Manchu frame from the Serial Squadron restoration. Collection of Eric Stedman.

In fact, a sequel serial entitled *Fu Manchu Strikes Back* was planned for the following year but was never produced. Brandon recalled, "They didn't do it because of too many protests from parent-teacher organizations, oriental organizations, and kids wetting their beds from nightmares!" There was additional pressure from the Chinese government to the U. S. State Department, as they were our allies during the war and so the shelved project was, sadly, never revived.

The first chapter of *Drums of Fu Manchu* played in the nation's cinemas on March 15, 1940 and the final thrilling moments were unreeled in the beginning of July. A 1940 review proclaimed that "Henry Brandon is the best of the cast, and is quite a terror as Fu Manchu."

In 1943, a feature version of the serial was edited together by Republic and released. The *Motion Picture Daily* wrote that *Drums of Fu Manchu* was "an action packed thriller with all of the 'poison dart' and 'death gas' sequences possible to cram into one film. It is a treat for the kids and a good picture for thrill-seeking adults. Formerly a Republic serial, the film has not suffered in the process, but members of the cast, with the exception of Henry Brandon, tend to deliver rather stilted performances throughout. Edward Todd and William Thompson deserve credit for a nice job of editing and molding the serial into an acceptable feature.

To Henry Brandon go honors for a very believable presentation of the fiendish Dr. Fu Manchu." Another 1943 review of this feature version from *The Film Daily* proclaimed that Brandon "makes a most devilish villain" and the *Motion Picture Herald* boasted to war-time audiences that "Fu Manchu proves that he could give lessons in cruelties and torture to Japanese and Nazis alike!"

Henry gives a vivid, unforgettable performance as Fu Manchu under thick, constricting make-up over an extended fifteen-chapter time frame. Impressively, he neither looks nor sounds like Henry Brandon and does compelling work over this long production period (the longest in Republic's history). With apologies to Boris Karloff, Christopher Lee and even Peter Sellers, Henry Brandon perhaps created the screen's definitive Fu Manchu.

Fu Manchu is *not* the most important role of Brandon's career, an argument can be made that either "Barnaby" or "Scar" fits that description. But Henry Brandon is not the star of *Babes in Toyland* or *The Searchers*. Henry Brandon IS the star of *Drums of Fu Manchu* – he is the whole show! That makes this serial his defining leading role and completely, devilishly iconic.

CHAPTER FIVE
The Searchers

By Henry Brandon's self-admission, he played Native American Indians over 35 times in movies and countless times on television. Henry was a cultured and educated man whose great joy was performing on stage, preferably in Shakespeare and Greek tragedies.

While Henry estimated in 1946 that he performed in some forty plays,[*] he went on to perform in countless others. Acting on stage, was his most fulfilling vocation.

Henry's solid experience, honed over the years gave him a distinguished presence on stage. His stature, booming voice, diction, and body language enhanced his performances. Not only did he star in many of these plays, but more established box office "names" sought out Henry as support for their own vehicles.

The name "Henry Brandon" never caught the eye of the typical moviegoing audiences during his career, but it did catch the eye the movie studios. Though he was not a product of the "studio system" in that he was not weaned, built up and set on course as "star material" for any film mogul, he did make a living as a character actor.

Henry understood drama, and as such he had the skill to interpret and enact dynamic character roles for film. Casting directors knew this. Henry could personify unspeakable evil, gentleness, even comedy, but his greatest talent might have been his *intensity* on the screen.

---

[*] *San Bernardino County Sun* April 11, 1946

Despite Henry's many Native American roles, he did not fit the stereotyped version of the "Hollywood Indian." He had blue eyes, wavy brown hair and was of German descent. Though he did not possess high cheek bones (as was a stereotype often portrayed in film), he did project a hawk-like stare as the part demanded. When Henry's fixed glare came into the scene, it was like a carnivore locking-in on its prey. These were the characteristics and acting skills directors could count on with Henry Brandon.

A Portrait of Scar from *The Searchers*.

It wasn't until 1948 that Henry was cast as an Indian medicine man," in the Bob Hope movie; *The Paleface*. Though Henry's face was covered and unrecognizable, he could still play it menacing at times and downright silly. It fit perfectly into the visual and physical humor that Bob Hope was renowned for.

Hope was at one point captured by Indians. All the Native American clichés were depicted incongruently and the cast was augmented by Hollywood Indians. There seemingly was one exception, Iron-Eyes Cody.* While Henry Brandon *portrayed* Indians, Cody represented himself as an *authentic* Native American. Iron-Eyes and Henry became friends during the course of *The Paleface*.

In the ensuing years between 1948 and 1956, Henry settled into a plethora of roles in the movies. There were two films in which he played Native Americans: *War Arrow* and *Comanche*. The former he played "Chief Maygro," the latter "Black Cloud."

Of all the American Indian characters Henry played in his career, none were as iconic as Chief Scar in John Ford's *The Searchers*. This epic was also Ford's crown jewel and correspondingly brought additional acclaim to John Wayne.

Henry had worked with Wayne before in *Wake of the Red Witch* (1948) and *Shepard of the Hills* (1941), John Ford had already established himself with numerous successes including the classic *Stagecoach* and four Academy Awards[†]

Ford knew what he wanted when casting for his films and most of them were an ensemble from his previous pictures. For the role of Chief Scar, Ford needed someone who was as physically imposing as John Wayne. It might be that Henry's brother, Hugo, may have had some influence on Ford. Hugo was a studio assistant cameraman (or as the 1940's census described it, an optical engineer) and had worked for Ford at Republic Studios.

In an interview with Henry in 1989, he recounted some of the dynamics of Ford and how he landing the plum role of Scar: "Ford spoke a smatter-

---

* The actor's real name was Espera Oscar de Corti (1904-1999) He was of Sicilian descent

† *The Informer* (1935), *Grapes of Wrath* (1940), *How Green Was My Valley* (1941) *The Quiet Man* (1952)

ing of many languages and he kind of loved to show off his knowledge. My brother told me before I went to the interview with Ford, 'If he asks you where you're from, say Germany.'"*

Henry was asked one question by Director Ford; "What is your background, Brandon?" When Henry replied, "I was born in Germany," Ford switched to German and Henry conversed back.†

Reflecting on that interview with Ford, Henry explained the irony of the role: "I became Scar by saying I was German!"‡ In truth, Henry's reputation as a consummate actor preceded him.

The Searchers was a big budget extravaganza shot on location utilizing the Technicolor filming technique. That meant Henry's piercing blue eyes would be displayed gigantically across the screen. Did his European genes contradict the notion that Native Americans had brown eyes? Henry had the nerve to ask his director about this one day. Fords response, "The exception, dramatically speaking, is always more exciting than the rule."§

Henry described Ford as; "Perverse! He was a genius. If you told him a joke, he'd scowl. If you told him something sad, he'd roar with laughter."¶

The Searchers was based on a novel of the same name by Alan LeMay. It was published in 1954 and was adapted for the screen. This wasn't your typical Western with non-stop action; the filmed version lets the images set the tone, and in "Vista Vision" this epic was canvassed in an almost panoramic effect. This also wasn't a typical "John Wayne" movie, as Ethan Edwards, the character he depicted was not a "hero" in the traditional sense. If anything,

---

*   "Talk of the Town" hosted by John Craig (Simmons Cable in Long Beach, California June 28, 1989

†   "Talk of the Town" hosted by John Craig (Simmons Cable in Long Beach, California June 28, 1989

‡   Ibid

§   "John Ford: The Searcher" by Scott Eyman and Paul Duncan Pg. 156

¶   "Talk of the Town" hosted by John Craig (Simmons Cable in Long Beach, ca.) June 28, 1989

Ethan Edwards was an anti-hero, a loner seemingly with a blood thirsty bent. The film was never intended as escapist fare.

Some call *The Searchers* a John Ford masterpiece of film making. It could be looked at as a psychological study of a revenge-seeking sociopath, not just in the personification of Ethan Edwards, but also in his archrival Chief Scar. Author Glenn Frankel who researched the original novel and film as a scholar, compared Scar and Edwards as "mirror images."*

Scar in war paint.

The story is set sometime after 1868 and tells the tale of a "white" girl who has been kidnapped and raised by a Comanche tribe. It might have been loosely based on an incident in 1836 in West Texas where Cynthia Ann Parker, who was only nine years of age, was abducted and raised by Comanche's. In the film, the young girl becomes one of Chief Scar's wives. The character of Scar was fictional.

---

* "The Searchers-The Making of an American Legend" by Glenn Frankel

The film opens with a striking image of the vastness and beauty of Utah's Monument Valley National Park, a favorite shooting location for John Ford that served as a substitute for Texas. John Wayne (as Edwards) is finally returning home after serving in the American Civil War in the Confederate army. Weather-beaten and hardened, Edwards enjoyed a short reunion with his brother, his wife, nieces and nephews at their shared ranch. Even the pioneer neighbors come out for the greeting.

We are introduced to the character; Martin Pawley (Jeffrey Hunter), a young man who has been adopted by the family during Edwards' absence. As the Edwards' clan enjoys their meal at the dinner table, Pawley comes in late. Edwards looks at him with disgust and tells him he looks like "a half-breed." Startled, Pauly admits to being one-eighth Cherokee and the rest Welsh and English.

In a couple of days the tranquility turns to tension after Edwards' arrival; it was suspected that cattle rustlers stole some fellow rancher's livestock and provoked a posse of locals to pursue them. Edwards, Pawley and the rest of the men-folk follow the trail.

Back at the ranch, the Comanche's descended on the Edward's frontier home in a war raid. The family sense their doom and shuttle Little Debbie Edwards (10-year old Lana Wood) through a window with her favorite rag-doll. She scampers away and as instructed, hides in the darkness behind her grandmother's tombstone.

The camera focuses on the child as unspeakable horrors [not shown] ensue at the house. Then an ominous shadow of a figure (ostensively created from a moonbeam) frames the helpless child. It is that of Chief Scar (Henry Brandon) whose face fills the screen. Though he is wearing warrior war paint, his expression is almost placid, until he sounds a hollowed buffalo horn to signal his warriors. The long note ends in a short eerie pitch. Cut! It is a powerful, unsettling scene, even more so because the director lets the audience surmise what might have happened.

Native American Gali Sanchez admitted to co-author Cassara that it was hard to watch this film, but his eyes were fixated on Henry. Sanchez observed, "Henry *moves* like a Indian."

In the daylight hours, the posse finally find their livestock many miles away but it is not what they had expected; a Comanche's lance has been emphatically driven into each bovine. Suddenly the posse realizes that they have been duped and drawn away from their families. Edwards says, "Stealin' the cattle was just to pull us out. This is a murder raid." The intended targets were the Jorgensen's family, the Edward's or both.

Edwards and Pawley ride swiftly back until they are stopped in their tracks as their worst fears are confirmed; their home is burned and gutted. Edwards runs into the house and sees the indescribable.

Edwards finds Debbie's little doll where she was standing last and deduces that she has been kidnapped to be raised as a Comanche. To Edwards, it is a fate *worse* than death. Rage fills his sensibilities and every pore in his body lusts for revenge.

With no home, no family and a purpose to pursue, Edwards and Pawley commit themselves to track down those responsible. Their quest is seemingly never ending; we know this by film flashbacks of letters received by Pawley's love interest (played by Vera Miles). The years are marked by the passing of Christmas seasons.

The slow, relentless hunt is punctuated by long stretches of scenery and cinematically takes the searchers over territories far and wide. After five years they finally get their first break in Mexico. It is there that they learn of Chief Scar and the Mexican name they call him, "Cicatriz."

A local guide agrees after a negotiated price, to introduce Edwards and Pauley (posing as traders) to Cicatriz. He guides the two into the Indian encampment. It is there that the two rivals finally meet, they are both the same height, rugged, determined and with hatred reflected in their eyes.

Edwards speaks first (as the soundtrack increases the tension). "Scar, huh?" As he is sizing up his opponent, he spits out the words: "It's plain to see how you got your name" There is a noticeable scar running down diagonally from the Chief's left temple across the bridge of his nose. They are standing almost toe-to-toe as Scar speaks in halting English; "You big shoulders, him (pointing to Pawley)…he who follows."

It's a veritable standoff between these two equally similar men. Edwards sarcastically says; "You speak pretty good American, for a *Comanche*; someone teach you?" Scar comes back with; "You speak pretty good Comanche, someone teach you?"

They retreat into a tepee to "talk trade." The guide encourages a smoke. Scar who is just as intense as Edwards, volunteers his conviction in words: "Two sons killed by white men. For each son I take many scalps."

Like a high-stakes poker game, Edwards plays his hand with outward confidence, We've seen scalps before." But the warrior chief shows his hand and motions for the (previously unseen) female Indian to display a symbolic "full-house," demonstrated by a row of scalps. There is a visible reaction when the searchers recognize the girl as Debbie, (Natalie Wood) now grown to maturity. She is one of Chief Scar's wives.

This is no time for a physical confrontation and besides, the chief has the house advantage. The parties coolly retreat. Away from the camp, the guide who has sized up the circumstances insists on giving back the coins he was paid as he does not want "blood money."

Pawley asks the seasoned Edwards why they weren't killed. He seethingly answers, "Some kind of Comanche hospitality I guess." Edwards picks up a rock and throws it to let off some steam.

The original objective all along was to find Debbie, and now that the searchers have discovered her, the two men differ over their next move. Pawley wants to sneak back to the Indian camp to rescue her. Edwards is convinced her marriage to Chief Scar has *soiled* her. The way he sees it Debbie is better off dead.

Pawley and Edwards disagree and for the first time, Pawley takes the lead. Just then, a shot rings out from an Indian, hitting Edwards in the arm. Pawley returns fire and kills the buck.

Debbie runs down to persuade the searchers to leave, "These are my people, go!" Edwards replies, "Living with a Comanche ain't living." Astonishingly he gets into position to shoot her, but Pawley stands in her way and pleads with Edwards not to fire.

The scene changes to Chief Scar donning his war bonnet, and riding toward the men, but his horse is shot out from under him. We see him spread out on the ground; the warrior face of Scar looks up intensely.

Pawley sneaks to the camp alone and finds Scar's lair. He crawls in looking for Debbie. Suddenly we see the bottom half of an Indian torso enter the tepee; the dramatic music lets us know it is Scar. Pauly turns and fires his gun, hitting the figure.

Moments later, Edwards enters the teepee trying to find Pawley. He sees the now deceased Scar (still out of the frame). In the most dramatic and disturbing scene in the film, Edwards grabs Scar's hair at the crown and yanks his head forward. This time the audience sees Scar all too well and; he is quite dead. Edwards throws Scar's head back to the horizontal position. He removes a long Bowie knife from his belt and brings it up towards Scar's scalp. Director Ford deemed it unnecessary to show what happens next.

Pawley finds Debbie but Edwards rides after her on his horse, bent on killing her now more than ever. She desperately runs toward a cave but Edwards overpowers her. He lifts Debbie up high as if to throw her unmercifully.

Debbie is overwhelmed and has no defense. She looks at him helplessly and Edwards remembers a moment like this years ago when he picked her up as a child, before the madness. His hate suddenly subsides and in a dramatic turn he lowers her and says, "Let's go home, Debbie." She collapses into his arms and is finally brought to the Jorgensen family who welcome her in celebration. The ending fades out as John Wayne's character looks at the reunion taking place and thinks he doesn't belong. Through the open doorway we see him ride away into the landscape. We hear the harmony of the cowboy band, "Sons of the Pioneers" on the soundtrack.

The Searchers was modestly received by some when it was first released. One columnist remarked, "It was just another Western, a very *long* Western." Unmistakably this was John Wayne's movie, and though Henry Brandon's Scar only spoke a few sentences, he was an excellent counter to Wayne's character. Scar remained in the audience's mind throughout and on the lips of the searchers making him more than just a central character. It was another nightmare-inducing performance by Henry.

As documented by Glenn Frankel in his amazing book chronicling the legends, the myths and the art of *The Searchers,* Ford incorporated many native Navajo Indians into some of the scenes of the film. "Henry made friends with all the Indians.'"* As a result the Navajo Indians of Monument Valley called a ceremony to make Ford, an honorary member of their tribe.† It was an honor the much-acclaimed director cherished, even above his many Academy Awards.‡

The American Film Institute currently rates *The Searchers* number # 12 in ranking of all American films ever created. For the genre of the Western category; it ranks number one.

---

*   Hugo Kleinbach as told to Co-Author Bill Cassara
†   "The Searchers-The Making of an American Legend" by Glenn Frankel 2013 Bloomsbury USA, New York
‡   Ibid

CHAPTER SIX
Edge of Darkness

HENRY KLEINBACH WAS PROGRESSING in his film career during the middle 1930's and his salary and duties were further subsidized by a government program called the Federal Theater Project.[*] However, not much is known about his private life during this time other than he lived with his parents in Glendale, California. He eventually moved out with his brother, Hugo to Los Angeles.

With anti-German sentiment raging in America when Hitler took over his country, Henry's Jewish agent,[†] tactfully suggested that the surname of "Kleinbach" was too "long" for a marquee. During the filming of *Garden of Allah* (1936) it was announced that Henry would be known professionally as "Henry Brandon."

Though Henry submitted his naturalization papers in 1938, by 1940 Henry was still listed in the national census as "Kleinbach." The legal name change came later in the year. Just before this time Hugo married and moved out. The census revealed Henry as a single occupant of a rental on Temple Hill Dr. in Los Angeles; he paid $25.00 per month for rent. He is recorded as being an "Actor/extra" and garnered over $4,000 in 1939. The average annual wage for a worker in that year was $1,000, so Henry was doing alright for himself

---

* *San Diego Union* September 18, 1938
† Abe Sugarman

Brandon is hiding a secret at the *Edge of Darkness.*

In 1939 Henry met Dolores Comley, a show business beauty. At the time she was a "box jumper"* assistant to the world-famous Dante the Magician. Both Henry and Dolores had exciting but separate careers; a romance blossomed nevertheless. They were married in Las Vegas on June 3, 1941. Dolores was seven months pregnant at the time.

Henry Richard Brandon Jr. was born on August 30, 1941, in San Francisco and it looked like the blessed moment would unite the young family. Unfortunately, conflict and dissent started to tear husband and wife apart; they separated two months later. (*For more details see Chapter 19 "Epilogue."*)

It was Henry who sought a divorce on the grounds of extreme cruelty. As the plaintiff, he cited:

---

* Professional Jargon term for "magician's assistant"

Glamorous Dolores Brandon. Collection of Rick Brandon.

The defendant [Dolores Brandon] willfully and wrongfully inflicted upon the plaintiff [Henry Brandon], a course of great and grievous mental suffering, that such course of conduct on the part of the defendant, consisting of acts of extreme cruelty, has caused plaintiff great bodily pain and suffering and mental anguish which impaired his health, destroyed his happiness and rendered his life so unendurable that the legitimate ends of matrimony were defeated and the continuance of the status of husband and wife between the parties hereto were rendered futile and impossible.*

Dolores Brandon onstage with Dante. Collection of Rick Brandon.

---

* Brandon VS Brandon Divorce papers and decree March 26, 1946

In an ironic example of art imitating life, Henry's personal conflicting "edge of darkness" was soon reflected in a cinema role for Warner Brothers, followed by an escape from his personal turmoil into the military.

In 1942 Warner Bros. big budgeted war film *Edge of Darkness* starring Errol Flynn went into production. Henry was cast as Major Ruck, a British agent. Shot during WWII, the storyline depicted the Nazi occupation of Norway and how it affected a simple fishing village of eight hundred citizens.

The film was based on a 1942 novel of the same name by William Woods and brought to life fictional characters based on true facts. The Nazi empire was on the move in 1940 and sought to exploit Norway and her people for their war machine efforts against the Allies.

The movie version was true to the book and was not light escapist fare for American audiences during the grip of the war. It is violent and often uncomfortable to watch. There is an implied rape of a key character, which was shocking for 1943 cinema.

The story takes place in an unnamed village, and there's an undercurrent of dissent among the villagers with the Nazi occupation. The villagers have been sitting in quiet rage, biding their time until English reinforcements come to aid their freedom. Talk is dangerous, and there are many who can't be trusted. There is turmoil within the respected doctor's house. Dr. Stensgard (Walter Huston) and his wife, (Ruth Gordon) are at odds with their son who allegedly joined the Nazis in Germany, but their daughter Karen (Ann Sheridan) disavows him as a traitor. This is one strong woman, she is the unwavering strength of this village.

Errol Flynn's character is durable enough as he persuades the members of the village to wait for a planned surprise attack, but this is less an Errol Flynn star vehicle than it is a moving, inspiring ensemble piece that included Judith Anderson. The villagers congregate at church where they weigh their options, the pastor preaches patience.

The story also focuses on the Nazi soldiers who have taken up a strategic position. Helmut Dantine played the sadistic Captain Koenig. The film is told in flashback after a horrific opening sequence that shows where Nazi soldiers arriving to find hundreds of dead bodies, both Germans and Norwegians.

Henry first appears at the beginning of the core flashback sequence as Major Ruck, a high ranking Nazi officer. In full uniform, he questions Captain Koenig about the layout of the town, as his stay will be brief. Henry's character demands, "I shall want a list of all the troublemakers in this town." The captain willingly obliges, intimidated by the sheer force of Ruck's Nazi command style and in so doing reveals the German stronghold. Henry's Major Ruck is cool, calculating, a quiet but deadly bully.

As the pressure mounts, the Norwegians are warned that anyone out at nightfall will be shot. This does not discourage the brave. Some of the townspeople hunker down with a hidden radio and each night they try to tune in for any information they can get over the airwaves. One night their perseverance is heartened by receiving a radio broadcast, in hushed tones, from Winston Churchill. The Prime Minister of England acknowledges the struggles of the people of Norway and encourages them not to lose faith. It is a tonic that soothes, at least temporarily.

Henry's Major Ruck returns to the occupied quarters and makes his presence known, to the astonished Errol Flynn and Ann Sheridan characters. He is a spy. In a sincere tone, he transforms from German to English, from evil to heroic, as he confides to the village insurgents that he is indeed an English intelligence officer who has infiltrated the Nazis. There are moments of skepticism, but this agent of the Queen divulges that reinforcements in the way of guns and ammunition are coming for them. Sure enough, he is good on his word as boats surreptitiously make their way to the outer shores. A boater in awe asks Henry, "An Englishman in that uniform? How do you do it?" He politely answers, "Do I ask you how to catch fish?" Henry is superb in his four key sequences, shifting from Nazi to ally, from black to white. His vocal pattern, his demeanor, the light behind his eyes transform in front of the audience. It's a master class in character drama.

Portrait signed "For Little Dolores, With Love, Henry" [1940]. Collection of Rick Brandon.

In another sequence, Major Ruck is threatened by a Polish woman who is desperate to get out of Norway. She'll reveal that he is a British spy unless he helps her. Henry plays shifting tones of this scene to perfection, not allowing the real danger to his character to undermine what he is trying to accomplish. He gets through to the girl, who backs down. Major Ruck is a brave, forceful personality, and Henry portrays the different layers with precision.

Despite careful plans for a united attack, there are many villagers who are hesitant, but this all changes when Ann Sheridan's character, Karen is sexually assaulted (off camera) by a German soldier.

As one villager puts it, "we're not afraid to die anymore." Like a match that is lit, the citizens are now galvanized to overtake their occupiers. The Germans think they were prepared for this and an epic battle is raged in guerilla-warfare style; old men, women, and even the pacifist pastor join in the fight against the Nazis. It is unrelenting bloodshed with massive losses on both sides, but the Germans are soundly defeated. These disturbing images brought realism to the viewers.

During the credits, President Franklin D. Roosevelt's [impersonated] voice can be heard addressing the courageous people of Norway in their plight. It is a powerful, deeply moving film that no doubt stirred the audience and evoked many war bond sales.

Edge of Darkness is a terrific and unforgettable motion picture, but it is frustrating for fans of Henry Brandon. His character is pivotal to the plot and involves a big twist when it's revealed that he is a spy, yet his name does not appear in the opening credits. For once, though, Henry Brandon played one of the heroes.

Henry's performance was not unnoticed; a fact he revealed to Don Leifert in an interview for *Cinemacabre Magazine:**

Q: Were you ever under contract to any of the studios?

A: No, never. There were several opportunities, but they never worked out.

Q: Why not?

A: Well, the war came along. I was offered a seven-year contract at Warner

---

*   *Cinemacabre # Six* 1984

Brothers. Warner told his people to give me a Clark Gable buildup, but unfortunately I was in basic training at the time.

After shooting wrapped up for *Edge of Darkness* in Monterey, California, Henry heard the call of duty and enlisted into the United States Army at the Presidio of Monterey on December 23, 1942. This presidio was unique because personnel were assigned for their language capabilities.

It would make sense that Uncle Sam would take advantage of Henry's skills as a fluent speaker of the German language. With his background in German culture and his acting abilities, he could conceivably have been assigned as a secret agent for the government much like his role in *Edge of Darkness*.

Despite limited existing records from the National Archives, we do get a glimpse of Henry's personal life prior to his military service. He was 6'2" 180 pounds, his permanent home address was 1119 Hacienda Place, Hollywood, California, and he was listed as married.

Henry was first assigned to Camp Beale, California, near Sacramento where he served two months for basic training. Seeing as Henry enlisted instead of having been drafted, it is clear that he had different ideas regarding his service to his country. Following boot camp, he was assigned to Washington and Lee University in Lexington, Virginia. Four weeks later, Henry was promoted to the rank of corporal. After two months he was promoted to sergeant.

As an as "Entertainment Specialist" in the army, Henry was not only a scriptwriter-- he also produced soldier shows, games and recreation. He was the master of ceremonies for various army shows overseas, at the Allied Forces Headquarters and even on Broadway *(see Henry Brandon Stage Credits Chapter 21)*.

The purpose of this special entertainment troupe was to boost the morale of the fighting men and to offer a distraction to the horrors of war. While in Italy, Henry produced and directed his old standby, *The Drunkard*. One can only imagine the chorus of "boos" and "hisses" directed by the boys at Henry's iconic villain character.

Henry with his unit overseas during World War II. Collection of Marcus Maier.

At the conclusion of the war, Henry received the WWII Victory Medal, Good Conduct Medal, American Campaign Medal, and the European African- Middle Eastern Campaign Medal. He was released from active duty with an Honorable Discharge on March 11, 1946.

Years after the war, a columnist by the name of Whitney Bolton caught up to Henry for an interview called, "The Night He Was for Shooting." It was conducted during Henry's run at the Carnegie Hall Playhouse where he was the male principal in *The Lady's Not for Burning*. Bolton asked Henry, "What was the toughest performance you ever gave?" Henry responded:

> Well, it lasted only 15 minutes for one night only, but if there had been a gun in the house I think I would have been shot. Just after basic training I was assigned to Fort Monmouth [New Jersey]. My last picture had been *Edge of Darkness* in which I played a British spy masquerading as a stuffy, arrogant young officer from

Berlin and Hitler's staff. I'd been at the fort only a few days and no one knew me—except one major. He came to me one day and said, "Brandon, are you a good enough actor, if we get you the right clothes, to play one of those charming-on-the-surfaces, arrogant-on-the-inside German officers and pretend it in a mostly ad-lib speech before more than 2,500 soldiers in training to kill Nazis?" Henry said, "I think so."

The Army arranged to borrow my film uniform from the Warner Bros. studio and also to show *Edge of Darkness* at the fort's theater after my speech. I went on first as a captured, but in his soul undefeated, German officer. I put on the uniform having agreed not to talk about the stunt in the barracks. It was agreed that all soldiers would be searched for arms before entering the theater.

I was introduced as a captured officer of the enemy and walked out to dead silence. First, I gave them the Viennese schmaltz charm; winning smile, ingratiating spirit, correct bow, a few nice words about America, but given with a slight and detectable edge of superiority. One soldier yelled, "Get that Nazi bum out of here," but one of the wonderful things about Americans happened, more than a score yelled back from all over the house; "Let the guy speak his piece. He's got a right to talk."

I held the charm bit for about six minutes and then, slowly, worked my way into icy, stiff, arrogance and from that to a final five minutes of insult. I told them with a sneer that they were going to get licked, that Germany was invincible, that Japan would lay them waste in the Pacific and we would trounce them in Europe. I ended with the prediction that the Axis would own the world.

The reaction was terrific and was what the observing officers wanted to see. Almost 3,000 enlisted men turned to rage and the urge to kill me. They had been indoctrinated against Nazis and they proved it. That's why I say that if there had been a gun in the house, I'd have been shot down. I gave them a mocking bow and walked off slowly and defiantly. It's a wonder they didn't tear the hall down in their fury.

A few minutes later the picture went on and when they saw me in it they realized they had been gulled and laughed in the sporting way Americans have when they are on the butt end of a joke.*

Henry elaborated further about his ethnic roles for author Scott Nollen that was published after Henry's death:

There are good and bad people of all races. I have played countless heavies of various nationalities and never felt that I was maligning any race by doing so. This includes Germans and my adopted nationality—American. I have never been ashamed of being German, only ashamed of a very corrupt and evil German government. I even got the guys in my barracks in the Signal Corps at Fort Monmouth, New Jersey, to say, "Dirty Nazis" instead of "Dirty Germans."†

When Henry returned from the war he found his marriage in ruins and he filed for divorce. He was promptly hired to continue his stage acting as Allesandra in the novel turned play; *Ramona* (for more details see Chapter 20 "Stage Synopsis and Theater Credits.")

---

* *News-Press* (Fort Myers, Florida) March 21, 1957
† "Three Bad Men: John Ford, John Wayne, Ward Bond by Scott Allen Nollen," McFarland, (2013) Pg. 258

CHAPTER SEVEN
Short Subjects & Other Appearances

IN THIS CHAPTER WE detail Henry Brandon's appearances in short subjects, beginning with his famous return to the Hal Roach Studios and the character of Barnaby in *The Our Gang Follies of 1938*. Following these we cover some of Henry's more unusual jobs including a rare gig with the Walt Disney Studios in reference footage for the animators and several appearances on the airwaves during the Golden Age of Radio.

The Our Gang Follies of 1938:

This comedy by Hal Roach Studios was a later entry for the "Our Gang" comedies. The series was in constant production starting in 1922. Over the years the kids who starred were replaced by younger children. In 1937 when this production was filmed, Carl "Alfalfa" Switzer, George "Spanky" McFarland, Darla Hood, Billy "Buckwheat" Thomas and Eugene "Porky" Lee were the headliners.

The "Follies of 1938" was a different expression from the usual neighborhood setting of the rascals. This was a twenty-minute extravaganza set with a musical theme. The show revolves around the "King of Crooners" (Alfalfa) who desires to sing grand opera.

The film opens with the gang and augmented members parading to the tent where the big show will take place. As things get under way, Alfalfa, who is billed all over every fence post and sign, announces he is through with crooning for all time and that nothing short of opera will satisfy him. Spanky was counting on him to head the line-up of local kid talent for his follies.

Alfalfa: "Porky and I decided that a voice like mine is a gift."

Spanky: "Well there'll be no opera in this show."

Alfalfa: "I'm going to take my voice where it'll be appreciated."

"Alfy" sets out with Porky for the Cosmopolitan Opera House where he seeks an audition from the impresario Henry Brandon, (who in this picture is billed as "Barnaby"). He is essentially the same character he performed in *Babes in Toyland* only three years earlier.

Barnaby terrorizes Alfalfa and Porky. Collection of Richard W. Bann

It's a villainous part in the grand tradition of stage melodrama where we also get to hear Henry's wicked laugh. In this film Henry is a young man of 25 years, then in his next scenes ages dramatically.

The two kids come marching in the stage door entrance interrupting rehearsals of opera "star" Geno Corrado. Alfy mimics Corrado in his own unique off-key rendition of *The Barber of Seville* with plenty of "Figaro's." Alphy projects an overconfident, rude but loveable characterization. After seeking the approval of his "peer" (Corrado) the professional singer insults him; "it's preposterous!" "Thanks" Alfalfa responds, "You're not so bad yourself." He then turns his attention to the boss, "Hey, are you the bull?" Amused, Brandon's character gently answers: "Why, yes I am."

Alfalfa: "Have you ever heard a voice like mine?

Barnaby: "Why no, come to think of it, I haven't."

Alfalfa: "Do you have room for me in your next show to sing opera?"

Barnaby: "I'm sorry. It's all set.

Alfalfa: "When do you need me?"

Barnaby now has a twinkle in his eye. He mocks a serious tone, puts on his spectacles and looks down at this timepiece.

Barnaby: "It's 2:32 now. Suppose you come back in 20 years?"

Alfalfa: "Can you put that in writing?"

Barnaby gives his secretary a knowing wink and says, "Give him form PBX." (It's a contract).

The scene cuts to the Follies where Spanky is nervously pacing while the show is going on. Thinking his star has regained his senses; he sees his lead male performer at the back door and eagerly opens it. Alfy has a superior attitude while Spanky explains the emergency.

Alfalfa: "My crooning days are over.

Spanky: "Over?"

Alfalfa: "Well take a look at this a contract to sing opera. That's all."

Spanky: "Suppose you lose your voice, then what will happen? You'll wind up with a tin cup."

Alfy has by now settled into (appropriately enough) a barber's chair with the sounds of chanting from the audience: "We want Alfalfa!" The star tunes everything out and drifts into sleep punctuated by snoring.

A dream sequence opens with Alfy and Porky back at the impresario's place of business. Barnaby has aged 20 years with grey hair and a bent back supported by a cane. He greets Alfalfa, "Ah, my little friend, I'm glad to see you but you are three minutes late. Give me the contract and I'll open up the 'Door of Fame' for you." Barnaby then literally opens up the door as Alfy and Porky enter. Every inch on Barnaby's body reveals to the audience that Alfalfa has been made a victim of a pact, perhaps with Faust himself.

Alfy returns to the stage where his adoring fans anticipate his signature off-key singing. Instead, he confidently bellows out, "I'm the Barber of Seville, I'm the Barber of Seville." A chorus of "boos" rings out from the audience; they are repulsed by this "high end" turn of events. It also triggers anger and the throwing of vegetables directly hitting Alfy right in the face.

We see Alfalfa getting thrown out, and landing on the sidewalk. Barnaby hunches over him and says, "You an opera singer, bah! I've waited twenty years for you. Take this tin cup and sing in the street where you belong."

Alfalfa is now humbled, shocked and afraid. He mutters: "Me, the great Alfalfa, singing in the gutter?" Barnaby lords it over him: "Yes, you signed the contract, don't forget, I have you in my power. Now don't play any tricks, remember I'm always watching." The camera follows the boys as they walk away. Off screen, we hear Barnaby cackling in a most sadistic manner.

Alfalfa dejectedly follows orders and walks the pavement. He gloomily repeats, "I'm the Barber of Seville…" For a moment he brightens up when he sees a flashy nightclub billed as "Club Spanky." Out of nowhere, Barnaby appears menacingly and barks: "You! Never mind Club Spanky, get busy and sing."

As the scene unfolds, Alfy and Porky catch old friend Spanky arriving in an expensive car. The well-heeled proprietor invites the boys into his nightclub. The inside of the club is dazzling with an impressive setting of fine dining and entertainment. "Cab Buckwheat" leads the swing band and soon Alfy is reunited with headliner, Darla, who flaunts her salary of "Hundreds of thousands of dollars."

A contract to sing opera in Our Gang Follies Of 1938.

Both Darla and Spanky beckon Alfalfa to sing for "old-time's sake," but he has an artist's pride. "I will not croon; I'm a slave to my art." As Alfy and Porky sit watching, the show begins with Spanky performing an intro-number which is followed by the delightful singing of Darla Hood. The show peaks with various kid musical numbers and builds to a climax.

Now swayed by the electricity of the moment, Alfalfa relents and offers to sing. To cheers, he approaches the stage and just as he inhales for his first note, we hear: "Stop, I say." It is the overwhelming voice, then the figure of the caped Barnaby descending. He glides to Alfalfa with a burst of evil laughter in all directions.

Barnaby imposes himself over the child and says, "You're supposed to be out on the street singing opera." Alfalfa pleads, "I want to croon." Barnaby reminds him, "I have your contract to sing opera. He grabs Alfalfa by the arm and devilishly laughs in triumph.

The shock of the dream startles Alfalfa to awaken. He is back to where he was before the dream, as Spanky and the audience plead with him to return and sing for the neighborhood audience. He can't get out of the chair fast enough and takes his rightful place on stage. Alfalfa sings the Bing Crosby hit, "Learn to Croon" to his adoring performers and female fans.

Our Gang Follies of 1938 was a lush production deserving of an Academy Award for the Best Short Subject of the year. For Henry Brandon, it was another nightmare-inducing performance.

In later years, Henry was asked to reflect on working with the Our Gang kids during this short. At a 1982 *Sons of the Desert* convention held in Detroit, Michigan, he offered his insights:

> I think they wrote [the Barnaby part] for me because they knew I could photograph as a young man and then as an older man. That was great fun, I had not seen too many of those shorts and I came away with such respect for those kids. They were incredibly talented!

Carnival in Paris:

This 1937 musical short by MGM features Henry as the male lead opposite Ann Rutherford. The setting takes place in a Paris museum's Egyptology department with the background of the famous Carnival of Paris, an annual festivity.

These types of short films augmented MGM's feature films in a package at Loew's theaters across America. Approximately 18-22 minutes in length, these two-reelers were sometimes lavishly produced with wonderful sets. They also served as a training ground of sorts because it seemed all actors, writers, directors, etc. started at this mini-feature level.

Rutherford was only 19 years old when this short was released. She had been acting since she was a child and graduated to MGM after playing opposite John Wayne and Gene Autry at Republic Studios. Her mother was an actress and her father was a former singer for the Metropolitan Opera.

It's easy to see why Rutherford was cast as the female lead in *Carnival of Paris*. She was a little pixie with big eyes and a vivacious personality that the camera captured perfectly. Henry Brandon had just come off from the role of the love-sick composer in *Metropolitan Nocturne* and garnered high praise. MGM noticed that. William Thiele, a Vienna native, was assigned the directorial duties.

Despite Henry's many "heavy" roles in his prior films, *Carnival of Paris* showcased him as a naïve, but dedicated mop-boy with high ambitions. He comes off as a fresh faced young man, with a certain European flavor perfectly suited opposite Ann Rutherford's character, "Lisette." She is a hungry waif from the streets whose immediate goal is to steal a delectable pastry from the dessert chefs at the fair. It's a wonderful scene, almost Chaplinesque in the physical chaos and then the chase by the French police who pursue her.

Lisette runs into a museum and scrambles into of all things, a mummy's empty sarcophagus. In the next room are three learned men discussing their latest artifacts, each offering a different opinion on its origins. In the middle of this spirited debate, Henry's character, "Louis" enters. He is a lowly janitor sweeping the floor, but who harbors great hopes of someday becoming an Egyptologist. Enthusiastically he interrupts the professors to offer his insight: "Pardon Monsieur Le Blanc, but in my opinion this mummy is…" He is cut off and humiliated by the director to "go back to your mop."

In the next scene, the professors are gone and Louis dejectedly drifts towards one of the new archives and discovers the girl. She begs him not to turn her in. Louis scolds her; "Do you realize you are desecrating the coffin of Netise the Pharaoh who lived in the year two thousand…oh never mind, get out of there."

After Lisette confesses she is in trouble with the police, Louis relents, "You think I pity you because you're a woman, don't you? I'd do the same thing for a dog or a cat." He offers her his bread. Though stale, she is very appreciative.

As Louis gives her worldly advice, Lisette is preoccupied with the dress-up carnival going on outside and all the delicious food. The revelers beckon the two to join in the festivities with a song. That does it; Louis smiles and takes the girl by the hand and says, "Come on!"

They exit the museum wearing the authentic Egyptian adornment from the exhibits and join the merriment, but the police recognize Lisette. Henry reassures her and they find themselves in line going on stage for the costume contest.

The judges are the Egyptologists from the museum; the young couple put masks over their faces. With their authentic looking "costumes" the judges decide they are the winners of the contest and award them 45 francs. They triumphantly join in eating, drinking and enjoying themselves for the duration of the carnival.

Things turn romantic when Louis suggests looking upwards and says; "Look at the stars. Would you believe it, five thousand years ago those same stars were shining over Egypt, over the pyramids, over Queen Ammenacha? What secrets those stars could tell. I shall learn them someday when I'm an Egyptologist."

They witness a shooting star and this being a musical, Lisette starts to sing, Louis joins in; "*Oh, falling star, on thou I wish and who could ask for more? Than who will come and hold me close with lips that say Je Vous Adore.*" They kiss and fall asleep on the park bench where they awaken the next day.

They run back to the museum to return the costumes and clean up, but Lisette inadvertently breaks a vase onto the floor alerting the policeman in charge of security. Lisette hides and hears a verbal assault towards Louis. "You cabbage head, brother of an ox, you're fired!"

In the next scene the two are once again sitting on the park bench. She tries to apologize:

Lisette: "I'm sorry you lost your position. Tell me you forgive me."

Louis: "I forgive you for everything, only please be quiet! Oh, stop sniffling; haven't you done enough to me already? My career is ruined."

Lisette reminds Louis that if he wants something out of life he must fight for it. She mentions a museum in another town and they begin to walk. They break out in a song, and then during their stroll, she develops a hole in her shoe. To cover it she takes a folded papyrus out of her pocket to cover it.

Louis: "Name of a name! Where did you get this?"

Lisette: "I must have picked it up off the floor from that vase I broke."

Louis recognizes the hieroglyphics as an important scripture. He tells the girl to "stay here" as he runs back to the museum to show the directors. With the new information he is able to identify and reconstruct the demise of their new mummified specimens. This wins applause and praise. "This is the most remarkable discovery of the age. We thank you, France thanks you. We will make you an assistant Egyptologist!"

Louis accepts graciously, and then runs off to find Lisette. As he starts to explain, she offers a solution to the vase: "I've solved the whole problem. I took the 45 francs and bought the museum a new vase."

Louis laughs and says, "Save it for when we get married, we'll put it over the fireplace." Lisette drops the vase in astonishment, "When we're married?" Louis reassures her, "Lisette, you are magnificent!" He kisses her and they walk off with musical accompaniment.

Henry is sincere and delightful in this extremely rare turn as a romantic lead in a musical setting. Sadly, his film career didn't offer any additional such as this.

Ghost Treasure:

This is an MGM short subject released as part of the Carey Wilson Miniatures series. *Ghost Treasure* is a one-reeler filmed in black and white but released in rustic sepia-tone on March 5, 1941.

In California's Death Valley, there is a hidden vein of gold first discovered back in 1843 by Mexican army officer Mariano Arguello (an uncredited Henry Brandon) and his men, all of whom perish mysteriously on their way out of the desert. Twenty years later another man walks out of Death Valley talking about his massive gold strike, but he's unable to find his way back to its location. Finally, in 1883, an old prospector named Pete Wilkins (Roman Bohnen) with $32,000 in gold and quartz, returns each month to remove additional quantities but never reveals the secret location. The three separate stories are connected by the theme of greed and how gold changes the human soul. *Ghost Treasure* is a *Treasure of the Sierra Madre*-morality play in miniature.

Peter Pan:

Possibly the most unusual job of Henry's career is also the most unsung – hired by Walt Disney Productions to 'perform' the role of Captain Hook, the primary antagonist of *Peter Pan*, for their celebrated 1953 animated feature.

The process of rotoscoping – tracing live action film footage of actors to create a more fluid, life-like style of animation – was created and patented by Max Fleischer, who utilized it in his famous Betty Boop, Popeye and Superman cartoons as well as his first feature length production *Gulliver's Travels*. At the Walt Disney Studios, rotoscoping was also used by animators for studying the movements of actors dressed in the costumes of the animated characters, performing their lines and acting out their movements – most often for dance sequences.

Live action footage was filmed for *Snow White* and *Pinocchio* and, most famously, of Bela Lugosi doing the movements of the evil demon Tchernobog for the climactic sequence of *Fantasia* in "Night on Bald Mountain."

In 1952, while *Peter Pan* was in production at Disney's Burbank studios, Henry Brandon was hired to 'perform' live-action sequences in full costume as the Captain Hook character for animator Frank Thomas. The voice-actor for this important role was Hans Conried, who also appeared in live-action footage. But, when you watch the film, see how Captain Hook is brought to life, he *sounds* like Hans Conried but he *looks* and *moves* like Henry Brandon.

Henry Brandon in full costume as Captain Hook for the Disney animators to study. Note the little doll stand-in for Tinkerbell. © Disney

In a 1987 interview with *Starlog Magazine*, Henry recalled "Hans Conried was playing Captain Hook; he had this fantastic, flexible voice. He could go up and down and was a wonderful vocal Captain Hook, but at Disney, you put on costumes and you would play scenes for the animators. Hans had been a radio actor all of his life and he wasn't very good with his body and his gestures so I was called in and had to learn all of his dialogue and songs. They put me in his Captain Hook costume and makeup and I had to play all of these scenes for the animators. So, I was the body of Captain Hook and he was the voice. I was there for two weeks. God, it was hard work!"

In 2017, the United States Postal Service issued a commemorative release saluting the ten most iconic Disney villains including Captain Hook. In a very real sense, Henry Brandon has been honored on a U.S. postage stamp.

Radio Broadcasts:

While Henry Brandon's acting career saw him divide his time almost equally between stage, screen and television, his appearances on the radio were far more infrequent, outside of interview programs in his later career. Here are two examples of jobs he landed during the Golden Age of Radio

The Villain Still Pursues Her:

Very much inspired by *The Drunkard*, **The Silver Theatre** brought *The Villain Still Pursues Her* to radio on this 30-minute anthology series with a revolving cast, hosted by Conrad Nagel. Broadcast live from The Silver Theatre in Hollywood on April 23, 1939, *The Villain Still Pursues Her* was described as the 'melodrama to end all melodramas' and starred Robert Montgomery and Helen Wood as the corny young lovers with Henry Brandon as evil Squire Doolittle.

Brandon was the natural choice, hired to recreate his *Drunkard* style role Squire Cribbs, as Ebenezer Doolittle, the mortgage holder on the Beaumont farm who tries to use this leverage in order to entrap beautiful, young Arabella into marrying him. The studio audience was encouraged to cheer the hero and hiss at Doolittle throughout the brisk half-hour.

Robert Montgomery plays Jack Bloodgood, a bank clerk who neither smokes nor drinks, and is wildly in love with Arabella Beaumont (Helen Wood), who proclaims that "lips that touch liquor will never touch mine!" Squire Doolittle happens by the family farm, and proclaims, "I just came on a social call to remind you of the little matter of the loan upon your farm house. It falls due at noon tomorrow!" He tells Farmer Beaumont that he'll forgive the note if he offers up his daughter's hand in marriage.

The Farmer tells Doolittle that his son is headed home with the needed cash. Henry replies, "So, you say your son Thomas is on his way home with that money? How interesting!" Doolittle chuckles, full of menace and exits, stage right, to waylay both the money and Thomas, wishing them a "good night to you all – and pleasant dreams!" The only thing missing are the Bogeymen.

Doolittle manages to get both brother Thomas and lover Bloodgood arrested on a phony murder rap. The audience boos wildly, having as much fun as Henry Brandon is, which inspires the outbursts. He cackles repeatedly with evil intent, walking away with the show and leaving his teeth-marks on the scenery.

The second act opens the next day, just one hour before the mortgage is due. When Doolittle arrives, he conveniently has a Deacon with him in case a marriage ceremony is to be performed. When Farmer Beaumont admits to Doolittle that he doesn't have the expected money to pay him, the villain oozes "What a pity!" Chuckling in triumph, he implores "my little buttercup" Arabella into an unwilling embrace. "No, no, a thousand times, no!" is her response, insisting in revulsion, "unhand me, villain!"

"You shall pay for this." Doolittle shoots back, then let's loose with a prolonged evil laugh. "So be it, but look to the clock. Six minutes to the fatal hour!" Jack and Thomas have escaped, making their way back to the farm in a blizzard. With one minute to go, Arabella still insists, "I can't marry you, Squire Doolittle! My heart belongs to Jack Bloodgood." Doolittle replies, "But you could learn to love me!"

Doolittle counts down the ticks… two seconds… one second… "Now! The farm is mine! Out! Out you go!" Intending to toss them out into the snow, she finally agrees to marry the scoundrel. The Deacon begins performing the ceremony but before it is concluded, Jack arrives with a thunderous "Unhand that woman!"

"So, you would foil me now, would you?" snaps Squire Doolittle, who pulls a gun on the group, only to be knocked out by Jack Bloodgood. The mortgage is paid off, the stolen money is recovered and the sheriff hauls Doolittle off with a snappy "Alright, Beetle-Face, let's go." Henry has the last word, threatening, "I'll go, but think not this is the end of this, Jack Bloodgood. I go to jail – yes, but the day shall come when I am released and on that day, I shall have revenge!" And with one last cackle, Doolittle is whisked away, making room for the requisite happy ending.

The Villain Still Pursues Her gives listeners a real sense of what it must have been like to be in the audience of *The Drunkard* and why that production was so popular for so long. It's nice to hear star Robert Montgomery thank Henry Brandon during the closing for being "a sinister villain."

The Life of Emile Zola:

The Lux Radio Theater was a long-running radio series devoted to bringing to life classics of the screen on hour-long radio adaptions, usually with one or more of the original movie cast members on hand to recreate their famous roles.

Just a few weeks after Henry stole the show on *The Villain Still Pursues Her* for **The Silver Theater**, he again appeared on radio in a **Lux Theater** adaptation of the classic Warner Brothers drama *The Life of Emile Zola* starring Paul Muni. It was broadcast live from Hollywood on May 8, 1939 with Muni recreating his screen role and Henry in the part of famous fall guy, Captain Alfred Dreyfus.

The *Zola* story begins in Paris of 1862 during the reign of Napoleon III, depicting the author's early life and early novels before becoming aware of the infamous Dreyfus case of 1894. Captain Dreyfus was wrongly accused of being a traitor, unwittingly framed by his superiors because they needed a patsy. Henry only appears in the second act of the drama, a naïve officer tailor-made to take the fall, and doesn't share any scenes at the microphone with Paul Muni.

Looking at life on Devil's Island, Dreyfus through his wife implores Zola to take up the case and the cause, which led to Zola's famous front page newspaper article, *J' Accduse!* The real traitor is discovered years later but the French Army is determined to save face. This means Henry's character is talked about throughout the one hour dramatization but he isn't heard from again, sadly.

The Life of Emile Zola works just fine as a 'greatest hits' compilation and Muni is terrific, but Henry Brandon gets little opportunity to make an impression in his short sequence as an innocent man thrown to the wolves.

CHAPTER EIGHT
Comedies

Henry Brandon had an impeccable sense of theatrical timing that worked well in the comedy genre. His long run in *The Drunkard* followed by his motion picture apprenticeship at The Hal Roach Studios taught him much about the business of film comedy, which he put to good use in movies with Joan Davis, Bob Hope, Martin & Lewis, Danny Kaye and Mel Brooks.

Big Brown Eyes:

This early 1936 Cary Grant film for Paramount is a tough one to categorize. It's not quite an 'A' picture but not really a 'B' either. *Big Brown Eyes* can't decide if it's a romantic comedy or a jewel heist thriller, but since Cary Grant and Joan Bennett spend the whole film wise-cracking and flirting, we're placing the amiable *Big Brown Eyes* here in the "Comedies" chapter.

Cary Grant plays police detective Danny Barr who loves manicurist Eve Fallon (Joan Bennett) and is on the trail of a jewel robbery ring. In his last film billed as Henry Kleinbach, Brandon plays half of the duo who steals the jewels, masterminded by Walter Pidgeon's Richard Morey, an insurance adjuster who also fences the hot ice. Henry's character is Don Butler, which we know from the end credits, as he's never referred to by this name on screen.

Early on is a bizarre sequence in which Grant's Danny Barr is attempting to get a jealous Eve to open her apartment door and let him in. To fool her, he throws his voice as a female, having a conversation with an amorous passer-by in the hallway. An unbilled Jean Arthur recorded the girl's voice, which Cary Grant mimes his lips to. It's incredibly strange, but Eve opens the door and Danny explains, "As a kid, I used to do a ventriloquist act." Eve retorts, "Which part did you play? The dummy?" *His Girl Friday* this ain't.

Henry finally shows up in a shocking sequence in a neighborhood park. They are meeting with Russ Cortig (Lloyd Nolan), to negotiate for their share of a recent heist. When they don't like the low-ball price Cortig offers, Henry's partner Patterson slugs Cortig, who pulls out a revolver and begins shooting at them! The two jewel thieves skeedaddle but we see one of the stray bullets pierce a baby carriage, killing the infant within! Pretty grim for a romcom.

With the police now searching for the Baby Killers in the Park, Morey expresses his displeasure with Cortig's short fuse and the trouble he causes. Getting Henry and Patterson on the phone, he negotiates direct on the price for the merchandise. Henry, bored with all the waiting, yawns while his partner handles the dickering. They decide to return to Philadelphia and conclude their business in person.

Here we are treated to another odd scene as Henry and his partner pack for the flight. Henry talks at length about his fear of flying and his mistrust of parachutes. "What are we gonna do?" he asks. "Fly over? I ain't stuck on them airplanes. They're too dangerous!" Patterson replies, "Go on, they're as safe as they can be!" but Brandon retorts, "They'd be a lot safer if you could keep one foot on the ground!" When his partner tells him that they'll give him a parachute that is guaranteed to open, Brandon/Butler confides, "I might have to jump 10,000 feet and if the parachute don't open, what good is the guarantee?" Patterson continues to mollify Butler, saying "If the parachute doesn't open, they give you a *second* parachute – you get it?" "Yeah," Henry laments, "I get it. I get everything but the second parachute!" It's so strange since he hasn't said much in this film yet. We don't know anything at all about these two crooks and they are suddenly doing a vaudeville routine. Was Director Raoul Walsh trying to humanize them, or just including a snappy sequence about failing parachutes? *Big Brown Eyes* is a definite misfire, but oddly fascinating.

They meet Morey at the local Art Museum as he attempts to educate the pair about the paintings on display. Henry and his partner are merely bored, as his pal asks, "That guy Rembrandt, he's dead, ain't he?" Yep… oddly fascinating! Morey offers the thieves the full $70,000 for the jewels if they also bump off Lloyd Nolan's character, who has become a liability even though he beat the Baby Killer rap with a crooked lawyer.

The duo arranges to meet Cortig at his apartment and kill him there, which is where Danny is hiding out on the balcony. They follow Cortig into his bathroom, watching him clip roses for a vase, and Nolan comments, "My motto is live and let live" and this is when Henry guns him down. As the killers leave, they notice Cary Grant's shadow on the ledge and pull him in. They call Morey who sees an opportunity to have others do his dirty work. He arranges to have Eve bring the money and collect the jewels while Henry guards Cary at the apartment with the corpse. However, Cary overpowers Brandon, gets the gun and handcuffs him, then heads back to the barber shop in time to protect Eve and arrest both Patterson and Pidgeon, wrapping up the case and movie – presumably picking up Henry Brandon later.

Big Brown Eyes doesn't make much sense but it's never dull and is often head-scratchingly entertaining. Henry's character Don Butler is as offbeat as the rest of the movie, which is worth seeking out for the Cary Grant hallway ventriloquist scene alone.

Half a Sinner:

Directed by silent comedy veteran Al Christie, *Half a Sinner* is a brisk and inoffensive bit of movie fluff that plays like Damon Runyon on a budget. With colorful characters like Slick, Red, Mrs. Breckenbridge and Henry Brandon's flirty gangster Handsome, Universal Pictures *Half a Sinner* breezes by in under an hour.

Brandon features prominently in the *Half a Sinner* title lobby card. Collection of Richard Finegan.

In fact, *Half a Sinner* began life as an independent production in 1939 for Grand National to be entitled either *Everything Happens to Anne* or *The Lady Takes a Chance*. After Grand National went out of business, Universal purchased the film and released it in 1940 as *Half a Sinner* (a title they must have liked as they had already used it for an unrelated film back in 1934.)

The plot concerns bored school teacher Anne Gladden (Heather Angel) deciding to have a day of adventure and spice up her life. Immediately, she crosses paths with Handsome (Henry Brandon) and his hood partner Red, who have just bumped off a thug under orders from their Boss Slick. They park their black limo in town and Red goes in to inform Slick while Handsome watches the car… and cutie Anne, who has bought a new dress, real silk stockings and ditched her school- marm glasses.

In his dark suit, trim mustache and dangling cigarette, Handsome hits on Anne, asking "All alone? Hasn't your Mother told you it isn't safe for a pretty girl like you?" When she brusquely replies that her six foot brother is coming to meet her, she notices the revolver in his belt. Henry persists, "Hey, you're kind of a cute trick, you know!" Anne resists his oily charm as Handsome gets more aggressive, telling her "Playing hard to get, eh? You'll soon melt! They all do!" Anne pushes Handsome backwards over a bus bench and jumps into his car, stealing it! It turns out the car is *already* stolen and with a dead body in the back seat that Handsome and Red haven't dumped yet. Even worse, Slick's black overcoat is covering the corpus and has his name in it.

The scalding tea attack in *Half a Sinner*. Collection of Rick Greene.

Their mobster boss tells Red, "I don't know how long you *want* to live, but I know how long you're going to live *if you don't get that coat!*" Red beats it after Anne, who has met Larry (John King) on the road with a disabled vehicle. She helps him; he discovers the body in the back seat, Red and a motorcycle copy follow them, the cop taking plenty of pot shots at the stolen car.

They all go chasing around town as Larry falls for Anne and – finally – Henry Brandon makes his way back into the festivities for the finale. Perhaps his character "Handsome" should have been called "The Seldom Seen Kid" since he's only in the first ten and the last ten minutes of *Half a Sinner*.

Red and Handsome track the hot limo to a deserted cabin and they follow Anne and Larry inside to get back that incriminating overcoat. A slapsticky fight scene follows with Anne pouring scalding tea onto Handsome's chest just before Larry knocks him out! Feeling compassionate, Anne spreads melted butter over Handsome's burned chest to help with the pain.

It turns out that Larry is the owner of the stolen car and has been playing along to be sure Anne was innocent of gangsterism. As the cops arrest the Boss and his thugs, Henry Brandon has been left buttered and unconscious, to be rounded up later.

Handsome's gangster pal Red is nicely played by Tom Dugan, about whom Henry Brandon said, "Tommy Dugan was a transplanted New Yorker whose single joy in life was practical jokes. His were epic in scope and were recounted at actor's gab fests on both coasts. Practical jokes were part of the joy in picture-making in the old days – this great art has practically died out on the treadmill of today's feature and TV making."

The Showman's Trade Review wrote up *Half a Sinner* in their June 1, 1940 issue, saying "An excellent supporting cast helps in the entertainment, with Constance Collier, Robert Elliott and Emma Dunn standing out and Henry Brandon doing nice underplaying as the gangster who considers himself a lady killer."

Crisp and cute, *Half a Sinner* is a pleasant way to kill an hour. Just ask the stiff in the back seat.

The Paleface:

There's something here to offend everyone, starting with the title. Keeping in mind that this was made in 1948 with comedian Bob Hope and Jane Russell, this ain't exactly a documentary. It was made for laughs and Hope as a dopey dentist dishes it out in this Technicolor title from Paramount.

Hope's character is called, "Painless Potter" and in keeping with his usual screen persona plays the horny coward way before Woody Allen put on a pair of glasses. They match him up with Jane Russell in this one and she is just as voluptuous as her signature film; *The Outlaw* made a few years before.

The Western genre has had many renditions for film comedy: Buster Keaton, Laurel and Hardy, W.C. Fields, Marx Bros. all succeeded with various combinations of clichés incorporating the famous theme "Go West Young Man, Go West."* They invariably included cowboys, Indians, shoot-outs, saloons and slug fests. *The Paleface* premise might have been influenced the most by *My Little Chicadee* (1940) in which Mae West lords it over her rarely sober husband, W.C. Fields. She is the one who shoots her way out of trouble and lets Field's character take the bows.

In *The Paleface*, Russell (as Calamity Jane) is roped into working for the government and needs a front to travel. She and her guns are standouts in this picture. Enter Painless Potter who takes the bait and believes himself to be married to Calamity. Forget the plot, Hope hams it up for the camera and dispenses his patented one-liners, sometimes directly to the audience.

With a snarl, Calamity often saves Potter's life but creates the illusion that he is the one skilled in sharpshooting. Potter and the townsfolk believe this too which eventually backfires on him.

The chicken ex-dentist is captured and brought to an Indian encampment. Painless is recognized as a great warrior, his reward is to be tortured by splitting him in half. This responsibility is entrusted to the tribe medicine man (Henry Brandon) named "Wapato." His headdress completely covers

---

* Attributed to newspaper editor Horace Greeley in 1865

his face in his scenes with Hope, but this does not stop Henry from having a ball with his character. A highlight of the film is his constant yelping and jumping around while throwing ritual powder at his intended victim.

The scene is set as Painless is bound to two limber trees tied to his legs. The idea is when the rope is cut; the extremities are pulled out, the rest of the body launches into the distance like a sling-shot. That is exactly what Wapato intended, but failed. Painless lucked out when the force catapulted him from his cowboy boots into a faraway tree.

When Wapato returns to the encampment he is met with scorn. The Chief demands he recapture his victim or he himself will be executed. This sets up a wonderful sequence where Wapato and Painless meet up in the wilderness and approach each other like wrestlers in a ring. Wapato is almost as cowardly as Painless and runs off into the distance. This sets up the best sight gag of the film; as we see Wapato running toward the horizon very far away, Painless goes through baseball pitching gestures with a rock and flings it high in the air. Seconds go by before we see (and hear) that it scores with a hit. Wapato does somersaults in the air as a result of the projectile's contact. This gag was used before in Laurel & Hardy's *Berth Marks* as well as countless Looney Tunes cartoons.

Painless has a dilemma: run away or return and rescue Calamity Jane. The solution is to run down Wapato and (off camera) exchange clothing. Painless returns garbed in the medicine man regalia, fools the Indians and saves his sweetheart. The last scene of the movie is a sight gag and has Hope addressing his movie audience, "What do you want, a happy ending?"

As an aside to this film, Iron Eyes Cody also plays an Indian Chief. He went on to play Indians through his whole acting career. It is from this film that Henry and fellow actor Iron Eyes first met and became friends for the rest of their lives.

Harem Girl:

Joan Davis was the star in a string of B-Picture slapstick comedies for Universal and Columbia Studios during the 1940's. Her character was a second-rate Bob Hope or a third-rate Lucille Ball, wise-cracking, man-crazy and cowardly.

Harem Girl, which features Henry Brandon in a straight-forward Arab baddie role, was her final comedy feature (it's easy to understand why) before going on to star in the mildly successful television series *I Married Joan* for three seasons on NBC.

Written by Elwood Ullman & Edward Bernds and directed by Bernds, the film feels like a protracted Three Stooges two-reeler, and for good reason. Ullman and Bernds worked together on many of the later Stooges shorts, as well as Bowery Boys pictures, and *Harem Girl* is cut from the same comic cloth.

The plot has Susie Stubblegrave (Joan Davis) buying a one-way ticket to the Middle East in search of romance and adventure. Susie hails from Cedar Rapids, Iowa and is a chocolate dipper in a candy factory. "When a boy took me home from the movies," she laments, "he didn't kiss me goodnight, he licked my fingers!"

Susie is accompanied by a pretty traveling companion, Shareen (Peggie Castle) who is really a Princess returning home to save her country from the clutches of Jamal. Lead thug and right-hand to Jamal is Hassan Ali (Henry Brandon) who sends two of his men to abduct Shareen and get rid of Susie in their hotel room. This first attempt is unsuccessful and when Jamal asks Hassan what happened, Henry humorously replies, "My men are imbeciles!"

Susie agrees to disguise herself as the Princess in an attempt to allow Shareen to secret off and find her desert rebel lover and his men. Stubblegrave drapes herself in silken veils and she's brought to the Palace to meet the chubby Bey she (or, rather, Shareen) is supposed to marry.

Abdul the Bey chases her around the room, imploring, "Take off your veil; I yearn to see your face!" Susie shoots back, "What are you, a Peeping Tom?" Yep, those are the jokes.

Henry as Hassan Ali, oblivious to the bland antics of Joan Davis in *Harem Girl*. Collection of Rick Greene.

The film is broad and bland and not terribly funny. In one highlight (and there only is one) Davis hides under Brandon's bed while he rests and a mouse runs up her pant leg. She jerks and jimmies and bolts up, upending the bed and dumping Hassan to the floor. Then Susie knocks him out with a vase and steals his keys, which unlock an arsenal of weapons that the rebels sorely need to win the day. As she escapes, she actually says, "Feet don't fail me now!" Hilarity reigns.

Susie does a comedy harem dance that seems to go on forever while Hassan attempts to escape his locked bedroom and warn Jamal that the keys are missing. And then something very curious happens… Henry Brandon disappears from *Harem Girl*. His character has been set up during this first half as the number two man to the main villain and he gets more screen time than Jamal gets… and then he's gone! His absence is quickly explained that Hassan has deserted, left town, packed all his belongings and simply took off! He must have read the back half of the script. It makes no story sense, which leads one to believe that Brandon got a better offer and asked to be released from the balance of this cheapie picture.

As the film concludes, we get a quick but welcome unbilled cameo from long-time Three Stooges stock player Emil Sitka, a chase sequence in a spooky dungeon and a climactic sword and gun battle which ends with Princess Shareen back on the throne and the French Foreign Legion helping out. The 70-minute comedy (that feels like 140 minutes) ends with Susie asking to join the Foreign Legion. She is told, "But, the Foreign Legion is for men!" Joan Davis looks directly into the camera and replies, "So am I, brother, so am I!"

Scared Stiff:
Dean Martin and Jerry Lewis made sixteen films as a team for Paramount and Henry Brandon appeared in two of them. The first Martin & Lewis comedy he scored a part in was one of their best, *Scared Stiff* from 1952.

Scared Stiff was their 8th film, the midpoint of their career and one of their last in black and white. Directed by Hal Roach Studios veteran George Marshall, it's a remake of Bob Hope's *The Ghost Breakers* and the material works just as well for Dean and Jerry. The film opens with a passionate smooch between Pierre (Henry Brandon) and drop dead gorgeous Rosie (Dorothy Malone) in a night club where she is a dancer and he is a waiter. She asks Pierre, "Am I going to see you later?" to which he responds in the lustful affirmative. A gangster enters the club and pulls Henry aside, telling him "The Big Boy wants to see you… now." He tells Pierre not to bother with his hat and coat, even though it is a cold and rainy night. Things don't look good for Pierre! He is bundled, soaking wet, into a waiting dark car.

Larry Todd (Dean Martin) arrives and the sultry Rosie kisses him even more passionately than she did Pierre. She asks the same of Dino, "Am I going to see you later?" He, too, confirms the date. While Larry sings "When I'm With My Baby," an exasperated maître de wonders where Pierre is, complaining that all of his tables are full with no one to wait on them. Myron the bellboy (Jerry Lewis) takes over for the missing Pierre, with predictably disastrous results that involve a large plate of spaghetti. This leads into Martin and Lewis doing a bit of their hilarious night club routine with Rosie supplying the pulchritude.

Dorothy Malone smooches with Henry (and Dean and Jerry) in *Scared Stiff*.

Afterwards, Myron tells Larry that Pierre was caught kissing The Big Boy's girl – and that girl is Rosie. He confirms that the gang took Pierre for a ride. Larry beats a hasty retreat and Rosie tells schnooky Myron that the Big Boy is also out to get his pal Larry. She kisses him passionately (the third man she's necked with since the picture started) and convinces Myron to intervene with the gang and save Larry.

This somehow works and Jerry Lewis gets to do his tough Bogie routine with the Big Boy's boys until he spies his other friend Pierre sitting there. Except poor Pierre is pretty deceased, Henry Brandon making a convincing dead-eyed corpse in Jerry Lewis' terrified arms. The shenanigans continue as the plot kicks in regarding a haunted castle in Cuba, but Henry Brandon is in and out of *Scared Stiff* in less than twenty-five minutes. The next Martin & Lewis film, *The Caddy*, also featured a part for Henry, thanks to his casting director buddy at Paramount.

The Caddy:

Henry Brandon's second Martin and Lewis appearance is in their final black and white film and one of their most popular, *The Caddy*. Dean and Jerry play a hopeful pro golfer and his caddy, competing in their first tournaments and rubbing shoulders with the California wealthy. Henry's character is called Mr. Preen, he's listed in the credits but, as he told co-author Rick Greene, "I'm really just a glorified extra in the picture." Indeed, Henry has more screen time throughout the various party and golf sequences of *The Caddy* than he had as Pierre in *Scared Stiff*, but he never speaks a word of dialogue.

Henry Brandon hovering in the background of *The Caddy*.

His character is one of many snobby rich folk populating several social gatherings at a Country Club in Santa Barbara and again at Donna Reed's gorgeous estate before a second golf tournament that Martin's character will be playing in. It's during these scenes that Jerry, who plays Dean's Caddy but is masquerading as a socialite to keep an eye on his buddy, sings a song "The Gay Continental." One can see Henry Brandon in the group around the pool, sitting near the diving board and watching Lewis sing the song, genuinely entertained by his spastic antics.

"We spent a week filming those pool scenes," Brandon told Greene, "and I got to see Lewis ad-lib constantly. He kept us all in stitches, all day long. He was just hilarious, singing that song over and over, trying different things." Henry recalled a prime example of Jerry's on-set tomfoolery. During the song, there is a sight gag that involves Jerry standing on the edge of the diving board and imagining falling in, and a big burst of bubbles occurs in the pool as if he'd taken the plunge. He continues his song, high and dry, circling the pool until the last verse when he does fall in. Brandon remembers Jerry secretly conspiring with the effects men who had rigged the air bubbles for the diving board sight gag. Everyone knew something was up because he had slipped off his wrist watch. They were saving Jerry's final plunge for the next day, since it was close to 5:00 PM. Henry elaborated:

> He sang the whole song in one take and then he went off the board and into the pool. The special effects men had seen him slip off his watch and they let him have it! A huge burst blew him up and out of the pool and into the air. He spit out some water and yelled "Gee, Ma, have I got gas!" That *had* to be an ad-lib! We laughed for ten minutes, everyone, the crew, and the extras. God, he was funny.

Henry can also be seen during the climactic golf tournament in Monterey, standing behind Jerry Lewis and watching the pandemonium, but never saying a word. He told Greene that he worked for over a month on *The Caddy*, laughing heartily at Jerry's antics, filling his bank account but doing nothing to further his career.

Knock On Wood:

After his back-to-back Martin & Lewis movies, Henry Brandon next appeared in two more Paramount Pictures comedies, this time with Danny Kaye and then Bob Hope. *Knock on Wood* came first, produced in 1953 but released in April of 1954. Like *The Caddy*, Brandon gets prominent billing in *Knock on Wood* and has very little to do. At least this time, he does it in Technicolor and gets to commit a couple of (off screen) murders. His character name of "Trenchcoat Man #2" gives you an idea of the importance of the role.

Written and Directed by Norman Panama and Melvin Frank, *Knock on Wood* is a kind of dry-run for their upcoming collaboration – *The Court Jester*. *Knock on Wood* is amusing and lots of fun, but nowhere near the pinnacle of classic comedy the trio (Panama, Frank, Kaye) would achieve with *The Court Jester*. The plot involves two rival spy rings trying to steal blueprints for a new type of doomsday secret weapon, with said blueprints ultimately being hidden in the hollow heads of Danny Kaye's two ventriloquist dummies – Clarence and Terrance.

In his early scenes, Trenchcoat Man #2 stands behind Trenchcoat Man #1 as they follow and watch the various people who have access to the blueprints. By the middle of *Knock on Wood*, Trenchcoat Man #1 has been knifed; leaving Henry's remaining spy to handle the action. When he finally does speak, another actor is dubbing Henry's lines in a British accent, and rather poorly.

In the best Hitchcockian style, Danny Kaye's Jerry Morgan gets the blame for Trenchcoat #1's death as well as rival spy Gromek, whom Henry actually murdered. Jerry is on the run around London and ends up at the estate of Godfrey Langstrom (Torin Thatcher), who is the master spy behind everything and Trenchcoat Man #2's boss. A gaggle of spies chase Jerry around the mansion and he comically eludes them, disabling Henry by slamming a large wooden table at him. When the gang pursues Kaye into the streets of London, Henry isn't with them. That table must have been pretty hard, as Trenchcoat Man #2 never returns to *Knock on Wood*.

Henry fares much better with Bob Hope than he did with Martin & Lewis and Danny Kaye in the fourth of the '50s Paramount comedy quartet, *Casanova's Big Night*.

Casanova's Big Night:

This is the second "Bob Hope movie" that Henry Brandon appeared in: this time he played Captain Rugello, an expert swordsman. The 1954 film was shot in splendid Technicolor with lavish sets and costumes. The all-star cast included: Vincent Price, Basil Rathbone, Raymond Burr, John Carradine, John Hoyt, Lucien Littlefield, Lon Chaney Jr. and the lovely Joan Fontaine.

Bumbling Bob retains his film persona as the randy fraidy-cat. His character is (Pippo Popolino), a meek tailor's apprentice who dreams of becoming a great lover. The film is loosely set in 18th century Venice when the famous lover, Casanova made his reputation.

The dashing figure of Vincent Price is briefly seen as the roguish rascal romancer who escapes his creditors. To succeed, he quickly talks Pippo into masquerading as himself and trades his royal garments in exchange for Pippo's horse.

The crazy plot involves some of Casanova's creditors to include the local merchants. One of them is (Fontaine) who plays a beautiful grocery clerk named Francesca. She helps concoct a scheme to aid and abet the chicanery in hopes that Pippo can actually fool the dignitaries.

Pippo's objective is to score with the women, while the creditors hope he scores with some appreciative coin. Basil Rathbone (as Lucio), the "real" Casanova's valet, is also bereft of money, so he readily helps out. The three venture off to romantic Venice to achieve their goals. Should they fail, their collective heads will most certainly be cut off.

The Doge of Venice is alerted that Casanova is due to arrive at the Royal

Ball. He does not know what he looks like, but the great lover's legend is known by all. Despite Francesca's warnings to Pippo to "try not to act like an idiot," he does just that.

Impersonating Casanova works tentatively despite his oafish behavior. It draws a Duchess to promise him a sum of money if he can seduce her son's future bride in a test of virtues.

For sadistic entertainment and to prove this is the real Casanova, The Doge of Venice summons his Captain from the front to engage Casanova in a fencing duel. Capt. Rugello (Henry Brandon) plays his part with convincing skill.

The scene is set at the ballroom with a royal audience looking on, and then an announcement is made: "Captain Rugello the fencing champion of the Venetian army will give you an exhibition of his skills. He has waited for a worthy opponent to come to Venice."

At this moment, Captain Rugello turns to the imposter with a challenge. "Signor Casanova, your fame as a swordsman is worldwide. I would deem it an honor if you would cross blades with me." Pippo's clumsy fencing is a comic gem especially when compared with the Captain's graceful moves.

Pippo wins the duel by accident but impresses all. He is still looked on as suspicious in the social settings. His awkward attempts at romance; battles with palace guards, imprisonment and escape all enhance the phony Casanova reputation.

It all ends as Pippo is sent to the gallows. Hope jumps out of his character and addresses the movie-going audience as Bob Hope. In an example of "knocking down the fourth wall of comedy" he offers an alternate ending where his neck is saved.

Henry Brandon's fencing, grace and athleticism was a skill he worked on seriously and serves him well in this entertaining Bob Hope comedy classic.

The Cobra Creeps! Henry Brandon in *Jungle Jim*.

CHAPTER NINE
Serials

IN DIVVYING UP THE various Henry Brandon cinematic genres into manageable groups for examination, his serials are one of the smaller categories, yet one of the most rewarding. He only appeared in four of them: *Jungle Jim*, *Secret Agent X-9*, *Buck Rogers* and one of the quintessential crown jewels of his career, *Drums of Fu Manchu*. His first and last serials, *Jungle Jim* and *Drums of Fu Manchu* offer significant main villain roles while in the middle two he plays mere henchmen, although his X-9 Blackstone ended up being a bait-and-switch final chapter surprise offering more screen time than his Cobra in *Jungle Jim*, already top-heavy with secondary baddies.

Since the iconic *Drums of Fu Manchu* was explored in great detail in Chapter Four, we will take a look at his initial trio of cliff-hanging chapter plays here, all of which were made at Universal Studios during the back half of the 1930s.

When asked by *Cinemacabre* Magazine to compare working on features with that of serials at Universal and Republic, Henry responded, "Well, you know in making an 'A' picture you might shoot anywhere from three to six or seven setups a day. On a serial you might shoot up to eighty-five a day! It was an enormous rush. The actor who could ad-lib his way out of somebody's fluffing his lines is considered the best actor on a serial lot. If you didn't stop, you were great! They would always congratulate you if you kept on going, made up lines or did anything not to ruin the take."

Jungle Jim:

Brandon's first serial, *Jungle Jim* came early in his film career, being produced in late 1936 and released from mid-January of 1937 through the end of March. *Jungle Jim* offered him a meaty main villain role called The Cobra. Like his Barnaby in *Babes in Toyland*, Henry is required to play the sinister Cobra much older than his actual age (he was 25 during the production of *Jungle Jim*) since we're supposed to believe that he is the father of leading lady Betty Jane Rhodes. As always, Henry rises to the challenge even though he was just nine years her senior.

Jungle Jim was a newspaper comic strip created in 1934 by Alex Raymond and comprised the top half of the full color Sunday page that focused on Raymond's other more famous creation, *Flash Gordon*. Both properties were procured by Universal Pictures from King Features Syndicate to be adapted for serials, with the first of three *Flash Gordon* epics produced early in 1936 and *Jungle Jim* coming on its heels. Inspired by the massive success of MGM's *Tarzan the Ape Man* released in 1932, the "Jungle Picture" genre was born and *Jungle Jim* was the first of *many* jungle serials and B-pictures yet to come.

The twelve chapters of *Jungle Jim* are brisk, action-packed and well-made – mainly in the wilds of the Universal City sound-stages with some location work done at Lake Sherwood. Even Brandon joked about this in an interview for *Starlog Magazine* in 1987.

> *Jungle Jim* was my first serial with Grant Withers and Evelyn Brent, a big star in silent pictures. She played my sister, Shanghai Lil and I played the Cobra, the villain. The film was set in darkest Africa – the Universal back-lot!

In fact, The Cobra's crumbling castle lair was built for use in Universal's horror classics *Dracula* and *Frankenstein* in 1931 and the iconic curved stairway had been most recently used in the first *Flash Gordon*. Things get off to a rousing start in the initial chapter, "Into the Lion's Den" with a violent storm aboard a ship off the coast of Africa.

It is 1920 and The Redmond's with young daughter Joan are aboard along with a variety of wild animals her father has caught and crated. The crates don't weather the storm; however, as one by one they crash open, releasing frightened lions, panthers and tigers among the more frightened passengers and crew.

There is a moment that packs a wallop as a roaring tiger leaps at little Joan in the ship's stateroom as her Mother pulls a loaded rifle off a wall rack and efficiently kills it. The Captain puts a hasty note in a bottle, informing whoever finds it that the Redmonds have been put in a life boat in the hopes of reaching the African shore.

Sixteen years later, two expeditions arrive to scour darkest Africa for Joan, who is now one of the wealthiest women in England (shades of Tarzan!). Jungle Jim (the virile Grant Withers) makes his cornball entrance returning from safari singing his theme song, "I'm Takin' The Jungle Trail" to reunite with his pals, the crusty Malay Mike (a scene-stealing Raymond Hatton) and Red, who doesn't make it out of this first chapter alive.

Red had been hired to lead the 'good guys' expedition searching for Joan Redmond, but he's murdered by treacherous Cajun La Bat, who covers up the killing by releasing crated animals that attack everyone in sight. Jim and Mike help subdue the animals and quickly take control of the 'good' safari, making it a mission of vengeance for their friend Red. The "evil" expedition is led by La Bat, Slade and a greedy Redmond relative who needs Joan out of his way. The rival safaris hit the jungle trail, both seeking a mysterious white Lion Goddess, who might be (and is) Joan Redmond. Henry's introduction as The Cobra in the first chapter is brief, but the Frankenstein castle lair and his neatly groomed goatee tell us he is to be the primary antagonist that Jungle Jim and his friends will face. Upon hearing that white men are in the jungle, The Cobra orders his natives to drive them out. His sister, Shanghai Lil (Evelyn Brent) throws a few barbs at her brother, but he ignores her. Luckily, we get more of Brandon in Chapter Two, entitled, *The Cobra Strikes!*

In the second episode of *Jungle Jim* a thrilling lion attack is called off by The Lion Goddess. When we again see Henry as The Cobra, he metes out jungle justice by sending a native to the whipping post. Dressed quite nattily in a crisp white linen suit and open collar, we discover The Cobra is an international crook on the lam, hiding out in his jungle fortress from Government Agents. Jim and Mike are captured and have their first (of many) encounters with The Cobra, who is pretending to be Joan's father.

Jungle Jim gets tough with The Cobra

For killing one of her lions in the preceding chapter, The Lion Goddess forces Jungle Jim to fight her fiercest tiger while The Cobra watches coldly and triumphantly from above. Jim kills the tiger armed with just a knife and wins their freedom. Henry warns his acerbic sister Shanghai Lil not to antagonize Joan as he can only control the spear-wielding natives through her influence. Before Malay Mike and Jim can leave, The Cobra dooms them by switching out their bullets for blanks.

However, by Chapter Three, Jungle Jim and Joan are pals and in the fourth chapter, her true identity is revealed by her loyal servant who was present on the boat during the storm while working for her real parents. During the fifth chapter, *The Bridge of Terror*, Henry Brandon has more to do than sit behind his desk and snarl. The Cobra and his warriors run up and down the Frankenstein steps in hot pursuit of an escaping Jim and Malay Mike. The duo pretty easily outsmarts the criminal and get away using a neat Indiana Jones maneuver with a whip.

At the end of Chapter Six, *Drums of Doom*, The Cobra again has Jim and Malay captive and exclaims to his chief warrior "Lala maloo kazanga zanti!" This gibberish, as delivered by Henry Brandon, carries great menace. He instructed his minions to broadcast via the drums that Jungle Jim is to be executed at sunset, knowing this threat will bring Joan racing back into his clutches. The episode ends with The White Cobra standing Jim and Mike in front of a native execution squad, pointing their deadly bow and arrows at the duo. "It looks like the end of the trail, Mike!" Jungle Jim exclaims to which Malay responds, "You're tellin' me!" as Henry leers down from a balcony above. The Cobra indulges in much balcony-leering throughout the twelve chapters.

The back half of *Jungle Jim* begins with Chapter Seven's *The Earth Trembles* as Joan saves her friends from a hail of arrows with a well-placed shield. She reveals to The Cobra that she now knows he isn't her real father and is leaving the jungle with Jim to claim her fortune. This isn't good for Henry's character for two reasons – with the Lion Goddess gone, his control over the natives vanishes and if they return to civilization, the police will soon set out to capture The Cobra and Shanghai Lil. He tricks Joan into agreeing to remain in the jungle by threatening her friends, then The Cobra sinks even lower into despicability by arming Slade and Redmond with enough weapons to finish off Jim and Malay before they can leave Africa.

Although the two evil factions have an uneasy truce, Joan's servant overhears The Cobra gloating (he gloats ubiquitously in most of the chapters) and reveals them to her friends. Before Henry can finish his Chapter Seven gloating, he hears a commotion and realizes once again his plans have gone awry.

Castle Dracula is attacked by a rival tribe AND a volcano erupts at the same time! You can't say these brisk two-reelers were dull! The Cobra seizes the opportunity and proclaims to the natives that HE is responsible for the eruption, threatening them with the fury of The Devil Mountain. The ruse works and as the eruption subsides, The Cobra tells the superstitious natives they've been punished enough and he is going to restore the sun. When that happens, Brandon's hold over them seems complete. Joan believes a rock slide has claimed the lives of Jungle Jim and Malay Mike. Grieving, she is tricked by Slade and Redmond to accompany them, not realizing they plan to get rid of her and steal her fortune. Showing some of Universal's cost – cutting measures in these later chapters, many of the music cues from the first *Flash Gordon* serial are reused here, much of them borrowed from Franz Waxman's *Bride Of Frankenstein* score from 1935.

The Cobra uses his new volcano-fueled influence with the natives to order the deaths of ALL the white people in the jungle, including Joan, via his drum network, to prevent ANY of them from returning to civilization. Joan is reunited with Jim and Malay, none the worse for wear after having a few tons of rock drop on them and as we make it to Chapter Nine, *The Devil Bird*, they are overwhelmed by bloodthirsty natives ready to carry out The Cobra's murderous orders.

The captured trio (again) are brought before The Cobra (again) back at the spooky Castle (again) and he bargains to take control of Joan's fortune. Jim and Mike escape (again) and Henry finally sees some physical action as Chapter Nine unfolds in a rousing fist fight. The Cobra doesn't make out too well in the battle, but his sister steps it up when Lil shoots Jungle Jim square in the gut as he falls backward out of a window! When Chapter Ten begins, the bullet to the stomach becomes a glancing flesh wound to the right shoulder, quite the cheat considering all of the cliffhangers up to this point have played fair with the audience. The brisk action sequence continues as The

Cobra gets trussed up with a rope lasso, then is knocked out by Jungle Jim who escapes (yet again).

In The Cobra's Castle is the eleventh chapter and features key supporting villain Redmond meeting a grizzly fate attacked by lions, leaving just Slade and The Cobra as antagonists. A British gent named Hawkins arrives by plane and is revealed to be a member of the Secret Police out to get The Cobra. He tells Jim that The Cobra and Shanghai Lil are wanted for murder in London, producing a wanted poster proving the point.

At the end of this penultimate chapter, The Cobra captures Jim and Mike one final time which leads into *The Last Safari*, the final thrilling chapter of *Jungle Jim*. With Hawks help, dropping hand grenades down on the natives huts below from his plane, the tables are finally turned and the cowardly Cobra abandons his sister and tries to escape. For the first time in the twelve chapters, Brandon is out of the Castle and on the run in the jungle. He knocks out Hawks and tries to steal his plane, but Jungle Jim bodily pulls him out and engages in a fierce climactic fist fight which results in those two instant movie black-eyes and signifies the end of The Cobra's reign of terror. Three planes arrive to haul away the surviving bad guys and Jim, Joan and Malay Mike return to civilization to claim her millions and live happily after.

Jungle Jim is a well-regarded Universal serial and just the beginning of a franchise that continued quite prolifically twelve years later. When Johnny Weissmuller concluded his run in the *Tarzan* series (which inspired Universal to produce this serial), he ironically assumed the mantle of Jungle Jim in a series of sixteen B-Pictures for Columbia from 1948 until 1955, when he *continued* to play Jungle Jim on a television series for twenty-six episodes through 1956!

Secret Agent X-9:

Henry Brandon's follow-up serial for Universal came on the heels of *Jungle Jim* in *Secret Agent X-9*, the first of TWO unrelated serials under this title. Produced and released in 1937, Brandon's role as Blackstone in *X-9* seems to be a step backward since he appears to be merely the number two henchman of a gang of jewel-thieves and not the primary villain… but appearances can be deceptful!

Like most serial source material, *Secret Agent X-9* also comes from the Sunday funny pages and King Features Syndicate, although X-9 is really more of an FBI G-man than a Secret Agent. Created by the dream team of writer Dashiell Hammett (*The Thin Man*) and artist Alex Raymond (*Flash Gordon*), *Secret Agent X-9* had a long, healthy comic-strip run from 1934 until 1996.

The plot of this first film version concerns the FBI tracking the activities of an elusive international thief named Victor Brenda and his gang - which includes Henry Brandon and Lon Chaney, Jr in one of his earliest appearances for Universal, years before *The Wolf Man* made him an iconic horror star. In an interview with *Cinemacabre* Magazine, Henry remembered Chaney, Jr:

> I appeared in several films with Chaney, Jr. This is a funny story. He was completely picture-oriented. He had grown up in the movies through his father, and I had started in the theatre. So, I would be playing in these serials, and he'd be the second or third man through the door. I was the heavy, you see. And we used to get in these enormous arguments about the value of stage training for film actors. He said he didn't think they needed stage training. He argued that he could get all the training he needed in films. Then suddenly, by a miracle, he was cast in Steinbeck's *Of Mice and Men* [ironically, for *Babes in Toyland* Producer Hal Roach]. He was chosen by Wallace Ford because Broderick Crawford, who'd created the part (of Lenny) wasn't available.

Brandon as Blackstone in *Secret Agent X-9*.

Wally Ford coached him in the part and Chaney became an enormous success in it. So I waited until it played a couple of weeks and I went backstage into his dressing room. He took one look at me and yelled, "Don't say it, don't say I told you so! You were a thousand per cent right about the value of stage acting, of developing a character and playing him for three hours in one evening." And, of course, his entire subsequent career was based on that one show.

In the first *X-9* chapter entitled *Modern Pirates* we meet both the forces of good and evil who will clash again and again in the subsequent episodes. When Blackstone (Henry Brandon) arrives after helping to fake Brenda's death in Belgravia, he makes his way immediately to a haunted Blackbeard pirate ship attraction which is where the gang cleverly holes up, awaiting their next assignment from the mysterious, shadowy Brenda as communicated via Blackstone.

Their new plan is to steal the Belgravian Crown Jewels, which are being packed up from exhibition in America to return to Belgravia. They manage to accomplish this with a heist at sea by using poison gas, knocking off a friend of X-9 and valued member of the FBI task force. Thus, this becomes (like in *Jungle Jim*) a mission of vengeance as well as justice for the X-Force. Using modern police methods (and lazy screen-writing), the team identifies a stray thread stuck to a match book cover which leads them to Blackstone via his tailor!

Henry gets much more screen time and action in *Secret Agent X-9* than he did in his first serial and this opening chapter includes a fierce fist fight with Agent X-9, who apprehends and arrests Blackstone. We also meet pert blonde Jean Rogers (that deep bedroom voice!) in between her first and second *Flash Gordon* serials. It isn't clear at first whether her Shara Graustark is one of the good guys or the bad guys! Like *Jungle Jim*, the score for *Secret Agent X-9* is lifted almost in whole from the first *Flash Gordon* serial, including many of the famous Franz Waxman themes repurposed from *The Bride of Frankenstein* giving all of these 1930s Universal serials a comforting sameness of identity that adds to the fun.

As the story continues in Chapter Two, *The Ray That Blinds*, Blackstone is released from jail due to a loophole in the law (this convenient "loophole" is never explained) putting him back in circulation and commanding the gang on behalf of Brenda. Henry underplays Blackstone, taking a different approach from Barnaby and The Cobra and showing his versatility even at this early stage in his film career. His Blackstone is suave and cool, seemingly the only one in the gang who has a personal relationship with Brenda.

A gang member, who stashed the stolen Crown Jewels in a safety box, hides the receipt for the box in the lining behind a painting at his art gallery. When he is killed trying to escape X-9 (taking a dramatic plunge off a building), Blackstone sends some of his thugs to the gallery with a powerful ray that illuminates the paintings so they can find the hidden receipt for the number to the lock box with the jewels from the heist on the boat. They are unsuccessful and, upon returning to the Pirate Ship hideout and bellyaching about Brenda's mysterious ways, Blackstone keeps them in line by sneering "When men get tired of working for Brenda, they can quit. But they *never* go to work for anyone else. Do I make myself clear?"

Blackstone grapples with X-9 (Scott Kolk) in an early chapter. Collection of Richard Finegan.

By the third chapter, *The Man of Many Faces*, we learn that Jean Rogers character is working hand in hand with the FBI as she discovers which painting has the disguised receipt and the battle is on for possession of said painting – racing back and forth from the Art Gallery to The Raymond Estate to FBI Headquarters and the Pirate Ship and back again.

Chapters Four and Five are spent chasing after the painting with the receipt and when X-9 finally gets it into FBI Headquarters, he discovers the corner of it has been cut out by Shara, who in another narrative shift now ISN'T working with X-9. She delivers the painting square to Baron Karsten (Monte Blue) midway through Chapter Five, when we learn they are BOTH working with Feds and against Brenda and Blackstone for the recovery of the jewels and confusion reigns, but mainly for the audience.

Tired of his henchmen's bungling, Blackstone heads out to the Raymond Estate personally where the receipt, now cleansed of oil paint, is hidden in a book. For the first time since the opening chapter, Henry has more to do than just bark and sneer at Brenda's goons.

Now, instead of everyone chasing after the painting, the receipt becomes the chapter play's MacGuffin. Blackstone retrieves it at gunpoint from X-9, revealing that Karsten is indeed part of Brenda's gang and is possibly Brenda himself. Karsten plays along, adding to the confusion and misdirection, so that even the gang think's he is Brenda. He manages to lift the receipt and put it back in the book, and then leaves with Blackstone. Gang member Ransom double-crosses Blackstone and takes the receipt from the book to head to The Farmers & Mechanics Bank and obtain the missing jewels for himself. However, Blackstone – who saw the receipt – knows where the jewels are and is there with the gang to nab Ransom when he nabs the jewels. But X-9 uses infra-red on the patch of painting pigment that the receipt had been hidden under and now the FBI has the Bank information – leading all parties there.

We finally dispense with paintings and corners of paintings and receipts to get to the jewels themselves. Except, when Blackstone takes the jewels from Ransom (sealed up in a metal box) he discovers HE has been tricked, they aren't in there! For once, X-9 is ahead of Brenda and got to the Bank first and switched out the jewels, now hoping to catch the gang and bring things to a satisfactory conclusion. But, it's only the end of Chapter 6 – the half-way point of this merry-go-round, so X-9 gets knocked out of a window to fall to his apparent death.

Blackstone and Baron Karsten (Monte Blue) capture Secret Agent X-9. Collection of Richard Finegan.

Where some of the chapter-ending cliffhangers in *X-9* are unique and exciting, the resolutions are often disappointing (the car didn't go off the cliff, it stalled at the edge of the cliff) and others outright cheats. It's one thing when additional footage is added to show how the hero got out of his peril (he leapt to safety before the car went over the cliff) but it is entirely another when, as in chapters six and seven, alternate footage is shown the following week. These chapter plays were designed to have a full seven days in between cliffhangers so that, when the kids saw the resolution, they'd scratch their heads and think 'Maybe I *didn't* see X-9 fall out of that window, I guess it WAS that other guy who fell…'when, in fact, having the luxury of rewatching sequences on DVD, it is clearly shown that X-9 fell out of the window at the end of Chapter 6 and at the beginning of Chapter 7, not the guy standing next to him who falls to his death. And at the end of that chapter, X-9 is shot in the stomach but when Chapter 8 begins, comic relief Pidge is shot in the wrist instead. Serials that didn't play fair with their audiences risked losing the engagement of that audience.

As the plot of *Secret Agent X-9* plays out, the jewels change hands several times, with the G-Men taking possession, then Blackstone gets them, then Blackstone loses them, then Blackstone forces Shara to help him get them back or his men will kill Baron Karsten, then X-9 rescues Karsten, then… well, you get the picture. X-9 finally discoveres the Pirate Ship hideout, not through crack detective work but because some of Brenda's men left tickets for the attraction in their pockets!

Fans of Henry Brandon are apt to be disappointed by the climactic chapters of this serial since Brenda/Blackstone is masquerading as Karsten and Monte Blue plays *both* roles for three episodes. Fake Karsten manages to get the jewels (before losing them AGAIN) and kills Tommy, one of X-9's best men and best friends. X-9 vows "If it's the last thing I ever do, I'll get Brenda for this!"

The big finale showdown between Brenda's men and the G-Men takes place in Chapter Twelve, *Crime Does Not Pay* aboard the Pirate Ship at night. There is a furious gun battles and one by one, all of Brenda's men are picked off or are captured except for Fake Karsten/Brenda/Blackstone and, of all people, Lon Chaney Jr. Brenda double-crosses Chaney as they escape, knocking him out and allowing him to be taken and finally, in the final few minutes of the final chapter of the serial, Henry Brandon returns as he removes the Karsten disguise and reveals that Blackstone and Brenda are one in the same. He discovers the jewels were switched *again* (as a master criminal, he falls for that trick a lot) and goes back to the pier where we first met Blackstone in Chapter One to get them from gruff Trader Delany. X-9 overhears Blackstone reveal himself as Brenda and has a furious fist fight with Henry Brandon's stunt double before beating the master villain senseless and taking him into custody.

His sleazy lawyer tries to get him off again, but ballistics tests prove that the bullets that killed poor Tommy match Brenda's gun and his fingerprints are on the getaway car. Brenda is put away for good, X-9 gets a Belgravian medal from the real Baron Karsten and the whole show ends with Secret Agent X-9 staring longingly into those luscious eyes of Jean Rogers.

Brandon didn't think much of *Secret Agent X-9* calling it "the dullest of the four (serials) I appeared in, because it was about cops and robbers. The kids had seen crime and gangster movies that were made for much more money." Though the serial could be tiresome and confusing, he was selling short the many pleasures of *X-9* including his own sophisticated performance, the more clever-than-usual episode ending cliffhangers (except for those cheaters) and the unique hide-in-plain-sight Pirate Ship base, a notion borrowed by Columbia for their first *Batman* serial in 1943, having the Dr. Daka gang based inside an active amusement park dark ride.

The following year, Henry Brandon would return to the sound stages at Universal City to wreak havoc in a much more imaginative chapter play for a rare foray into the realm of fantasy and science-fiction.

Buck Rogers:

Henry's third and final serial for Universal was based on the *Buck Rogers* comic strip, which in turn began life as a science fiction novella published in 1928 by Phillip Francis Nowlan. The daily comic strip adaptation began in 1929 and the classic full color Sunday strip began in 1930. In the strip, Buck was a Rip Van Winkle in space, in suspended animation for 500 years and awakening in the year 2419 AD. The comic strip was called *Buck Rogers In The 25th Century A.D.* and was soon a booming franchise, appearing in Big Little Books, a radio show and then – following the wildly popular Flash Gordon chapter plays, a serial for Universal Pictures.

Shot in the latter third of 1938, *Buck Rogers* (Universal shortened the print title for the movies) was initially released on February 2, 1939 and completed its first run at the end of April. For Buster Crabbe, it came between his second and third Flash Gordon serials. For Henry Brandon, it came at another career crossroads.

Henry began his film career in an iconic leading role as Silas Barnaby at The Hal Roach Studios. He continued playing the lead villain roles in his first two Universal serials but here, seemingly takes a backward move playing NOT the lead heavy Killer Kane but one of his many look-a-like thugs, a minion named Laska. For Henry, the decision – as many of his career choices – was an economic one. He told *Starlog Magazine*:

> They called me in and told me they were going to do "Buck Rogers." They had me down for the second heavy. I was a little miffed because I had played the *first* heavy in "Jungle Jim". I asked why I couldn't play the first heavy (in *Buck Rogers*) and they explained that the first heavy worked one day on an office set. The second worked three weeks. I was convinced. I was the guy Killer Kane sent out to do all the dirty jobs, which kept me in front of the cameras *all* the time.

Buck Rogers is, for all intent, another *Flash Gordon* serial but without the vivid imagination and unusual planets and fun monsters of those films, not to mention a complete lack of romance. In *Buck*, the heroes go back and forth and back and forth and back and forth to Saturn throughout the twelve tedious chapters until the final battle with Killer Kane, for which Henry's Captain Laska is sadly absent.

The first chapter of *Buck Rogers* is called *Tomorrow's World* and sets up the premise quickly. Buck Rogers and his young pal Buddy Wade are on a dirigible in a raging snowstorm. They crash on a mountain top and a canister of experimental gas called 'Nirvano' places the duo in a state of suspended animation just as the wreckage of the airship is buried by an avalanche.

1940 becomes 2440, as evidenced by the leftover Flash Gordon space ships flying around with those little sparks shooting out of the exhaust pipes. Melting ice has unveiled part of the dirigible and one ship stops to investigate, using a ray-gun to melt a doorway and allowing for the retrieval of Buck and Buddy, still alive and VERY confused. This all takes place to the usual strains of Franz Waxman's *Bride of Frankenstein* used in both of the

Flash Gordon serials as well as Henry's previous chapter-plays *Jungle Jim* and *Secret Agent X-9*. This common musical language gives the Universal films of this period a "shared Universe" identity in much the same way that the appealing tunes of LeRoy Shield and Marvin Hatley gave the Hal Roach comedies of the early 1930's their special vibe.

Captain Laska (Brandon) and his minions in *Buck Rogers*. Collection of Richard Finegan.

The future men, some kind of soldiers, bring their 'prisoners' back to a secret mountain base and then they 'beam' off the ship into a lab – twenty-five years before *Star Trek* would make this activity commonplace. Buck Rogers is looked upon as a scientific miracle. We see, via a television screen, Killer Kane, who is a 25th Century racketeer, capture one of the "good" pilots in his attempt to discover the secret entrance Buck and Buddy were just brought through. Rogers immediately volunteers to help the scientists with a strategy to slip through Kane's planet-wide blockade and fly to Saturn for assistance. Wilma (Constance Moore) accompanies them as Buck's idea of a decoy ship seems to work and the three comrades are off to Saturn! However, they have been followed as we get our unceremonious introduction to Henry Brandon's Captain Laska. He fires upon the ship with Buck and friends, mortally wounding it as it plummets down, and thus have our first *Buck Rogers* cliff hanger!

Laska and the Zombie Helmet. Collection of Richard Finegan.

Chapter Two is called *Tragedy on Saturn* and Brandon finally gets into the thick of the action! Buck and his pals escape the doomed ship by using anti-gravity belts to land safely on the surface of Saturn (which is, in reality, the popular Vaquez Rocks filming location near Canyon Country, California – used previously in the opening scenes of Universal's *Werewolf of London*.)

Captain Laska reports to The Leader that he has destroyed the rebel ship and everyone aboard, but he's commanded to follow the wreck down and be sure. In his first *Buck Rogers* fist fight, Laska is beaten and captured NOT by Buck Rogers, but by little Buddy! How humiliating. Everyone is shuttled to the ruling council of Saturn on glass bullet monorail cars. Laska convinces the council that Buck and company are dangerous revolutionaries, which calls for a quick escape *back* along the bullet track and onto a stolen Killer Kane ship to fly home. The radio is broken so they can't signal their Earth friends that it's them in the ship, so when they enter through the secret gate, they are seemingly destroyed.

They survive, buried in wreckage (again), but back on Saturn, Captain Laska has the council fully deceived. A treaty is prepared to help Kane wipe out the anarchists on Earth, which Henry takes back to our planet. "I think our troubles are just about over!" gloats Laska, quite prematurely. Using an enemy uniform from the rubble of the stolen ship, Buck infiltrates Kane's stronghold as a spy. Buddy joins him, as they happen to have a teenaged boy-sized uniform aboard the ship as well. Chapter Three concludes with Buck interrupting the signing of the treaty and showing Saturn's Prince Tallen how Kane uses zombie helmets to rob Earth people of their free will. Rogers quickly sways the Prince's allegiance to the Rebels and they all escape to be shot by a ray gun!

The reveal in Chapter Four, called *The Sky Patrol*, is that it is a paralyzing ray, not a deadly weapon. Once again Buddy comes to the rescue as he shoots out the ray (he was only partially paralyzed) and releases them from its hold. They escape in the Leader's own patrol ship, to which Kane, when informed of this indignity, hilariously replies, "You Blockheads!"

At the end of Chapter Four, Henry Brandon finally shows up again on Earth in a rocket pursuing the escapees. He bombs the stolen ship while Buck and Buddy hide behind a nearby rock formation.

The Phantom Plane is Chapter Five in which Laska shares a rare scene with Killer Kane, who tells him "Being a kindly ruler, I shall give you a chance to redeem yourself!" He sends Brandon *back* to Saturn to get a treaty in place before Prince Tallen can return and report on what a big meanie Killer Kane really is. The Leader continues, "If you succeed, there is an empty chair at my Council table," since he just removed a naysayer and turned him into a mindless zombie with the zombie helmet. Laska likes Kane's invitation and does that smile/sneer that assures more danger for Buck Rogers.

Laska presents Buck Rogers (Buster Crabbe) and friends to the Council on Saturn. Collection of Richard Finegan.

Meanwhile, Buck, Tallen and Wilma take off for Saturn (again) in ship Z-9 upon which a test of their new invisibility ray should allow them to ease by Kane's planetary blockade unseen. The cloaking device capability works and the rebels arrive on Saturn (again). But Laska has prepared a trap for Buck on the surface of Saturn. They board his seemingly deserted command ship and when Buck demeaningly sends Prince Tallen back to their ship to fetch a wrench, they realize that Captain Laska has trapped them inside his ship. "We've got them right where we want them!" gloats Brandon, once again prematurely. He gasses the friends, who collapse and head into the next chapter completely unconscious, a state that most of the audience wishes they shared with the protagonists.

The mid-point of Buck Rogers, Chapters Six and Seven, present Captain Laska at his most despicable. He murders one of the helmet-wearing zombies to take the filament from the helmet so he can secret it into Prince Tallen's hat and zombify him. In front of the rulers of Saturn, Tallen is forced to lie about Buck and get them to ratify the treaty with Earth in Killer Kane's favor. It's looking like Laska is going to get that seat at the table! Meanwhile the other robot men start throwing Vasquez rocks at Buck and Wilma, but only brain their own comrades allowing our heroes to escape and run right to the Council – not knowing Tallen is under Laska's control via the amnesiatic filament. Tallen brands the confused Buck and Wilma as enemies as Brandon whispers sweet lies into his ear. Buck grabs Tallen and escapes in a bullet rail car. Laska closes the steel gate and the car crashes and explodes into Chapter Seven, *The Primitive Urge*.

They are unhurt – of course – and Laska, who tries to murder the Prince, is revealed finally as a deceitful traitor to Earth *and* Saturn. They capture Henry, but he escapes in another bullet car. Buck removes Tallen's helmet and he returns to his senses. Captain Laska makes it back to his space ship, unties his bound men and takes off... but not for Earth. He is fearful of returning to face The Leader in failure.

Buck Rogers and the Council sign the treaty that finally allies Saturn with the Hidden City of Earth. Laska, using his last Helmet Zombie, is able to control the Zuggs (kind of like The Mole Men but not as ugly) because they worship the helmet, for some reason. Brandon finds himself in command of an instant alien army with which he causes an uprising and takes control of the Council room. Before he can radio Kane for reinforcements, Buck destroys the radio and is overwhelmed by Laska's Zugg army! Revolt! And 'revolting' is the perfect word for it, as Chapter Eight – *Revolt of The Zuggs* – unfolds.

Buck escapes (again) but Laska blasts at him with a ray gun and misses. As Laska tries to use the Zuggs to seize control of the Council, Buck removes the Zombie Helmet and quells the Zugg riot. He has Captain Laska imprisoned in a dungeon on Saturn, effectively removing Henry Brandon from the next few chapters in which Buck and Wilma travel back to Earth (again).

Chapter Nine is one of those budget-saving recap chapters that most serials have, reminding viewers of plot points from the early chapters and repeating footage. In Chapter Nine, Henry appears in flashback footage only. Embarrassing as it was the first time little Buddy beat and captured Laska back Chapter Two, they hadda pick THAT scene to rerun here. Chapter Ten features no new footage with Henry Brandon either, but in Chapter Eleven the secret entrance to The Hidden City is discovered by Killer Kane's forces. Buck takes a captured enemy ship BACK to Saturn (again) for an incredulous THIRD TIME in eleven chapters – where he discovers nasty Captain Laska has been a busy boy during the previous two chapters. Upon Buck and Buddy's arrival, he learns Laska has escaped and taken Prince Tallen captive and is blackmailing the Council with his safety. Laska begins bombing the surface from his ship, blowing up the Palace and bringing us at long last to the final cliffhanger of *Buck Rogers*.

Buck is unhurt (naturally) and goes after Laska to free Tallen. In the ultimate Henry Brandon indignity, Buck rescues the Prince and once again it is Buddy who shoots down Laska with a ray gun for his final capture on Saturn. He is imprisoned and Buck and Buddy return to Earth (again and again and again) for the final battle with Killer Kane and the story's resolution.

Years later, Henry Brandon met with classic film historian Richard Finegan in June of 1979 to sign dozens of publicity stills from serials, westerns and crime movies that Brandon had appeared in. On the back of many of these glossies, Henry added background information about his co-stars and on one such still from *Buck Rogers* that featured David Sharpe, Philson Ahn and Tom Steel, he wrote:

David Sharpe and Yakima Canutt were the premiere stunt men of their day. Davie was probably the more versatile. He could function in any (genre) while Yakima was limited to Westerns and any film concerning horses. Tom Steele and I both appeared at a symposium at The Museum of the Living Image on serials last month (May, 1979). I made *four* serials and Tommy was involved with *82* of them. Philson Ahn is the brother of the well-known Korean actor, Philip Ahn. He rather reluctantly took acting jobs that his busy brother couldn't fulfill. He ran the family restaurant in Panorama City, California.

In a strange footnote for this serial, Henry Brandon again wrote to collector Richard Finegan on the back of a signed still from *Buck Rogers* with his Laska character dressed in black and Buster Crabbe as Buck: "When Buster Crabbe died, the *Los Angeles Times* had a still of *me* from this picture accompanying the obituary. I thought everyone knew that black was only worn by villains!"

Buck Rogers is a difficult serial to get through with its painfully repetitive story line and unfavorable comparison to the previous two *Flash Gordon* films. Even more challenging is the fact that, though it was a better payday for Henry Brandon for the actor than the much briefer role of Killer Kane would have been, it is a definite career step backwards from a "Vicious Villainy" standpoint.

All that changed, however, in Brandon's fourth and final serial with his epic portrayal as the insidious Dr. Fu Manchu for Republic Pictures in one of his three most iconic performances – *Drums of Fu Manchu!*

CHAPTER TEN
Westerns

WHEN DIVIDING UP HENRY Brandon's career roles into genres, he made more Westerns in motion pictures and on television than any other category. When subdividing Westerns further, he played cowboys and Indians about equally but he was "bad" about 90% of the time.

Wells Fargo:

Director Frank Lloyd's epic generational story of the founding of the Wells Fargo freight lines is more of a drama than an action-packed Western, but it does have several exciting sequences and, in a throw-away role, Henry Brandon.

Joel McCrea stars as Ramsay Mackay, first a break-neck driver then a founder of many of the Wells Fargo branches and the key man who devised the trails and got the mail and gold shipments where there were going. From Buffalo to New York to St. Louis and finally out to Los Angeles and San Francisco, Ramsay survives robbers, Indian attacks and even the Civil War in his quest to assure that the Wells Fargo wagons always arrived at their destinations.

In one brief scene at about the mid-point of *Wells Fargo*, Henry Brandon shows up as Larry, a new hire by Mackay to run one of the branch offices of the company. He assures Mackay he'll bring in new customers for Wells Fargo and brings him some mail to deliver on the current stage. That's it, Larry never reappears and one wonders why Paramount hired Brandon for such an insignificant part that any extra or bit player could have enacted. *Wells Fargo* is sprawling and entertaining, but for fans of Henry Brandon, it's hardly worth the trouble.

The Marshal of Mesa City:

Barrel-chested George O'Brien headlines RKO's thrilling *The Marshal of Mesa City* (1939) with fourth-billed Henry Brandon as Duke Allison, an infamous gunfighter brought in by a crooked sheriff to go up against the new Marshal. Allison enters the picture as quite the dangerous adversary but ends up in a surprisingly different place as the narrative unfolds. When the smoke clears and the last bullet has been fired, *The Marshal of Mesa City* stands as one of the twelve finest Henry Brandon performances on film.

The lively story takes place in Mesa City, Arizona in 1880, a corrupt town run by sleazy sheriff Jud Cronin (Leon Ames.) Luckily ex-Marshal Cliff Mason (George O'Brien) happens by during a stagecoach hold up and takes an interest in Mesa City – and a special interest in pretty school teacher Virginia King (Virginia Vale.) He quickly becomes a threat to Cronin both personally and professionally, so Cronin enlists the special talents of killer Duke Allison to eliminate that threat.

When the new Marshal passes an ordinance prohibiting firearms in the Mesa City limits, Cronin tells his mob that "Duke Allison is coming to town. I sent for him." The gang is suitably impressed indicating that quite the showdown of titans is coming.

Henry Brandon shows up at exactly the midpoint of *Mesa City*, in a black hat, black suit and black tie. He checks in with his new boss as Jud tells the gunfighter, "He's fast, Duke. You better give it to him the first chance you get!" Allison retorts, "I never draw on a man until he draws first." Jud asks, "Suppose he beats you to it?" to which Allison chillingly replies, "He won't."

To goad Marshal Mason into a confrontation, Duke walks through the saloon with a waiter following him, whiskey shots lined up on a tray. One by one, he offers the bar patrons a drink, then throws that drink into each of their faces with that patented Brandon sneer. Finally he is face to face with the Marshal. The suspense is electric!

In a tense confrontation, Cliff shows Allison what kind of a man he is. One of Cronin's mob pulls a hidden gun to take a pot shot at Cliff, who draws like lightning and shoots the man. At the same time, with the same speed, Allison draws and levels his gun at Mason's stomach. "Sucker!" sneers Allison, who doesn't fire – he has a gunman's code of honor and is shocked that Cliff allowed himself to be vulnerable, going for the hood instead of him. Duke holsters his gun, respectful of this Marshal who bet his life on that code. It becomes clear that Duke Allison won't be doing any dirty work for Jud Cronin, even though Cliff warns Duke that he has to check *his* guns, too.

Henry Brandon as Duke Allison in *Marshal of Mesa City.*

Later, Cronin's cronies set a trap for the Marshal at the saloon, using a drunk with a revolver as bait. The Marshal gets the drunk, but the gang members get the drop on him and are about to murder him in cold blood.

Suddenly, Duke Allison wanders in and announces, "I'm checking my gun, Marshal!" sliding the six-shooter along the bar to Cliff, who quickly turns the tables on the hoodlums. When one of them tries to shoot the Marshal, Duke shoots the gun right out of his hand! Allison sidles up alongside Cliff and asks, "What are we going to do with them, Marshall?" The Marshall regretfully informs his new ally that he has to arrest *him* too – for not checking his guns! Duke is a bit incredulous but goes along with the plans of this man who has earned his respect.

The corrupt judge fines each of the gang members a mere ten bucks for carrying firearms, but hits Allison with a massive fifty dollar fine! "I guess that makes me worth five of these tin-horn bad men!" comments Duke Allison wryly. When he goes to pay his fine, his pal the Marshall tells him, "Please, this one is on me!" and clinks out the coins with a grin.

The tone of *Marshal of Mesa City* has shifted to a buddy movie as Henry Brandon takes a rare left turn from hired killer into Butch & Sundance territory. This vibe feels quite rewarding for Brandon buffs used to his career of vicious villainy. In fact, to get around his no gun ordinance, the Marshal suggests, "Say, Duke, how would you like to be a Deputy Marshall?" Allison is nearly dumbstruck. "What? Me, a law man?" He has to say it again, disbelieving. "Duke Allison... Lawman!"

Cliff goes after one of the killers and tells Duke to keep an eye on the town while he's gone. "Okay, Boss!" he replies, a twinkle in his eye at this surreal turn of events. Brandon plays this shift just beautifully, winning the audience sympathy and easing into the sidekick role of Deputy Duke.

As the various thugs in town see Allison walking the streets with his badge, they actually laugh out loud at him, which grates on the gunslinger. The sheriff confronts Duke and tries to arrest him as "a known killer" but the Marshal arrives in time to back up his partner, telling the skunk sheriff that there is a showdown coming between the two forces, after which Duke adds, "You're a dirty crook!"

Cliff (George O'Brien) and Duke triumphant in *Marshal of Mesa City*. Collection of Richard W. Bann.

Things come to a head when one of Cronin's toughest men challenges Cliff to a fight. The Marshal takes off his guns and goes into the back room with the thug for a ferocious fist fight, which Duke and the others can only hear. It goes on for some time as they wait to see who will walk triumphantly out of the closed door. The Marshall finally punches his opponent *through* the door, settling that question, to which Duke merely grins widely. After all the ribbing he's taken, Deputy Duke now polishes his badge proudly with his sleeve and ambles out after his pal, whistling with joy! The sequence is simply delightful and Henry Brandon owns it!

The climax finally comes with the crooked sheriff rearming his entire mob for a showdown during a dance planned for that evening. The Marshal dances with Virginia while his Deputy watches from the sidelines. However the next dance is 'ladies choice' and suddenly Duke is surrounded by four eager women all vying for his attention! Unfortunately, the most aggressive of them who pulls him onto the dance floor is so homely that she looks like (and probably is) a man in a wig and dress. Allison is wildly uncomfortable during the dance and breaks out in a big smile when the Marshal is tipped off that the gang is approaching, telling Duke, "Come on, we have work to do!"

The brave duo easily nails one of the killers, but the Sheriff turns the tables on them, claiming his "prisoner" was murdered and arrests Cliff and Duke. They go along with the charade, knowing a US Attorney will arrive in the morning to strip the sheriff of his badge. However, Cronin sets fire to the jail, leaving his prisoners inside to burn to death!

The mayor arrives with a sledge hammer which they use to smash open the back wall, freeing the duo. Cliff reclaims his guns to go get Cronin once and for all. He tells Duke to remain behind, saying "This is my fight!" But Duke refuses, retorting, "Your fight? They tried to barbecue me too!" He relents with a grin and the pair stride side by side toward the Cronin gang, each of their four fists holding a gun. Smoke from the jail fire is billowing behind them as they walk forward with nerves of steel. The imagery in this final showdown is just incredible for a B-Western with the two heroes walking forward, forward in a hail of bullets, forward into the smoke until they both disappear in the haze, guns still firing! The sequence is presented with surprising artistry for a low-budget oater.

Finally, the shooting stops. The camera pans over the gang, a dozen men, all sprawled dead around the streets… and we see only one man is left standing. It is Cliff. At his feet, lies the body of Duke Allison.

The Marshal cries out, "Duke! Duke, are you all right?" Allison raises his head slowly. He is hurt bad. "Did… did we get 'em?" "Yes," is all the Marshal can manage. Duke is dying. He says, "Me… a Lawman. I can't get over it." Before he expires, he spies Cronin, still alive! On a balcony, aiming his gun at Cliff's back! A shot rings out! Duke gets him, saving his friend's life… and then he dies. "Thanks, Duke," the Marshal chokes out. Fade out.

The 1939 reviews for *Marshal* ranged from mediocre to strong, but most singled out the impressive performance of Henry Brandon. Women's University Club was unimpressed, but wrote "the one original character is Duke Allison (Henry Brandon) who is neither all good nor all bad and who has a dash and swagger all his own." Even stronger words came from the *Showmen's Trade Review*, who stated "standing out is the work of Henry Brandon, a young character player, who plays the killer with a style which marks him for bigger spots in the future."

The Marshal of Mesa City is barely an hour long and Henry Brandon is only in the last thirty minutes, but he creates an antihero that becomes a hero in Duke Allison. Even RKO's press materials got it right, referring to Brandon's part in the pressbook as "the menace who becomes a hero." So many of Henry's film roles are one-dimensional characters without an arc, but Duke Allison emerges as one of his most impressive, most important performances.

The Ranger and the Lady/Bad Man of Deadwood:

Henry Brandon played the heavy in a pair of Roy Rogers B-Westerns in 1940 and 1941 for Republic Studios. The first of the two was *The Ranger and The Lady* and takes place in and around Texas on the Santa Fe Trail in 1836.

Jane Faber (Jacqueline Wells)[*], is the owner of a trading goods wagon train headed through Santa Fe. When thugs commanded by General Augustus Larue (Henry Brandon with a droopy black mustache) attempt to extort a 'toll' from her, she boldly refuses. Rangers Colt (Roy Rogers) and Gabby Hayes arrive and take the men into custody, returning to town to confront Larue. That is a mistake, as Larue is running Santa Fe while President Sam Houston is in Washington negotiating to bring Texas into the United States.

Larue orders Roy to enforce his dictates and collect the toll from the Faber party. Roy objects, saying, "The Texas Rangers have no right to col-

---

[*] Best remembered as Laurel & Hardy's *Bohemian Girl* leading lady

lect toll in Mexico (territory)" but he is bound by duty and evil Larue is in charge. After he reluctantly leaves, Brandon murmurs to his henchman, "I'm afraid that young man may interfere with our plans!"

At Bent's Fort, Colt and Miss Taber clash as she continues to refuse to pay the toll. Roy takes her into custody and a long ride back to Larue, which seems to be exactly what Taber wants. As they camp that night, Roy has the opportunity to serenade her, but she resists his charms. In fact, the next day back in Santa Fe with Larue, she chides that Colt isn't very good at collecting taxes but he's a great dancer and singer! Brandon says snidely, "Perhaps the Captain could arrange to give singing lessons to the rest of our Rangers?

Miss Taber invites General Larue to partner with her on a monopoly – refusing entry on the Santa Fe Trail to all traders but *her* concern, which Brandon accepts. Captain Colt is horrified, knowing this will undo all of President Houston's work toward Texas and statehood. He refuses to enforce this monopoly and Larue fires him, glad to be rid of the singing do-gooder.

Roy and Gabby form a rebellion against Larue's forces and help other traders get across the Texas border. Soon, Rogers is captured and brought to Larue, who proclaims him guilty of treason, to be shot at sunrise. Then Larue makes some smooth moves on Miss Taber, but she deflects them easily. She is secretly the daughter of a man that Larue framed and had killed and she's been planning his downfall as revenge. Taber decides to help former Ranger Colt escape his doom.

She is successful and Colt manages to ride out and save returning Sam Houston from a Larue-arranged ambush, then returns to take down Henry Brandon! During the climactic gun battle, Brandon finally does more than sit behind a desk and scheme, taking up a revolver and shooting the Rangers. He admits to Taber that he framed and murdered her father, saying "He stood for the Republic, I stand for myself!" As he aims at Captain Colt through a window, Miss Taber has her revenge when she shoots him dead in the back. Brandon seems to get shot in the back a lot. It's an occupational hazard for a cinema scoundrel.

Ranger & The Lady lobby card.

The following year saw *Bad Man of Deadwood* hit the nation's screens. This time Gabby and Roy run a traveling medicine show and Henry Brandon is a crusading newspaper editor named Ted Carver. For a change of pace, Brandon may NOT be the "bad man" of the film's title.

Roy Rogers is Bill Brady, a marksman in Professor Gabby's show. Henry wears the same droopy mustache as in the previous film, rallying the decent folk of Deadwood against the town's corruption and the colorful Ripper gang. These good guys gravitate immediately toward Brady and ask his help to clean up the town.

A convenient plot twist gives Professor Gabby an inheritance of $36,000, which he claims at the local Deadwood bank in thousand dollar bills. He is promptly robbed of his windfall by the Ripper gang. Brainstorming that afternoon with Brady and Carver about how to get that money back, they decide to break into the bank that night to see if anyone in the Ripper gang deposited the stolen money. Even Henry Brandon's Mr. Carver is in favor of this idiotic plan, which of course goes horribly wrong. The Ripper gang is there in force to shoot up and capture the GOOD GUYS *robbing* the bank! Yep, that's how this twisted little picture unfolds.

They get away with the deposit records and Carver is forced to print up **WANTED** posters for the apprehension of his friends. Linda (Sally Payne), the romantic lead of *Deadwood*, is shattered by Brady's apparent guilt and Ted Carver chooses this moment to clumsily hit on her, knowing Brady is also romancing her. It is this moment that we get an inkling that maybe – just *maybe* – Henry Brandon's character might be in contention for the title character.

With Roy Rogers on a *Bad Man of Deadwood* lobby card.

Next, Roy and the good guys rob the outbound stage hoping the stolen money is on board and finally their befuddling strategies pay off. The money is all there, going to banks in other parts of the country along with proof that Ted Carver is behind all the evil shenanigans! It was Henry Brandon who tipped off the Ripper gang of the idiotic plan to rob the bank and it is Henry Brandon who IS the *Bad Man of Deadwood,* suddenly all is right in the universe.

Carver knows he's been identified as 'bad' and has to move fast. He has the Ripper gang attack the Judge and steal the money back, but the two key Rippers are scared and decide to leave town with the loot. Carver arrives and catches them packing, saying "I don't have to ask if you've got the money!" His voice is full of patented Brandon menace and he guns them both down in cold blood. And *there* is our vicious villain of vintage cinema!

Carver manipulates the sheriff, pinning all the wrong doing on Bill Brady and rallying the town against our hero. He leads the posse to a back entrance at The Gap (really the Iverson Ranch in Chatsworth, California), where they are holed up, to catch them "like rats in a trap." But Brady is guarding the back entrance and even though Carver hits him with a shot from a hidden derringer, Brady keeps them pinned down. When they rush him, Ted Carver is gunned down. Henry dies beautifully, showing the bullet's crushing impact, then stumbling and twitching on his death drop into the bramble. The cavalry arrives in time to gun down the crooked sheriff before he gets Brady.

There is a lot of plot packed into *Bad Man of Deadwood's* brisk 52-minute running time, and much of that plot is deliciously bewildering. That, and the fun reveal of Henry's skullduggery, make *Bad Mad of Deadwood* easily the best of his two Roy Rogers pictures. To demonstrate how quickly these B-Westerns were churned out, the first day of shooting for *Bad Man Of Deadwood* was on a Saturday, July 19th where they completed twelve camera set-ups – and the picture was completed, edited, scored, printed and released into theaters about six weeks later on September 5th, 1941.

Under Texas Skies:

A fast-moving and entertaining B-Western, *Under Texas Skies* was a Three Mesquiteers adventure released by Republic Studios in 1940 and features Henry Brandon as the primary antagonist.

Republic's wildly popular Three Mesquiteers series ran from 1936 through 1943 and comprised a whopping fifty-one features! The trio, played by different cowboy stars at different times, were Stony Brooke, Tucson Smith and Lullaby Joslyn. *Under Texas Skies* was the thirty-second entry, the twentieth time Robert Livingston played Stony (a role also played by John Wayne in eight pictures) but the first time both Bob Steele and Rufe Davis played their roles of Tucson and Lullaby. Therefore, this film is a kind of origin story for this incarnation of the trio.

It is 1859 and the opening title card informs us "threats of Civil War caused the withdrawal of Federal troops from Southwest territories, leaving our frontiers unguarded and prey to a reign of outlawry unequaled in American history!" Tom Blackton (Henry Brandon) tells Texan Sheriff Brooke that "we can handle" patrolling the borders, letting upstanding cowboy Tucson Smith (Bob Steele) know that his services won't be needed. Right out of the gate, we know Blackton is up to something, as in the next scene he hires deputies from among his cattle rustling gang, fooling the naïve Sheriff and setting himself up pretty nicely.

Half the gang works for the law, the other half continues their rustling duties and soon the headlines read: **MYSTERY RAIDS CONTINUE and SHERIFF UNABLE TO CONTROL BAD SITUATION**.

The situation quickly goes from bad to worse, when Tucson captures one of the "deputies" named Talbot and brings him in to the jail. Despicable Blackton sneaks around back of the jail and aims through the bars… not at his own man, but he kills Sheriff Brooke in cold blood, blaming it on innocent Tucson Smith! Blackton arrests Tucson, proclaims him guilty and schedules his hanging!

Some of the honest citizens start a street brawl, allowing Tucson to escape from jail to the wilds of the Iverson Ranch in Chatsworth. It is here that Stony and Tucson reunite (they were childhood pals) but not before Stony is told his father, the former Sheriff, was murdered.

In a tense scene in town, Blackton informs Stony of his father's killing, convincing the grief-stricken hero that Tucson is the murderer. He deputizes Stony to go bring his friend in, but it isn't long before the square-jawed cowboy realizes who the real villain is. He is nearby when marauders stop a stagecoach, kill the driver and unleash a hail of bullets on the inhabitant inside – a circuit judge coming to give Tucson a fair trial. Stony brings the corpse of the judge into town and crafty Blackton has him remain behind and fill out paperwork while his own men go after the marauders, confirming Stony's suspicions about the corruption infesting the town.

When the new Sheriff sends his thugs to gun down Tucson, Stony joins them and pretends to pump several bullets into his friend, completely fooling Blackton. When the ruse is later discovered, Stony slugs Blackton and knocks him right off his horse and escapes to join his two pals and rally the good town folk toward a climactic confrontation in the Overland Trail. Here a cattle drive is due to be rustled by Blackton's gang, so the heroes put Henry Brandon front and center, first to be shot when the gang attacks in the pass! Blackton is visibly distressed, a cold sweat breaks out all over his slimy face, as he licks his cowardly lips.

In the gorge; the rustlers begin firing and Blackton screams out, "Don't shoot! It's me! Blackton!" admitting his guilt to the whole town. During the melee Blackton makes a break for it as his men are slaughtered by the honest ranchers. Stony chases after him and pulls him off his horse (again) for a fist fight. Blackton pulls a knife, but falls on it during the battle, killing himself and saving the town the bother of a trial.

A 1941 review of *Under Texas Skies* appeared in **The Film Daily** and proclaimed that "Brandon is effective as the principal villain in the piece." *Under Texas Skies* is a lot of fun but a fairly typical entry with Henry Brandon playing his stock bad Western grease ball.

Hurricane Smith (1941):

Henry Brandon appeared in two unrelated films named *Hurricane Smith* for two different studios. This first *Hurricane* was released by Republic Studios in mid-1941 and is a Western thriller. Henry plays Sam Carson, a desperado with a facial scar that spells trouble for star Ray Middleton. The film was unavailable for viewing in preparation of this book, but the following review from the August, 1941 edition of **Film Bulletin** gives a good indication of the plot and Henry's contributions:

> A mildly entertaining, somewhat improbable adventure programmer, *Hurricane Smith* is acceptable as dual-fare. The players are capable and well-cast, if lacking in marquee strength, with the picture's chief claim to distinction being the straight-forward portrayal by Ray Middleton in the leading role. Bernard Vorhaus' direction stresses action whenever possible, but the script dawdles considerably just before the climax.
>
> *Hurricane Smith* is a roving rodeo cowboy who meets and falls in love with Jane Wyatt, a newspaper reporter, and persuades her he can marry and settle down. But before the marriage, Smith encounters two train robbers (J. Edward Bromberg and Henry Brandon) and in the gun-fighting and resultant confusion he is unjustly accused of murder because he carries a facial scar similar to Brandon. Smith keeps the girl – his only possible alibi – out of the trial, and after being condemned to death, he again encounters the robbers on his way to prison. This time the score is evened when Brandon is killed and Smith escapes with the stolen money.

The film then picks up two years later and concerns Middleton clearing his name and exposing Bromberg for a happy ending. Henry's Sam Carson is the secondary villain who is killed about half-way through *Hurricane Smith*.

Old Los Angeles:

This is one of those "hoss oprys" that Republic Studios cranked out for the Western crowd in 1948. As suggested by the title, this is supposed to be one of the stories taking place 100 years prior during the California Gold Rush era. Any resemblance to the history of Los Angeles is fiction, but the title sure made a marketing splash.

Bill Elliot was the star in this one. He had been featured in starring roles of this kind for many years and became better known as "Wild Bill Elliot" from the Red Ryder series. As Bill Stockton, he avenges his brother who was murdered by bad guys. The heavy in this film was John Carroll.

Where does Henry Brandon fit in? He plays Larry Stockton, a genteel sort who is an honest and sincere character. For the people that were in line at the popcorn counter and late for the first five minutes, they missed Henry in one of his best action sequences.

The film starts with stock footage in a montage of California beauty contrasted with images of manmade destruction. The voiceover tells us that "A team of outlaws; burning, looting, murdering without rhyme or reason."

Enter Larry along with his Mexican companion, Miguel. They are leading a 20 mule team carrying sacks of gold to Los Angeles. Along the way they encounter a shady character that is the front man to an ambush. Larry is at ease because he recognizes him as "a friend." He naïvely tells this bad guy (we know this because of his black hat and snake-oil mustache), that they are taking the gold to Los Angeles for charity. The guy invites himself to ride down the canyon with them.

Once down the hill they are confronted with gunshots fired at them from five different members of the gang. One of the bullets finds Miguel who slumps; Larry gets hit over the head and is subdued. Once he gets on his feet, Larry scolds them terribly: "No wonder Mexicans are suspicious of Americans, you double crossing renegades!"

The renegades threaten Larry with a branding to which he defiantly responds: "Go ahead, see what it gets you." The bad guy reveals a different strategy; he takes out a claim paper and demands Larry sign it over to him. Though wounded, Miguel yells: "Don't sign anything Larry." He is shot for his troubles.

Larry relents and signs the document under duress, but warns them: "When you get to the recorder's office, you'll find me there waiting." The mustachioed bad guy says, "You won't be waiting for anyone." This is the best moment of the film and we're only six minutes into it. Larry simultaneously handles all the evil doers by trading haymakers, kicks and attitude. What makes the extended scene memorable are the dramatic close-ups of Henry framed in back-light.

Larry wins the fights and tries to run for his life towards the mountains. He is shot in the back, and for every 12-year old boy watching, it defined a cowardly and dastardly deed.

For the rest of the film, Bill Stockton seeks revenge for who was responsible. In the process there is romance, singing, and justice served in the end. Andy Devine supplies much needed comedy relief.

While the film is all Bill Elliot's, *Old Los Angeles* is memorable in that the whole point of the film is based on vengeance for Henry's character's demise. It is also refreshing to hear Henry's sincere, natural voice, not heard since *Carnival of Paris*.

Cattle Drive:

Kurt Neumann's *Cattle Drive* released in 1951 offered up a starring role for Joel McCrea that became one of his personal favorite films, a coming-of-age character drama masquerading as a Western. Young Dean Stockwell is Chester Graham Jr., a spoiled, rich brat traveling with his widowed father Chester Graham Sr., railroad tycoon. They are traveling out West together and Chester Jr. gets separated and lost, getting 'adopted' by a large cattle drive headed to Santa Fe and run by Dan Matthews (Joel McCrea).

Henry Brandon plays Jim Currie, one of the hands working the drive and a pretty snarky fellow, always needling Matthews and now the boy. "Its bad luck to pick up strangers!" warns Currie, looking to blame each bad turn they face on the youngster. Chet has a friend in chuck wagon cook Dallas (Chill Wills) who calls beans "Texas strawberries."

Cattle Drive lobby card.

Chet quickly gains respect for Dan and learns the ways of riding, roping and rustling. It makes a man out of him, but there are lessons yet to be learned. The midpoint highlight of *Cattle Drive* is the horse race between Dan and Currie, each riding their fastest horses Blaze and Lightning. As expected, Dan wins the race, but afterwards Chet reveals that the night before, he rode Lightning ragged to be sure his friend won. Dan gives back the winnings and Currie snarls, "The no good soft livin' little sneak!" Matthews explains that "there is no satisfaction in winning unless you can win fair and square!" Chet has a growth moment and apologizes.

Dan and Chet capture a stunning wild black stallion they call Midnight.

Currie wants to shoot the horse, but Dan hopes to break and train him. The dumb kid accidently lets Midnight loose and Brandon takes a shot at the escaping horse, only to cause the entire herd to stampede for a rousing action climax! Working together, they manage to get things under control but Dallas' chuck wagon is smashed to pieces and Midnight gets away.

Henry as Jim Currie in *Cattle Drive*.

Chet is unharmed and apologetic and Brandon's Currie even admits he caused the stampede after taking a shot at the wild horse. Turns out Currie isn't bad, he's just cranky. The cute ending sees Chester Sr. and Jr. signing on with Dan for another cattle drive – together. And for a pleasant change of pace, Henry Brandon doesn't end up with a bullet in his belly!

Wagons West:

Monogram produced this handsome 1952 B-Western, filmed mainly on location in Simi Valley, California in the Cinecolor process. Rod Cameron stars as Wagon Master Jeff Curtis, taking a wagon train west under the direction of the crooked Cook family. Fifth-billed Henry Brandon plays nephew Clay Cook, the chief antagonist of *Wagons West*.

Things get off to a rousing start with Henry's first appearance as Clay Cook at a meeting of the folks on the wagon train. Curtis has befriended young Ben Wilkins (Michael Chapin), who had run off with his dog. Clay, who is sweet on Ben's older sister, rushes up to the youngster, shouting, "Where have you been? Your sister's been worried about you! What's the idea of running off like that?"

Clay Cook (Henry Brandon) knocked down in *Wagons West*.

Clay Cook is dressed in a rich burgundy shirt, black hat and black bandana. His perpetual scowl and slanted, petulant body language tells us that Cook is a real stinker. He and Curtis clash immediately which leads to his taking an ill-advised swing at the Wagon Master. Clay misses and gets knocked on his can, pulls a gun but is much too slow as Jeff beats him to the draw. When he reholsters his gun, Clay asks, "Why didn't you shoot, Curtis?" to which Jeff replies, "You might be useful on this trip." As Jeff turns to leave, Clay sucker-punches him in the back of the head. This leads to a vicious bar fight broken up by the Sheriff. Clay angrily threatens, "There won't be any lawman to look after you on the trail, Curtis!" and stomps off.

On the trail, they run into some friendly Indians who may try to steal a horse or two, so Jeff takes first watch that night – the same night that Clay saw him kissing his 'fiancé' Ann (Peggie Castle from television's *Lawman*). Cook's Uncle tells Jeff one of his nephews will relieve him at midnight – to which Clay says, full of menace, "I'll relieve him!"

At midnight, Clay Cook sees the Indian chief leaving after Jeff gave him some trinkets so they wouldn't steal any horses. Clay pulls out his rifle and shoots the Indian in the back! Jeff angrily accuses Clay of murder, shouting, "You're a brave man! You just killed an unarmed Indian chief!" Jeff takes full charge of the Wagon Train, ordering Cook to keep his troublesome nephews out of the saddle and on their wagons. We next see Henry complacently driving a wagon on the trail, leaving before the Indian tribe can mobilize.

Soon, they enter Cheyenne country but Uncle Cook doesn't seem too worried. This is because he plans to make a fortune selling illegal arms to the tribe. He contrives to break away from the wagon train with his wagons for just this opportunity.

A suspicious Jeff catches Clay with a wagon full of rifles, leading to a dramatic moment where his Aunt slaps his face, ashamed that her husband and nephews are selling arms to the Cheyenne that will be used against their own people. Clay is bound and brought back to the encircled wagon train, awaiting a furious attack from the Cheyenne when they don't get the promised rifles.

For the climactic attack, Clay is foolishly unbound and given a gun to fight off the Indians. His greedy Uncle is killed by an arrow and finally Clay turns to kill his rival Jeff by shooting him in the back at the peak of the attack. Before he can pull the trigger, little Ben jumps out of a wagon onto Henry's back, shouting and spoiling his aim. This leads to a big fist fight between Clay and Jeff, and is a fight that Clay seems to win! With Jeff prone on the ground, Clay again pulls out his revolver to shoot him, but instead is shot and killed by an Indian. The settlers fight off the Cheyenne and Jeff brokers for safe passage, gets the girl and we have our happy ending.

Wagons West, with its location filming, rich red, green and brown Cinecolor photography and rousing musical score is at the high end of the usually cheap Monogram productions. For a B-Western, it does the job with style, thanks to director Ford Beebe, who cut his teeth on silent films, westerns and serials. In fact, he co-directed all three of Henry's Universal serials, *Jungle Jim*, *Secret Agent X-9* and *Buck Rogers*. Beebe, who also directed Henry in *West Bound Limited*, fully indulged his friend's penchant for teeth-gnashing villainy in *Wagons West* to great effect. Clay Cook is a one-note character, but it is a note that Henry Brandon knew how to play masterfully and he gets as much from the role as can be expected. *Wagons West* is one of the best Monogram pictures and a cracker-jack of a movie.

Pony Express:

A lush, sprawling 1953 Technicolor Western, *Pony Express* is the story of the friendship of Buffalo Bill Cody (Charlton Heston) and Wild Bill Hickok (Forrest Tucker) and their attempts to launch the Pony Express, which would down the time of mail delivery from the East to the West from 21 days to about 10 days. While the concept sounds a bit dry and businesslike, the film is an expertly crafted thrill ride with exciting action set-pieces and terrific performances.

One of those performances belongs to Henry Brandon, playing Joe Cooper, the manager of the Overland Stage Line who doesn't want to lose the lucrative U.S. Mail franchise to this Pony Express idea. Cooper schemes with Evelyn Hastings (a ravishing Rhonda Fleming) and her unscrupulous brother (Michael Moore) to get Buffalo Bill and Wild Bill out of the way.

Brandon portrays Cooper with the right amounts of smarm and slime, seeming to be the primary villain in *Pony Express* for the first two-thirds of the picture. When Charlton Heston and Henry Brandon first clash, real sparks fly. It's a great deal of fun to watch these two pros verbally spar. Heston and Forrest Tucker have an easygoing Butch and Sundance-type chemistry that is also a delight as the centerpiece relationship of *Pony Express*.

When Cody survives a tense encounter with Chief Yellow Hand and his tribe, he heads back to town to confront Cooper about selling rifles to the Indians as a ploy to eliminate him and his pal. Joe Cooper reveals his yellow streak and attempts to escape through the back, sacrificing a minion to Cody's blazing gun. There follows a suspenseful cat and mouse sequence in a corral with Buffalo Bill stalking Cooper, who manages to get on a horse but is gunned down by Cody. Thus ended Henry Brandon's participation in *Pony Express* about 70 minutes in. Other baddies take his place for the third act, but the real good vs. evil tension of the film ended with that bullet in Henry Brandon's back.

War Arrow:

In the early 1950's, Henry Brandon appeared in three Technicolor films for Universal International starring Maureen O'Hara: *Flame of Araby*, *War Arrow* and *Lady Godiva of Coventry*. The middle film of this trilogy, *War Arrow* from 1953, was the only Western and is easily the best of the three.

Directed by George Sherman, *War Arrow* stars O'Hara as Cavalry widow Elaine Corwin and Jeff Chandler as Major Howell Brady. Therefore, here's the story of a man named Brady (that pop culture reference will become clear shortly) who has a crazy idea to battle the Kiowa Indian tribe whose uprising is overwhelming the stymied Army forces in Texas. Brady's idea is to recruit the equally deadly but neutered Seminole tribe, transplanted from Florida to Texas, to pit against the Kiowas.

The chief of the Seminoles is our man Brandon, playing Maygro with long loose grey hair and a cowboy hat. When Brady brings Maygro to camp for initial discussions about his plan, supporting character actor Noah Beery says about the intimidating chief, "That fella could charm the Rocky Mountains into going south for the winter!"

Maygro readies his rifle in *War Arrow*.

Maygro resists the idea of returning to their warrior ways and killing other Indians in exchange for an entire valley of their own to live in. When Brady persists, Maygro takes the decision to his people. "I am your leader," he proclaims, "When we were driven from Florida, we pledged to keep peace. We knew it would be hard. You want new leader – say so!" The Seminoles bow their heads in subservience indicating Maygro is to remain in charge. But as things look bleak, the rampaging Kiowas attack the encampment and this changes everything. When Henry and his right hand Indian played by a young Dennis Weaver see the new repeating rifles they will get to use as weapons, the deal is all the sweeter.

Maygro and Brady strike up an immediate rapport and mutual respect. The scene where Brady's men train the Indian warriors to use the repeating rifles is quite entertaining. Maygro goes first and blasts off three shots, hitting each target with expert precision. Weaver does even better and it's clear these Seminoles are even better on the rifles than the Army officers! Back at the Fort, the career cavalry men ridicule the plan and demeaningly refer to the ragtag troupe as "Brady's Bunch."

Tense confrontation between Brandon, Jeff Chandler and John McIntire in *War Arrow*.

The romance between Brady and Widow Corwin is pretty goopy stuff, the real rewards of *War Arrow* derive from the training and action sequences with Brady's Bunch and the Kirk/Spock relationship of Brady & Maygro. Their first skirmish with the Kiowas arrives at about the midpoint of the film and is a rousing sequence. The second battle goes even better as Brady, Maygro and the Bunch wipe out most of a band of Kiowa marauders.

The climactic battle at the Fort between the massive Kiowa army and the much smaller Bunch is an Alamo-style finale, but with a more satisfying conclusion. Brady's Bunch has been well-trained and using some unconventional fighting methods, wins the day. It's thrilling and extremely entertaining when it is Henry Brandon's Maygro who knocks off the Kiowa Chief, signaling ultimate victory.

As Brady prepares to ride off into the sunset with his woman, Maygro tells his friend, "The days will be long 'til you return," and one wonders if he'd rather spend time having new adventures with his Seminole partner in the Texas wilderness than head to a desk job in Washington with his gorgeous redhead. *War Arrow* gives Henry Brandon a rare protagonist part – in fact, one of his strongest co-lead performances – and one wonders if his Maygro set the stage for the coming iconic role of Scar in *The Searchers*

Comanche:

Henry Brandon played a pivotal role in this one as Indian renegade "Black Cloud." *Comanche* was released in March of 1956, two months before Henry's iconic "Chief Scar" in *The Searchers*[*]. The star of this Western saga is Dana Andrews (Jim Reid) as a Calvary Scout who talks robotically in his dialogue. Kent Smith plays Comanche Chief Quanah Parker, with subdued passion.

This film has a beautiful opening scene that takes place in Durango, Mexico. Quaint villagers are about to take part in a wedding; the festivities are about to start when a galloping herd of "Injuns" storm in, they are led by Black Cloud. As people are in a panic, they are overwhelmed, killed or kidnapped. While on horseback, Black Cloud grabs the gowned bride and sweeps her up onto his horse. Henry performs this very physical and potentially dangerous stunt himself, again proving to be a master of cinematic horsemanship.

---

* *The Searchers* actually started filming June of 1955 almost a full year before release

Brandon as Black Cloud in *Comanche* with Linda Cristal.

On their way back to the encampment on the United States side, they come across pioneers making their way across. They are attacked and two are captured. Black Cloud instructs the warriors to "burn them." Before that happens, Quanah Parker descends onto the scene. Henry's character shows Chief Parker, "fresh Comanche scalps from their wagon," Black Cloud declares, "Mexicans are enemies but white eyes are worse. For each Comanche scalps, take ten of theirs." In a bit of a power struggle, Chief Parker orders them released with their horses.

The U.S. Government sent a naïve Commissioner to this war zone seeking peace with the Comanche's. (Where have we heard this one before?) The Commissioner appoints Scout Read to broker the deal, and *oh yeah*, politely ask for the captives back.

Read is compelled to give a dissertation to the Commissioner (and also the audience), a cuff-sleeve historical background on the war that Spain started against the Indians in Mexico, and ultimately against the Americans and Indians. There were episodes "many seasons before" that treaties were in place and violated leading to the desecration of the Comanche nation. Read is sympathetic to the plight of the Indians. It also happens that Read is first cousin to Quanah Parker, *small world, eh?*

Scout Read dutifully heads to the Comanche encampment with his trusty sidekick; "Puffer" (Nestor Paiva) the Gabby Hayes* type comedy relief. He has the propensity to whip out a deck of cards when the opportunity presents itself. Before they leave, Read bestows upon Puffer an old woman's curly wig. Puffer gleefully wears it on his bald head.

On the way towards the camp they encounter two Indians; one dead the other seriously wounded. They inform Reid that two "Buffalo hunters" attacked them, he then passes out. This is a revolting development because Black Cloud descends upon them and has a slightly different take on what transpired.

The two Americans are captured, bound; and are marched back to Comanche headquarters. Quanah Parker promises a slow death to the prisoners if his brother dies. They are tied up and taunted by Black Cloud and the warriors. Fortunately, the Indian did not die and divulged what really happened to him. The captives are freed much to the disgust of Black Cloud.

---

*   Gabby Hayes played many cowboy sidekicks of the Western film era of the 1930's and '40's. He's an older grizzly faced character.

So what does Puffer do? He takes off his wig and shakes it like a mop at the Indians, who scatter at the sight, all, that is, except Black Cloud.

Relieved the Americans were telling the truth, it has earned Reid the opportunity to present the terms that the U.S. Government proposed: a peaceful solution and their own reservation to live on. Meanwhile during the negotiations, Puffer ingratiated himself to a large warrior named "Flat Mouth," (Mike Mazurki) into a game of blackjack. In one of those "comedy relief" moments, Flat Mouth beats Puffer in a hand.

Black Cloud fights Jim Read (Dana Andrews) on a *Comanche* lobby card.

Chief Parker announces to his followers that he will honor the negotiated peaceful settlement. He explains, "The Americans are like weeds, like drops of rain, there's no end to them." He articulates that he wants his children to grow up without the constant threat of war.

Black Cloud disagrees fiercely: "Reid speaks with crooked tongue." He repeats the Chief's words mockingly, "A treaty with honor!" He then spits on the ground.

A confrontation ensues when the Chief exclaims, "I walk the path of the Americans. Those that violate my word, leave me now. Those that do will become my enemies and I will hunt them down and kill them myself."

Black Cloud is defiant: "I will not, if you make peace with the Americans and Mexicans, there are others who think like I do." Most of the warriors stay with the Chief but a few go with Black Cloud. Before he rides off, he tries to grab the Mexican girl he kidnapped until the Chief tells him that part of the treaty requires the release of the captives. Now Black Cloud is really enraged as he is exiled out.

Things finally come to a head later in the film when Black Cloud is surrounded by the U.S. Calvary on one side and high behind him is Chief Parker and his army on the bluff. To show he means business, Quanah Parker has Flat Mouth pick up one of Black Cloud's warriors and throws him down a cliff. He then yells out, "Black Cloud, you die." The film climaxes with the Calvary charging Black Cloud's warriors, naturally Reid and Black Cloud fight to the death. It is Reid who is the victor by way of strangulation via a choke hold.

Henry's role created quite a contrast in energy compared to the other actors. Despite his Halloween looking wig, he conveys intensity and believability, making this an entertaining film if one can forgive the cliché's.

Hell's Crossroads:

Republic Pictures produced this black and white widescreen (Filmed in Naturama) low-key Western in which Henry Brandon does a magnificent job as the infamous outlaw Jesse James. *Hell's Crossroads* stars Stephen McNally as Vic Rodell and a young Robert **(*The Man from U.N.C.L.E.*)** Vaughn as Bob Ford, both members of The James Gang.

The picture opens with a group of men riding up on their horses to the outskirts of Muncie. They are led by 6th billed Henry Brandon as Jesse James with a full black beard and the requisite black cowboy hat. He gives orders to the men, who disperse and take up positions around the seemingly deserted town. This is Sunday morning and everyone is in church. Jesse waylays the local Express Agent by rifle point and forces him to open the office so they can rob the safe.

Hell's Crossroads title lobby card intimates Henry's Jesse James is the focus of the film, but he's a supporting player. Collection of Richard Finegan.

Tension builds as, across the street, the man who runs the hardware store sees what is happening and sneaks out back to the church to alert the Sheriff. As they force the Express Agent to open his safe, he threatens, "Someday you men will pay for this!" to which Jesse replies, "Yeah, you might be right, Pop," then sees all the cash in the safe, adding wryly, "but today, I guess, the Express Company will have to pay!"

As they mount their horses to leave, the town folk pulled from church by the Sheriff open fire! After an exciting shoot out leaving several dead, the James

Gang escapes with the money. One of the gang has a leg wound. Vic Rodell was hit and that night Jesse himself digs the bullet out. He splits the gang up; Jesse and Frank James to Saint Jo, while Vic and Bob are sent back "home" to Bob's father's ranch, so that Vic's leg can heal without attracting attention.

In these early scenes, Henry is commanding as Jesse James. He's a man in charge and good at his job, which just happens to be robbing banks and killing people. Henry doesn't play James as evil, which is quite interesting. He underplays the part as an experienced, matter-of-fact strategist. It's a refreshing twist on Jesse James and Brandon does not disappoint.

However, the middle third of the movie follows Vic and Bob on the ranch with Jesse James out of the action. We find out that Vic had been in love with Bob's sister Paula (Peggie Castle from television's *Lawman*) and broke her heart. She married another man, a bank teller who was later killed during a robbery… by Jesse James. But when the two are reunited, their old feelings quickly resurface – as does the animosity of Paula's father, who always felt Vic to be no good. The soap opera conflict plays out with Bob getting caught and arrested by the Sheriff and Mr. Ford begging Vic to get Jesse and break his son out of jail before the boy is lynched.

Vic rides out to round up Jesse James, who is living under an assumed name with a loving wife and children in a nearby town. Henry Brandon brings new surprises to his portrayal showing Jesse to be a devoted family man, warmly embracing his lovely wife, saying he'll be gone for a few days. She reminds Jesse he'll miss that evening's church bazaar – he promised the minister he'd help out. Jesse responds, "Tell him I'm sorry, I had to leave town on business. And tell the children I'll be back as soon as I can." This sweet domestic scene with Jesse James' *other* family is both jarring and heart-warming, humanizing the bank robber.

The men round up the rest of the outlaws, riding toward town in a montage shot at Republic's favored Iverson Ranch location. Ever the strategist, Jesse tells them, "We'll split up and ride into town separately. If Bob's still okay, we'll wait it out." The James Gang are all in place when the angry lynch mob approaches the jail. Incredibly, Jesse James and his men have become the protagonists of *Hell's Crossroads* and we actually find ourselves rooting for these killers much like audiences would root for Tony Soprano forty years later.

Jesse James robs the safe in the opening of *Hell's Crossroads*. Collection of Richard Finegan.

In a terrific sequence, the James Gang expertly stages the breakout and rescue of Bob Ford using the lynch mob to extract the boy from his cell, then getting him away from them. They shoot into the air, frightening but not killing the town folk.

Later, Vic goes to see Jesse to quit and follow his heart. James allows his old friend to do so as the gang continues robbing its way around the Midwest. One headline reads: **JESSE JAMES RAIDS MINNESOTA – GUN BATTLE FOLLOWS DARING BANK ROBBERY.**

Urged by his father and sister, Bob meets with the Governor to beg for leniency as he's the newest member of the gang and hasn't killed anyone. The Governor agrees – if he brings in Jesse James, dead or alive. Bob's plan is to wait until Christmas, when Jesse always returns home to his family.

At Christmas, we see Jesse James hanging ornaments on the tree in his living room when there is a knock at the door. Bob Ford has arrived and is warmly welcomed by Jesse and his wife. "You caught me playing Santa Claus!" he tells his former Gang member. Henry expertly plays these domestic scenes, which adds to the sense of dread as we know what is coming. When James is up on a ladder, putting the star on the top of the tree, Bob savagely shoots him in the back! Then, in shock over what he's done – Jesse is the first man he's killed – he bolts from the house like a coward while Jesse's wife breaks down beside the body of her dead husband. A headline reads **JESSE JAMES MURDERED – FAMED OUTLAW SLAIN IN OWN HOME**. One hour into *Hell's Crossroads*, and the story of Jesse James comes to a brutal end.

The final act plays out with the James Gang gunning for retribution against Bob and Vic and their attempts to survive. It's still exciting but once the anchor of this movie – Jesse James – is removed, the finale feels empty and adrift, as its power player has been taken out. *Hell's Crossroads* is an important addition to Henry Brandon's filmography as it shows he can play a villain in shades of grey rather than in all black. He's so good in the role that, even though he isn't the star of *Hell's Crossroads*, he monopolizes the film with the sheer subtle power of his portrayal. This is one of his dozen best film roles and is a must-see for Brandon buffs.

Two Rode Together:

This 1961 Western was directed by the legendary John Ford and for the second time, he cast Henry Brandon as a Native American. It starred the iconic Jimmy Stewart along with Richard Widmark, Shirley Jones, Linda Cristal and for comedy relief; Andy Devine.

This movie is a classic (slap). No, it's a dog (slap). No, it's *schizophrenic*. It's a John Ford flick folks so it's sure not going to go in a straight line; it zigs and zags and just when things start making sense there are contradictions. Ford wanted it that way.

Brandon reunites with John Ford in *Two Rode Together*.

Unlike *Stagecoach*, this one is slowed down and concentrates on character study, or perhaps even a sociological/psychological study. It seems to explore areas of the Indian wars that *The Searchers* didn't touch; in this case, following what happened to those victims and families that were impacted.

Instead of playing a young renegade, the now 49-year old Henry Brandon was cast as Chief Quanah Parker, a real figure in Western and Indian lore.*

---

* Chief Parker was the child of Comanche Chief Peta Nocona and Cynthia Ann Parker. Cynthia was the child who was captured by Indians and then re-captured by the white's. In *The Searchers* she was cast as Natalie Wood.

Henry essentially played the son to the father Indian chief character he portrayed in *The Searchers* five years earlier. We told you this Western movie was schizophrenic.

This personality disorder even affects good ol' Jimmy Stewart. He's not the "ah shucks," stuttering, everyman in this film. He is a selfish, greedy politician, cynical and dare it be said, a murderer. His unexpected personality reminds one of his ambiguous role in *Vertigo*, only this time the era is during the Comanche/America wars of the 1870's.

To be fair, this film takes us into unchartered territory and examines the horrors of the results of kidnapping, prejudice, lynching and even insanity. It was astonishing for a Western film in 1961 to explicitly depict such subject matter.

Marshall McCabe (Jimmy Stewart) is the law in Tascosa, Texas[*] and he's got things pretty well laid out for himself. He gets 10% of every business in town, plus he stays at the local bordello. The proprietor, Madame Belle Aragon (Annette Hayes) is a very strong willed female and has been cultivating the thought of marrying the Marshal. He is slow to bite.

The Marshall has survived the West by being cynical and untrusting of people; despite this he was able to cultivate a trading relationship with Chief Quanah Parker who represents the Comanche Indian tribe in the southwest. Over the years Marshall McCabe was able to trade goods and even weapons with the Chief. He is the only white man who earned this trust, sort of.

McCabe understands the Comanche language, which makes him very valuable. He is so essential that the US Cavalry calls on him to do them a "favor," specifically to approach the Chief and bargain for the release of the 15 or 20 kidnapped children they allegedly abducted over the past few years.

It was 1st Lt. Jim Gary (Richard Widmark) who approached the Marshall (who was busy drinking beer at the bordello). Lt. Gary appeals to the better side of the Marshal, but when he shows disinterest he is threatened with

---

* (also the town that set the setting of Jimmy Stewart's character in *Winchester '73* (1950)

handcuffs if he doesn't follow him to Ft. Grant. The only reason he agreed to go was to get away from the amorous Madame.

The commanding officer of the fort, we learn, is under increasing pressure to either make war with the Comanche's, or negotiate to get their children back. It's been many years since the kidnappings have taken place and Major John McIntire knows it will be a task with a low percentage of success. He offers to make the Marshall a financial deal based on the amount of people he brings back, supplemented by army scout pay.

There is a large population of civilians at the fort that are all seemingly victims of Indian past misdeeds. Shirley Jones is a young woman who remembers her younger brother being captured by Indians many years ago. If he is still alive that means he was raised as a Comanche. Her parents have not adjusted to this fact, especially the mother (Jeanette Nolan) who is downright delusional.

Marshall McCabe and the Lieutenant set out to Comanche territory to negotiate with Chief Quanah Parker. He is not happy to see them, especially because he recognizes Lt. Gary dressed in civilian attire.

Despite plentiful Winchester repeating rifles to trade with, the Chief is still suspicious. Henry Brandon's character says: "It's been many years since I traded for glass beads and red flannel." The chief tells the men they are in violation of a prior treaty by trespassing on their lands.

While in negotiations a new character arrives: he is a fierce younger male wearing a Mohawk hair style. His name is Stone Calf and is head of the "Buffalo Shields" tribe. He has no respect for Chief Parker and shows him up. Marshall McCabe plays on the Chief's disgust of this new threat. The bargain is made and the Chief releases two captive "whites;" a teenage boy (Running Wolf) who was completely assimilated into the Comanche nation and is violently opposed to his new captors. The young lady, Elena (Linda Cristal) has been Stone Calf's "woman" for the past five years.

Elena remembers her Mexican culture and speaks English; she tries to dissuade McCabe and McIntire to return her to her people. She warns them that Stone Calf will kill them. The Lieutenant's idea is to hurry back to the fort before anything happens. Marshall McCabe disagrees; his brainstorm is to remain behind with the woman and make camp. An argument breaks out until the Lt. has to order his temporary soldier to comply. The Marshall draws his gun to make his point again, and it works. As the Lieutenant and his captive ride off, he sits with Elena in the dark wilderness by the campfire.

Sure enough, Stone Calf approaches them brandishing a knife; his figure is illuminated in the fire. No questions asked, the Marshall shoots him dead. So it leaves viewers to ask, "Was this self-defense or premeditated murder? Was Jimmy Stewart's character eliminating the rival to Chief Quanah Parker to gain favor?" If it is any clue, the last words Chief Parker had for McCabe were he didn't trust him.

Back at the fort, there is a big welcome and excitement in seeing the captive boy. Jeanette Nolan's character believes that this wild thing is her long lost son. Running Wolf spits, fights and resists all attempts to cooperate. He is placed in the hoosegow temporarily until she brings the boy food. He is unresponsive and angry. She cuts off his bindings and then purrs to him, "You are my Toby, and I'm going to cut your hair so you'll look like a nice white boy." That did it; he wrestles the knife away from her and stabs her in the chest. Upon discovery of this savage act, the towns-people capture and hang Running Wolf.

Marshall McCabe rides back the next day and introduces Elena, but she is not well received. She is cruelly treated by the women especially with their quite personal questions. McCabe has seen enough, as he cares for Elena. His solution is for them to ride out of the fort and back to Tascosa. Upon arrival he discovers everything has changed; his former deputy is now the Marshall and has taken over business. McCabe and his now love interest is not bothered at all; he continues to ride into the sunset much to the consternation of the Madame.

Looking at this film with modern day perspective, it is incredibly disturbing on all accounts. This wasn't the typical Western. Director Ford dared to explore the tragedy of war from both sides; he was a WWII veteran and brought to the lens the hypocrisies of history. The topic of "race cleansing" in this film was and is uncomfortable to watch. Ford deserves credit for inducing the audience to react empathetically towards the Native Americans.

This was Henry Brandon's last film role as an Indian, although he would continue portraying Native Americans in the medium of television. Thanks to this film and *The Searchers*, he would forever be linked to John Ford's cinema.

Mission to Glory: A True Story:

This bland and boring theatrical release looks and sounds like a television movie and features Henry Brandon in one of his final movie roles: as an actor he has virtually nothing to do. *Mission To Glory* is the true story of Father Kino, a priest who wandered the American West a few centuries ago building Missions and converting Indians to Christianity. The film is filled with impressive star-power, offering roles to Ricardo Montalban, Cesar Romero, Joseph Campanella, Keenan Wynn and Henry's dear friend Anthony Caruso in the Indian chief role that Brandon *should* have played.

Instead, Henry plays Father Canion (pronounced "Canon"), one of Kino's black robed superiors who pops up a few times to offer his assessment of Father Kino, of his challenging situation, or to bring new information about Army troops coming to "punish the evil doers." He doesn't actually *do* anything and he looks about as bored as the audience is. What a shame that Henry Brandon's final Western movie had to be *this* one.

It's a tough picture to sit through. Even the battle scenes between the Spanish Army and the Indians are by-the-numbers 'arrow hits and stunt falls from red rocks' sequences. For completest or religious movie fans only.

CHAPTER ELEVEN
"A" Pictures

Trail of the Lonesome Pine:
This was an important feature film (released in 1936) as the first Three-Strip Technicolor full-length movie and the first feature shot on location. Henry Brandon had a prevalent part. He was still going by his birth name of Kleinbach and everyone in the business knew him from his "Drunkard" persona. There was a write-up about it in *The Los Angeles Times* on Jan. 16, 1936:

> Audiences continue to hiss the villain, Squire Cribbs enacted to the hilt by Henry Kleinbach in "The Drunkard," now in his one hundred and thirty-second weeks at the Theater Mart. It was Cribbs who lived and died a snake in the grass, who found no practice too low to stoop to in his Mephisthophelean efforts to ruin the hero and to bring his pure wife and child to privation, grief and shame. But the vile Cribbs is defeated in fifteen arching scenes and our hero rescued from the gutter and restored to his happy fireside.
>
> The young Kleinbach declares that the character he plays in the forthcoming release of *The Trail of the Lonesome Pine* makes his familiar one in the current melodrama a positive "sissy."

In his new screen role, Henry played a scruffy backwoods ornery cuss, bent on physical vengeance. As Wade Falin, he personified the worst of human character and solidified the very essence of a nasty screen heavy.

The film, *Trail of the Lonesome Pine* was based on a novel of the same name first published in 1908 by John Fox, Jr. The book was an important slice of American literature and a best seller for years (even inspiring a song of the same name in 1913), that told the story about the battle of the fictional Tollivers and the Falins, who were not unlike the battling Hatfields and the McCoys. The family feuds across hilltops, struggles against nature, literacy and progress served as the backdrop of this drama. There really was a famous pine tree that was part of the natural boundary between Kentucky and the Blue Ridge Mountains of Virginia.

A dramatic moment late in *Trail of The Lonesome Pine,* Brandon is far right with his arm in a sling. Collection of Rick Greene.

In prior years there were three silent film adaptions (one even directed by Cecil B. DeMille) and many stage productions of this title, so there was much anticipation for the new version. The production was shot entirely in the outdoors with the newly perfected Technicolor film process. Substituting for the Appalachian Mountains, the on-location venue was Big

Bear Valley in California – looking crisp and lush with hues of greens, yellows and browns never seen on screen before.

The film starts with Dave Tolliver (*Henry Fonda*) who is suffering from a gunshot wound to his arm, courtesy of the feuding Falins. Jack Hale (*Fred MacMurray*) is an outsider who comes whistling into the territory. He is an engineer and his quest is to build a mutual junction adjoining railroad tracks through both properties. During the course of his duties, Jack notices a vein of coal that could be easily mined and worth a fortune. He also notices a Tolliver girl named June.

Educated man that he is, Jack cannot fathom the long seeded hatred between the two families. Saving the life of Dave (by doctoring him up) and offering guaranteed riches does him no good. They are distrustful of the outside world and have no sophistication reading, writing or banking.

If Dave is the hot-headed young one, then Henry Kleinbach (as Wade Falin) is his equal. Acting as an intermediary between the families, Jack appeals to their commonalities. Jack also appeals to June, which further incites Dave. Even little Buddy Tolliver (played by 8-year old Spanky McFarland) idolizes the city guy and wants to someday also become an engineer. The child actor steals every scene he is in, as a likeable, natural little boy.

Despite the promise of a better financial plight, hatred still runs deep between the families, culminating in an action sequence of cinematic beauty. It featured an extended fist fight between Dave and Wade, on a trail in rocky mountain terrain. They each get their licks in but the match ends when Dave wallops his rival who falls down a twenty foot ravine. We learn that Wade suffered a broken arm in the skirmish because in later scenes his arm is in a sling.

A 1936 newspaper carried the story of the brutally authentic fight sequence:

> So realistic were the fight scenes between Henry Fonda and Henry Kleinbach in *The Trail of the Lonesome Pine* that both actors required hospitalization at their conclusion of the scene.*

---

* *Augusta Chronicle* January 29, 1936

After further plot developments things get really nasty. A suspicious fire breaks out at the campground headquarters of the engineer and railroad workers. The camera lets the audience see the likely culprit sneaking under the steam shovel; it is Wade filling the underside with dynamite. Worse yet, little Buddy was fooling around inside on the seat when the unthinkable happened, the steam shovel blew up. This is possibly the nastiest thing that Bogeyman Brandon ever did on screen – until the climactic sequence.

The story dramatically shifts gears as a result of the child's screen death. A funeral is seen, but the most tear wrenching moments were elicited when we see Buddy's dog crawling towards the grave.

It took the death of a child for sensibilities to settle in: the longstanding murderous feud no longer made sense. Unarmed, Dave Tolliver makes his way to the Falin cabin. A heartfelt apology is extended to the family. The father, Buck Falin, (in an extended sincere handshake) is remorseful for not initiating an apology first. With renewed spirit, and a peaceful sentiment, Dave turns and starts to head back to his cabin. Then, in one of cinema's most shocking "**stinker**" moments, Wade sheepishly addresses his father: "For a minute I almost believed you." Henry's character then grabs a rifle, shoots through the window and hits Dave *in the back*. In outrage, Buck emphatically empties his revolver into his own son.

Buck carries the mortally wounded Dave back to the Tolliver cabin. Dave volunteers that he fell on his own gun, thereby nobly ending any animosity. As Dave is dying, the fathers make peace and June is free to marry Fred MacMurray's Jack Hale.

This film made box office stars of Henry Fonda and Fred MacMurray. For Henry Kleinbach, he solidified the perception he could play despicable villain roles with the best of them. The type-cast was set.

The Garden of Allah:

If you were hoping that Hollywood could produce a three-strip Technicolor film featuring the burning Arabian sands, *The Garden of Allah* is the movie for you. In this epic, seemingly every pebble was highlighted at dusk along with a few camels, tents and toothless people.

In this story of religious guilt and hokum, the two stars Marlene Dietrich and Charles Boyer, strike an unlikely pair of lovers in this thinly disguised soap opera. Dietrich looks positively wax-like through the radiant veils, silks and gowns. Boyer looks confused and he should be. He spent his special purpose in a monastery to learn the craft of the special wine only he knows the recipe of. The rest of the brothers of the monastery are helpless without this.

The location "oasis" for this 1936 Selznick International Picture was shot near Yuma, Arizona. The irrigated water was brought from the Colorado River five miles away.*

Henry himself confirms this in a notation on the back of a scene still from *Drums of Fu Manchu* for collector Richard Finegan, discussing bit player Jammel Hassan: "Hassan was primarily a technical advisor on films involving Arabs in Hollywood. He was a native-born Moroccan. I shared a tent with him at Buttercup Valley, out of Yuma, Arizona during location shooting of Selznick's *Garden Of Allah*. He was one of the greatest poker players of all time and used to fleece the grips in their after-hours table stakes games."

It is fortunate that Basil Rathbone and John Carradine are featured prominently; it needed all the help it could get. There were plenty of extras for this extravaganza and it is significant that Henry Brandon was given screen credit. It was in this film that he changed his name professionally. This occurrence was picked up by the print media: "Young Henry Kleinbach, young screen character actor, he changed his name to Henry Brandon. He has an important role in *The Garden of Allah*."†

---

* *San Diego Union* May 17, 1936
† *Pittsburgh Post-Gazette* May 28, 1936.

That important role was as "Hadj," a non-English speaking son of the desert with a comical bent. Despite juicy descriptions of him involved with some action scenes, they were edited out in the final cut. He is, however, developing his considerable skills of scene stealing, as he inhabits the background shots of several sequences, shifting from one foot to another, raising his eyebrow, chewing his fingernail and generally calling attention to his simple character. At one point he even gives out with a superb James Finlayson-type "D'oh!" Indeed Brandon's few scattered scenes offer *The Garden of Allah* it's only expressive comic relief -- but it is not enough. In a word, this film is *Pepe le Pue*(trid).

Conquest:

The famous story of the ill-fated love affair between Napoleon Bonaparte and Marie Walewska, *Conquest* is a glossy MGM romantic drama illuminated by the star-power of Charles Boyer and Greta Garbo. And, oh yes, Henry Brandon shows up in one scene with one line.

Before we analyze that one scene and one line, let's take a look at where Brandon's film career was in 1937, the year *Conquest* was produced and released. 1937 was, in fact, one of Henry's busiest, bustling years. He starred as the lead villain in two serials for Universal (*Jungle Jim* and *Secret Agent X-9*), he acted opposite against Humphrey Bogart in *Black Legion* at Warner Brothers, he played the lead heavy in the Poverty Row production of *Island Captives*, had a solid supporting character role with Joel McCrea in the excellent Paramount Western *Wells Fargo* and he made his triumphant return to The Hal Roach Studios reviving his role of Barnaby in *The Our Gang Follies of 1938* (produced at the end of '37 and released the following year), among other features and short subject roles.

Why on Earth would Henry Brandon take a job that amounted to a bit part of a character who doesn't even have a character name (he is 'Staff Officer') in *Conquest*? For several good reasons; it was a job at MGM, the grandest and, biggest of the movie production studios in Hollywood. It was a Greta Garbo film, which meant EVERYONE would go see it and it would be a box office success. It was an 'A' production with big money being spent on sets, costumes, script with no expenses spared. Henry Brandon would have been foolish *not* to take the small job.

Conquest begins in 1807 as Napoleon conquers Poland and follows his meteoric rise and fall right through to his Waterloo. Intertwined with the battles, the victories and the defeats, is woven the real story, a moving story of love and loneliness and politics. Brandon shows up at about thirty-five minutes in, heralding the arrival of Napoleon at the estates of Ms. Walewska, announcing, "I'm afraid we inconvenience you, Madam…" But before he can continue and make the "request" of allowing the battle-weary men to stay the night at her mansion, Napoleon breezes into the foyer and dominates the remainder of the sequence. However, our Henry Brandon – old Silas Barnaby, evil Fu Manchu, The Cobra himself – got to play a scene and deliver a line to Greta Garbo, the biggest movie star of the 1930's in one of her most famous sound pictures.

I Met My Love Again:

This 1938 Walter Wanger-produced drama stars Henry Fonda and Joan Bennett and features Henry Brandon in one strange sequence that is worth the price of admission and foreshadows – of all things – Fu Manchu!

I Met My Love Again begins its romantic journey of a dozen years in 1925 small-town Vermont with fresh-faced college youngsters Julie (Joan Bennett) and Ives (Henry Fonda) falling in love and getting engaged. But things don't work out as planned when one snowy-evening a few years later Julie meets and is captivated by a smooth-talking writer named Michael Shaw (Alan Marshal) and impulsively elopes with him. They move to Paris where they have a daughter.

It is in 1930 Paris where we experience Henry Brandon's bizarre sequence. The couple lives in a bohemian artist colony full of writers, painters, dancers and other quirky types. One fateful night they attend a party hosted by Bruno the Painter (Henry Brandon) who, despite being named Bruno, is an imperious oriental artist. Henry wears long Chinese ornamental robes and sports a thin drooping mustache, heavily lidded eyes and smokes his cigarette in a long black simmering holder. His appearance is startling and odd. Michael arrives inebriated and shoots up the place with two revolvers, damaging the skylight and the ceiling, but no one other than the landlord gives the shocking behavior of "that crazy American" much thought. It is evident that Shaw behaves this way frequently and poor Julie is trapped in a marriage with a crass alcoholic who will never finish his great American novel.

The oddball international gathering of peculiar artistic-types is an embryonic version of the wild parties that *Auntie Mame* would throw twenty years later in the film version of that stage success, also with Henry Brandon in attendance. But this Brandon is Asian and when Bruno first speaks, it is with the *exact* voice and mannerisms of Dr. Fu Manchu, the insidious leader of vengeful Si Fan bent on world domination still two years in Henry Brandon's future. Bruno could almost *be* Fu Manchu, the frustrated artist painting with his Italian meat sauce, scorned and misunderstood, seeking his revenge.

Bruno is showing off his latest painting, done in "a new technique of painting" utilizing food. He explains to an astonished Shaw "that setting sun is of catsup, that brown earth is of Italian meat sauce, that green grass is of spinach. It is utilitarian." Moody Michael replies that he doesn't like the painting because, "it smells" and "no matter how good it is today, tomorrow it will be garbage!"

Bruno takes offense and the two nearly come to blows. Julie begs mercurial Michael not to fight and land in jail again. He seems to agree, but then engages Bruno in a mock duel with his empty revolvers. When Shaw fires, his gun merely clicks. Tragically, he has handed Bruno a weapon with one round remaining and the catsup-painter fires almost point-blank into the writer, fatally wounding him. It is a horrifying moment capping off a wacky scene that sends widowed Julie back to Vermont and a second chance with her one true love.

I Met My Love Again was a box-office failure and hasn't aged well, though. Fonda and Bennett make appealing leads and the attraction of experiencing Henry Brandon as a foreshadowed Fu Manchu make the film worth seeking out.

Three Comrades:

If Henry Brandon's thankless one-line role in *Conquest* is what led to his being cast in MGM's *Three Comrades*, then it was worth every syllable. *Three Comrades* is a unique cinematic experience in Brandon's filmography even though the part of Valentin, the man with the eye patch, isn't all that much larger than his role in the Garbo picture. But, oh, how it resonates!

Based on a novel by Erich Maria Remarque, the literate screenplay by the legendary F. Scott Fitzgerald is simply terrific. *Three Comrades* stars Robert Taylor (Erich), Franchot Tone (Otto) and Robert Young (Gottfried) as a trio of German pals who survived the horrors of World War I together. The story opens in November 1918 as the Great War has just ended and Germany is licking its wounds. We meet the Three Comrades at their favorite haunt, a bar run by Alfons (Guy Kibbee). They toast each other and their return to normal life, something that simply isn't possible.

Two years pass and it is 1920. We find the cynical Comrades lamenting the social uprising in Germany as not what they risked their lives for. Life is tough but together they somehow survive and meet the luminous Patricia Hollman (Margaret Sullavan) who falls in love with Erich and the trio becomes a devoted quartet.

In addition to the wonderful Guy Kibbee, the stellar supporting cast includes Lionel Atwill, Henry Hull, Charley Grapewin, Monty Wooley, George Zucco and Henry Brandon – a literal dream team of Hollywood's finest supporting players! Imagine Atwill, Zucco and Brandon all in the same picture and *none* of them are villains!

Brandon's enigmatic Valentin in *Three Comrades*.

Henry Brandon makes his first appearance in a scene about twenty minutes in. He is one of the denizens of Alfons' bar, sitting alone and drinking his beer, looking both intriguing and pitiful with his black eye patch. Otto describes Henry's Valentin as "another one for whom the war will never stop!"

He calls to the quartet at their table, saying, "Tomorrow is the anniversary of our first attack on Chemander Dam!" and raises his glass to the memory, smiling wistfully. There is an aura of tragedy about him, slumped at his table, a broken man in the wake of his World War. A war that he lost, a war that they *all* lost.

Erich tries to fit into Pat's wealthy world, but can't. He returns to his friends to get drunk, but Pat follows. In a Germany ravaged by the ramifications of losing, at least the Three Comrades have each other – and now Pat. Henry Brandon has only his memories. Valentin isn't even a whole man as his eye-patch clearly denotes.

At the midpoint of *Three Comrades* comes Henry's second scene. Erich and Pat get married in a private ceremony at Alfons' Bar. Valentin comes striding up for a drink but the door is bolted. He peers in between the shutters and sees the Comrades in the midst of the wedding ceremony, joyous and celebrating. Valentin will forever be the man on the outside of life, looking in. He has been left behind. Director Frank Borzage could have included a close-up of Brandon, peering in with his one eye to devastating effect, but didn't. The fact that this just isn't his story makes the exclusion of such a close-up all the more devastating.

As 1920 comes to an end, the civil unrest intensifies and riots break out. Erich is focused on a severe health crisis that Pat is facing and the other two Comrades get drawn into the conflicted Germany that allowed Hitler to rise to power. When one of the friends is killed during a melee, the remaining two focus on a mission of vengeance. These theatrics could easily have shifted into maudlin soap opera, but in the hands of this expert cast, a great director and equally great script, *Three Comrades* is riveting film-making.

Brandon's third and final scene as Valentin comes at Christmas time. One of the Comrades is dead, Pat is away being operated on and Erich finds himself once again at Alfons, lonely and dejected. One of the girls at the bar asks Robert Taylor to play a song on the piano and he chooses one to fit his mood – sad and sentimental. As the patrons gather around and sing, Valentin remains in the background, listening but not participating, hovering to the extreme left of the screen in his only medium shot in the scene. He lives on the fringes of his own camera angle!

At the end, *Three Comrades* is deeply moving. If your eyes aren't filled with tears, then you are as lost as the enigma called Valentin. Henry Brandon is only in three short scenes in *Three Comrades*, yet he portrays a character so profoundly damaged and solitary that his memory lingers. Valentin haunts the perifery of the film, a lost soul. It is an absolute masterpiece.

The Last Train from Madrid:

Henry Brandon did two small cameo appearances in Dorothy Lamour star vehicles at Paramount, where she was under contract, in late 1937 and early 1938. The films were *The Last Train from Madrid* and *Spawn of the North*.

The Last Train from Madrid is a suspenseful thriller about refugees fleeing Madrid during the Spanish Civil War. After the opening titles, the first thing we see is Henry Brandon in a dramatic, moody close-up. He is a radio announcer, speaking urgently, sweat glistening on his face, looking furtively back and forth from his script to the microphone.

"Attention! Attention! An announcement of vital importance! The last train for Madrid will leave tonight at twelve o'clock sharp! Due to Governmental reasons, railroad communications linking Madrid to Valencia and the sea coast will be destroyed immediately after the departure of this last train. Special passes will be issued by the Office for Municipal Defense. But here is a warning, Citizens; these special passes will be issued *only* to accredited persons or those who have important business outside Madrid and to certain members of the military." And with that well delivered warning, Boy Announcer Henry Brandon sets up the plot of *The Last Train from Madrid*, never to be seen again. His bit in the next Lamour picture is even shorter, but places him squarely in the middle of an action sequence.

Spawn of the North:

In 1938, Paramount produced a sprawling, two-fisted all-star vehicle for George Raft, Henry Fonda, Dorothy Lamour and John Barrymore called *Spawn of The North*, the story of the Fish Pirates of the Alaskan frontier.

The story is treated like a Northern, a snow-capped, iceberg-filled Western where fish are wrangled instead of cattle. When we meet Raft as Tyler, Fonda as Jim and Slicker the seal, we quickly grasp these finely etched characters as if their rich history up to this point was real. *Spawn of the North* is deeply entertaining, rooted in the chemistry of the Raft-Fonda best pal's friendship.

However, for Henry Brandon buffs, the pleasures of *Spawn of the North* offer next to nothing. He shows up about one hour in as a ship captain named Davis, who had been searching for lost fish traps but found Fonda's First Mate instead. He was, as Davis matter-of-factly intones, "Deader than a herring."

As fast as he floats in, Henry Brandon floats out, not to be seen again, not even listed in the films closing credits. *Spawn of the North* is a terrific picture, but Brandon fans are sure to be disappointed.

Beau Geste:

That legendary year 1939, the year of *Gone with the Wind* and *The Wizard Of Oz*, that ultimate Golden Age of Hollywood pinnacle output year – a year which also saw *Stagecoach, Mr. Smith Goes To Washington, Ninotchka, Destry Rides Again, Son Of Frankenstein, Of Mice & Men, Gunga Din* and *Goodbye Mr. Chips*. Henry Brandon appeared mainly in B Pictures and a serial that year but did participate in ONE of the great classics of 1939, William Wellman's terrific action-packed thriller *Beau Geste*.

Probably Gary Cooper's best film, Paramount's *Beau Geste* is the rousing story of three brothers (Cooper, Robert Preston, and Ray Milland), French Foreign Legionnaires whose tight, wise-cracking friendship rivals that of the six-fisted trio from *Gunga Din*. The film opens with a double mystery – who stole the valuable sapphire 'Blue Water' and who set fire to the Legion outpost eerily staffed by dead soldiers?

Henry's one short scene takes place early on in the Foreign Legion sequences but is both riveting and shocking. All three brothers find themselves under the brutal command of the sadistic Sergeant Markoff (a crackling good Brian Donlevy) and this scene is the first example of his sick cruelty. Two deserters have been recaptured and brought back to the Fort for punishment. One of these unfortunate souls is Renouf (Henry Brandon), the only one of the two who is able to remain on his feet after their near-fatal desert ordeal. Markoff informs the men, in front of the entire company, to set an example, -- that they have a choice: They can either stay and be executed for desertion or go back into the Sahara and "escape"' again.

Henry is virtually unrecognizable as he begs Markoff, "Let us stay…water…water!" but the Sergeant has made the choice for them. Back into the blazing heat they go, facing a horrific, slow death in the unforgiving Sahara Desert. Beau Geste will soon face the evil Markoff himself, but Henry's fate sets the stage for that climactic confrontation.

Henry Brandon only appeared in a handful of all-time classic 'A' pictures and *Beau Geste* is certainly one of them. It is as powerful, entertaining and alluring today as when it was made in that fabled year of 1939.

Nurse Edith Cavell:

This feature film produced in 1939 is a tribute to a legend in the long history of English heroes of the Great War. During the 20th century she is synonymous as the "Joan of Arc of England" for her virtues, guile, and sacrifices. It was shot in Hollywood and distributed by RKO pictures.

The movie is a biography of the famed nurse played by British actress Anna Neale. In 1914 when the movie begins, we see her as head of a hospital in Germany-occupied Brussels. As a nurse she is the consummate professional; her mandate is to save lives whether or not they be citizens of Germany.

Amazingly, no scenes in this movie depict war battles. Most of the footage is devoted to the drama of Edith's dedication in the hospital and sending fugitive soldiers across the Dutch border. To accomplish this, she must interact with the secret underground while keeping the pesky Germans away from her business. Despite being a British citizen, Nurse Cavell had earned the trust of the Germans with her dedication to professional duties. This enabled her to have a little bit of free reign.

Unfortunately for the nurse, a German double-agent had cunningly infiltrated among the Underground. He was seemingly a trusted soul who could speak both English and German. The culprit was Henry Brandon (of course), playing the role of Lt. Schultz. As the ambitious German spy, he both looks and acts sly and sneaky, right in his talent wheelhouse. Brandon is only in a handful of scenes in *Nurse Edith Cavell*, but he adds an element of real danger and suspense to the proceedings, making a worthwhile contribution to a film that can be tough to sit through.

When word reaches headquarters, the good nurse is suddenly arrested for treason and held as a prisoner until her trial. Neale is unemotional throughout the whole affair, taking the word "underplayed" to a new level. George Sanders takes up the slack as the prosecutor as he chews up the scenery in his inimitable fashion.

Edna May Oliver, as Countess de Mavon has the best line in the film: She addresses Lt. Schultz (after looking at him up and down in disgust) and says "You worm!" The scene is supposed to be played straight but it is unintentionally funny. Comedienne favorite, Zasu Pitts is in this one as well. Her talents are wasted, but she did have that *face*.

The climax of the film is the firing squad execution of Nurse Edith Cavell; it was based on the true event of 1915 at the beginning of the war in Europe. The horror of executing a female nurse took on international outrage. During the time between imprisonment and trial, many attempts at diplomacy failed, further fueling world-wide anti-German sentiment.

Since the first Great War, Edith Cavell has been hailed as a martyr for her courage and sacrifice. In 1939 the film was also a good propaganda piece for English and American audiences during the period ramping up to World War II.

In a nice mention, an August 1939 review of *Nurse Edith Cavell* in *The Film Daily* has Henry listed "among others who appear in lesser roles" but noted for his "splendid acting."

Florian:

Historical 1940 drama from MGM is really, getting down to the heart of the matter, a love story between a man, a woman and a horse. Robert Young stars as the Austrian trainer and caretaker for a magnificent white stallion named Florian and the picture follows their adventures during and after a civil war.

Henry Brandon has an unnamed, unbilled blink-and-you'd-miss-it bit as a horse groom. He probably landed the job due to his experience with horses and his acting abilities, although neither talent is utilized. If you love horses, you'll tear up at the ending. If you love Henry Brandon, you'll also tear up - over the missed opportunity.

The Shepherd of the Hills:

The first of Henry Brandon's three films with John Wayne was also Wayne's first appearance in Technicolor, 1941's *The Shepherd of The Hills*, produced by Paramount. Containing many of the same plot beats and locales as the earlier *Trail Of The Lonesome Pine* (both pictures were directed by Henry Hathaway), *The Shepherd of the Hills* ends up as not much more than a hillbilly soap opera and a big disappointment for Brandon fans.

Shepherd is the story of a moonshiner family named Matthews and how a mysterious stranger coming to their backwoods mountain community changes everything. The Duke is Matt Matthews and his jug-swilling brood includes Marjorie Main, Ward Bond and Henry Brandon. Not only does Henry's unbilled character not have a name, he doesn't utter a word of dialogue in the finished film. He is there during the supper scenes and during a climactic sequence where a blind character regains her sight, doing and saying nothing more than providing local color in Technicolor.

The Shepherd of the Hills is a beautiful looking film of moonshiner drama, but for real thrills, romance and a juicy nasty role for Henry Brandon, stick with *Trail of the Lonesome Pine*.

Northwest Outpost:

This 1947 Nelson Eddy musical drama was significant for Henry Brandon for two reasons while still being barely a blip in his long filmography. A story of intrigue at Fort Ross, a Russian settlement in California during the 1840s, Henry plays a Chinese Junk Captain who doesn't even appear until the film's final ten minutes in a role so minor it barely registers. So why is Republic Pictures' *Northwest Outpost* significant?

Henry as a Chinese Boat Captain with Hugo Hass in *Northwest Outpost*. Collection of Rick Greene.

First, it is his first motion picture job since returning from his WWII army service, possibly as a result of Republic's gratitude for the boatloads of money that his *Drums of Fu Manchu* serial made for the company.

Second, his Chinese Junk Captain is quite the homage to that Fu Manchu character, looking and even sounding like the insidious Doctor. His first line, to Ilona Massey's Natalia, is "Your cabin is this way, Missy" done in full Fu intonation, sounding almost threatening. Henry does little more than direct people to their cabins and misremembers who may or may not be on his ship. It's a throwaway job, but a welcome return to the cinema after a long four-year absence.

Joan of Arc:"

A sumptuous but dull 1948 Technicolor feast, *Joan of Arc* stars luminous Ingrid Bergman as the teenaged Joan in this overlong humorless biopic that offers up a three-strip Henry Brandon in chainmail armor with virtually nothing to do. Directed by Victor Fleming *(Gone with the Wind, The Wizard of Oz)*, *Joan of Arc* is one of those movies like *Titanic* - we all know how it ends, so the point is the journey, not the tragic destination.

Brandon in full armor in *Joan of Arc*.

Henry's sequence is at almost the film's midpoint – The Battle of Orleans in 1429. Joan is now a religious figurehead, there to help lead the French troops to victory over the invading British. Brandon plays Captain Giles de Rais, one of the men who looks upon Joan's arrival with doubt and scorn. With a jet-black van dyke beard, a pointy metal helmet and a chain-mail vest over his armor, Brandon cuts an imposing figure. He is also completely mute, having no dialogue at all, merely shown in several striking close-ups and medium shots.

Captain de Rais listens as Joan engages in verbal sparring with Captain La Hire (Ward Bond), who believes the young girl to be either a charlatan or a fool. She brings them all around, and they ultimately rally around her as she leads them to victory. It's interesting to see Henry in these scenes with Ward Bond, as in just a few short years they'd be working together on several solid episodes of his television series **Wagon Train.**

During the battle sequence, the film's action highlight, Joan takes an arrow through the shoulder but still rallies the troops to conquer the English. Henry isn't visible during the fighting and one might presume him to be lost, but we do see Captain de Rais one final time, cheering the Dauphin (Jose Ferrer) as he is crowned King. The new King ultimately betrays Joan, the woman who put him on the throne, and the story meanders to its fiery conclusion without any further participation from Henry Brandon.

The nearly two and a half hour epic is tough to sit through, but Bergman and Ferrer are both excellent. Even though Henry Brandon doesn't have a word of dialogue, save some cheering, he looks intimidating in his pointless close-ups. *Joan of Arc* isn't worth sitting through just for those. However, pyromaniacs will have a ball.

The Fighting O'Flynn:

A love letter to the classic silent films of his famous father, Douglas Fairbanks Jr's *The Fighting O'Flynn* produced at Universal Studios in 1949 is a charming, romantic, boisterous old-fashioned adventure movie. Fairbanks Jr. plays a swashbuckling soldier of fortune returning to Ireland at the time of the Napoleonic Wars with a minor but amusing part for Henry Brandon.

A subtitle tells us this is "a story of plots and counterplots, of intrigue and violence," and that it surely is. But mainly it is the full-throttled story of O'Flynn and how he foils the villains, wins the love of the girl, and has a grand time doing so. Fairbanks commands the screen with his father's infectious high spirits in a performance that traces directly back to Robin Hood, Zorro and D'Artagnan. If you love the original Fairbanks silent classics and don't yet know *The Fighting O'Flynn*, you must immediately seek this film out-- and be swept away to high adventure!

Nearly one hour into the fun, O'Flynn decides to single-handedly capture a French castle in order to prove his devotion to the object of his affections Lady Benedetta (Helena Carter). Here Henry Brandon appears as Lieutenant Carpe, a French officer under the command of General Van Dronk. When O'Flynn walks up to the castle and demands to be admitted, Carpe replies, "Let him come in and be questioned. We will shoot him later!" Henry dusts off his light French accent from *The Corsican Brothers*, which also starred Douglas Fairbanks, Jr.

O'Flynn is brought before the General for questioning and his pack of Irish lies is so complimentary to Van Dronk, that he delays the execution so the two can drink all night and shoot the breeze, much to Carpe's chagrin. As Henry stomps out, O'Flynn comments, "Unpleasant fellow!" The two drink the night away knowing that death comes with the dawn. However, Fairbanks drugs the General, who passes out soundly. Carpe returns outside the door with news of the arrival of a special envoy regarding the invasion. O'Flynn allows Carpe to enter, who sees his General's body and exclaims "You've killed him!" and then attacks O'Flynn.

Fairbanks easily bests Brandon and knocks him unconscious. He tricks the envoy into revealing his treasonous plans, but Carpe has returned to consciousness in the back room and sneaks in with a pistol to capture O'Flynn. "You must have a terribly thick skull!" complains the Irish prisoner to Carpe, who arranges for a firing squad to be assembled to have this nuisance dealt with.

Fortuitously, O'Flynn's friends have accidentally found the long lost O'Flynn fortune hidden in the O'Flynn well and are able to bribe the entire firing squad into shooting blanks, thus saving O'Flynn from an O'hail of O'bullets. His friends spirit the "body" away right under Lieutenant Carpe's nose!

The Fighting O'Flynn plays out without any further participation from Henry Brandon's Carpe to a finale filled with stunts, excitement, chases and love. Fairbanks Jr. produced the film and wrote the screenplay, just as his Father did when he was the first superstar action hero of the cinema.

Vera Cruz:

This is an "A" picture if ever there was one, shot in Technicolor "Superscope" at various locations in Mexico. The 1954 film had quite a cast going for it: Gary Cooper, Burt Lancaster, Cesar Romero, Jack Elam, Ernest Borgnine, Charles Bronson and of course, Henry Brandon.

It is interesting to note that this film was produced by Lancaster's own production company and Burt made the most of it. His character is Joe Erin with a sadistic and sociopathic bent. He not only wears a black hat, he is also clothed in all-black attire. He smiles like a crocodile to signal his displeasure. *

Cooper (as Benjamin Trane) is a loner similar to his role in *High Noon*. He wears a white hat and is a survivor of the American Civil War on the side for the South. He was unfortunate in that the last act of war was on his plantation and it was destroyed. He came to Mexico in hopes of seeking quick money.

Vera Cruz is a port in Mexico and the plot revolves around the period during the Mexican Revolution of 1866. During this era, France occupied Mexico and imposed Emperor Maximilian on the people. Despite this for-

---

* The mannerism is reminiscent of Richard Widmark's trademark idiosyncrasy from the 1947 film, *Kiss of Death*.

eign rule, the Juarez army of nationalists went to battle to take back their country.

Many American fighting men were drawn to the cause; some were adventurers, opportunists or criminals and all were seeking fortunes. Most have little loyalty to either side. Erin surrounded himself as head of a loosely knit gang by the likes of Ernest Borgnine, Jack Elam and Charles Bronson. Don't turn your back on these guys.

That searing Brandon intensity at full throttle in *Vera Cruz*

There is an early scene that establishes what is at stake in the war. The Americans were surprised in their encampment when a large contingency of delegates representing the Emperor ride in. It is headed by Marquis Henri de Labordere (Cesar Romero). With great flair he introduces himself and flatters Erin (his reputation preceded him).

Suddenly, a Juarez General rides in and beckons the men to join their cause; they can pay nothing for their services. To counter, the Marquis offers the Americans a princely sum and position if he but joins with the Emperor. A standoff ensues as they are speaking; the Juarez army surrounds them. The situation is at an impasse in a high risk, high gain maneuver. There is a promise by the general that they will meet again, and they do (at the end of course).

The Juarez sympathizers in Mexico easily outnumbered Emperor Maximilian's supporters. To counter this, the Emperor encloses himself with professional soldiers from France including Captain Danette (Henry Brandon).

An invitation is extended to the Americans to ride to the palace in Mexico City to be received by the Emperor. They can hardly refuse. Once there, the Marquis escorts Erin and Trane inside the palace where a grand ball is taking place. The setting is very enchanting, the people beautiful and there is plenty of food, drink and music.

The opportunity presents itself for the Marquis to introduce Captain Danette to Trane and Erin while the two uncouth Americans are hovering over the glamorously prepared buffet. The Captain clicks his heels in good militaristic manner when announced.

> **Marquis**: "May I present Captain Danette, you'll find something in common to talk about with this gentleman (Trane). As a soldier he fought with the Confederate Army."
>
> Capt. Danette: "Then I fear we have little in common. You see, I've never fought for the losing side."

The Captain is a rigid soldier; his hair is closely cropped and he sports a scar over his face.[*] He is fastidious in his demeanor and is one who takes pride in his most colorful uniform. There isn't a speck of untidiness on this soldier until Lancaster's character (Erin), accidently on purpose, waves a chicken leg in the air and brushed it against the Captain's chest.

---

[*]   Henry's "Captain Danette" is very much like the character Eric Von Stroheim was famous for as "The Man You Love to Hate."

The glaring Captain watches the vulgar American stuff his face with food to the point where an attempt at washing it down with drink results in gross spillage. Capt. Danette sarcastically remarks; "Be careful Monsieur, some of your wine is going into your mouth." The reaction from Erin is one of insult, but he regroups to flash the Captain with a toothy smile thereby marking him for death later. The verbal confrontation escalates as Erin picks up a whole cooked chicken and starts to devour it.

Capt. Danette: "Your etiquette amazes me, monsieur. I had no idea you knew what hand to use."

The put-down compels Erin to break off the Tiperillo-looking smoking devise from the Captain's lips. With that the Captain removes his Class-A white gloves and slaps Erin across the face. Though highly insulted, Erin's attention is diverted when Countess Marie Duvarre enters the room. She walks right past Erin, who mutters: "Ho-there chicky baby" (or something similar), then removes the Captain's pristine white gloves, wipes his dirty mouth and shoves them back into the soldier's breast pocket. The Captain glares as Erin and Trane watch the Countess move on; the pair both look at each other and then do a synchronized affirmative nod.

Part of the fun in this film is that Trane and Erin do not trust each other; they lie, make alliances, and easily cast these aside for their own personal gain. Because of their shooting skills, they are offered a handsome sum of money to help escort the Countess (The Emperor's wife) through tough Juarez territory to Vera Cruz. The entourage is headed by Captain Danette's royal army and is augmented by Trane and Erin's fringe support of the cutthroat, raping wild bunch.

Erin and Trane figured out that the carriage transporting the Emperor's wife is also carrying three million ducats worth of gold under her seat (one has to suspend disbelief in physics here) which they plan to steal when they get the chance. It turns out the Empress also has her greedy motives to intercept the gold once they reach port. Complications ensue.

Henry with Gary Cooper and Burt Lancaster in *Vera Cruz*.

While at a campsite during the evening, Capt. Danette orders his men to ride away without the Americans. Erin starts to run at them and is shot in the arm by the Captain. It's only a flesh wound and Erin asks Trane to dig the bullet out with his knife (no telling where *that* has been).

The film reaches its climax when all parties converge at a plaza in a gun fight over the gold. During the skirmish, Captain Danette is thrown from his horse and winds up on his back, helpless on the ground. Erin is there to greet him and in a desperate attempt to defend himself, the Captain rolls to grab his military lance. Erin kicks the Captain in the face and then picks up the lance. Their eyes meet for a second as they both recognize the situation they are in. A sadistic smile is flashed on Erin's face as he plunges the steel lance into the Captain's throat.

Erin still has gold fever but is thwarted by Trane who announces his intentions to make sure the gold goes to the rightful people of Mexico. This culminates into a showdown of epic proportions between the two. Gary Cooper's "Trane" is the winner and walks off with a señorita chasing him as the movie fades out.

This film is dazzling; the beauty of Mexico and their Aztec ruins serve as an excellent backdrop and a refreshing change from "Westerns" shot on flimsy set stages in Hollywood. It broke many rules at the time and opened up a new genre. This was *The Good, the Bad and the Ugly* of its time.

Henry again displayed what made him such an essential character actor; he played his scenes with stark realism, contempt and superiority blazing in his eyes. That robust voice is fully utilized when he barks at his army. All things considered this is one of the top films to showcase Henry Brandon; he is recognized very highly by film buffs for this role while chalking up another show-stopping death scene.

Bandido!

Not really a Western, *Bandido!* was a solid star vehicle for Robert Mitchum released in 1956 by United Artists and featuring Henry Brandon in a modest supporting role. It's a big, loud, and tremendously entertaining action picture with bullets flying and grenades exploding and very little for Henry to do.

Brandon appears on and off throughout *Bandido!* as Gunther, a smarmy arms broker who brings Kennedy (Zachary Scott) and his wife (Ursula Thiess) over the border into Mexico to peddle guns and ammunition to the Regulares during their 1916 conflict against the rebels. Shot in Cinemascope on location in Mexico, Henry's Gunther is a businessman intent on getting these needed weapons to the military so that can wipe out the rebel faction led by Colonel Escobar (Gilbert Roland). The role Brandon plays isn't very interesting and he seems there merely to provide expository dialogue and to ride a horse.

With Robert Mitchum in a lobby card from *Bandido*. Collection of Rick Greene.

There is only so much Henry can do with dialogue like "Put your men along this bank and behind the warehouse. The pier will give them protection from the barge!" Mitchum as a cynical competing dealer named Wilson plays it cool as a cucumber, selling to the opposition and falling in love with Kennedy's wife. It's his picture all the way, and *Bandido!* is exciting and funny with an intense climax filled with carnage and a high body count. Indeed, Brandon's Gunther is one of those presumed blown up by a barge full of dynamite, but the script has so little interest in the character that it isn't bothered with showing his potentially explosive demise. Henry gives it his best – he always does – but his bland character give him little opportunity to shine…or explode.

The Ten Commandments:

In 1956, Cecil B. DeMille's epic *The Ten Commandments* was (up to that point) the most expensive picture ever made and has since become a part of all of our lives via annual television screenings and its consistent ranking on Top Ten Motion Picture lists. It cost an astounding $13,000,000 to make but grossed well over $100 Million worldwide on its initial release. The stellar cast included Charlton Heston as Moses, Yul Brenner, Anne Baxter, Yvonne De Carlo, Edward G. Robinson, Sir Cedric Hardwicke, Vincent Price, Judith Anderson, John Carradine, Nina Foch and, playing a small part in a big picture, Henry Brandon.

The good news for Brandon fans is one doesn't need to sit through the seemingly endless 220 minute run time to enjoy Henry as the Commander Of The Hosts in *The Ten Commandments*. He appears in the very first dialogue scene… after the Overture, the filmed introduction by Cecil B. DeMille, the Main Credits and opening narration by Cecil B. DeMille.

In fact, Brandon speaks the third line of dialogue in the film, asking rhetorically of his Pharaoh what nation would be foolish enough to draw the sword against mighty Egypt. The High Priest has come with information of a prophecy that their enemy comes from within, that, a male child born into slavery will rise and lead the Hebrew slaves out of bondage. Brandon's Commander sneers, "Then let the Hebrews die!"

Rameses proclaims just that, declaring, "Every newborn Hebrew man child shall die. So let it be written, so let it be done!" Then the armored Commander of the Hosts strides off to see that his Pharaoh's directive is bloodily carried out, making this role easily Henry Brandon's most despicable.

After Baby Moses escapes via the floating basket in the reeds, the story moves forward in time and leaves Henry behind. But it is nice to see him part of such an illustrious cast in one of the biggest motion pictures ever made, a film that has become as much an annual family holiday tradition as *The Wizard of Oz* and *It's a Wonderful Life*.

The Life, Loves and Adventures of Omar Khayyam:

Another mid-1950's Paramount production that Henry had a bit part in was *The Life, Loves and Adventures of Omar Khayyam* with an all-star cast including Cornel Wilde (as Omar), Debra Paget, Michael Rennie, Raymond Massey and cult favorite Yma Sumac.

Fanciful and old-fashioned, *Omar Khayyam* takes place a thousand years ago in the ancient Persian Empire. Khayyam is a poet, a mathematician and a student of the stars. He secures a place in the Shah's palace as an astronomer working on a new calendar and this is where we first see Henry Brandon, who plays "Commander of the Guards."

Brandon is bearded and wears purple robes studded with big brass buttons and a metal helmet that sports a sharp spire wrapped in a white turban. He hovers in the background of scenes throughout the film, now and then spouting pronouncements such as "All guards are alerted!" and listening and watching and looking very interested in the happenings of the Court.

Because he is part of the Shah's (Raymond Massey) inner-circle of advisors, Brandon worked throughout the production of the picture without contributing much to the proceedings. His character didn't even have a name and, as such, isn't much of a character. The Commander's best line, about the arrival of the Shah's son, is "He will come through the South Gate tomorrow night!" Not very compelling, and Henry must have been bored silly spending weeks wrapped in his turban and marking time to the next, hopefully meatier, role. For every *Bandido* or *Omar Khayyam*, there was thankfully a *Land Unknown* or an *Okefenokee* to balance the acting scales.

The Buccaneer:

The Ten Commandments isn't the only epic Cecil B. DeMille production that Henry Brandon had a bit part in. *The Buccaneer* is another DeMille remake of an earlier production that he was slated to direct following *Commandments*, but DeMille got sick and brought in his son-in-law Anthony Quinn (yes, *that* Anthony Quinn) to direct while DeMille handled the role of Executive Producer.

The Buccaneer is not a swashbuckling *Sea Hawk* adventure, but a tale of the War of 1812 as filtered through Cecil B. DeMille's cheese cloth. It's wildly entertaining, old-fashioned movie storytelling. DeMille brought back Charlton Heston, who is terrific as war-weary General Andrew Jackson, stealing every scene he is in, along with Yul Brynner as the infamous pirate Jean Lafitte. When these tinsel town titans share the screen, sparks fly.

Not so much for Henry Brandon, who plays 'British Major' and shows up almost ninety minutes into the proceedings. His three or four camera shots all depict him on horseback and it's easy to surmise that the reason he landed the minor job was because of his extensive experience riding and controlling horses on camera. He doesn't say anything and when the battle begins, it is his stunt double who falls from the horse.

Lafitte's pirates join forces with Jackson's civilians and Kentucky rebels, along with their flints and gun powder to win the day. Their long-range rifles cut the British forces – including British Major Henry Brandon – to ribbons.

This fun 1958 slice of American history was DeMille's final film. He died shortly after its release. While Brandon fans are sure to be disappointed, it is well worth enjoying *The Buccaneer* to bask in the banter of Heston's General Jackson with just about everybody he talks to.

Auntie Mame:

This landmark film debuted in 1958 after a two-year run on Broadway. It was based on a novel with the central character played by Rosalind Russell, repeating her role from the stage.

Shot in Technicolor and projected to the screen in "Technirama," all the intense theatrical colors of the sets, costumes and personality of Russell's Auntie Mame is brought vividly to life. She is a diva, a talkative, eclectic social hurricane capped off by her exotic long-tipped cigarette holder.

Auntie Mame presides in her luxurious penthouse over Park Avenue in New York. She is rich but generous and lives life to the fullest; "Life is a banquet." Her evenings are filled with people of the theater crowd, with music, poetry and a bottomless champagne glass. Her favorite beau is Henry Brandon's character, named "Acacious Page." He is a beatnik bohemian who transcended Greenwich Village culture to that of extremely high modern art form.

This film was shot to make it look like a stage play and for that it succeeds all too well. Despite venturing to all corners of the earth, all the "location scenes" were shot at Stage 11 of the Warner Bros. Studio in Hollywood.

One really has to suspend disbelief taking in this film; the opening of the party takes place in 1928. The film continues in chapter-like sequences over the years and the period clothes help to define the era.

The plot has to do with a ten-year old nephew being delivered to his Auntie Mame. His father has just died and it is specified in the will that his sister will become the boy's guardian. Naturally, this is a big surprise to the aunt especially when the nephew is received right in the middle of a party. Her first thought is to offer him a martini.

The maternal instincts kick in but the aunt's objective is to raise the child in free expression. As she escorts her nephew around the party, he is introduced to a number of exotic people. One of them is Henry's Acacious Page, who is in mid-sentence while reciting poetry. Auntie Mame informs the boy that Mr. Page is an educator; she wastes no time in asking if her nephew could go to his school. Acacious answers, "For him, yes! In this boy I see a head of fire, dirt and air." The nephew asks if they wear uniforms at his school. The response: "At my school we wear no clothes." Unfazed Auntie M. responds; "It'll be good for his libido."

Encouraged to take notes on words the boy doesn't understand, he finally gets to ask his aunt the meaning of: libido, inferiority complex, stink, blotto, free love, bathtub gin, monkey glands and even Karl Marx." It was *that* kind of a party, and the film has only just begun.

To counter Auntie Mame's carefree liberated character, the Trustee of the boy's father (played by Fred Clark) tries to monitor his progress; he wants the boy enrolled into a "God-fearing Christian institute." Auntie Mame's bold philosophies contradict the uptight trustee at every turn.

Baldheaded Clark plays it like Edgar Kennedy might have; always burning at the indignation put upon him.

The rest of the movie graduates from set to exotic locations around the world, where Auntie Mame knows all the most important people. Forrest Tucker is a Southern gentleman who invites her down to his estate. Auntie Mame is out of her element with the clan to say the least.

Back at home the nephew is now grown up with his own pursuits in life. A colorful figure is Peggy Cass in a wonderful role as an unwed mother, further pushing the envelope of controversy for a 1958 film.

Henry Brandon's Acacious Page shows up during the ending scenes in Mame's penthouse. He is most welcome there. The film does not go into detail but in the original novel, there is an illustration on the front cover of Acacious and Mame sharing a bed.

Henry's *West Bound Limited* (1937) co-star Polly Rowles had an important connection to *Auntie Mame*, as he explained in a written caption on the back of a scene still from the B-Movie to collector Richard Finegan:

> Polly Rowles later created the role of the actress Vera Charles in the Broadway production of *Auntie Mame*. Polly, being a native of Pittsburgh, was able to lapse from beautifully exaggerated stage diction into a drunken mid-Western (drawl.) This, Coral Browne, excellent English actress that she is, was not able to attempt in the film. You may remember that I played Acacious Page, the Greenwich Village schoolmaster (nude classes for the kiddies) in the Warner Bros production.

Henry's flamboyant portrayal of Page, as one of Mame's outrageous entourage, was a unique and offbeat character role that added a striking contrast to his cinematic repertoire of rogues.

Henry recalled for author Richard Tyler Jordan:

It wasn't an enormous role, but I was dying to be in the movie so I accepted the part." Brandon recalled Director Decosta simply said, "I want a performance, this character is sort of a pompous ass." Brandon replied, "Great, I'm basing him on a ham actor who used to hang around Sardi's bar. I used to see this guy pontificating all the time with very elegant speech, which I think was covering up a Bronx accent. So that's who I was doing in the film."*

The Big Fisherman:

In the wake of Biblical epics like *The Ten Commandments, The Robe* and *Ben Hur* comes 1959's *The Big Fisherman*, a religious picture released in a 70mm road show edition, but nowhere near the success of its gargantuan predecessors. As the opening title sets the stage, *The Big Fisherman* takes place in Arabia during the memorable years of the First Century AD. It is the story of Jesus Christ (never referred to by name) and his disciples just about up to the time of crucifixion.

Indeed, it plays like an overlong Technicolor prequel to one of Henry Brandon's very first television gigs, "Hill Number One" on *Family Theatre* in 1951, which was the story of the Easter resurrection. There Henry played Cassius Longinus (see the 'Television' chapter for full analysis) in a startling role that is one of the most significant of his career. In *The Big Fisherman*, he is also a Roman career soldier, Pro Council Menicus, but he undergoes no character arc as moving as the one he played on television eight years earlier.

We first see Menicus leaving a pub and attacked by three peasants. He is holding his own, but would soon be overpowered... and killed... by the three assassins until a stranger joins in the fight. That stranger is Prince Voldi (John Saxon), on a mission following his beloved Princess Fara (Susan

---

* "But Darling, I'm Your Auntie Mame! The Amazing History of the World's Favorite Macap Aunt" by Richard Tyler Jordan Capra Press 1998

Kohner), both pledged by blood oath to kill Herod (Herbert Lom, a few years before *his* blood oath to kill Inspector Clouseau!) Vowing to help his new friend, he brags, "I have eyes and ears in every part of Judea!" but repays Voldi's assistance by putting him under arrest! Menicus correctly guesses Voldi's mission to kill Herod.

Henry is fully decked out in First Century Roman armor, looking and acting regal and imperious. As the familiar story of Simon Peter and John the Baptist plays out, Menicus has several scenes pursuing and arresting insurgents. He is fooled, however, by Princess Fara, now as Esther and working in Herod's household. Herod's evil ways are his undoing, and although Fara never completes her mission of vengeance, Menicus arrives in his final scene with a scroll documenting Herod's evidence of misrule and takes him into custody to escort him to Jerusalem. The long narrative ends with the lovers being unable to remain together, as each has his and her own mission to fulfill as the events of the crucifixion loom.

Brandon is splendid in *The Big Fisherman*, adding an air of Roman superiority to the proceedings, but it is a minor addition to his filmography.

CHAPTER TWELVE
"B" Pictures

The Preview Murder Mystery:
After *Babes in Toyland* and *Trail Of The Lonesome Pine*, Henry's third feature film role was an unbilled cameo – and a very funny one - as the mysterious Bat Man in the 1936 Paramount murder chiller *The Preview Murder Mystery*. The film stars Frances Drake and Reginald Denny with Henry playing a sensitive horror film star who is afraid of his own shadow!

The movie takes place almost entirely on the sound stages, back lot and offices of World Attractions, Inc. as a series of murders threatens the very studio itself. While the police and studio publicity agent Denny work to unveil the identity of the murderer, productions continue on the various stages. They listen in on one production – a horror film starring The Bat Man (Henry Brandon).

The camera zooms in on a ghoulish-looking fiend with a pale white face and dead blackened eyes. The angled background is a slanting stylistic nod to *The Cabinet of Dr. Caligari*. Entering to his left is a gruesome gnome made up similarly and startling the actor. Suddenly, Henry's character calls a halt to filming, frustrating the director.

"I'm nervous... I'm afraid!" bemoans Henry, to which the director exclaims, "You... the Bat Man... Afraid! In pictures you scare kids until they can't sleep at night and in real life you're afraid of a shadow!"

Ashamed, The Bat Man explains in a whiny voice, "You don't understand! Certain things make me ill! That's why I'm a vegetarian – I can't eat meat! And with all these murders going on around here…"

As The Bat Man in a brief but hilarious role in *Preview Murder Mystery*. Collection of Rick Greene.

The director gives up and dismisses the company and this self-contained little sequence ends Henry Brandon's role in *The Preview Murder Mystery*. However, he's very funny as the cowardly Bela Lugosi-type actor and makes this snappy thriller worth seeking out.

Killer At Large:

This fast-paced 1936 Columbia chiller is a study in frustration as the brilliant set-up gives us a Henry Brandon performance like we've *never* seen before as the strange serial killer Mr. Zero – then the screenplay gets lazy for a rushed finale that turns this master criminal into a stupid thug. Mr. Zero is *almost* a classic Henry Brandon villain and *Killer At Large* almost one of his Top Twelve films, but not quite.

The story begins at Whitley's Department Store, where Tommy Braddock (Russell Hardie) works in the jewelry department and Linda Allen (Mary Brian) has been promoted to a store detective. Also working there is the bizarre Mr. Zero, who stages store window displays with his wax mannequins with the signage:

CAN YOU GUESS WHICH IS MR. ZERO?

and

CAN HOLD A POSE LONGER THAN ANYONE IN THE WORLD

The current tableau has the crew of a ship and pedestrians gather in dozens to peer into the window and guess which one is Mr. Zero, positive that this one moved or that one blinked. After a few minutes of this offbeat set-up, the drapes close and Mr. Zero (Henry Brandon) is revealed to the camera. He has thick messy black hair, a pale complexion and a strange drooping right eye.

A porter unwisely enters by a side door to clean and Mr. Zero rasps in a startling throaty voice, "I left orders for NO ONE to come in here. Close that door and don't open it again." The porter is shaken and leaves quickly, muttering, "T'aint natural"

That night, the store manager Mr. Bentley is murdered and the safe robbed of all the jewels in its inventory. As a decoy, Mr. Zero hires a pretty blonde to ask to see some expensive necklaces, giving him the opportunity to stage this clever robbery. But she can't resist stealing a gold compact and is caught by Linda Allen. She bluffs her way out of this dilemma without the store pressing charges, but then finds her problems are much more serious.

When she meets up with Mr. Zero at his secret wax works headquarters, she asks for her cut of the job. Brandon, his hair wildly askew, his dark eyes narrowed into cruel slits, tells her, "Suppose I told you that you weren't just mixed up with a burglary. What if I told you there was a murder committed in that store tonight?"

Distressed, she replies, "That's something I didn't bargain for. Give me my cut, I'm getting out of here!" Mr. Zero confides, "No. You're not, you're staying… permanently!" Henry Brandon delivers these cliché ridden lines with such an eerie tone and stilted speech pattern that they deliver quite a chilling jolt. As he approaches the blonde to murder her, he lets loose with a horrifying giggle-laugh that would have done The Joker proud. One wonders if this performance helped to inspire the creation of The Joker.

Even though Mr. Zero comes relatively early in Brandon's film career, he had never portrayed such an unhinged killer before. Twelve minutes in to *Killer At Large*, it is clear that Mr. Zero is a uniquely terrifying role in the Brandon Rogues Gallery. Then, sadly, it all falls apart.

Linda and Tommy decide to play amateur detective since the police think Tommy may have stolen the jewels. They figure out how Mr. Zero got the combination to the store safe and track him back to his Wax Works from the store employment records. That night they break into the back mannequin warehouse while Mr. Zero inventories all of the jewels he stole up front. After a "slapsticky" sequence with wax figures of gangsters, knights and a mummy, Mr. Zero realizes there are intruders in his warehouse just as two workmen arrive to take away a coffin-shaped box. One of these men is Lon Chaney Jr. in one of his first small screen roles. Brandon and Chaney, who became lifelong friends, would work together again the following year in *Secret Agent X-9* and again years later in *Raiders of the Seven Seas*.

Henry Brandon wrote to fan Richard Finegan about *Killer At Large*, "Chaney was the 'second man through the door' to my lead heavy in this little epic and later in the serial *Secret Agent X-9*. This was before his big break in *Of Mice and Men* which was the beginning of his career as a star of horror flicks."

Mr. Zero (Brandon) with his henchmen including Lon Chaney Jr. in *Killer At Large*. Collection of Richard Finegan.

As the two men drive off with the crate, Linda notices that their truck says WESTERN CEMETERY on the side. Before Mr. Zero can take care of his unwanted guests, the police arrive in force. The clever criminal takes the place of one of the wax monks in a display. While Mary explains to the police how she discovered Mr. Zero's robbery plans, he overhears everything she says and plots his revenge. They all race off to the Western Cemetery in pursuit of the men with the coffin.

The mob of detectives and policemen apprehend the two men, who are burying the coffin at the cemetery after midnight in broad daylight. Inside the box is the body of the blonde shoplifter and the stolen jewels. And it is at this point that *Killer At Large* falls apart with a lapse in logic when Mr. Zero does something incredibly stupid. As he watches hidden in the bushes as his men are arrested, his coffin dug up and his second murder victim revealed, *he pulls out a revolver and takes a pot shot at Tommy*, grazing his arm in front of a dozen police officers. Then he vaults over the cemetery wall and into his car, followed by the dozen police officers.

Wait, what? This master criminal, this cunning, creepy monster of wax and shadows with his messy hair and his twitchy eye, loses his temper and reveals himself to a squadron of the law? It is here that the marvelously built up threat of Mr. Zero devolves to just that… zero. A common, stupid, hot-headed thug. It's an epic screenplay fail that torpedoes the film.

Somehow he escapes leading to the headline **KILLER AT LARGE** and the final fifteen minutes of *Killer At Large* concern Mr. Zero's attempts to bump off Linda and Tommy – instead of, say, disappear and plan a new wave of terror and murder? He returns to Whitley's Department Store in a false beard to spy on the young lovers with his one good eye. One attempt to hit them on the heads with a flower pot from an apartment window fails (what has *happened* to this screenplay!) so the next day Mr. Zero knocks out the driver of their taxi cab and has them in his clutches. Tommy grapples with Mr. Zero as they drive through the city. The criminal leaps out of the taxi and onto another car, allowing the hack to crash-- but the kids are unharmed.

The next day's headline reads **MR. ZERO STRIKES AGAIN** when it should read **MR. ZERO CRASHES A TAXI CAB**. Tommy and Linda are tired of these shenanigans and use themselves as bait to catch Mr. Zero. A trap is set, he easily falls for it, is machine-gunned to death by a cop and the movie quickly ends in a rushed and disappointing finale.

A good review for *Killer At Large* appeared in an October 1936 issue of *The Film Daily*, stating that Mr. Zero is "played spine-chillingly by Henry Brandon, one of those maniac killers that makes things distinctly warm for organized law before the net is closed. It is fairly entertaining cinema fare for average fans who like a dash of the Frankenstein sort of thing in their cinema diets."

Killer At Large was shot over two and a half weeks in August of 1936 and released just before Halloween. The running time is less than fifty-five minutes. The first half of those fifty-four and a half minutes contain a masterful build-up of one of the most disturbing killers Henry Brandon would *ever* portray – and he is **superb**. However, the screenplay takes a left turn into stupid thugdom and Mr. Zero is robbed of his quirky brilliance. It is a cinematic tragedy.

Black Legion:

This is first film in which Humphrey Bogart got top billing, a full four years before his star-making turn in *The Maltese Falcon*. Henry Brandon plays a significant supporting part in the first half of this brisk 83-minute Warner Brothers social shocker.

This tough Ku-Klux-Klan allegory story is one that ONLY Warner Bros. could have made! As startling as their *Public Enemy* or *I Am a Fugitive from a Chain Gang*, this is the story of the "Black Legion," a secret society of prejudiced white supremacists who use fear, intimidation and violence to force foreign "undesirables" from their town.

Bogie is Frank Taylor and Brandon is Joe Dombrowski, blue collar coworkers in a machine plant in Everytown, USA. The shop foreman is promoted to upper management, which means a new foreman will be needed. Popular Frank Taylor is thought to be the shoo-in for the job, but Henry's Dombrowski is studious and hard-working, coming up with better methods to insure productivity. He always has his head in a journal while the other guys chew the fat and brag about women.

When Taylor is predictably passed over for the promotion, his dreams of a new car and other luxuries are crushed. Joe, whom Frank feels has been "sucking up to the Boss" gets the job based on skill and dedication, his collar shifting from blue to white. The seeds of conflict are further sown when Frank hears a radio broadcast from the Black Legion lamenting about how foreigners are stealing jobs from 100% American workers with the rallying rant of "America for Americans!"

Humphrey Bogart and Henry Brandon in *Black Legion*. Collection of Rick Brandon.

Taylor's resentment for Dombrowski affects his job performance, although it's a bit hard to take him seriously wearing that Jughead hat right out of Archie Comics. Joe tells Frank he's making too many dumb mistakes, that he's better than that and should pay attention to his job. Another slimy co-worker senses a possible Black Legion recruit and says, "I see that greaseball's been picking on you too!" He invites Bogie to a secret basement Legion meeting with thirty or forty like-minded prejudiced 'Americans.' Frank is swept up into the insanity, fueled by hate and jealousy.

The Black Legion vows to purge the land of these foreigners like Joe Dombrowski, wearing black robes and black hoods with a white skull and crossbones design on the front. At gunpoint, Frank Taylor takes the sacred oath to God and the Devil, pledging allegiance to The Black Legion. Stern stuff!

Taylor's first assignment is to attack Joe Dombrowski and his elderly father at night, beating them and burning down their farm house egg business, then taking them away, bound and gagged. As their every worldly possession burns to the ground, the duo are forced to board a freight train out of town and are warned never to return! Later Bogie and his cronies laugh and drink beers, celebrating the success of their violent scare tactics. Dombrowski does not return and Frank Taylor gets his job.

Next the marauders indulge in further violence, vandalism, floggings and beatings until it spirals out of control. Frank commits a cold-blooded murder, killing his best friend Ed Jackson (Dick Foran) which leads to a sensational trial and the ultimate crushing of the evil Black Legion.

Black Legion is a glimpse into "what might-have-been" if Henry Brandon had NEVER played Silas Barnaby, The Cobra and Wade Falin and only landed traditional supporting-player roles. He's very good in the part, creating immense sympathy as dedicated Joe Dombrowski. But a career of "Joe Dombrowski's" would have assured Henry's place in cinema obscurity. His teeth-gnashing, scenery-chewing bad guy roles, thankfully, have proven otherwise!

I Promise To Pay:

Henry plays "Fancyface," a slick henchman for gangsters running a loan shark racket in the entertaining and fast-moving *I Promise to Pay*. Released by Columbia in 1937, the picture stars Chester Morris (just a few years from playing Boston Blackie) and Helen Mack as Eddie and Mary Lang, Leo Carrillo as the Big Boss Richard Fara and Marc Lawrence as Henry's fellow henchman "White Hat."

Eddie Lang is a low-wage bookkeeper at a firm that has annual bonuses coming up soon. He is targeted by a shill who steers mugs into the waiting arms of the loan racket so they can be plucked like pigeons. Eddie borrows fifty dollars to take his family on a week's vacation not realizing that the firm's bonuses have been cancelled. He can only pay a few dollars a week instead of the agreed upon ten – which all goes to interest anyway. As the Boss tells sidekick Fancyface, "Not one sucker in ten pays the loan off" and they end up paying ten dollars per week *permanently*.

When Lang only pays two dollars the next week, they grab his pay envelope and take out the other eight. The following week, when he refuses to pay more than two, Fancyface and White Hat pick up Lang and take him for a ride. Fancyface tells him, "Now listen, Lang, we're only asking for what you signed the note to pay!" He pulls out the signed agreement which now has added verbiage about outrageous interest payments. When Lang balks, they threaten him, and then his children! Then they reveal that, also in the car, is one of Lang's co-workers and loan victims… unconscious and beaten bloody!

Eddie Lang is in a tough spot. He steals ten bucks from the office petty cash, argues with his wife and his work begins to suffer. When he is guilt ridden from stealing those ten bucks, he returns it and confesses – and loses his job.

To contrast Lang's hard times, Farra's floozie sees a new car on the street that she thinks is "cute", so the Big Boss has Fancyface steer the owner over and he buys the car on the spot, right on the street, in cash! Then Farra *gives* the old car to an astonished Fancyface.

The Lang family moves to a different city to escape the gangsters, but they track them down. Fancyface and White Hat find Eddie laying pipe at a new job and beat the tar out of him. Lang remains unconscious in a ditch until a night watchman finds him and has an ambulance bring him to the hospital.

District Attorney Curtis (the great Thomas Mitchell) easily convinces Lang to testify against the racketeers and together they build their case. Ten members of the gang are arrested, but not Fancyface. When Farra begins to feel the heat, he drills Fancyface about what he did to Lang. Henry admits he "took a poke at him" which spooks the Boss, calling his torpedo a "thick-skulled stupid lug!" He explains to Fancyface that he is guilty of kidnapping and assault. Escalating the situation, he sends White Hat to kidnap the Lang children, but the criminal is caught in the act and jailed. Then he and Fancyface head out to take care of Lang before he can testify. As Eddie arrives for the hearing, Fancyface guns him down with two bullets in the back right on the stairway at the Hall Of Justice in front of dozens of witnesses.

Racing away, a nervous Fancyface hits a truck and both men are caught.

Believing Lang dead and the electric chair waiting, Fancyface squeals on Farra like a little girl. The loan shark ring is smashed!

If this was a Warner Brothers film; Lang would have perished, his death the motivator for the other victims to step up and testify; but this is a Columbia Picture, which means Eddie Lang is fine and there are happy endings for all. All except Fancyface, who shot a man in the back and won't ever see another day of freedom.

Chester Morris is great as Eddie Lang and Henry Brandon provides solid sinister support in this exciting crime drama, making *I Promise to Pay* a must see for buffs.

Island Captives:

One of Henry's earliest appearances in what would be considered a 'B' picture was for Poverty Row studio Falcon Films. Part murder thriller, part shipwreck survival epic, *Island Captives* from 1936 is short, stiff and padded.

Brandon gets third billing as Dick Bannister, the son of the head of the International Cannery Company, a firm looking to add the fruit plantation of Mr. Carsons to its holdings. The movie opens with a long montage of idyllic shots of South Seas paradise – lots of them. Indeed, it is nearly four minutes into this short 53 minute film before anyone says anything.

A radiogram arrives from Mr. Bannister, Dick's father, threatening Mr. Carsons, "THIS IS YOUR LAST CHANCE. JOIN US OR FIGHT = BANNISTER." Son Dick (and he turns out to be just that) volunteers to take the steamship Caroline to Tahiti and convince Carsons' daughter Helen to sell out. Meanwhile, Bannister's lawyer Hudson has a henchman murder Carsons with a shotgun blast in the back!

Dick Bannister stiffly romances Miss Carsons (Joan Barclay) on board the Caroline heading to Tahiti. Henry is young and gangly here, still learning his screen camera craft. She gently rebuffs his advances as she's interested in the ship's radio operator Tom Willoughby (Eddie Nugent.) Brandon reverts to type when he tries to bribe Tom to lose copies of some incriminating radiograms, then threatens him. But before they come to blows, the ship hits a reef and starts to sink! Another long 'ship sinking' montage follows to pad out the running time, followed by yet another idyllic South Seas montage, making it clear that the slim plot isn't enough to fill an hour, even with padding.

A lifeboat with five survivors from the Caroline arrives, including Tom, Helen and Dick. A grubby brute named Kelly runs this small island and he informs the Caroline crew that it will be two months before a supply ship arrives and there is no working radio available. The port town is comprised of people hiding from the law and local natives. Halfway in to *Island Captives*, the slender plot takes a left turn from a murder story about fruit plantation control to a shipwreck survival drama.

The first night, evil Kelly arrives at Helen's hut to have his wicked way with her, but Tom arrives to beat him senseless and stand guard. The next morning, young Bannister insinuates that Tom was less than a gentleman and the two clash. Tom insists that all five of them must stick together against the dangerous Kelly and his men. Kelly sends four thugs to take care of Tom and Dick so he can snatch Helen.

They all outmaneuver Kelly and take refuge in a cave, but Henry's character shows his true despicable nature by betraying his companions and revealing to Kelly where they are hiding. The double-cross doesn't pay off as Tom has a climactic battle with Kelly and Dick Bannister, soundly beating them both as the Coast Guard arrives to save them.

Bannister is hauled off to jail with Kelly's crew and Tom and Helen get married as the film ends with a third South Seas montage and clocks in at just under 53 minutes. Brandon is much more comfortable during the second half of the narrative when Dick Bannister reverts to type as a slimeball in this minor entry in his filmography.

West Bound Limited:

This low-budget 1937 Universal drama is the story of a railroad man, an attempted robbery and a spectacular train crash that destroys his life. It stars Lyle Talbot, Polly Rowles, Frank Reicher and 4th billed heavy Henry Brandon as a sleazy small-town telegraph operator named Joe Forbes.

During the stormy night a train is roaring westward, stopping at Hargrave to offload the cash payroll for a local mine and a coffin. Dave Tolliver (Lyle Talbot) is the station master and telegraph operator. As the fury of the storm mounts and two trains are speeding toward one another on opposite tracks, the coffin lid opens and a shadowy man disguised in a black raincoat and black hat rises out intent on robbing that payroll. Using a gun, he forces Dave to turn over the briefcase with the cash, but they are soon involved in an exciting fist fight. They slam against the switches, altering the train route.

With the struggle, Dave notices his assailant has an unusual tattoo on his forearm – a snake wrapped around a sword. Dave is knocked down, the robber flees, but the station master gives chase, leaving his post. They exchange gunfire in the darkness of the woods, and Dave sees he hits the man in the shoulder, causing him to drop the case but he gets away. Sadly, Dave isn't able to get back to the station in time to prevent a massive head-on collision between two engines. Headlines scream:

27 DIE IN RR CRASH – WORST WRECK IN G.R.&N. HISTORY!
DAVE TOLLIVER ON TRIAL FOR CRIMINAL NEGLICENCE

Disbelieving his story about an attempted robbery and a tattooed man, the jury finds Dave Tolliver guilty of manslaughter. As they drag him from court, he has quite the emotional outburst, screaming over and over, "You can't send an innocent man to prison…You can't send an innocent man to prison!"

Dave is sentenced to five years in jail but escapes by leaping off of the train bound for the pen. He eludes the posse and lives a life on the lam, moving from town to town, working menial jobs. Dave ends up in another small town, meeting old Pop Martin (Frank Reicher) and his pretty daughter Janet (Polly Rowles). Pop runs the local train station and their boarder, Joe Forbes (Henry Brandon) takes the night shift.

With Polly Rowles in *West Bound Limited*. Collection of Richard Finegan.

Henry's first appearance sets the tone for his nasty little coward's character. He arrives back from a shift, wanting breakfast and is alone in the kitchen with Janet. They argue about his recent "proposal" which she declined. He has evidently been pretty fresh about it and keeps pressing the matter, putting his hands on her arms and shoulders. Finally, Janet slaps his face, hard! "I've taken about all the high-hat from you that I'm going to!" Joe threatens her menacingly… and there is a knock at the door. Tolliver, now going under the name of Bob Kirk, asks for some work in exchange for a meal. Janet's demeanor immediately changes and we see this is a compassionate woman, who agrees to feed Bob and give him some odd jobs. Joe turns away in disgust at the 'hobo' and she throws Joe out, bags packed. Greasy Joe refuses to leave and 'Bob' steps in, saying, "I think you better leave… NOW!"

Joe's yellow streak causes him to back down and leave. In conversation with Bob, Janet reveals that Pop spent over a year in the hospital a few years ago. He was injured in the train wreck that Bob/Dave was blamed for. Meanwhile, up in the train office, Pop collapses at the switches, the victim of a heart attack. Bob pitches in, knowing how to telegraph, and covers for the kindly old character. He decides to stay and repay Janet's kindness by covering for Pop while he recovers so he won't lose his job, his pension and his home. He even convinces Joe Forbes to go along with the ploy, saying it would ruin his chances with Janet if he doesn't.

Grappling with Lyle Talbot in *West Bound Limited*. Collection of Richard Finegan.

A month passes, and the railroad men constantly needle Joe about losing Janet to the "hobo" – which causes nasty Forbes to try to blackmail Janet into marrying him or he'll reveal that Pop was sick and they'll lose everything. Pop overhears and pulls a rifle on Joe, and that yellow streak pops up again! He backs off, believing that Janet is now engaged to Bob, as the two have fallen in love.

Through a chance meeting, Joe discovers that Bob is in fact the missing fugitive Dave Tolliver and he tips off the local sheriff, who heads down on the next train to arrest him. The climax is a mirror of the opening scenes, with a dark rainstorm, two trains headed toward each and a fight scene between Bob and Joe, who attempts to hold him at gunpoint for the sheriff but is easily knocked off balance. The furious fist fight ends up with Bob breaking Joe's arm, remaining to fix the switch that saves the trains (and the sheriff's life) at the cost of his arrest. However, as Pop fixes Joe's broken arm, the dragon tattoo is revealed! Joe Forbes was the man who attempted to rob the station house for the payroll four years ago! The bullet scar on his shoulder proves it! Cue the happy ending as the sheriff hauls Henry Brandon's Joe Forbes away to meet justice.

Decades later, Henry Brandon met with historian Richard Finegan in June of 1979 to sign scene stills from a variety of his B-Pictures and serials including several from *West Bound Limited*. On the backs of these pictures, Henry added extensive notations about his *West Bound* co-stars that offer great insight and humorous anecdotes:

> During the location filming in Santa Cruz, California, Polly Rowles was the only girl on the set. She was treated like the virgin queen by all and sundry. Every night, we all lit out for the local bars and bordellos, leaving her behind in the hotel. Apparently, she had her fill of this, because one day during shooting I was wandering around without my suit coat. Now, I have very long legs and a short torso. Polly waited for a break in the usual din and called out in good round tone, "Henry, has your asshole always been that far from the ground?" Well, the whole set collapsed. From then on, she was one of the gang.

Henry also wrote of a scene featuring Lyle Talbot in the same film:

> I believe it was 1937 – I went to New York to look for a play. On my first night I wandered down 45th Street looking for a

familiar face. I peered down into a little bar and, sure enough, there was Lyle Talbot holding up the bar. He was feeling no pain and greeted me like a long lost benefactor. (He) told me that our movie *West Bound Limited* had played SIX MONTHS on Broadway! The joke was that our "good" movie had actually CLOSED the theatre six months earlier! I went by the next day and there it still was on the marquee – *West Bound Limited!*

West Bound Limited is a quick-moving, plot-packed little charmer with young Henry Brandon at his oozing, sneering cowardly nastiest! For Brandon fans, it is essential viewing.

The Last Warning:

Universal produced a series of "Crime Club Productions" during the late 1930's and 1939's *The Last Warning* is the third of three starring Preston Foster and Frank Jenks as wisecracking, hard-drinking detectives Bill Crane and Doc Williams. Its standard "B" mystery fare, fun but forgettable and features Henry Brandon in an unbilled bit part as "Willie the Creep."

Bill and Doc have been hired by millionaire John Essex to protect him and his sister from The Eye, a mysterious criminal who sends threatening notes and takes pot shots at him. After his sister is kidnapped, the duo visits likely suspect fortune-hunter Paul Gomez at his apartment.

This is where we briefly see Willie the Creep, who answers the door and has riveting dialogue like "What do you want?" and "There is no one here by that name." He delivers it, however, in a Russian accent. When Willie realizes these are detectives, he bolts from the apartment like a frightened rabbit, returning only as they are leaving. Realizing his pal Gomez is unharmed, he actually gets a line with a laugh, saying, "Too bad, Paul, I expected to find you dead. What a hero you would have been!"

Pirates of the Skies:

After finishing *The Last Warning*, Henry continued to report to Universal City to work on *Pirates of The Skies*, a crime drama starring Kent Taylor and *Poppy* herself, Rochelle Hudson. Henry plays Jake Austin, the pilot for a clever criminal organization run by Lucien Littlefield.

Littlefield plays Dr. Amos Pettingill, a benign and charming old man who runs a Rest Home as a cover for his gang's activities. We first meet Brandon's Jake Austin, seemingly a patient on the porch of the Home, who complains that their afternoon beverage doesn't have any scotch in it! A homing pigeon arrives with a message from their spy on the inside of the air patrol and Jake remarks, "Looks like a visitor, Doc!" Pettingill reads the messages and tells his thugs, "Gentlemen, our vacation is over!" which leads to their next job – robbing the Owens National Bank. The robbery goes smoothly as the crooks change from one car to another, and then they board Jake's getaway plane.

The Pirates of the Skies attack Kent Taylor. Collection of Richard Finegan.

The gang embarks on quite the crime spree with a successful wave of robberies over several months, knocking over banks and stealing diamonds, all the while eluding the authorities. During one job, they kill a bank guard.

Nick Conlan is an irresponsible pilot who doesn't follow the rules. He lands a job with the Air Patrol and he finally spies Jake and the gang on a getaway in the air, but they are too fast and he loses them. As a result, his fuel line is dislodged and he has engine trouble – right in the area of Pettingill's Rest Home! Jake and the Doc watch the plane coming down, worried about discovery. But Jake tells him that the trouble "looks legitimate, Doctor. Relax!"

Nick lands in the same field that the gang has been using, their plane hidden in a false haystack. Pettingill and Jake greet him, with Henry introduced by "This is my nephew, Jacob Austin." The Doc tells Nick that this is "a convalescent home for tired businessmen" as the gang quickly don blankets and take their places on the restful front porch, guns under the blankets!

Nick sees some fuel containers which arouse his suspicions, while Jake has his fingers on the trigger of his gun behind him in a suspenseful sequence. He leaves unmolested but thoughtful, planning to return to the Rest Home at his earliest convenience. When he reveals his suspicions to the Air Patrol, they aren't interested and fire him for disobeying orders. But their man on the inside sends a homing pigeon (of alarm) back to the Home and he's caught by Nick's estranged wife Barbara (Rochelle Hudson). The heat is on, Barbara is taken as a hostage and Jake readies the plane for a getaway.

Nick steals a new, fast plane when he hears about his wife's disappearance and zooms out toward the Rest Home. The climax is pretty exciting stuff, with gentle Lucien Littlefield smashing out the window of their plane and shooting down an Air Patrol pursuer... then taking aim at Nick! But the faster plane forces Jake's down, back at the Rest Home air field, into the waiting arms of the law. They are all arrested without much fuss as Nick reunites with Barbara for the typical Universal happy ending.

Even though Henry Brandon appears throughout much of *Pirates of the Skies*, the part of air pirate pilot Jake Austin is as bland as they get and

Brandon doesn't have much to work with. The result is a role that blends in with the rest of the gang and offers no opportunity to shine. *Pirates of the Skies* is an exciting little caper movie, but not terribly interesting for fans of Henry Brandon.

Conspiracy:

Released in August of 1939, RKO's *Conspiracy* is a taut war thriller about an American on the run in an unnamed European country that begins with a bang. That bang is Henry Brandon!

This is one of those movies that Brandon doesn't make it out of the first five minutes alive, but what a five minutes! On a freighter approaching port during a dense fog, Captain Steve Kendall (Allan Lane) discovers a member of his engine room crew, Mr. Carlson (Henry Brandon), in the radio room sending an unauthorized message. Carlson tries to bluff his way out of the situation by speaking in halting English, but Kendall isn't buying it. The grease-smudged Carlson is forced to pull a gun on his Captain and has him complete and send the radio message. The recipient we see at the other end is none other than Dwight Frye (*Dracula, Frankenstein*) who transmits a code back. During this response, we see a hand ease through the cabin door with a gun, which both Carlson and Kendall see in a mirror, and both start firing at each other!

Carlson dashed onto the deck and dives overboard into the frigid water. Second Mate Wilson begins firing at the swimming figure, but misses... until someone turns on a spotlight, making the fleeing spy an easy target. Carlson is drilled with several bullets and sinks into the ocean, dead as a mackerel.

This exciting opening sets the stage for a tense spy thriller in which we learn that Brandon's Carlson was a member of that country's underground – fighting for freedom. *Conspiracy* tells the rest of its story focused on the "Hitchcockian" adventures of Kendall and Nedra Carlson (Linda Hayes), who is Carlson's sister. Henry Brandon dutifully kicks this B-effort into high gear with a slam-bang sequence worth seeing.

Ski Patrol:

Universal Studios produced this mildly entertaining 1940 war picture with cardboard thin characters including an underdeveloped role for Henry Brandon. *Ski Patrol* begins at the 1936 Winter Olympics in the Tyrol as we meet a trio of Gold Medal recipients who will figure into the derring-do after the war in Europe breaks out a few years later. Henry plays Jan Sikorsky, a man who joins a group of skiers in a snowy mountain bunker that blocks the path of the Germans from entering Finland.

There is a "Dirty Dozen" vibe with the group in the bunker, awaiting each mission with impatience and raw nerves. At one point Henry's Sikorsky bemoans, "How can we fight 'em cooped up here like rats in a hole!" It's difficult to relate to these characters since we don't know much of anything about any of them save the three whose Olympic back story we received in the opening scenes. They are differentiated by character types – the coward, the psycho, the tough guy, the brave leader, the cheerful positive guy and so on. When they jump to act or react, we can't relate.

One example is after an attack by ground forces that the team drives back. They capture a prisoner, who confusingly seems to be an American, not a German. When he is brought into the bunker, Jan Sikorsky leaps up and begins to strangle him! The others pull Brandon off of the P.O.W., Jan urges, "I say we kill him now!" What is the motivator for such extreme violent behavior? It's never explained so Sikorsky's actions are merely startling and out-of-place.

The German forces are unable to fight past the group, so they decide to dig into the mountain at the base and blow the whole thing up, giving them clear passage into Finland. The film's climax shows the remaining troops skiing down the mountain, armed with their own explosives intending to blow up the enemy before the enemy can blow them up. Halfway down the mountain, they get pinned down by a machine gun nest. Jan Sikorsky sacrifices himself for the team and the mission by skiing directly into the machine gun stronghold and blowing them – and himself – sky high.

Another element of confusion for film buffs is the extensive use of Hans Salter's recent score for *Son of Frankenstein* during most of the action sequences. *Ski Patrol* is a frustrating film experience thanks to a half-baked script that even Henry Brandon can't do much with.

Doomed To Die:

The popular successes of the Charlie Chan and Mr. Moto film series at 20th Century Fox led Poverty Row studio Monogram to launch their own oriental detective series starring Boris Karloff as Mr. Wong. Based on the James Lee Wong stories by Hugh Wiley, there were ultimately five films in the series produced between 1938 and 1940. The fifth and final Wong with Karloff was called *Doomed to Die* and features Henry Brandon in a meaty supporting role.

The mystery begins with newspaper headlines proclaiming that the Wentworth Castle passenger ship was involved in a suspicious fire at sea leading to its sinking and 400 lives lost. Curtis Wentworth of Wentworth Industries is inconsolable and calls in his staff lawyer Attorney Victor Martin (Henry Brandon) to witness his signing of insurance papers related to the loss, as well as a new last will and testament. As we all know, as soon as someone signs a new will in a mystery movie, they are "doomed to die."

As Victor Martin, Henry is respectful, upstanding and clean cut. He expresses concern that his employer may commit suicide, but Wentworth assures him otherwise. They discuss a mysterious cargo that was aboard and Martin urges Wentworth to go before the Maritime Commission first thing in the morning and come clean, as he'd advised the older man to do when he first became involved in this "shady deal." Wentworth agrees, and then the red herrings file in, one by one.

There is his business rival, Paul Fleming whose son (Dick), is in love with Wentworth's daughter (Cynthia). Wentworth is violently opposed to the union. And we also have a terminated drunk chauffeur and a sleazy blackmailing office manager.

Boris Karloff and Henry Brandon in *Doomed To Die*.

But seriously... you're reading this book for a reason - that Henry Brandon was among the greatest, most versatile of screen villains in cinema history. Do you really think Monogram would hire The King of the Bogeymen to be a mere clean cut lawyer? Of course not, our Henry is the killer, as well he should be!

Young Dick goes to visit Old Wentworth to make a final plea for his daughter's hand. He refuses and they argue. A shot rings out! Cyrus Wentworth of Wentworth Industries has been murdered and the prime suspect is poor Dick Fleming.

Series regular reporter Bobby Logan (Marjorie Reynolds) is friends with Cynthia Wentworth so she recruits Mr. Wong to take the case and discover the truth. Wong examines the passenger list of the ill-fated Wentworth Castle and finds that the sinking and the murder are connected. That night, someone drives by and takes a shot at Wong, winging him in the left arm, resulting in a mere flesh wound.

This leads to the first meeting of the silver screen's two greatest Fu Manchus when Mr. Wong interviews Attorney Martin. In real life, Henry Brandon was dear friends with Boris Karloff and his wife, whom he knew from the theatre. This friendship of two of the greatest of movie bogeymen would endure for decades.

Martin sings the praises of Mr. Wentworth, exclaiming, "I owe him whatever success I've had!" He floats the suicide theory again, then reveals that large sums of money have been disappearing from the company's reserves and he and Wentworth were hoping to identify the culprit.

That night, a likely culprit in the form of the drunken chauffeur breaks in to burn papers from the company safe as Mr. Wong watches from the shadows. Attorney Martin comes charging in, firing his gun at the escaping figure, nearly shooting Mr. Wong. As events build to a climax, it turns out that this is a smuggling caper and Mr. Wong correctly identifies Henry's lawyer as the culprit. Brandon was the one who took the poor shot at Karloff early on, and he says his only regret is that he didn't kill Mr. Wong when he had the chance. Then he's hauled off to jail, mystery solved.

The Monogram mystery and horror films, especially those with Boris Karloff, Bela Lugosi and George Zucco, have a cheap, cheesy charm that give the cut-rate productions an allure they don't deserve, but offer up anyway. *Doomed to Die* is probably the weakest of the Wongs, but still a fun way to kill sixty-eight minutes. Henry recalled at the 1982 Sons of The Desert Convention in Detroit:

> I worked only once with Boris on a Monogram Picture when he played Mr. Wong, the detective. It was the last one because this was just before Pearl Harbor and nobody wanted to see a sympathetic Japanese detective after Pearl Harbor. Imagine, *I* played the heavy in a Boris Karloff picture!

Dark Streets of Cairo:

Around the same time that Universal produced *The Mummy's Hand* in 1940, they also made *Dark Streets of Cairo* on many of the same sets, with the same brisk, wisecracking humor, the same Hans Salter music and the same lead villain in the ominous George Zucco. While it would have been wildly cool to see Henry Brandon interacting with the undead Kharis, he did land a plum supporting part opposite Zucco in *Dark Streets of Cairo* playing an Arab knife-thrower named Hussien.

George Zucco dooms Henry Brandon in *Dark Streets of Cairo*. Collection of Richard Finegan.

Dark Streets of Cairo begins with the announcement that the Wyndam archeological expedition has unearthed the famous Seven Jewels of the Seventh Pharaoh with plans to take them back to America. This news is greeted with much concern by the secret criminal organization The Defenders, a "cultural brotherhood" that steals back unearthed treasures to keep them in their native Egypt. The Defenders is masterminded by Abadi (George Zucco) and one of his henchmen is the deadly Hussien (Henry Brandon.)

Playing an Arab again after his performance in *Garden Of Allah* of four years earlier, Henry's Hussien is appropriately Egyptian in his sun-darkened skin, his fez and thick black goatee. He has won the plum assignment of switching false diamonds with the real Seven Jewels, but Abadi has grave concerns – with an accent on "grave." Hussien, he believes, is too impetuous for the job but agrees to let him proceed.

That evening, our two American protagonists Dennis Martin (Ralph Byrd) and Jerry Jones (Eddie Quillan) enter a café looking for girls. Jerry is smitten with the beautiful assistant in a knife-throwing act, and that knife thrower happens to be Hussien. Henry makes a convincing knife-thrower (as he would again twenty-seven years later on an episode of television's ***Mr. Terrific***) but allows his jealousy to inflame his better judgment. He growls to his assistant, "You were flirting with that American!" She replies that she was lonely and his chilling response is, "I will see that it does not happen again" Impetuous indeed!

After his main act throwing knives at the girl, he tries to goad Jerry to come up and face his blades. "Perhaps you are afraid?" Hussien taunts. "Afraid?" boasts Jerry, "Listen, Sphinx-face, if anyone talked to me like that in my country, why, I would…" "And?" Hussien challenges, "Why don't you?" Jerry chuckles, "'Cause I'm not in my country!" However, Hussien successfully convinces him to come up and begins throwing knives at him, intending to kill the American with the final knife. At the last moment, Jerry ducks to pick up his shoe and the fatal knife misses. Hussien covers by saying, "I am so sorry, my foot slipped!" to which the wise-cracking Jerry replies, "That's your story and I'm stuck with it!"

Even though Hussien didn't kill Jerry Jones, he *did* knife the Professor in the back when he switched the jewels, drawing unwanted attention to the

Defenders and angering Abadi. He is brought before his master, squirming and sweating. As Abadi confronts his disciple, Hussien jabbers, "It was an accident! I beg you, Abadi, I brought you the jewels! I fulfilled my mission!" But the cold, calculating Abadi will have none of this. He turns away and says simply to his executioner, "Attend to him!" sealing Hussien's doom. As Hans Salter's *Mummy* music throbs in the background, Henry Brandon is strangled and out of *Dark Streets of Cairo* at the half-way mark.

Brandon offers solid support to George Zucco in *Dark Streets of Cairo*, his hot-headed Hussien bringing about his own demise. The film is a solid Universal thriller well worth seeking out.

The Son of Monte Cristo:

Zorro on a budget, *The Son of Monte Cristo* was a fun United Artists release during the holiday season at the end of 1940 starring Louis Hayward as the swashbuckling offspring and Joan Bennett as Grand Duchess Zora. It was directed by Rowland V. Lee, just coming off of another 'Son' picture, the third in Universal's Frankenstein series, *Son of Frankenstein*. Henry was cast in a rare "good guy" role as Lt. Schultz, a member of the Lichtenburg underground, fighting alongside future Lone Ranger Clayton Moore as Lt. Dorner against a subdued (for him) George Sanders as evil Count Zurko.

The plot begins in the tiny country of Lichtenburg in 1865. The nation is called "the jewel of the Balkans" but has seen happier times, since they are now under the greedy thumb of Count Zurko and his plans to control and subjugate the people of Lichtenburg. Both Henry Brandon and Clayton Moore work as palace guards, pretending to be loyal to Zurko, but they are really inside men with the underground working to free Lichtenburg from tyranny. They soon connect with the son of The Count of Monte Cristo, who aids them in their quest.

Hayward is fairly amusing as the foppish version of the Count, tired of being compared to his famous adventurer father. He creates a black masked hero called The Flame to fight by night and his first task is to free Von

Neuhof (Montagu Love) from the dungeon before he is executed for treason. During their first meeting with the Count, Brandon's Lt. Schultz wryly comments "You must have a high opinion of our country!" as he laments the fact that Von Neuhof, one of their greatest citizens, is to be hung and that the Grand Duchess is a prisoner in her own palace.

They plan a daring rescue and because Brandon plays the sidekick to a sidekick, he is expendable. This makes him the movie's sacrificial lamb, dying in a hail of rifle bullets while his friends escape with Von Neuhof at the film's midpoint.

The Son of Monte Cristo clips along to its predictable conclusion. On its original release, *The New Yorker* brutally assessed the film as "arranged for young persons, or for those of arrested mental development"! But it is modest fun on a modest budget with Henry Brandon fighting – and perishing – on the side of the angels.

Underground:

This Warner Brothers propaganda picture, released in 1941 months before the United States entered the Second World War, was firmly anti-Nazi and offered Henry Brandon a role as a 'good' German working on the side of the *Underground*.

Philip Dorn plays Eric, the leader of the Berlin-based underground movement, informing the German people of the truth about Nazi atrocities via a series of illegal radio broadcasts. Barely one step ahead of the authorities, they lose their truck and broadcasting equipment in a tense sequence and have to rebuild their resources.

About a half-hour in, during a meeting in which the team is discussing building a new radio unit, Joseph (Henry Brandon) arrives, all smiles and with good news. Their member Hoffman, arrested and imprisoned in a concentration camp for two years, has been released and will rejoin the movement that evening. What they don't realize is that Hoffman has been tortured into helping the Gestapo round up the underground leaders and this meeting is a trap.

That night at a local café, key members of the underground gather to meet with Hoffman to determine if he is genuine in his intent or actually a pawn of the Nazis. At a background table, Joseph waits for the signal to call Hoffman and let him know the rendezvous point. Hoffman immediately informs his handler of the meeting, betraying his comrades, compromised by the years of Nazi terror. The central committee of the underground movement is in grave danger!

Shortly before Hoffman arrives at the café, four Gestapo members arrive in plain clothes, ready to take action. A grim-faced Henry Brandon realizes Hoffman has betrayed them and they all need to make their escape from the café. As Hoffman arrives, he sees Joseph and a Gestapo officer who notices and identifies him as a member of the underground. He guns down Joseph on a staircase and Henry gets to enact another fine death scene. Joseph grasps the bannister in his death throes, staggering then collapsing and he perishes – the first "sacrificial lamb" death in *Underground*.

Hoffman is confronted later that evening and told of Joseph's murder by the Gestapo. Eric gives him a loaded gun so he can do the right thing… which he does, killing himself. A typical exciting Warner Brothers drama, the story unfolds in a series of suspenseful set pieces as the underground attempts to avoid capture and death at the hands of the Nazis.

It's nice to see Henry Brandon fighting with good guys in *Underground* and almost startling to see him broadly grinning in his first sequence. A gripping, entertaining pre-WWII propaganda film.

Two in a Taxi:

Columbia produced this social drama about the economic challenges of an independent taxi cab driver in New York City with Henry Brandon as a supporting character called The Professor. Released in July of 1941, *Two in a Taxi* has a dash of romance, a bit of action and stars Russell Hayden as struggling hack driver Jimmy Owens.

Jimmy dreams of owning his own gas station with buddy Sandy Connors

(Noah Beery Jr.) but can't seem to scrape up the needed $300 deposit. All the cabbies hang out at the same coffee shop, which is where we get to know one of them, The Professor (Henry Brandon) who always seems to be there, reading books and wryly commenting on the hopelessness of it all.

Brandon appears in four coffee shop scenes, sprinkled throughout the picture. He sports a thick black mustache and a defeatist attitude. One of the cab drivers tells him "Reading won't get you no fares!" to which his response is, "No, but it makes you see things clearer. The world is pretty much the same, all the time, all over. You've got to be… philosophical."

Later, when Jimmy faces insurmountable odds in keeping his license, much less raising the dough for that gas station, The Professor offers "A cabby's got no right to dream. We live in a world of reality!" What a Debbie Downer Henry Brandon is in *this* movie! His socialist stances offer a big picture commentary that still gives way to the happy movie ending where the little guy comes out okay.

Two in a Taxi is short and not-so-sweet offering up Henry in a role that must have grated, but a paycheck is a paycheck, whether you're a struggling hack driver or a struggling actor.

Night in New Orleans:

One of Henry's last films before he went into the service to serve during WWII, *Night in New Orleans* offers a minor role in a comic murder mystery reminiscent of both *The Thin Man* and *Charlie Chan* series.

Produced by Paramount, *Night in New Orleans* stars Preston Foster and Patricia Morrison as Steve and Ethel Abbott, a married couple who solve crimes with the help of their cowardly Black valet Shadrach Jones (played by *Casablanca*'s Dooley Wilson.) During a dark, foggy night early on a beat cop remarks "Swell night for a murder!" and indeed it is – a man is murdered and one of the chief suspects is Lt. Steve Abbott.

Henry's scene comes about forty minutes into the mayhem when Ethel visits the Mississippi Inn, a gambling joint on the banks of the river. Brandon plays a tough casino croupier who can't believe Ethel's luck at the craps table – not knowing she is using Shadrach's crooked dice that always throw a seven. "I been here eight years," he says incredulously, "I've never seen one like that!" When Mrs. Abbott heads backstage to visit one of the show girls who is also a suspect, Brandon discovers that the dice are loaded and sets off in pursuit. Instead of a showgirl, Ethel finds a second murdered man with a knife in his back and dashes off in alarm, chased by Henry Brandon and a confederate.

She eludes them by batting Brandon in the face with her purse, and brings her husband to see the new body… which, of course, has vanished. Then Henry and his casino thug pal corner them again in the dressing room and threaten them with some rough stuff. Ethel snaps off the lights, Steve clobbers Henry with a handy fire extinguisher and the couple escapes by diving into the river as Brandon stares in disbelief. He sets off in hopeless pursuit but we don't see him again during this *Night*.

Night in New Orleans is fun murder romp with appealing leads. Patricia Morrison (also known as Sherlock Holmes' *Woman in Green*) has the sexiest overbite this side of Gene Tierney. Henry Brandon is only in one sequence playing an inconsequential role.

Canon City:

A gritty, tense prison-break picture, *Canon City* is the true story of a December 1947 breakout from the Colorado State Prison told in a film-noir documentary style. It was produced by Eagle-Lion and released by United Artists in 1948 and featured Henry Brandon as one of the dozen members of the gang who participated in the well-planned escape.

Scott Brady plays Jimmy, one of 1,200 prisoners at the maximum security (but not maximum enough) prison up in the Colorado mountains. He's in for a murder he committed seventeen years ago, so parole is still a good decade away. Jimmy is an unwilling participant in the coming breakout, but ends up pretty much running the show.

Six of the members of this dirty dozen are in solitary, including Henry Brandon's character Freeman. Brandon doesn't have much to do for the first half of the film, but once they escape from solitary and Freeman steals one of the guard uniforms, he finally stands apart from the mob. Humorously, when the Warden heads back to the prison to take charge after his night on the town, the movie theatre he's leaving has *The Noose Hangs High* on the marquee, an Abbott and Costello comedy that is also an Eagle-Lion release.

The newspaper headline blares:

12 DESPERADOS ESCAPE FROM CANON CITY PEN.
Most Spectacular Prison Break In Western History

Half of the escapees are quickly captured or killed, leaving six who invade the Smith family home, including Jimmy and Freeman. Showing his typical movie villain nature, Brandon stares at the seventeen-year old daughter Maxine with inmate lust. He roughs up the Uncle a bit, looking for guns, and then takes terrified Maxine outside to locate a spare gas tank. Sinking to a new low (at least, in this picture) Freeman threatens to hurt Uncle if Maxine doesn't "cooperate." He growls, "Don't get excited, nobody's going to hurt you. I haven't seen anything like you since I got locked up!" Freeman assaults her and she screams, but Jimmy intervenes and tells him to leave the women alone. The dangerous group tries to leave in the family car, but the coppers arrive and the climactic shootout begins, the Smith home getting peppered with flying bullets.

Henry nails a guard, but when they try to escape through the back, he is shot down in the snow. Freeman is wounded, not killed so they drag him back to Colorado State Penitentiary and draw a big, bold X through his mug shot on the board, number ten out of twelve to be recaptured.

Within 61 hours, all are either dead or back in solitary, bringing an end to this highly entertaining crime drama.

Hollow Triumph:

Hollow Triumph would make a good double feature with *Canon City*, also an Eagle Lion release, as both are gritty crime dramas that are tough little potboilers. *Hollow Triumph* is more in the film noir style and director Steve Sekely's use of darkness, shadow, negative space and low angles is masterful.

Henry Brandon plays a cheap hood named Big Boy, part of a gang that pulls jobs with Paul Henreid's Johnny Muller. As *Hollow Triumph* begins, Johnny has just been released from prison after serving time for a payroll robbery. "You'll be back!" the Warden tells him. They set him up with a job and cheap room, but he goes right back to his old gang.

A camera angle dripping with noir in *Hollow Triumph*.

When Big Boy arrives, he bursts out with a big grin and exclaims, "Hey Johnny! Good to see you, chum!" We don't often see Henry Brandon smiling and exuding sheer joy in the cinema, so it's a little startling, but feels authentic. Johnny seems disappointed that his gang all have legit jobs, with Big Boy dealing in a poker joint. Johnny immediately plans a risky heist, pushing them into robbing a gambling club run by a hood named Rocky Stansyck. They are reluctant, but Muller reminds Big Boy and the others that he took the rap for them and spent years behind bars. The gang agrees and what follows is a tense sequence showing how the robbery goes wrong in spite of Johnny's careful planning.

Three of them enter the club with guns hidden while Big Boy is stationed in the utility area, ready to pull the switch to plunge the club into darkness in order to make their getaway. Big Boy is discovered moments before he is to pull the master switch and Henry has a brutal fight with a club thug in a confined space. This scene is shot from a low angle with no music. It's thrilling and expertly edited, intercut with the robbery concluding but with the lights still on.

Big Boy savagely clubs his adversary, knocking him out and then he pulls the power switch down. However, when the gang exits the club, the outside parking lot lights are on a different circuit and snap back on, illuminating all five of them. The two getaway cars are piled into, Big Boy needing a bit of help as he is still groggy from his fight. As the cars screech off into the night, Rocky's goons fire bullets into the rear windscreens of both cars and Big Boy loses control of his, crashing it into a tree.

Three of the gang are caught, including unlucky Big Boy. Rocky pulls them from the disabled car and has one of them beaten until he reveals the name of the man behind the daring robbery – Johnny Muller. Then, surprisingly, Rocky tells Big Boy and the others, "Okay, you can go." Big Boy is incredulous. "Just walk away?" he asks Rocky. The Boss confirms, "Just walk away." As they leave, Rocky turns to one of his men and says, "You're not going to let them get away, are you, Bullseye?" Bullseye grins and we know that Big Boy's moments are numbered and that number is a low one. Exit Henry Brandon from *Hollow Triumph*.

The rest of this suspenseful chiller deals with Johnny discovering he looks very much like a psychiatrist in Los Angeles, so he kills him and takes his place, thereby inheriting the very real troubles of this man's life. As his brother says early on, "Sooner or later, it always catches up with you!" Indeed it does.

Brandon is in *Hollow Triumph* for less than thirteen minutes, but he still makes an impression and the film is well worth seeking out. It's one of the better film noir pictures.

The Scarlet Angel:

Yvonne DeCarlo and Rock Hudson spar and fall in love in the romantic 1953 adventure *The Scarlet Angel* produced by Universal International in glorious Technicolor. Yvonne is saloon girl Roxie McClanahan and Hudson a worldly deck-hand named Panama, in port in New Orleans during 1865. The Scarlet Angel is the saloon, owned by Pierre (Henry Brandon.)

Up to no good with Tol Avery and Yvonne De Carlo in *Scarlet Angel*. Collection of Richard Finegan.

Brandon's Pierre is only present during the first ten minutes and the last ten minutes of *The Scarlet Angel*, but he's still the primary scoundrel of the movie. We first see him behind the bar at The Scarlet Angel serving Panama, who pays for the whole bottle. Pierre races upstairs to tell Roxie with a French flavored accent that "he flashed a bankroll that would choke you!" He has her engage in their customary activity of romancing and drugging Angel patrons so Pierre can rob them, but Panama is too smart for the duo.

When the Sheriff arrives to arrest Roxie for yesterday's robbery victim, the smitten Panama asks Pierre if he's going to help his partner. Pierre refuses, so Panama obliges by starting a distraction – a massive barroom brawl that begins with his belting Henry Brandon so hard that his double crashes backwards through a window!

Pierre takes several additional slugs to his chin as Roxy and Panama escape into the next hundred minutes of convoluted plotting which sees Roxy taking the place of a dead Civil War widow and bringing her child to the husband's wealthy society family. Several years pass and in the end, Roxy chooses love over money to be with now Captain Panama.

Pierre returns in the final few scenes of *The Scarlet Angel*, having closed his joint to travel cross country and blackmail Roxy for $25,000, threatening to reveal her secret and snatch away the young boy's inheritance. Brandon says he'll lie and say that Roxy had the child back at his bar, that he isn't the Caldwell heir - but his strawberry birth mark reveals otherwise. Pierre's plan is foiled and the raucous tale ends as it began – with Rock Hudson clobbering Henry Brandon's face followed by a massive barroom brawl.

Henry made two Universal films with the exotically beautiful Yvonne De Carlo in 1952, *The Scarlet Angel* and *Hurricane Smith*. He had been linked romantically with Ms. De Carlo in the press a few years earlier, one such write-up on August 15, 1950 noting, "Yvonne De Carlo and Henry Brandon were dancing dreamily at the Biltmore Bowl." They certainly developed a close friendship, as Henry later wrote about the filming of *The Scarlet Angel*:

> During shooting, Miss De Carlo complained bitterly to me that the studio had given her a "stock boy" as a leading man. It was Rock Hudson's first co-starring picture; little did she know that he was to become a great box office star.*

---

* Henry's recollections as written on the back of a still from the *Scarlet Angel* for Richard Finegan

CHAPTER THIRTEEN
Sci-Fi, Swashbucklers, Jungle Thrillers & Other Potboilers

The Corsican Brothers

This 1941 film was based on an adventure tale by Alexandre Dumas, *The Corsican Brothers* is a full-blooded swashbuckler with Douglas Fairbanks, Jr. playing twin siblings who were born Siamese. Based in Corsica, it's the violent tale of a vendetta between two Italian families – almost a pirate version of *The Trail of The Lonesome Pine*.

Akim Tamiroff is head of the Colona family, out to obliterate the Franchi clan in one fell swoop, on the occasion of the birth of the twins engagingly played by Fairbanks. "I've grown tired of slitting their throats one at a time," he chillingly confides. "This is the chance I've been waiting for – to wipe them out – to be rid of the Franchi family root and branch, forever!"

He successfully does so, murdering the parents of the twin boys Lucien and Mario, who escape with the family doctor and are separated in a miraculous operation. Lucien grows up as a forest bandit while Brother Mario is raised in Paris amidst wealth and culture.

Henry Brandon's solitary sequence takes place twenty years later at a performance of an opera, also attended by Mario Frenchi. Brandon plays the Marquis de Raveneau as a pompous, dandified soldier, bragging to his friends that he'll get a dinner date with a gorgeous brunette theatre-goer that evening or pay 1,000 francs. Mario also taken by the girl's beauty, overhears and snatches up a couple of ice cream sundaes, spilling them on purpose all over Henry's pressed trousers.

Early in *The Corsican Brothers*, Douglas Fairbanks Jr. duels with Henry.

Mario laments that the Marquis will never be able to dine with his lovely companion with ice cream all over his pants, adding, "You'll lose your thousand francs!" to which an enraged de Raveneau responds, "You'll lose your *life!*"

They engage in a furious sword fight, right there in the theatre lobby on the grand staircase. It's an exciting sequence, intercut with shots of Mario's brother Lucien, many miles away yet telepathically connected to his brother. Mario is the better fighter and bests the Marquis, winning the duel and knocking the sword from Henry's hand. Fairbanks smiles and offers the sword back to a chagrined de Raveneau, and then turns and walks away. This is when OUR Henry makes an appearance by stabbing the twin in the back! Across the miles, Lucien feels the searing pain of the blade, and the story of reunion and revenge continues without a further appearance of the Marquis de Raveneau.

The Corsican Brothers is a solid thriller with strong performances and able support from Henry Brandon in this exciting early scene.

Wake of the Red Witch:

In the second of his three films with John Wayne, Henry Brandon plays Kurinua, a South Seas native, in the flashback sequences of Republic Pictures *Wake of The Red Witch* (1948). It's a significant and unusual role for Henry for several reasons. First, he's a good guy, the second in command of the village on a friendly South Pacific island where lurks an *unfriendly* monster octopus. Next, his make-up for the part of Kurinua drastically alters his facial features.

John Wayne and Henry Brandon in *Wake of The Red Witch*.

In the early 1980s, Henry told co-author Rick Greene that the *Red Witch* make-up supervisor inserted several cotton balls into each of his nostrils to distend and flatten out his features, rendering him almost unrecognizable – especially from the front. He made it clear, he's *not* wearing a false nose, it's the cotton shoved up in there that did the trick.

Wake of the Red Witch is the story of Captain Ralls (John Wayne), a brutal but fair ship's captain and his quest for both pearls and gold. This high seas adventure begins in 1860 from the perspective of new First Mate Sam

Rosen (Gig Young). However the middle third of the picture is comprised of a lengthy flashback sequence which includes all of Henry Brandon's scenes.

When the Duke scuttles his ship The Red Witch with its cargo of $5,000,000 in gold bullion, he makes for port at the tropical island where his ship's owner resides – bearing quite the grudge for Captain Ralls! This is where the flashback begins at about forty-five minutes in. Henry arrives with much island pomp and circumstance to welcome The Red Witch and her crew. Kurinua is not only dark skinned with a broad flat nose, but he has a mop of thick blonde hair! He shakes hands warmly with Captain Ralls and one can't help but think to just a few years into the cinematic future – that the last thing Ethan and Scar would ever do is to shake hands. It's a kind of alternate universe moment.

It is the Festival of the Half-Moon with a big native feast honoring the sunken pearls guarded down below by a monstrous octopus. Several native divers try to go down and are attacked, unsuccessful. Henry wisely intones that "only Tarotato (their deity) can save the pearls!" However, Wayne is goaded into diving down to confront the octopus and get the pearls, and he does exactly that, retrieving getting the chest of giant pearls and evading the writhing tentacles – but then goes BACK DOWN to face the monster in battle! Armed with a spear and a knife, he engages in hand-to-sucker combat with the sea beast, which looks just a little fake, but not too fake. [Republic's Lydecker brothers do good work on special effects.] From above, our Kurinua looks down with great consternation. Perhaps those cotton balls jammed into his nose are making it difficult to breathe?

The Duke jabs and jabs at the creature, tentacles swirling around him until an inky blackness fills the screen. He did it! The tentacles untangle and Ralls surfaces. That night, Kurinua sits at his friend's bedside, watching over him as he recovers from his ordeal. They return to the joyous festivities for a defining Henry Brandon movie moment. Kurinua is holding a wicker basket with the carved-out eye of the octopus in it! He announces, "Tarotato says to burn the eye of the demon and spread the ashes to the wind!" Just when you believe you've seen everything Henry Brandon can do on screen, there he is –

bare-chested with curly blonde hair, a fat nose and an octopus eye in a wicker basket in his hands. He tosses the eye into the flames beneath a massive stone idol. Cheese simply doesn't get much tastier than *Wake of the Red Witch*.

Blonde, broad-nosed Brandon and the infamous eye of the octopus.

Captain Ralls is given all of the pearls but a greedy and jealous Henry Daniell places him under arrest and attempts to turn the tribe against him. Daniell pulls a pistol, they grapple, the Duke punches him and the fool falls backwards into the fire pit with the burning octopus eye. Ashes to ashes.

Kurinua proclaims it "justice" and an example of "the wrath of Tarotato!" Ralls is horrified at having accidentally killed a man and abandons the pearls, boards his Red Witch and loses his love, the beautiful Angelique (Gail Russell) as well as his self-respect. This is where the flashback – and Henry Brandon's role – ends, but it is the undeniable highlight of *Wake of the Red Witch*, the John Wayne film that everyone remembers as "the one with the octopus." *Reap the Wild Wind* is "the one with the giant squid." There, that's settled.

The Tarzan Series:

The Tarzan film series was at a crossroads in the late 1940's. After a long, successful run first at MGM as 'A' productions, and later at RKO demoted to 'B' status, Johnny Weissmuller had concluded his iconic run in the title role. Weissmuller wasn't the first screen Tarzan, but he was the first to portray the Jungle King in an expensive, glossy picture. The first few Tarzan films from MGM were massive hits, spawning an entire Jungle Picture genre that continued for decades in both features and serials. Indeed, Henry Brandon portrayed the key baddie in his first serial, *Jungle Jim* at Universal in 1937.

Johnny Weissmuller played Tarzan from 1932 to 1948, the first half-dozen at MGM with Maureen O'Sullivan as Jane and then another six at RKO with Brenda Joyce playing Jane in four of them. Weissmuller made a superlative Tarzan the Ape Man, but after a total of twelve cinematic adventures, he was getting a bit old and stocky to continue convincingly swinging from vines and rescuing Jane. Producer Sol Lesser made the risky decision to recast the lead role in 1949. It worked for Charlie Chan, it should work for Tarzan.

Lex Barker stepped into the Ape Man's loin cloth, doing a fine job in his series of five Tarzan jungle thrillers. Brenda Joyce provided initial continuity, playing Jane again in the first of the Barker episodes, *Tarzan's Magic Fountain*. Henry Brandon played significant supporting roles in the first and last of the Lex Barker African quintet.

Henry recalled for *Starlog Magazine*:

I did two Tarzan films with Lex Barker down at Selznick. You ran around with very little on. That was in the days when they weren't using black actors in featured roles because they would automatically not be released in the southern states. So, there were all these white tribes down in Africa. Where the hell are there white tribes in Africa? I was always the chief. I was taking the place of a black actor who *should* have been playing the part and nowadays would.[*]

Tarzan's Magic Fountain:

Lex Barker assumes the Tarzan mantle in this fantasy thriller in which Cheetah discovers a diary in a plane crash belonging to long lost aviatrix Gloria James (à la Amelia Erhardt) and brings the journal to Jane. It seems that Ms. James didn't die in the crash, but has been living for twenty years in the mystical Blue Valley. Hidden away, the Valley is the source for a mystical geyser of youth that keeps everyone in this Shangri-La young and healthy.

It's a film-buff's treat to see Evelyn Ankers *(The Wolf Man, The Ghost of Frankenstein)* playing Gloria James after her long string of Universal monster movies, looking radiant. She hasn't aged a day since her disappearance, but is needed back in England to clear a man wrongly serving time for murder. Tarzan goes off to fetch her and send her back to civilization.

The inhabitants of the Blue Valley are a simple people, but there is a contingent of insurgents who go against their ruler's wishes, fearful that Gloria will reveal the location of their secret valley. Henry's character Siko leads this group. He appears bare-chested and wears a kind of reverse leopard-print headband. Gloria James is young and beautiful, looking half of her real age of fifty. Tarzan explains to a doubtful Jane that she'll quickly grow old now that she's left the Blue Valley.

Some greedy trappers backtrack Tarzan's path to locate the Blue Valley

---

[*] *Starlog Magazine* January 1987 #114

and steal the secrets of the magic fountain. Siko wrongly assumes that Tarzan directed the safari to their mountain hideaway. They kill the men with massive flaming spears and Siko vows, "Only Tarzan knows the way here…I will go…I will kill him!"

Tarzan's Magic Fountain lobby card. Collection of Rick Greene.

As Brandon stalks Tarzan, Cheetah warns her master and Siko and Tarzan engage in a brisk hand-to-hand fight scene. Tarzan judo flips Siko, who bites him on the wrist to escape! Then the Lord of the Jungle breaks all of his arrows and refrains from killing him, sending Siko back to The Blue Valley with the message that Tarzan is still their friend and has kept their secret. Henry doubts this, glowering with sheer hatred, murder burning in his gaze.

Gloria James returns to the jungle, now old and grey-haired, wanting to return to live out her life with her new husband in the Blue Valley. Tarzan refuses to guide them back, a man of his word. Jane decides to guide them alone, Tarzan watching over them from above and Siko stalking Tarzan as they all make their way back to the lost tribe in the Blue Valley.

Siko (Brandon) and Tarzan battle in *Tarzan's Magic Fountain*.

Back in the village, Henry rabble-rouses his people against Tarzan and the intruders. "Death to Tarzan! Death to the Betrayer!" he shouts, convincing several followers to capture and bind Tarzan in a cave. His plan is to blind Tarzan so he can never again find his way to the Blue Valley.

At last we see the glowing geyser of youth, whose waters have the power to restore youth and heal the sick. As Tarzan struggles with his ropes, Siko heats up a devilish two-pronged pitchfork in a fire to a white-hot temperature! Tarzan escapes with Cheetah and sets out to the mountaintop where Jane is under siege by flaming arrows. They make their getaway, leaving Gloria and her husband to live a happy life as members of the Blue Valley tribe. Henry's Siko pursues them up the mountain, but resourceful Cheetah causes an avalanche of boulders that bury and kill him in one of Brandon's more unusual death scenes – the only time in his screen career that Henry was murdered by a monkey!

Tarzan's Magic Fountain ends on a note of comic fantasy as Cheetah drinks a sample he stole from the geyser and turns into a baby chimp!

Tarzan and the She-Devil:

In 1953, Lex Barker made his fifth and final appearance as Tarzan for producer Sol Lesser in RKO's *Tarzan and The She-Devil*. Henry was brought back to again play a jungle native, the Locopo Chief M'Tara.

This time around, Tarzan gets involved with a gang of elephant-murdering ivory poachers led by the white 'she-devil' of the title and a pre-***Perry Mason*** Raymond Burr as Vargo, a swarthy unshaven brute of a man. In other words, the typical Henry Brandon role.

Brandon as Chief M'Tara in *Tarzan and the She-Devil*.

But in *Tarzan and the She-Devil*, we are treated to Henry as M'Tara, the Chief of the Locopo tribe and a good friend of Tarzan. Brandon is dark-skinned, barefoot and bare-chested with several native necklaces around his neck. It is so refreshing to see Henry's M'Tara laughing with Tarzan when Cheetah discovers a boomerang and tries to throw it away, but it clobbers him.

Vargo's armed men raid the Locopo tribe and shanghai them to work a massive elephant herd. Tarzan sneaks into camp, knocks out two guards, unties the bound Locopo men including M'Tara and throws the poacher's rifles down a well.

But the poachers don't give up so easily and head back into Locopo territory, rousting up Henry's tribe again, capturing Tarzan and kidnapping Jane to compel Tarzan to do what they want and to lure all the elephants into a death trap. But Jane escapes, although Tarzan and everyone else believes she is dead. Burr, attempting to compel the broken-hearted Tarzan to call the elephants, tortures him with a whip. He is SO going to get it!

It a unique and disturbing experience to see Henry Brandon in chains, beaten and half-starved and forced to do slave labor. He is usually the one putting enemies into chains. The movie wraps up quickly and we don't see much of Henry in the finale, where Tarzan realizes Jane is alive. He calls the elephants, to stampede the camp and kill the She-Devil and Vargo. Barker's final Tarzan movie is rousing and typical, with a standout performance by Raymond Burr and Henry Brandon as one of the good guys.

The Golden Horde:

During the first half of the busy 1950's, Henry Brandon's motion picture work saw him bouncing back and forth between Paramount and Universal, one significant assignment being his portrayal of Juchi, the son of Genghis Khan in *The Golden Horde*. The Technicolor Universal release from 1951 cast Brandon as the cocky, belligerent Juchi – brown skinned, armored and bearded, looking almost exactly like a Star Trek Klingon but for the huge feather planted squarely on his helmet.

Juchi's infamous father sends him from Persia to the city of Samarkand to pillage and destroy it. Accompanying him are an advisor and warriors of The Golden Horde. The films protagonists are Christian Crusaders led by Sir Guy of Devon (David Farrar) who are charged with protecting Samarkand and its Princess Shalimar (exotic Ann Blyth). Above the gates of the city reads a prophecy HE WHO COMES TO DESTROY SAMARKAND SHALL HIMSELF – BE DESTROYED. There you have the plot.

The cocksure Juchi and his barbarian soldiers arrive, immediately confronted by the Crusaders and first blood is spilled in a contest of one-upmanship that fully displays the testosterone in the palace. An English arrow hits its mark, then Juchi's arrow splits that one cleanly, à la Robin Hood. Brandon gives his trademark smirk of superiority at his marksmanship skills.

Working with the Princess to divide and conquer the conquerors, the old astrologer gives Juchi a prophecy about a mighty force arriving to wed the Princess Shalimar and together, rule the world. Henry is positive HE is the man referred to as the seeds of dissent are firmly planted to divide the Horde.

Brandon on horseback in *The Golden Horde*. Collection of Del Kempster.

Shalimar sends her ring to Juchi that night, summoning him, and does likewise with his Captain. The whole middle third of *The Golden Horde* involves the clever Princess pitting Juchi and those loyal to the son of the Khan against the Captain and his men until they clash in battle. As the picture builds to a climax: Henry has yet another notable death scene – worthy of the finest Klingon – getting a spear through the belly.

In fact, The Associated Press ran a silly story on February 4, 1951 while the film was in production. Embarrassingly headlined **Actor Has to Wear Falsies**, it read:

> Actor Henry Brandon had to wear 'falsies' for a movie scene. But unlike the feminine variety, his padding didn't show. Playing the son of Genghis Khan in *The Golden Horde*, Brandon was supposed to meet a horrible death by being impaled on a lance. To cushion the shock, special effects men made a king-size pad a foot in diameter with sponge rubber and a steel plate base. The actor wore it around his waist under his costume.

With this flashy death-by-spear, Brandon misses the climax but makes a final appearance as Juchi's corpse when Genghis Khan finally arrives in Samarkand at the denouement, also tricked by Sir Guy and Shalimar into returning to Persia with the cold, bloody body of his son.

Henry Brandon turns in his usual solid lead villain performance with plenty of action, a fun death and leaves modern fans wishing that he *had* played a Klingon opposite Captain Kirk fifteen years later. It would have been GLORIOUS.

Flame of Araby:

Universal Pictures cast Henry Brandon in three Technicolor Maureen O'Hara-starring vehicles in the early 1950's – *Flame of Araby, War Arrow* and *Lady Godiva of Coventry*. *War Arrow* is covered in the Westerns chapter, so here we review *Flame of Araby* and *Lady Godiva*, which offered him two colorful opportunities to shine in supporting baddie roles, although only one of them had a script worthy of his considerable skill.

The first, and best of these Maureen O'Hara films is 1951's *Flame of Araby*. Henry plays a lusty pirate named Malik in a sleeveless black wooly vest, strutting around with his deadly dagger. Brandon looks magnificent as the scoundrel Malik. He is loyal to his Barbarossa captain, played with zest by Brandon's old friend Lon Chaney Jr.

Unlike the later *Lady Godiva*, Henry shares no scenes with Maureen O'Hara in *Flame of Araby*, his scenes sadly confined to the first third of the film. We first see him with his bawdy pirate crew after successfully pillaging Tunis; spurning the sensual advances of a gorgeous brunette. Malik throws her to the floor, but she rises, smiling and kisses the pirate passionately. This makes the wench his woman.

Later, as Malik is preoccupied with drinking grog, she is claimed by another of the Barbarossa crew – until Brandon expertly knifes him in the back, killing him instantly. Malik explains, "He broke the law of the Brotherhood by attempting to steal my woman!" and Chaney proclaims the death was merited. Henry gets to keep his wench!

That is, until Bedouin Chief Jeff Chandler arrives in Tunis and the fickle brunette throws herself at *him* while Malik continues to drink. Henry challenges the rival to a duel for the woman and while Chandler isn't interested in the whore, he will defend his honor. The duel is quick, as before Malik can even raise his arm to throw his murderous knife, he is killed by the Bedouin's slingshot blow to the head. Just 24 minutes into *Flame of Araby*, Brandon's participation is ended with his bloodied head striking the stone ground.

It's a shame, as Malik had the potential of being a terrific lead henchman role-- if it weren't for that slingshot!

Lady Godiva of Coventry:

In this 1955 costume drama set in 11th Century England, Brandon plays Bejac opposite Maureen O'Hara in the legendary title role. The film looks and sounds like a female-driven version of *The Adventures of Robin Hood* but it ends up as a dull story of political intrigue that neither excites nor titillates.

The plot casts Henry in a thankless role as a medieval thug. His first scene is nearly thirty minutes into the picture and he merely loiters, glowering in the background. Bejac happens to be very good at glowering and he gets ample opportunity to do so throughout the balance of the film.

At 45 minutes in, Brandon still hasn't spoken a word of dialogue but continues to stand menacingly behind the leads. In fact, Henry Brandon's mastery of the camera is hilariously demonstrated in a scene where a disarmament agreement is to be signed and George Nader moves to potentially block Brandon from view. Henry angles his head to the left to remain visible. Bejac may not say anything, but by God, we're going to see that bearded, scowling face!

Finally, more than fifty minutes in, Bejac has his first line, summoning the Captain of the Guard. It is hardly riveting, and what few lines Henry does deliver are with an odd French accent that doesn't quite work. The plot finally embraces Bejac when he is captured, stripped to his skivvies and thrown into a jail cell before the climactic ride of Lady Godiva. He is later released, and says of injured Saxon hero Nader (playing Leofric), "He will live long enough to reach the gallows!" But it's too little, too late.

That anticipated unclothed ride of Lady Godiva is treated like a funeral march. O'Hara is clearly not nude, wearing a flesh colored body stocking and the only merit of the sequence is a Technicolor view of the famous Universal back-lot's European street where the Frankenstein Monster, the Wolf Man and Sherlock Holmes all once roamed.

In the weak squib of a finale, an exciting battle sequence is averted and Henry merely slinks off with his Norman conspirators to jail.

Hurricane Smith: (1952)

Henry Brandon appeared in two unrelated movies both entitled *Hurricane Smith*. The first *Hurricane* was released in 1941 and was a Western made for Republic Studios. The second *Hurricane* came over a decade later, a Technicolor pirate movie produced at Paramount Studios. Surprisingly, Henry played characters named "Sam" in both films!

The 1952 *Hurricane Smith* is a pirate picture with very little pirating going on. The film stars Yvonne De Carlo as Luana, part of a group posing as scientists that charters the stolen vessel 'The Lady Betty' for an expedition really after the hidden treasure of the infamous pirate Hurricane Smith (a bland John Ireland.) Henry Brandon plays one of the shanghaied crew of the

Betty, 'recruited' in Australia and looking grubby throughout the film with a week's worth of beard growth, a ripped sleeveless shirt and smoking a stogie.

Although he does appear throughout the film as one of the key crew members that stands out from the crowd, his character Sam is rarely focused on, only appearing in two and three shots and never in a close-up. He does fine work, looking concerned when Hurricane Smith dives overboard to fight a shark then shouting triumphantly when Smith wins that fight. He also engages in a bare-chested arm-wrestling match as those rascally pirates are wont to do, losing the match to the ship's champion and later, tying down the mast in a long sequence where the seeds of mutiny are sown. Sam is always there, doing his duty, swabbing that deck and adding local color to the proceedings.

His two big scenes come late in the film. First, after a pirate buddy is unjustly whipped, Sam is the voice of reason when mutiny talk bubbles up again. "Not so fast, mates!" Sam urges. "I was in a mutiny once. It wasn't pretty. About fourteen mates were hung for it!" When the whipped man persists, Sam continues, "That kinda talk will get you nowhere. It will get you into trouble and you've had enough of that for one day!"

But during the climactic mutiny, Sam is the first one to join in and take up arms against the captain. His first order of business is to break down the door of sultry Luana's locked cabin. Sam obviously is hoping to have his wicked pirate way with Luana but she shoots him, almost point blank in the gut, and Henry Brandon plays yet another convulsive death scene at the hands of a beautiful woman.

Hurricane Smith is predictable sea-going fun with lots of Henry Brandon having little to do. He would play a similar part on a 1964 **Walt Disney's Wonderful World of Color** television episode with a much more satisfying result.

War of the Worlds:

Over the course of his long film and television career, dastardly Henry Brandon has had quite the repertoire of notable screen demises, but possibly the most unusual of all his movie deaths was in the 1953 sci-fi invasion classic the *War of the Worlds*.

The cowardly cop shortly before meeting the Heat Ray in *War of the Worlds*.

H. G. Wells seminal 1897 novel is a cornerstone of science fiction literature and had been equally indispensable when updated and infamously adapted for radio in 1938 by Orson Welles and then updated again for the big screen by Producer George Pal in 1953. Starring Gene Barry (television's *Bat Masterson*) and pert Ann Robinson, Paramount's *The War of the Worlds* featured ground-breaking special effects that won an Academy Award and offered Henry Brandon the chance to go where no man had gone before… actually, where three men had gone before.

When the first meteor lands, it doesn't leave a big crater because it hit "sideways." It is determined to be radioactive, so the sheriff leaves three deputized men to stand guard. These are the first three victims of the Martian heat ray, which leaves them as nothing but body- shaped ash piles. The fire can be seen from town, so the sheriff and Gene Barry are picked up by Patrolman Henry Brandon and they drive up the hill to investigate.

The trio arrives at an ominous scene of billowing smoke as Henry exclaims nervously, "Hey, look at the cars!" and shines his patrol car searchlight on the remains of a vehicle, then onto the ashy body shapes. When the heat ray again rears up from the opening in the meteor and points in their direction, Officer Brandon jumps back into his car, *leaving the other two men* and drives away – but he doesn't get very far. The cowardly patrolman is the fourth victim of the Martians, disintegrated, car and all, by the deadly weapon.

After decades of being shot and stabbed, Henry Brandon is dissolved in a green flash by a Martian heat ray! It is an iconic sci-fi death, a definite high point demise in the Brandon pantheon of movie murders, but in his *next* rare science fiction film, he faces the retro threat of… dinosaurs!

The Land Unknown:

Universal International had transformed in the 1950s from the studio that gave us *Frankenstein, Dracula* and *The Wolf Man* to the leading producer of science fiction epics like *It Came From Outer Space, This Island Earth, The Deadly Mantis, The Mole People* and their 1957 "lost world" thriller, *The Land Unknown*. Henry Brandon gets fourth billing in this dinosaur picture, probably one of his ten or twelve most significant and best remembered roles.

The Land Unknown follows the exploits of three Navy men and a beautiful reporter who follow in Admiral Byrd's footsteps to explore a polar oasis area of Antarctica on helicopter X-3. The expedition is led by a slab of cardboard named Commander Roberts (Jock Mahoney), who takes a shine to spunky Margaret Hathaway (Shawn Smith). The copter predictably crash lands in a dense fog more than 2,500 feet below sea level when something that looks like a pterodactyl flies by and bumps their rotors. The quartet lands in one piece but the tube assembly is bent and they don't have the needed spare parts to allow them to take off again.

The Land Unknown **portrait. Collection of Rick Greene.**

As they explore their lush, humid surroundings, they realize this is a land that time forgot with bubbling lava pots, massive prehistoric foliage and a multi-tentacled woman-eating plant! The valley is stuck in the Mesozoic era, which Roberts deduces when they find the corpse of the pterodactyl that hit their helicopter. "It isn't safe here," Jock intones, delivering his lines with a square-jawed sincerity. On cue, the dinosaurs attack.

The dinosaurs of *The Land Unknown* are either komodo dragons blown up to building size or men in suits àla Godzilla – there is no Harryhausen stop-motion excitement to be found *here*. The T-Rex suit is particularly ludicrous and lumbering, well below Godzilla-standards. It does blink, though.

The group makes a dash for the copter, which can't fly. But the blades do spin, which slice into the Rex as a deterrent. But it still loiters, hoping the snacks will leave the spinning tin can soon, until a piercing sound drives him away in fear. This is where Henry Brandon finally enters the picture, and once he does, he owns it.

While the blinking Rex attacked, someone raided their camp and stole their food. During another lizard attack, Maggie is separated from the group and a strong swarthy arm snakes around her from behind and abducts her. We see this man is barefoot as he carries the unconscious girl to a homemade canoe and paddles off with his blonde prize.

The trio of men find human footprints and follow them to the lagoon's edge. Brandon takes Maggie to his Crusoe-type cave and we finally get a good look at him. Henry has a thick mop of unkempt black hair and a full scraggly beard. He carries a large conch shell around his torso on a leather lanyard – this is what produced the sonics that drove Blinky away. Brandon has an angry scowl and an air of superiority, despite his caveman-like appearance. He revives his helpless captive and does his best Bond villain soliloquy, telling her, "This whole valley is mine! Everything in it belongs to me – including you!"

Henry Brandon is Dr. Carl Hunter who crash-landed ten years earlier during a 1945 expedition with three other scientists. He was the only survivor, revealing that he's had to outthink the beasts to survive. Hunter destroyed their eggs, keeping the dino population manageable and using the shell noise to rule over them. Lust overcomes the need for talk and he savagely attacks Maggie just as Jock and the other men arrive. The Commander tries to understand Hunter's mindset and to befriend him, but Hunter is too far gone. He wants them to trade the woman for the location of his copter wreck so they can salvage the spare parts and leave, but Roberts is in love with Maggie and will have none of that.

Man vs. Dinosaur Puppet in *The Land Unknown*.

They cautiously leave and Hunter rants about being alone during the nine-month Antarctic nights; we further understand the solitude this man had to endure over a decade of horror. Brandon emotes here somewhat restrained but full of angst. His Dr. Hunter is a very effective performance as the only character in this film with a character arc – and a surprising one at that!

Hunter follows the intruders and saves Maggie from the tentacles of the woman-eating plant, then disappears into the jungle. She decides to offer herself up to the brute in order to save her friends and heads back to his cave via the life raft. He sees her approaching and, knowing of the dangers of this large lagoon, paddles off to meet her, two large flaming torches ready at the bow.

Some *thing* is bubbling under the surface, and it turns out to be a monstrous plesiosaurus, which soon is towering above her, ready for lunch. Hunter blows his shell, drawing the beast toward him instead of away. He boldly shoves a burning torch into its gaping mouth! It dives under, then attacks him again. Henry only has one torch left! He lunges and scores another direct hit, finally driving it off. Hunter then brings the unconscious girl back to his cave and revives her for some adult fun, but one of her friends arrives before he can assault Maggie.

A furious fight takes place and Henry almost slices the man open with a nasty curved blade when he himself gets knocked backward against a stone table, which knocks him out. Jock stops his pilot from torturing Hunter in a brutal attempt to discover the location of the wreck, saying "We're not going to dig our way out of here through human flesh!"

When Maggie goes to help Hunter, who has a head injury, he softens and gives them the map to his wreck; then he asks to be left alone. His decade with these prehistoric beasts has turned him, out of necessity, into an animal but this human compassion has helped to heal his soul. As the men leave for the wreck site, Maggie remains to help Hunter, knowing she will now be safe with him.

Henry Brandon exudes animal magnetism in this *Land Unknown* in a part unlike any previous role he's had. You can feel his male hunger for Maggie and see the darting cunning in his eyes. It's a terrific part, never overplayed, with seething sexual desire bubbling under his surface like the lava pots that dot the primordial landscape.

With the helicopter repaired and taking off, Hunter escorts Maggie to rendezvous with the ship via his raft and the sea beast comes back for another round with his old enemy. She faints again as he shoves flaming torches into that singed toothy mouth. Maggie is hoisted up via an air wench and the Plesiosaurus makes one last run at Henry. This time, it dives under and topples the raft, knocking Hunter unconscious with his massive fin. Jock shoots a flare into its mouth (you'd think it would be pretty tender in there by now) and dives off the copter to haul Hunter's prone form into the ship. Four people crash-landed but it is *five* people who finally leave the land unknown. They make it out of the volcano crater and the look of sheer wonder on Henry Brandon's face when he spies the aircraft carrier and their certain salvation is joyous!

Brandon reminisced in a *Starlog Magazine* interview:

> Working on *The Land Unknown* was very difficult for me because it was a very strange photographic process which I didn't understand at that time. You couldn't move sideways when you were doing medium and close shots. You had to be very static in your movements, because they had *preshot* all the second unit stuff with the miniatures and prehistoric animals. When I was fighting the dinosaur, I was really fighting air.*

The Land Unknown offers Brandon a strong part with quite the acting arc, beginning as the primary human antagonist and becoming sympathetic, even heroic at the finish. Hunter reclaims his humanity and Henry Brandon actually lives at the conclusion, a happy ending for a nice change of pace. Not quite so happy for Universal International, as *The Land Unknown* cost them slightly more than $800,000 to produce. This is more than the lavish Technicolor *This Island Earth* and the 3-D chiller *It Came from Outer Space*, making *The Land Unknown* the most expensive 1950s sci-fi movie made at Universal.

Raiders of the Seven Seas:

Henry Brandon gives an engaging performance in *Raiders of the Seven Seas*, a low budget *Sea Hawk* with a very broad tone from 1957. Produced by Global Productions and released through United Artists, *Raiders* brings together an expert cast with John Payne and Donna Reed as unlikely swashbucklers and features Henry's friend Lon Chaney Jr. in one of his best post-Universal horror roles.

Payne plays Barbarossa, one of the famous pirates raiding the seven seas, although there is only one sea depicted in this tongue-in-cheek potboiler. Barbarossa commands the screen with a smile, a wink and a *very* healthy

---

* *Starlog Magazine* January 1987 #114

libido! It begins with Barbarossa escaping from Morocco via some Indiana Jones-style derring-do and capturing an entire Spanish ship with just a knife, echoing Douglas Fairbanks in *The Black Pirate*. The ship's cargo includes prisoners to be sold into slavery in Tortuga, all of whom are only too happy to serve under their new 'Captain' Barbarossa. This includes Chaney's lovable cutthroat Peg Leg.

Brandon as Captain Goiti in *Raiders of the Seven Seas*.

Brandon plays Havana-based Captain Goiti, who is constantly bickering with Salcedo (Gerald Mohr) about how to best serve their Spanish masters. Henry is flamboyantly attired in a bright red uniform and an air of superiority and experience. When Barbarossa arrives, he easily gets the best of them and kidnaps the lovely Alida (Donna Reed with a brunette wig) which has both Salcedo and Goiti in hot pursuit while remaining at odds.

Goiti's impressive death throes in *Raiders of the Seven Seas*.

The film tries to set up a Robin Hood/Maid Marian relationship between Barbarossa and Alida, but it's hard to take serious because Payne never does. However, Raiders takes an ill-advised tone shift about fifty minutes in when Brandon and Mohr discover Barbarossa's base while they are out marauding and they murder (off-screen) all the women and children in the encampment! This is shocking, and instantly sucks the sense of fun right out of the picture, which never quite recovers.

Since Salcedo fails to apprehend Barbarossa, Goiti is promoted to the rank of General and is tasked with bringing the pirate in and rescuing Alida. The film's mood shifts even darker when crew member Renzo (Anthony Caruso) betrays his comrades and brutally murders poor Peg Leg with a dagger to the heart, framing Alida for the killing. This sends Barbarossa into a rage of revenge with a plan to attack the capitol in Havana.

The scheming Salcedo tricks Captain Goiti into giving him 1,500 troops to nail Barbarossa, knowing he leaves them virtually unprotected from the pirates impending attack. With Goiti dead, Salcedo will again be in command.

This confrontation sequence is Henry's best in *Raiders*, as his Goiti is inebriated and pompous, holding court for his foppish friends and society hangers-on. He is loud, lively, condescending and wildly entertaining. The next morning has the enraged Barbarossa storming the fort and easily conquering the undermanned facility.

Brandon spies Barbarossa, who has fallen to the ground during the battle. He sneaks up behind him to kill him but things don't quite work out. Henry Brandon has had some pretty unique and memorable movie deaths, but this ain't one of them! Before he can stab Barbarossa in the back, he is skewered in the stomach by a little boy! His writhing death throes are pretty impressive, and he dies with supreme grace.

Raiders of the Seven Seas wraps up with an exciting escape, the pirate getting the girl and capturing another ship for new adventures. This is a split personality movie whose two halves don't mesh well together, but it remains an entertaining effort with good roles for Henry Brandon and his two pals Lon Chaney and Tony Caruso.

Captain Sindbad:

In 1958, Columbia Pictures released what is probably the best of the Ray Harryhausen special-effects extravaganzas, the eye-popping monsterfest called *The 7th Voyage of Sindbad*. Six years later, MGM released a King Brothers (*Gorgo*) production named *Captain Sindbad* with Henry Brandon in a significant supporting role, but a sequel to *The 7th Voyage of Sindbad* this ain't.

Captain Sindbad was filmed in Munich, Germany at the Bavaria Studios in 1963 during a frigid winter, the centerpiece production of Henry's extended European sojourn that also included a **Walt Disney Presents** television episode and several stage productions. Guy Williams (shortly to play the lead on television's **Lost in Space**) makes an engaging, confident Sindbad and the main heavy is portrayed by the superb Pedro Armendariz as El

Kerim. *Sindbad* was Armendariz' second to last film role before he portrayed Kerim Bey in the second James Bond thriller *From Russia With Love*, a film he wouldn't live to see.

Brandon as Colonel Kabar in *Captain Sindbad*.

As a juvenile fantasy film with the name Sindbad in the title, there are certain expectations an audience is looking for – expectations that *Captain Sindbad* fails to deliver on. The budget was evidently spent on sets, costumes and importing talent in front of and behind the camera, leaving very little for special effects, which are mostly laughable in this broad adventure.

In Baristan, a nutty magician named Galgo the Great (Abraham Sofaer) makes it rain and snow indoors with cheesy effects that would flat out embarrass Ray Harryhausen. He lets the Princess Jana (Heidi Bruhl) know that her beloved Sindbad is returning from his latest voyage, but that he won't make it back safely. We see Henry Brandon's Colonel Kabar arrive in the city with great fanfare, at the side of his master El Kerim (Armendariz coincidentally sharing his character name with that of his *From Russia with Love* Bond ally). They are in a full procession of troops and elephants to take control of the capitol city.

Kabar is dressed fully in black, from his turban to his silken ornate robes and menacing black gloves. Brandon plays the role fairly straight as compared to the juicier performances given by Galgo and Kerim, however he gives the role surprising subtext for a children's fantasy, as we see later in the film. Kabar arrives in the quarters of Galgo, demanding that the Princess be brought before his master, El Kerim. She is absent, having been turned into a bird to fly out and greet her beloved Sindbad, still at sea.

Sindbad's boat is attacked by birds carrying large rocks, dropping them onto the decks. After only a few hits, Sindbad cries, "Abandon ship!" which the crew quickly does. Not much grit in this incarnation of monster-fighter Sindbad.

The crew is seemingly lost but Sindbad makes it back to Baristan thanks to some fishermen. He quickly finds that his crew also made it back and determines that the quickest way into the castle to face El Kerim and rescue the Princess is to steal cantaloupes and be accused of a crime. Kabar reads off the list of charges from a scroll as the Princess unwittingly reveals Sindbad's identity to the court. He runs Kerim through with his blade, to no ill effect.

Sorcery has removed his heart to some safe place and he cannot be killed. El Kerim decrees that Sindbad will face a deadly challenge in the arena the next morning. Finally, monsters are coming!

The next morning, with the entire population of the city watching from the bleachers, Sindbad is brought out to face some horrifying creature snorting and roaring from behind a large gate. When Henry Brandon informs his foe that, at the express order of his Excellency El Kerim, Sindbad will combat this coming horror with NO weapon, you can sense in Kabar his displeasure at the inequity of the contest. Kabar has respect for the warrior that Sindbad is and definitely seems at odds with his master El Kerim. Henry expertly conveys this undercurrent of emotion, even camaraderie for Sindbad and it is both surprising and oddly affecting.

Fifty minutes into this creature-less Sindbad movie, will we finally have our monster? Nope. The budget was spent on sets, costumes, talent, and therefore the massive dragon-like monster is – and must be – invisible. He leaves big three-toed footprints and green sparks, though. O, wherefore art thou, Harryhausen?

Sindbad easily evades the transparent beast by climbing up a tapestry, toppling one of those massive fiery torch-thingies and causing a riot, during which he escapes. Enraged, Kerim threatens to kill anyone aiding Sindbad and doubles all taxes. Col. Kabar wisely advises against this and suggests, instead, that an act of generosity would be a better course, advice that El Kerim follows. One thousand gold coins are offered for the capture and killing of Sindbad!

While Sindbad and his men journey to a nearby tower that contains Kerim's beating heart, the villain forces the princess to marry him-- or die. She chooses death, so Kerim arranges a mass execution, which Kabar reluctantly follows. Sindbad is warned that "untold horrors" surround the dark tower, which means that finally the monsters are coming! Well, sort of.

There are some ambulatory weeds, a big chained door and lots of jungle noises. Then a fog swamp, a sink hole and some rubber alligators.

Dawn approaches and the Princess and her usurped father are to be crushed under elephant hooves. Before the crushing occurs, Sindbad finally battles the one and only monster of *Captain Sindbad*. We get a ten or twelve-headed hydra puppet whose close–up heads don't match the long-shot heads; but a monster is a monster. The crew rolls a fake boulder onto the fake hydra puppet, which roars and topples into a fire-pit. This shouldn't hurt a real dragon, but it kills this one. Then Sindbad battles a massive gloved fist (needs to be seen to be disbelieved) which moves very slowly, finally getting to the red, beating heart of El Kerim.

Throughout the movie, Kabar has been nothing but loyal and patient with his master El Kerim. He is suddenly determined by Kerim to be a traitor and is jailed for siding with Sindbad. We never see him again. Lucky Kabar.

With the nutty magician's help, Sindbad defeats Kerim and marries the Princess and this endless disappointment finally comes to a colorful conclusion. *Captain Sindbad* is a slice of cheesy schlock in Brandon's filmography, but at least Henry got a trip back home to Germany out of the job.

CHAPTER FOURTEEN
Z Pictures

IN A LONG FILM career comprised of over one hundred roles, Henry Brandon was in his share of great films, good films, entertaining films and potboilers. He never gave less than 100% of his considerable acting skills whether he was playing a leading role, a supporting role or a cameo role. Henry was in dozens of B pictures and – as one would suspect – a handful of what can only be categorized as "clunkers" or Grade Z films. All of these come in the back half of Henry's film career and most can be categorized as "exploitation" films. There aren't that many of them, surprisingly, but when Henry found himself cast in a stinker… well, they could be quite pungent!

Okefenokee:

Filmed on location in the Florida Everglades in 1959, *Okefenokee* was one of just two films that Henry Brandon appeared in that year. Not a studio production, it was an exploitation picture released by Film Service Distributing Corporation on the bottom half of a double bill with *The Monster of Piedras Blancas*.

Narrator Patrick McGeehan tells us at the film's outset that "deep in the Florida Everglades, the Seminole Indians lived for centuries in what once was a tranquil sanctuary." The coming of the white man ended that tranquility, at least as far as *Okefenokee* is concerned when we see third-billed Henry Brandon as Joe Kalhari arriving on a flat mosquito airboat for a questionable meeting.

Kalhari sits like a king on a throne, surrounded by his minions. He is a criminal, involved in smuggling gold, narcotics, diamonds, international agents and saboteurs. Clean shaven and shot from low angles, Joe Kalhari glides through the twisting Everglades water ways like an anaconda.

Okefenokee's **Joe Kalhari (Brandon) up to no good.**

One of his first despicable acts is to murder his Seminole guide so he can't talk, leaving the bullet-riddled body to the alligators in the reeds. Asked by his sidekick why they have to knock off all the redskins, Kalhari snaps, "And as soon as they get wise, we gotta hit 'em! Quit worrying!"

All of the outdoors footage in *Okefenokee* was clearly shot silent and poorly dubbed in later. The unnatural sound adds greatly to the cheese factor and gives the film an artificial feel. The constant flow of menacing music by Jack Shaindlin (who also contributed to the early Hanna-Barbera cartoons at this same time) is another cheesy aspect of this production for us to embrace.

The murdered guide was a cousin to the film's protagonist Chekika (Peter Coe) who tries to find out what happened to the missing relative. His investigation leads him to a sleazy bar called The Blue Heron run by blonde

Ricki Hart (Peggy Maley) who happens to be Kalhari's main squeeze. She reports back that Chekika is asking too many questions and might be dangerous. "Let him," Kalhari replies. "The alligators in the glades eat up all the evidence, if the vultures don't find him first."

He tells Ricki that if this new Indian becomes a threat, he'll do away with him immediately. His murderous talk turns *himself* on and he savagely kisses Ms. Hart. Henry's normally black hair is Florida sun-bleached to varying degrees throughout the picture. He looks particularly robust and bronzed in *Okefenokee*.

That night at The Blue Heron, Brandon plays table games dressed in a white linen suit and open collar print shirt, oozing sleaze and boasting, "I have yet to be beaten!" Chekika arrives and meets Kalhari for the first time. Joe has no information about the missing Seminole and almost immediately makes a racially insensitive remark, putting him at odds with Chekika, who leaves. Kalhari decides that the inquisitive intruder is to be gator bait as he snarls the most shocking line in the movie, "The only good Indian is a dead Indian!" It's a quintessential Brandon movie moment because it is at odds with a screen career in which he played a multitude of good Indians, bad Indians and dead Indians.

Kalhari arranges for a drop point at Shark Harbor Channel via short wave radio and uses another Seminole water guide; this one is Chekika's younger brother. They meet up with a seaplane and pick up two fugitives, whom they deliver miles away to a waiting car. As the long flat boat speeds through the waterways, Brandon, on an elevated platform, hovers above everyone in his white ball cap and black soul.

He has his "enforcer" rifle butt the young guide in the middle of a mangrove swamp. Instead of shooting the boy, Kalhari circles back and drives his boat over the body, the large blades of the propeller doing the dirty work. Not a pleasant way to go.

Chekika searches the Glades all the way to Miami, but finds no one who has seen his missing brother or cousin. When Ricki informs Kalhari that it was the little brother of Chekika he killed the previous night in the swamp and the police are going to be called in, he shuts down the smuggling operation to make a run for it. Kalhari tells Hart to keep her bar open for a few days and then meet them in Havana. She refuses and he snaps, "Then consider yourself replaced!" Ricki slaps Kalhari, and then he strikes her hard, across her face, nearly knocking her down the stairs! "You're safe as long as you keep the joint open – now get out!"

Brandon as sleazy Kalhari in *Okefenokee*.

Chekika beats the truth out of a drunken thug who works for Kalhari and now knows who killed his brother. He gathers up the entire Seminole tribe in their flatboats in hot pursuit of Kalhari's gang. The offbeat showdown of a dozen or so Indian mosquito boats with thundering motors converging on Kalhari's boat makes for a unique cinematic climactic chase.

Kalhari is on the run for his life, playing hide and seek in the mangrove inlets, hoping to make for the open sea away from the Seminoles. His escape sea plane is sighted and lands. They make a run for it, but before he can get there, the Seminoles converge on the solitary craft, throwing deadly spears at Kalhari! He manages to get aboard and the plane roars to take off! Chekika speeds his craft directly at the water plane in a suicide ram. This sequence is intercut with extreme close-ups of Henry Brandon's writhing features, building tension expertly if obviously. The motion picture camera was *never* so close to Brandon's trademark facial grimace.

Chekika jumps off before his boat collides with the plane in a fireball explosion in one of Henry's best screen deaths – blown to blazing pieces! *Okefenokee* is most definitely a turkey, but thanks to Henry Brandon's sleazy Joe Kalhari, it is a most tasty turkey with a big helping of Limburger cheese on the side.

Search for the Evil One:

Ambassador Film's production of *Search for the Evil One* released in 1967 is possibly the very worst film that Henry Brandon ever appeared in. It is one massive hunk of aromatic cheese that lays there for 70 long minutes, even though Henry does his best as Nazi Martin Bormann, working with an aging, addle-brained Adolph Hitler (yep, he's still alive) to revive the Fourth Reich and take over South America.

Lee Patterson stars as Anton Becker, a Jew pretending to be German for no reason other than that's what the script calls for. His stiff, one-note acting skills permeate the entire film with an air of amateurish blandness. Becker is recruited by an Israeli spy organization to penetrate a secluded castle on the outskirts of Buenos Aires and gain the confidence of exiled Martin Bormann because they suspect that Hitler's death in 1945 was faked and he is living in this castle. They base this hypothesis on a man's gnarled hand in the frame of a cropped photograph. It is, they believe, Hitler's hand. And if Hitler's hand still exists, then the rest of Hitler MUST be nearby as well.

A flashback confirms that Hitler had his double in the bunker as the

Allies were bombing him and Bormann personally puts a bullet in the hapless lookalike's head then stages the "suicide." Martin takes Adolph to Madrid, Hitler shaves his mustache and they head down to South America to hide and rebuild, but mostly hide.

Becker, whose parents and sister were murdered by the Nazis during WWII, agrees to help the Israelis and manages to get himself invited to the Castle by an old German girlfriend. Henry first appears in the present riding up on his horse at the front of the Castle, greeting this newcomer with feigned warmth and plenty of suspicion. Brandon easily commands the screen as literally the only one with talent in the entire production, both in front of and behind the camera.

Later, the Germans go deer hunting with bow and arrows. Henry speaks in a thick German accent but shows some restraint, giving Bormann quite an air of menace. He is a very dangerous man, although during the deer hunt he falls down a mountainside and Becker runs up, concerned. Because of this, Bormann is suddenly convinced of Becker's sincerity that a true German heart beats within his chest. It makes no sense whatsoever; especially as the next sequence has Becker invited to attend a full blown Nazi propaganda meeting in a bunker at the Castle. The Germans are in full dress uniform, swastikas and "Sieg Heiling" and all.

After listening to a recording of Adolph Hitler, the REAL live Hitler joins them, dramatically introduced via a convenient spotlight. He is grey-haired and grey-mustached and launches into a typical fervent speech, threatening to eradicate the Jews for good this time. Bormann at his side is clearly his Number Two, a loyal caretaker. Hitler is disoriented and rambling, talking about assassinating both Jews and journalists. Brandon has him escorted away for a 'rest' and he tells Becker about the coming Fourth Reich and their takeover of all of South America.

"In his moments of lucidity," Bormann explains, "he still has the vision to tell us how to succeed! He is old and talks too much. Sometimes he forgets where he is. He never leaves his bunker. No matter how old he is, no matter how sick he is – HE IS STILL THE FUEHRER!" Brandon works himself up into a frothy Nazi frenzy and this is easily the best scene in the picture.

"In the coming veeks, you vill be able to prove your dedication to our sacred cause!" Martin Bormann continues to explain to Becker, who pledges allegiance to that cause. Later that night he is caught signaling to the Israeli forces in the woods. Bormann enters and reveals that they knew all along that he was a spy working with Israel. He guns down the old German girlfriend in cold blood and takes Becker away to be tortured.

A half dozen Israeli troops emerge from the woods and engage in a gunfight with a like number of Nazis in as unexciting a gun battle as was ever lensed for a motion picture. Meanwhile, Martin Bormann armed with his bow and arrow, hunts down Becker on the wooded hillside around the Castle a'la *The Most Dangerous Game.*

Before that can play out, the Israelis start shooting off mortar fire and blow up most of the Nazis. Becker escapes in the confusion, Hitler potters around believing he's back in the 1940's and Bormann gets blown up. Nutty Adolph keeps talking to Henry Brandon's corpse until he is blown up too. This is when *Search for the Evil One* truly embraces exactly what it is… a bomb.

To Henry's credit, he never goes hammy with this awful material and portrays the only character without a monotone in the whole picture. His Nazi diatribe is fairly entertaining, but it's not worth sitting through this whole amateurish mess to get to it.

Gentle Savage:

This 1973 *Billy Jack*-type exploitation film is about a lowlife American Indian who is wrongfully accused of raping an underage white girl in a film populated with foul-mouthed, ugly people and, somehow, Joe Flynn from *McHale's Navy*. Wildly politically incorrect in the 21st Century, the film is a brutal, inept, joyless experience filled with one savage beating, murder and explosion after another.

Henry Brandon appears in one mercifully brief scene as a grizzled Indian holy man in a graveyard. When a character brings his murdered brother's body to him, Brandon says, "This is sacred burial ground. You cannot leave your brother here." Insultingly, another actor was brought in to loop the dialogue, so it's not even Henry's voice coming out of his own mouth. This is a terrible movie to be avoided at all costs.

The Manhandlers:

It's a sign of the times that some of the worst films that Henry Brandon appeared in were at the tail end of his career – 'tail' being the operative word for *The Manhandlers*, an exploitation film released in December of 1974.

Henry plays a greasy Italian mob boss named Carlo with slick jet black hair. As the film's key heavy, he shows up immediately, in the pre-credits sequence, meeting with a sniveling pimp named Leo. Leo and his partner have been blackmailing Carlo with an incriminating tape, and Carlo wants the partner identified. "Give me his name, you son of a bitch!" snarls Henry, who is soon engaged in a gunfight with Leo. Carlo shoots him and then, for good measure, shoots his prone corpse in the back! "Schmuck!" exclaims Carlo, "I didn't want to do that. What good are you to me now?" As gooey red blood drips from Leo's mouth, Carlo strides away to the strands of 70's wah-wah soundtrack guitar music and we know this will be a Henry Brandon we aren't accustomed to seeing in motion pictures.

After the credits, Carlo attends Leo's funeral, watching for who his mysterious partner might be. Katie Farrell (Cara Burgess) is Leo's beautiful niece who inherits his massage parlor business, The Loving Touch. She goes to check it out and is shocked to find two topless girls giving full service to a john. "This is a brothel!" Katie realizes, showing keen insight and impressive intelligence.

Carlo sends his good-looking nephew Frank Spinelli (Vince Cannon) over to "The Loving Touch" to explain things, but Frank finds himself attracted to Katie. Henry, meanwhile, visits one of the hookers that Katie fired to get the name of Leo's blackmailing partner. She reveals it is a lawyer named Ratchet, then accuses Henry of killing Leo… which is unfortunate for her. Carlo has his Oddjob-type thug come in and "give the broad a hug, a nice big hug!" That ties up one loose caboose.

Brandon then tracks down and confronts Lawyer Ratchet, who doesn't have the tape and threatens Carlo. That's not a good idea as Carlo coldly guns him down and, like Leo, plants the final silenced shot into Ratchet's twitching back.

The Manhandlers at The Loving Touch are now reopened for business, giving genuine massages. This doesn't sit well with the local Godfather Vito Fennuchi who berates his lieutenant Carlo for losing one of his profitable prostitution businesses and threatens him to fix it. Henry Brandon then drops an 'F' bomb, sending his crusher over to convince the girls to turn over 50% of their gross for "protection."

It turns out that the missing blackmail tape contains evidence that Carlo is a stoolie talking to the Feds about Mob activity. Katie finds the 8-Track tape among her Uncle's cartridges and Carlo decides to handle her personally. As usual, Henry brings real menace to his role as Carlo the Informer, amidst a sea of bad acting, a bevy of breastage, lame humor and graphic mob violence.

The climax (one of them, anyway) was filmed at a vintage Long Beach amusement park called The Pike and it's fun to watch Henry Brandon stalking Cara Burgess on the various old-time rides. They are on a ferris wheel, dodgem cars, and Carlo even mows down metal bunnies at the shooting gallery as he follows his prey. Carlo is unaware that HE is also prey, being followed by two Mob goons, sent by Frank. When he finally corners Katie on a deserted dodgem car and begins to strangle her, he is interrupted by the Mob, who take him for a ride to be rubbed out.

The Manhandlers is a typical 70's exploitation cheese-fest at about the same low level as *Search for the Evil One*. In both films, Henry is easily the highlight.

Assault on Precinct 13:

One of John Carpenter's early efforts, the *Halloween* and *The Thing* [1982] masterminded, wrote and directed *Assault on Precinct 13* in 1976. He cast Henry Brandon as a weary veteran desk sergeant named Chaney for this suspenseful gore-fest. While *Assault on Precinct 13* is far from a clunker like most of the "epics" in this chapter, it is most definitely an exploitation flick in the wake of *Dirty Harry* and *Death Wish*. Indeed, one wishes Brandon's Chaney had made it further than the midway mark of this 90 minute feature as it would have been nice to see him in action against these well-armed gang punks on the rampage.

Desk Sergeant Chaney in *Assault On Precinct 13*.

The gang in question is called "Street Thunder" and they converge on a soon-to-close police station in fictitious Anderson, California, one of the worst of the Los Angeles ghetto communities. In fact, Chaney's boss, the precinct Captain complains to Lt. Ethan Bishop (Austin Stoker), there to take over for the last night of command, that there have been twelve stolen cars, three burglaries and eight aggravated assaults – and it's not even 8:00 PM yet! Nice neighborhood.

Bishop grew up a few blocks from the Precinct, so it's a turf he knows well. He has just a few cops and a few female clerical staff, some prisoners being transferred to Death Row and grizzled front desk Sgt. Chaney on hand when a man bursts in, claiming his daughter was killed and the gang responsible is following him. When the phones go dead and the lights go out, unsuspecting Officer Chaney heads outside to his car to radio from there. It is there that Henry Brandon gives us – via the exploding blood packets so enamored by director Carpenter – one of his most violent screen deaths yet. Out in front of the station, Street Thunder lets loose with their first deadly volley and three silenced bullets take out Chaney, who collapses in a shower of gore.

The balance of the film has the Death Row inmates joining forces with the cops and girls of the precinct to hold off the massive army of gang members until help can arrive. It's more like a classic Western at this point and it's engaging, thrilling stuff. Too bad Henry Brandon was earmarked for first blood and missed out on all the action.

Run for the Roses:

This 1977 film is a dull horse-racing drama about a dysfunctional wealthy family of race-horse owners who always come in second at The Kentucky Derby. *Run for the Roses* offers up Henry Brandon in a thankless role every bit as boring as the film is.

Vera Miles, Stuart Whitman and Sam Gomez star with support from Henry Brandon as Jeff, a slightly snooty horse trainer and companion of Clarissa (Miles), the family matriarch. When a colt is born lame, she offhandedly gives the animal to young Juanito (Panchito Gomez) who names him Royal Champion. Juanito raises the needed down payment of $300 for an operation to straighten Champion's crooked knee and the horse responds immediately to the surgery.

When Clarissa and Jeff see Champion working out and looking smart, she says to her trainer, "I want Champion back. I never should have given him away in the first place." Jeff's response is "But you did." The role of Jeff is one of those "But you did" parts for Brandon, who spends most of his meager screen time responding to Vera Miles and making no worthwhile contribution to the plot.

Run for the Roses contains flat acting, looped dialogue and a predictable script which add up to a bland film experience. Henry must have been bored stiff trying to make Trainer Jeff interesting. *Roses* was a rare failure for him, although the real culprit is the hackneyed script.

As Champion makes the rounds, winning key races at Santa Anita, Del Mar and Bay Meadows, they set their sights on winning the Kentucky Derby. The family makes up, the wealthy get wealthier, Henry Brandon smiles and everyone has a happy ending. Does Champion win the Derby? This film doesn't have enough imagination for a surprising ending, but thankfully, there *is* an ending.

Run for the Roses was produced by Pan American Films and released by Kodiak Films. Henry would make one more film in the 70's and two in the 1980's, sadly wrapping up his movie career with one Z Picture after another. One almost wishes he would have called it a day after the superb *When the North Wind Blows* in 1974. But then we never would have had the loopy delights of *Wizards of the Lost Kingdom II* to bookend his motion picture filmography.

Hollywood Knight/Hard Knocks:

The last 'bad' cowboy Henry Brandon played was Curley in the schizophrenic *Hollywood Knight* (aka *Hard Knocks*, aka *Mid-Knight Rider*) which starts out like a pornographic film but ends up as a bland drama of redemption. Produced in 1979, *Hollywood Knight* is also notable as the only film in which both Henry Brandon and his significant other Mark Herron worked, although the two share no scenes together.

Written, Produced and starring Michael Christian as male prostitute Guy Montgomery, *Hollywood Knight* can be an uncomfortable viewing experience for classic movie buffs. The story begins with a voice over by the lead character, who tells us, "Sex is something everybody seems to hide. They all want it. They all need it. It's how I make my money. Sometimes it seems glamorous… it's not."

The opening montage cuts together scenes of excessive nudity and violence. In these days of chapter stops and fast forwarding, Brandon fans are advised to skip ahead to the point where Guy, on the run believing he's killed a porn filmmaker who drugged him, ends up on a ranch in rural America. The owner is Keenan Wynn as Jud, who hires Guy as a ranch hand.

After a few weeks of hard work, the pair heads into town to stop at a bar for a beer. Here we meet Henry Brandon as Curley, a nasty cowpoke with a bad attitude, lounging at a table with two buddies. When waitress Sally heads over to Guy and introduces herself as the hostess, Curley leeringly adds that she is "the hostess with the mostest!" Then he laughs it up.

Brandon plays Curley like an updated version of Clay Cook from *Wagon's West*, a smart-mouthed hateful jerk. He's also got some history with Jud, who punches Curley in the face after he teases Sally for spending time with "old men and queers." This leads to a generic bar fight and the pair getting arrested.

After Jud and Guy get released, the Sheriff asks Curley to bury the hatchet with the old man. He visits Jud at his ranch and extends his hand in friendship. Suspicious, then accepting, Jud shakes Curley's hand, which is a mistake. Curley beats Jud senseless (off screen) and the police mistakenly chase Guy, who thinks they've come to arrest him for what happened back in Hollywood.

Curley joins the posse out to get Guy which leads to a brief scene that *could* have been the highlight of *Hollywood Knight* for Brandon fans. Shiftless and lazy, Curley takes time off from the posse's manhunt to loaf by a creek. He pulls of his cowboy boots and dips his feet in the water, croaking 'Blood on the Saddle' in his best Johnny Cash voice. Sadly, the sequence is poorly lit and staged, robbing it of any comedic impact.

After a harrowing night in a dark cave with bats and tarantulas, Guy crawls out into daylight, torn and bleeding, near the edge of a precipice. There to meet him is Curley, evil in his eyes and a deadly smile on his lips. He kicks helpless Guy toward the ledge and a horrible death. Brandon's murderous grin is spine-chilling as he grinds his boot into Guy's cave wounds. Before he can deliver the final kick, the sound of a rifle cocking stops him cold. Keenan Wynn's Jed, recovered from the beating, is there to save the day.

"I was just shaking him up a bit," Curley explains lamely, taking a rifle butt in the face. Jed pulls Guy up off the ledge and the male prostitute gets a happy Hollywood ending. *Hollywood Knight/Hard Knocks/Mid-Knight Rider* is a rough exploitation film to get through with Keenan Wynn and Henry Brandon giving it their best efforts but ultimately unable to rise above the bland script, poor acting and direction with enough violence, nudity and vulgarity to make *The Manhandlers* feel like *Mary Poppins*.

Wizards of the Lost Kingdom II:

Henry Brandon's film career both begins and ends with his playing the despicable lead villain in a make-believe fantasyland – but from there *Babes in Toyland* and *Wizards of the Lost Kingdom II* have nothing further in common.

"Across the Sea of Dreams... behind the Curtain of Time... lies the land of ultimate fantasy" reads the tag line for the ad campaign of *Wizards of the Lost Kingdom II*, released by New Classics in 1989. When the ad hype is more entertaining than the picture, you've got problems.

Henry Brandon appeared in more than one hundred feature motion pictures during his long career and this last film he made, *Wizards of the Lost Kingdom II*, is the easily the worst film he ever appeared in.

WOTLKII begins with a montage of all the best action shots yet to come in the hopes of convincing the audience not to storm out of the theatre. Intercut with these bland shots of lightning strikes and glowing swords and people getting mock-impaled are close-up shots of the three main wizard villains laughing maniacally. Laughing – no doubt – at the audience, as if in mockery that the film's producers now have their hard-earned ticket money and they are stuck in the theatre to watch this abomination of a motion picture. Henry is one of these wizened wizard villains, looking straight at the camera, a flashlight from below illuminating his wrinkles, laughing in a low, throaty bellow with perhaps just the slightest look of apology in his craggy eyes.

Indeed, in a December 12, 1988 letter to his friend Marcus Maier, Henry wrote:

> Wednesday morning I'm going to Venice (California) for a showing for the cast of Roger Corman's *Wizards of the Lost Kingdom II* starring David Carradine. It is a perfectly dreadful film I made a couple of months ago. I am the lead villain and I will probably have crawled under the seat in front of me by the time the house lights come up.

WOTLK II plays like *Star Wars* meets *Lord of the Rings*, but with none of those films imagination, scope or talent. Produced after the initial *Star Wars* trilogy and the rousing success of the first *WOTLK* (that was sarcasm), part *II* follows the familiar character beats found in *A New Hope*, *The Empire Strikes Back* and *Return of the Jedi*.

"The age of heroes came to an end," a self-impressed voice-over tells us. "And in their place evil wizards rose up to oppress the Three Kingdoms. As ever, it was the people who suffered." (No doubt, a reference to the theatre audience.) "Some tried to fight back." (Perhaps they asked the theatre manager for their ticket price to be refunded?) "But the magic and the soldiers proved to be too much. And the rule of tyranny grew. And at last there remained only one hope (Luke?) to rid the Kingdoms of this terrible darkness... Caedmon of Nogg!"

Caedmon of Nogg? We'd be better off with Egg of Nogg since Caedmon is a fat, old, gray-bearded bumbling cave-dweller and a truly terrible actor.

He is the last of the good wizards and the "Obi-Wan" of *WOTLK II*, if Obi-Wan had just finished playing the Catskills after indulging in way too much pastrami on rye. Caedmon, as his talking bubbling cauldron informs him, must face three bad wizards – the most powerful evil Lord of them all being Henry Brandon's character, Zarz of Edark. The thought of Brandon playing this adventure's Darth Vader with Shakespearean relish on top of a deep-fried corn-dog is actually quite appealing: could it possibly be worth slogging through the film for? We shall see…

"What can I do against forces such as these?" asks Caedmon of the verbose kettle. He is told to embark on a journey to find the one with purity of heart who can reunite the Three Kingdoms. So our ersatz Obi-Wan sets out to locate a Luke Skywalker-esque boy hero with a special birthmark in his armpit. IN HIS ARMPIT! Meanwhile the reign of terror grows worse which we see depicted via an increase in lethal sword fights in the streets.

The old, fat guy tries to trick young boys into raising their arms so he can examine their pits (yes, this is really the plot) to find the mystical tattoo. Luckily, the first boy he tricks is The One and his magical training begins ala Yoda and Luke, only stupider. He is Tyor, played with all the acting skills of piece of wood by Bobby Jacoby. Rather than instruction in mastering his powers to levitate heavy objects, Caedmon teaches the boy to make a roast chicken appear.

Next up, they seek out "The Dark One" (David Carradine) in a seedy bar (like in *Star Wars*, only stupider) in search of their Han Solo character. Carradine tells them "I'm just a simple bartender," but Caedmon will have none of that. "Dark One," he implores, "we need you if we're going to overthrow these evil wizards!" But he's busy with the bar, so they move on to a matte painting of a castle to enlist the aid of an imprisoned Prince.

The dubbing of this movie is terrible to the point of distraction, even worse than in *Captain Sindbad*. In the castle they meet three blonde maidens in a prison cell and a guy in a Don Post werewolf mask chained to a wall. (That mask must have put quite a strain on the budget. Some of those run as much as eighty dollars). We are now seventeen minutes into *Wizards* (it feels like forty-five) and still our only sign of Henry Brandon was when he was laughing at us during the opening credits.

***Wizards of the Lost Kingdom* II poster art featured Henry prominently. Collection of Bill Cassara.**

There is a pig beast with fangs that attacks the werewolf mask in a lethargic fight as the duo rescue Prince Ermin and his three bimbos. Suddenly, outside there is a big unconvincing fight scene with people on fire, making this senseless movie make even less sense. The first of the three bad wizards appears to attack the boy in what amounts to a game of freeze tag. They take his amulet and then a mystical sword stolen from the second bad wizard played by Sid Haig (*Spider Baby*) as the film gets harder to plod through. The acting is uniformly horrific, with even David Carradine embarrassed and sleep-walking through his role.

An idiotic chase scene in a castle hallway that seems to steal the old Three Stooges running- through-doors routine but without any laughs whatsoever stops the plot cold and tries the patience of the battered and bruised audience. At one point when Carradine rejoins the cause and his wife Idun (Susan Lee Hoffman) nags at him about being a mercenary without a job, he says "These are hard times for heroes, kid!" They are a lot harder for the audience, David.

We are fifty minutes into the abysmal *Wizards II*. And it's a feat of sheer endurance for viewers yearning for the promise of some prime Henry Brandon theatrical villainy. And finally… it comes!

At fifty-five minutes we hear *that laugh!* Henry Brandon as Zarz appears, in black and leopard print with a full grizzled beard. He says to a captured Carradine, "Ragged warrior, prepare to *die!*" Brandon puts some punch on that word "die," his eyes wide and aflame. It's as if a switch has been flipped! Suddenly, this steaming pile of a film comes to life thanks to Henry Brandon chewing the scenery.

Haig's Donar asks of his Master how they will find the boy wizard, to which Zarz replies, "He rushes to us – to his *doom!*" Then he cackles with maniacal laughter and all of this tedium is SO worth it. Carradine faces the monster of Zarz in the dungeon, something with tentacles and teeth that we barely see; thankfully so. Carridine escapes and engages in bloodless play-acting slow fighting like little boys in the backyard with plastic swords. While Henry is off screen, this hunk of rot begins to smell again.

Thankfully, Henry and the boy wizard Tyor are engaged in a contest of wills in which Zarz hopes to draw him to the dark side (sound familiar?) by killing his second in command Sid Haig. Sid seems all too eager to have his throat cut and escape the final act of the film. "Surrender the Chalice of Magic and I'll let you go free, Zarz!" Tyor drones in a flat monotone. Zarz compensates by laughing with fervid glee, his eyes almost popping from his head. He wryly comments to Donar, "And you told me he had no sense of humor!" Zarz continues, "Step forward, Lad. I'd like to see you up close before you *die!*" Brandon is just barely over the top here, relishing the silliness of it and owning the movie completely.

He continues needling the young slug, saying, "Aren't you afraid you are too weak to defeat me? Even with the sword and the amulet? Do you even know how to use their power?" The kid shows his abilities by turning the amulet into a fried chicken, which one of the guards begins eating. Then David Carradine reappears from the dungeon, fighting and killing forty or so of Zarz's men in more poorly staged fight sequences, as Henry simply sits and watches.

As the fighting moves outdoors, Zarz shows the boy visions of a skull in the chalice from the palace, trying to trick him into joining their evil dictator club. Dazed by the vision, Zarz takes possession of the powerful amulet and strings it over his neck, cackling, "It's mine! It's mine!" and having a bit of trouble getting it over the bat's wings on either side of his hat.

"No magic can touch me now!" Zarz proclaims triumphantly and brags to Haig, "Who is the greatest villain of all, now, Donar?" But jealous Donar snits, "I should be able to wear that half the time!"

Old Caedmon conjures up flames to incinerate the two evil wizards but Zarz counters with a spell, intoning, "Cava Eema Voll!" causing rain to fall indoors extinguishing the blaze. "Any more tricks?" he asks fumbling Caedmon, who merely mutters, "Well…I tried!"

Donar reaches for an axe to kill Tyor with, but the boy shoots mystical lightning from his fingers and fries Sid Haig to death, after which the kid collapses from the strain. Zarz is delighted, saying "You've eliminated my last rival, for which I'm grateful. But you've been a naughty boy. You must be punished!"

Trying to snap out of it, Tyor mumbles "Wakey makey achey" and his body starts glowing until we see his skull in the only special effects of *Wizards II* that aren't terrible. Before Zarz can impale the boy, The Dark One returns, saying, "Hold it, Rat Head!" He gives the boy wizard back the enchanted sword to slay Zarz, who continues to cackle with glee. They have a lumbering fight in which Zarz knocks the boy down, preparing to give the death blow. Tyor gives himself bigger biceps so he can throw the sword across the room and impale Zarz right in the belly, killing him and winning the day. Tyor pulls the amulet off of Brandon's corpse, having the same trouble with the bat wings snagging on his black hat.

Zarz's death is not terribly satisfying as even Henry believed. In a story he related at a Sons of the Desert gathering in Northern California in April of 1989, [one month after the film was released], Henry told the audience that he approached director Charles B. Griffith to ask if it might not look better if he had a blood capsule in his mouth so when he was impaled, some of the crimson would drip down for an effective demise. Horrified, the director refused, citing, "This is a *family* film!" to which Henry replied with a deep, throaty Zarz laugh at the inane contradiction.

Good prevails, evil is vanquished and Henry Brandon's final motion picture camera shot is of him impaled to a wall with a magic sword. And while it is disappointing that Henry's last movie role was in such a stinker of a film, there is a poetic feeling of full-circle cinematic finality to the proceedings. He ends where he began and when Zarz gleefully asks, "Who is the greatest villain of all, now?" the question is most definitely rhetorical.

CHAPTER FIFTEEN
When the North Wind Blows

"I Think It Is My Best!"

As Henry Brandon entered the twilight years of his film career, something astounding, important and wonderful happened. Something called *When the North Wind Blows*.

By 1974, the year that *When the North Wind Blows* was produced and released, Henry's television career was winding down, with less than ten projects yet to come and even fewer movie roles. While some of them from this period were 'typical' Brandon adversary-type roles – Martin Borman in *Search for the Evil One*, Carlo in *The Manhandlers*, the Nazi officer in *To Be or Not to Be* and the evil sorcerer Zarz in *Wizards of the Lost Kingdom II* – about half of these remaining parts were most unusual, even atypical.

Henry, looking wise, weathered and experienced, was called upon to portray religious men in *Mission To Glory: A True Story* and *Gentle Savage* and, almost shockingly so late in his career, landed the starring role in an extraordinary motion picture called *When The North Wind Blows*.

Produced on a modest budget by Schick Sun Classic Pictures and filmed entirely on location in Alberta, Canada, *When the North Wind Blows* gives us a Henry Brandon star turn that is expertly done and deeply moving. Indeed, if we had to select a fourth film to join *Babes in Toyland*, *Drums of Fu Manchu* and *The Searchers* as an iconic Brandon performance, it would certainly be this one.

When the North Wind Blows one sheet

Directed with unflinching honesty by Stewart Raffill, *When the North Wind Blows* explains that there is a legend which tells us that every one hundred years; winter is so extreme that no living thing in the brutal North can survive. These extreme winters begin when the North wind blows and this story, told in flashback by an old bearded man named Boris watching tigers in a zoo, is one of them.

It is approximately around the turn of the century. Siberian tigers, starving due to the horrific cold, are coming down from the mountains in search of food. These hungry tigers attack both livestock and man. It's been so many years since the younger men have even seen a tiger that they find this difficult to believe.

Henry Brandon plays old Avakum, a man that his best friend Boris describes as "a quiet man… a gentle man of the wilderness." Avakum has a massive grey wooly beard and a thick, full head of grey hair to match. He dresses, as do all the men, in huge fur caps and bulky fur jackets. Avakum, visiting Boris from the Siberian Mountains, joins in on a tiger hunt for a pair of tigers to keep a watchful eye on Boris' cocky son, who has never seen or hunted tigers before.

The youngsters not only disregard the wise input of the older man, but they are flat out disrespectful. Brandon, as usual, acts circles around the younger actors, inhabiting the role of Avakum as if he personally lived those six decades in the frigid wilderness.

Boris' foolish, argumentative son does exactly what Avakum warns him NOT to do – he wounds one of the tigers they are stalking, making it even more dangerous. It attacks and mauls the boy, who is severely injured before Avakum can shoot and kill it. The boy is also hit by the bullet and they rush him back to the village. When Brandon tells his friend, "I'm sorry" the suppressed emotion in those two words and in the moment is deeply moving. He failed to keep him safe, as he had promised he would.

The angry townspeople, hearing that the two had argued over their approach to the hunt before the shooting, begin to wonder if Avakum had shot the boy intentionally! Idiots. This leads to a tense scene in which Avakum tries to leave on his dog sled and a group of men attempt to stop him, thinking he should remain nearby until they know if the boy will survive his wounds. Henry's character is angered by this foolishness and they back down, threatening to come after him should the boy die. Avakum's return to the mountains as the weather worsens is virtually a death sentence, and when Boris hears about the idiocy of the townsmen, he heads off to catch up to his friend, apologize and bring him back to the safety of shelter.

Believing he is a hunted man, Avakum evades the pursuit and the film becomes a survival epic with Henry Brandon as the sympathetic leading character. He finds an old trappers hut to live in and that night, as the camera slowly zooms in on his craggy, weathered face, *When the North Wind Blows* has found its protagonist. His lead husky finds him and becomes his only companion. The next morning, the pair bags a wild turkey – and nearby, the surviving tiger hunts deer. The dog's joyful barking over the turkey scare away the deer, angering the hungry tiger. When Avakum and the tiger find themselves face to face, he raises his rifle but can't pull the trigger to kill the magnificent but deadly beast. The tiger pads off and that night in the hut, Avakum is concerned to discover he only has two bullets left.

This role of Avakum is an acting tour de force for Henry Brandon who takes full advantage of every twist and turn of the very active plot. Chased up a tree by a famished, massive black bear, his dog comes to the rescue and lures the bear away, but is killed, leaving Avakum truly alone. It is a heartbreaking moment when he finds the husky's bloody body in the snow. That night he stares into the evening fire, his face aflame with emotion.

For most of the picture, when Henry is not onscreen in the village sequences, they are all talking about him, about his past, if he'll survive. Avakum is the focal point of *When the North Wind Blows*.

Two months have passed and the winter is at its brutal peak. We see wolves chasing Avakum, whose rifle is now useless: And he can use only sharp branches to defend himself. Perched up a tree in a blinding snow storm, his face caked with snow, the wolves circle menacingly. How will Avakum survive?

Henry with one of his tiger co-stars in *When the North Wind Blows*. Collection of Rick Greene.

The tiger returns and chases the wolves off, beginning an unusual relationship between man and tiger. The tiger seems to remember that this man did *not* pull that trigger and mutual respect develops between the two.

A hunting party (led by a pre-***Grizzly Adams*** Dan Haggarty) goes into the woods to capture the tiger for a zoo and to see if the old man somehow survived. Hearing the commotion of the bloodhounds cornering the tiger, Avakum goes to investigate. The tiger is roped, then netted. Avakum arrives and angered, shoots one of the trappers in the leg with his homemade bow and arrow. Both Avakum and the tiger escape.

Henry Brandon now appears to be a wild animal, chasing down squealing boars and gleefully roaring through the forest! Hunting alongside him, but not too close, is the tiger, who nails the boar but allows Avakum to slice off a leg for his dinner. Somehow, these two creatures of the forest have become allies. The snows begin to melt, birds return, the long brutal winter is over. Avakum, his woolen parka off, basks in the feel of the warm sun on his face and shirtsleeves.

The next day, using his wits and swimming underwater, he catches two ducks and roars in effusive triumph! He shares the duck dinner with the tiger, now his constant companion. But there is a delightful twist coming as Avakum hears some unusual cries in the forest and discovers two newborn tiger cubs. His tiger is a female and these are her cubs! He embraces them, and names them Terrick and Lika.

This remarkable film now takes on a new tone, the story of man vs. nature and an unlikely friendship turns the duo into a family of four. Avakum lives out in the open and helps to raise the tiger cubs as they grow alarmingly fast. The scenes of Henry Brandon playing with these cubs are just delightful, especially at one point where he howls, "Hey, let go of my leg!" Later they frolic in a lake as Avakum laughs and literally exudes sheer joy. Indeed, the press kit for *When the North Wind Blows* includes this interesting paragraph:

While filming *When the North Wind Blows* in Alberta, Canada, Brandon was required to do scenes with two of the tremendous snow tigers that are also featured in the film. "After becoming acquainted with the tigers, I was able to understand their feelings,' explains Brandon, 'and knowing how to work with animals of their size and strength is very important."

Rifle shots ring out! Hunters have come and wounded the mother tiger, who limps to Avakum to die. It is horrifying. He attacks the men with the bow and arrow, getting one in the leg, but they shoot at him and hit him! Avakum is wounded, but not killed. He becomes the surrogate mother to the tiger cubs, feeding and caring for them.

The villagers, especially Boris, are startled to hear that Avakum is still alive and possibly shot. Boris sets out in search of his friend. They find a fresh grave with the mother tiger in it, determining he can't be badly wounded if he was able to dig this hole. Avakum is pursued to the river's edge, where he plunges into the swift current, escaping and making it safely out of the rapids to the other side. This is indeed a vigorous role for 62-year old Henry Brandon, but he's having a ball, and his enthusiasm shines through his unforgettable performance.

When the North Wind Blows lobby card. Collection of Bill Cassara.

Boris sends everyone home, remaining alone in the wilderness to try and find his friend. At dusk, Avakum dries his clothes near his campfire, the young tigers at his side. There is a delightful scene where one of the tigers paws playfully at Henry's head, demonstrating the genuine rapport he had with his feline co-stars. Avakum hears Boris shouting his name and, with some hesitation, finally confronts him, asking "What is it you want with me?"

Boris tells him his son is fine, no one is after him, and pleads with him to come back. Avakum asks, "I should grow old and useless in a place where people think age is an illness? Go back to your world, leave me in mine." This powerful ageism theme resonates even today. Your world is unnatural, uncivilized, says Boris. Avakum responds, "It is the most natural thing in the world!"

Boris finally understands. It is time for him to leave. He gazes back wistfully at Avakum in the distance, kneeling with his two tigers at his side, then turns to go. "That was the last I ever saw of Ava," his voice over tells us, "We were the closest of friends and yet we were from different worlds."

While it seems as though the film is wrapping up on this hopeful note, there is another dramatic twist yet to come. We see a long panning shot of the gorgeous Siberian wilderness – and the two now fully grown tigers romping along with their more scraggly-than-ever "Dad" Avakum ice-fishing through a hole for their supper. He is smiling and laughing as his tiger kids play with their wriggling fish.

That night as he feeds them, Henry says aloud, "I'm worried about you two. One of these days you're going to have to hunt for yourselves." His concern is justified, as the next day the zoo hunters return with many horses, dogs and equipment. They capture one of the tigers, then corner and net the other. Since the youngsters are somewhat tame and used to humans, it isn't that difficult. Later that night, Avakum calls for his tigers, but they don't come. The look of concern on his face is heartbreaking.

Once again, Avakum is alone, without purpose. He spends a miserable night and the next day sets out in search of his tigers, calling out their names in vain. Things go from bleak to worse when a snow storm hits and some wolves attack Avakum. He tries to fight off the pack by hurling sticks and branches, somehow keeping them at bay. At this point, Brandon looks more like one of the wolves than a man. He sleeps in the safety of a roaring campfire and the next morning finds a town, his first encounter with civilization in nearly a year.

Avakum finds his tigers imprisoned in a backyard wooden pen and uses an axe to free them. The trio runs happily back into the woods, as Boris' narration tells us that "such a man cannot be defeated." Jaunty harmonium music indicates that this, finally, is the happy ending we were hoping for, that Avakum and his tigers cheerfully survive together in the wilderness… where the north wind blows…

The press materials for *When the North Wind Blows* were eager to point out that Henry's part "in this adventure film is quite a unique one for him. As the wiry old trapper, Brandon marks his first performance as a character his own age."

It's not easy to find *When the North Wind Blows,* never having had a proper home video or DVD release (as of 2017) and being produced by Schick Sun Classic Pictures, an obscure company, but it is well worth seeking out. Henry Brandon is compelling and dynamic in this late starring role and he's clearly relishing every moment. At 109 minutes, *W.T.N.W.B* is nearly two hours of Brandon at his most engaging. Henry modestly told co-author Bill Cassara, "If you ever get a chance to see it, I think it's my best." The authors concur.

CHAPTER SIXTEEN
Television

FOR HOLLYWOOD'S EXPERIENCED CHARACTER actors, the coming of television after WWII was boon to their bank accounts. Where stars like Humphrey Bogart, Jimmy Stewart, James Cagney, John Wayne and Clark Gable made rare, calculated appearances on television, versatile character players like Henry Brandon had a new outlet to land a wide variety of roles in faster, cheaper productions which were ground out like little pig sausages. Since many of these series were long-running shows with ongoing featured casts, the scripts often stressed interesting character byplay rather than action and gave the industry's character actors many opportunities to shine opposite consummate actors like Richard Boone, Robert Duvall, Leonard Nimoy and Ward Bond.

Beginning in 1949, Henry Brandon began his lucrative "second career" with early television appearances intermingled with his motion picture work. For the next thirty-eight years, Brandon landed frequent roles on programs of every type, from science-fiction and Westerns to detective, drama and even religious and comedy programs. And immediately after his vivid portrayal of Chief Scar in John Ford's *The Searchers* hit the big screen in 1956, Henry began playing Indian chiefs on the small screen, portraying Native Americans as often as he played cowboy roles.

Many of the first television programs were adaptations of long-running radio series and Henry appeared on such TV series as **Suspense** and **Light's Out** before landing a long series of supporting roles in Western programs, which made up a hefty fifty per cent of his video gigs. Fans never knew where Henry might pop up during the Golden Age of television, going from many appearances on *Wagon Train* and *Lawman* to *The Loretta Young Show* or *77 Sunset Strip*, even inspired casting on comedy programs like *Mister Ed* and *F-Troop* and *Mr. Terrific*. After television got a couple of decades under its belt and grew more sophisticated, the roles for Henry Brandon continued to come on programs like *The Rookies* and *Night Gallery* and *Murder, She Wrote*. In all, he appeared in about as many TV programs as he did motion pictures.

1940s

Suspense:

The earliest existing example of Henry Brandon's fledgling television career is his second known appearance, which occurred during the second season of *Suspense* on CBS. On radio, *Suspense* was among the very best examples of the mystery/adventure program, utilizing the full scope of "the theatre of the mind" in its panorama of exotic excitement, shocking murder and edge-of-your-seat thrills. The initial television seasons, however, limited by live performances, a lack of editing and cheesy organ music, were not very compelling viewing. Henry's episode was broadcast in the middle of the season and aired in the final days of the 1940's. It was called *The Case of Lady Sannox* and was based on a story by Sir Arthur Conan Doyle. Second billed Henry Brandon portrays Dr. Douglas Stone and the Lady Sannox of the title is top-billed Stella Adler.

Dr. Stone is described as the most brilliant young surgeon in all of London, but is throwing his career away carrying on a very public affair with the married Lady Sannox. They rendezvous in the garden at a party at her flat, Henry speaking in a wandering British accent, having to toss off silly phrases like, "Rot! I said rot!" and still come off as a jealous, possessive, self-absorbed surgeon. Lady Sannox flirts, teases and tortures her lover and they share some fiery yet angry passionate kisses several times. Her husband, Lord Sannox approaches from the garden (he raises orchids) and may – or may not- have seen them embracing. After some banter, Dr. Stone makes an appointment the following week to view his rival's greenhouse and when Sannox leaves, he asks his paramour if she would marry him, if she could. Divorce isn't simple in England, she replies and Henry offers to make her a widow on the morning of the greenhouse visit.

Bug-eyed Brandon in *Suspense*.

Earlier that same evening, he brought a man back from the dead during surgery. "On the operating table tonight, I cheated death" he intones loftily, "I must make that up, you see?" By murdering her husband! Henry portrays Dr. Douglas Stone with a thick slice of fully cooked ham – mugging for the television camera and eyes a-popping. Rather than this performance being an example of how he approached Shakespeare on stage, it's closer to the florid melodrama of *The Drunkard*.

On the eve of his planned murder of Lord Sannox, a swarthy Muslim foreigner in a fez arrives at Dr. Stone's home begging him to come save his wife from a horrible fate. She has been cut on the face by a poisoned dagger and, appealing to his vanity, only a genius with the scalpel of Dr. Stone's ability can save her. Henry accompanies the pleading Muslim and they go to a strange dark part of London that seems to be made of cardboard. Per Muslim tradition, when Dr. Stone arrives her face is covered and we suddenly know exactly where this predictable story is going. She is drugged with opium and he slices away at her face for a few seconds then gasps in horror. The woman is... Lady Sannox! The Muslim is... a heavily disguised Lord Sannox in a rubber nose, getting his twisted revenge on the lovers. Henry lets loose with a couple of unfortunate deep bellowing screams and that previously mentioned thick slice of ham becomes an entire 400 lb. porker.

In the quick finale, we are told Dr. Stone is in an asylum, Lady Sannox is permanently disfigured from the two-second procedure and Lord Sannox is arrested to face justice of some vague sort. Some of these early episodes of *Suspense* were written by a young Rod Serling, but this one sure wasn't. *The Case of Lady Sannox* aired live on CBS on December 27, 1949.

1950s

Family Theatre:
The first episode of *Family Theatre* was called *Hill Number One* and surprisingly features one of the most significant performances of Henry Brandon's entire career. This is a religious story – a story of faith. It begins during a war – it could be WWII or The Korean Conflict – with a group of jaded soldiers griping about the hill they've been tasked to overtake. A Padre arrives as it is Easter Sunday, and they gather around him to hear the story of the First Hill – the site of the crucifixion. This is the story of the resurrection of Jesus Christ. Joseph of Arimathea arrives before Pontius Pilate to request the body of Christ for burial in a concrete vault.

About fifteen minutes in, Henry Brandon as Cassius arrives, in breast plate armor and spear, with shocking news for Pilate. He tells him, "This Jesus we crucified was the Son of God! I've never seen a man die as this man! Never before have I seen a man die loving those who put Him to death!" Cassius tells of a great earthquake at the very moment of Jesus' death. To be certain He was deceased, Cassius describes how he drove his lance into the body of Jesus, how His blood flowed from His heart onto his face, that the blood cured him of a lifelong affliction. Cassius is transformed – and becomes a Roman, who worships at the foot of the cross.

Brandon's sincerity in this role is compelling. He approaches the character of Cassius with a Shakespearean demeanor. We believe that HE believes Christ is the Son of God.

Later, Brandon arrives at the crypt on horseback. He pledges to Mary that he'll guard the body that no harm will come to it. He tells her the story of driving his lance into the heart of Jesus. "He has opened my heart – as He has opened my eyes!" Cassius intones. Brandon delivers these challenging lines with moving passion. This, then, is one of the most important roles of Henry Brandon's career. He begins "Hill Number One" as the most despicable villain of all time – the Roman who killed Jesus Christ – then is transformed at the base of the cross into a Christian – the *first* born-again Christian. Henry is terrific, performing with a larger-than-life honesty that is almost startling.

In his final sequence, he rushes into to awaken Pilate, breathless and wide-eyed, with more news. "He is risen! He is risen! Jesus is Risen!" Again, Brandon's sincerity has the power to move viewers to tears. Here, in these earliest days of his television career, is a deeply heartfelt performance that reverberates with honesty and passion. Making "Hill Number One" even more required viewing is the fact this is the film debut of James Dean. Henry is so good that the Producers of **Family Theatre** brought him back the following year to perform in "A Star Shall Rise." The magnificent "Hill Number One" was first broadcast on March 25, 1951.

Rocky Jones, Space Ranger:

One of Henry Brandon's earliest television appearances was in a genre that he had the least exposure in – science fiction. Although referring to **Rocky Jones, Space Ranger** as 'science fiction' is a bit of stretch as it was really just children's programming in the **Captain Video, Space Patrol** and **Tom Corbett, Space Cadet** vein.

As Brandon explained to co-author Greene in 1984:

> I never cared much for sci-fi, never really understood it. I had a few roles in television where I had to spout that gobbledygook, I didn't understand a word of what I was saying!"

Indeed, Henry's usually smooth delivery was impeded by the "technobabble" required of such roles as Rinkman, the fugitive, traitor and space pirate villain of *The Pirates of Prah*, a three-episode run of **Rocky Jones** from the first season.

In the slow moving episodes, the plot involves Rocky and his sidekick Winky (Scotty Beckett of Our Gang) searching for a hijacked space ship CM-7 and later using Cold Light (the power of invisibility – an early version of **Star Trek's** cloaking device) to overcome the evil Cleolanta (Patsy Parsons) and her minions. Head minion Rinkman offers Henry the juiciest role and he makes the most of this lame opportunity. Indeed, **Rocky Jones** is a poor man's *Flash Gordon* without the imagination, special effects or interesting characterizations with star Richard Crane's wooden one-dimensional acting quite lethargic.

Rocky talks in a virtual monotone that induces sleep: what zest there is provided by Brandon's nefarious Rinkman and his fellow Hal Roach Studios alumni Beckett as girl-crazy Winky. Even worse are the special effects, which consist of rocket ship models taking off and landing in front of background paintings and little else. **Rocky** was produced on film instead of video, which offers a much stronger picture and allowed for the longer episodes to be edited into feature film programmers. The *Pirates of Prah* was one such effort, becoming *Manhunt in Space* shortly after these three episodes aired in May of 1954.

When *Cinemacabre* Magazine asked Henry how long it took to film this three-part early television series, he responded, "They shot them very, very quickly. I think it was about three days or two-and-a-half days per episode."

Stories of the Century:

Westerns were among the most popular programming in the pioneering decades of television and Henry Brandon probably appeared as both cowboys and Indians in this genre more often than any other. He racked up meaty roles on such shows as **Maverick, Have Gun – Will Travel, Gunsmoke, Lawman, Wagon Train, Broken Arrow, The Texan, The Deputy, Zane Grey Theatre, Gunslinger, Branded** and many others, even playing an Indian on the screwball comedy show **F-Troop**.

This was a half-hour anthology series 'based on official newspaper records and files' and was produced by Studio City TV Productions, a division of Republic Pictures. Its main title was dramatically branded into the pages of an open book. Henry portrayed the title role in a 1955 episode called *Nate Champion* which concerned the activities of this "famous and notorious character" who was one of the most-feared big-scale cattle rustlers in history. Told **Dragnet**-style by Matt Clark, Railroad Detective, his deep monotone delivery unfolds a fast-paced and exciting half-hour of television that wracks up quite the body count in its brisk 26-minutes.

Things begin with Nate Champion being run out of Colorado by the Cattlemen's Association, who have no proof but know he's a rustler. He's put on a stage to Wyoming where he meets Englander Roger Benton and his ward (and daughter of his late partner), Joan Jameson. Thinking fast, Brandon poses as Joe Baker, Cattle Buyer and quickly takes Benton for all he's worth, setting himself up in the rustling business again with a new gang of cutthroats.

The cast of *Stories of the Century* in 1955's "Nate Champion" episode. Collection of Rick Greene.

Henry looks natty but slimy and he off-handedly has ranch owner Old Man Riley gunned down when he figures out his property is being used for rustling. But Henry's got nothing on Joan Jameson, who quickly shifts from spoiled brat to cold-blooded murderess with a bullet to the gut for poor, disbelieving Benton. She races to help Champion with dummy receipts for the stolen cattle but Clark and Jonesy put it all together in a typical Western shoot-out climax complete with corny hands-in-the-air death throes. Nate Champion, in a hail of bullets, inexplicably lights a lamp in broad daylight so it can be shot out and turn his shack into a fiery blaze, giving Brandon a juicy flaming death scene. The B-Western easily made the transition from the big screen to the small in compact little oaters like this one. The episode aired on February 2, 1955.

Soldiers of Fortune:

A few years before John Russell began a four-season run as Dan Troop on **Lawman** (which featured Henry Brandon in two notable episodes), he starred as Tim Kelly on the syndicated adventure series **Soldiers of Fortune**. With his sidekick Toubo Smith (Chick Chandler) the two men travel the globe as adventurers offering their services for hire. In an early Season One episode called "The Greatest Beast", the duo find themselves in Tibet looking into the mysterious death of a fellow 'soldier' named Singer. They are offered $10,000 to discover who... or what... killed the man by a mining company seeking mineral concessions. Henry Brandon plays Ki Yang in full Fu Manchu mode with bald cap and a vocal inflection very close to that of the criminal mastermind he portrayed in his final serial appearance fifteen years earlier. In fact, **Soldiers Of Fortune** was filmed on the Republic lot, where Henry starred in *Drums Of Fu Manchu* looking and sounding much like he does in this striking episode.

Henry Brandon as Ki Yang in *Soldiers Of Fortune*.

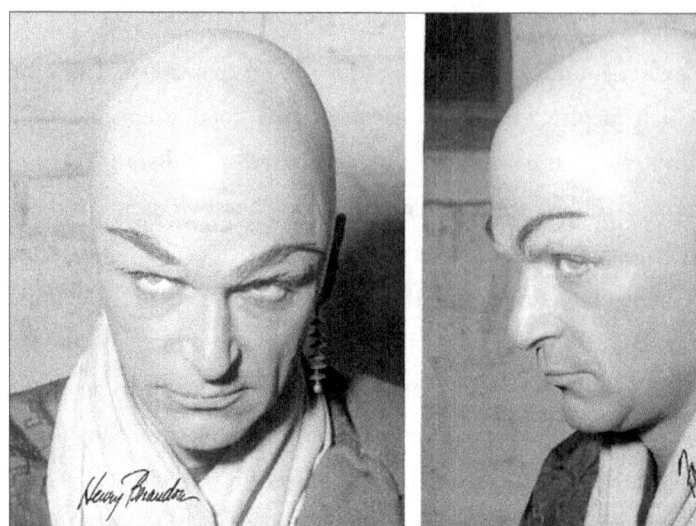

Make-up test photos for Brandon as Ki Yang in *Soldiers Of Fortune*. Collection of Eric Stedman.

Kelly and Smith are taken captive by Ki Yang, who explains he is the High Llama and was present when Singer died, acting as his guide. A fearsome beast killed him, bent his rifle and disappeared… a beast that isn't specifically called out as a Yeti, but the implication is definite. Ki Yang offers to guide them up the mountain as he did for the deceased Singer, and although he is quite shifty and evasive, Tim Kelly agrees. Of course, up the mountain in a fierce wind storm, Ki Yang shows his true colors by cutting Toubo's rope in an attempt to murder him. Tim catches the rope and saves his friend, then heads up to deal with Yang.

Henry has a marvelous shot, thinking he's succeeded in murder, the biting cold and horrific winds pummeling him… and he smiles! It's delicious but short-lived as Tim Kelly arrives and the two struggle in a fight. Toubo follows and sees the 'monster' – really a pile of rocks that Ki Yang prepared to startle climbers – and he shoots at it. This causes an avalanche which buries Ki Yang, who, unlike Fu Manchu, perishes. "The Greatest Beast" is an exciting episode of a solid two season series and its great fun to see Henry

Brandon again portray an Asian baddie. This syndicated show first aired on February 20, 1955.

The Adventures of Jim Bowie:

The series which tells of the man who used his famous knife instead of a gun began its second season with a slam-bang episode entitled *Epitaph for an Indian* which featured Henry Brandon as the despicable Quint Oxley. He rules a backwoods Louisiana town with a grip of fear, owns the Tavern and owns the Sheriff. Jim Bowie (Scott Forbes) makes a promise to a dying friend to deliver some money to his father Crawford Green, a half-breed who lives in Oxley's town. After some run-ins with Oxley's lackeys and an unhelpful Sheriff Pete Webber, Quint Oxley finally appears and Henry infuses him with all the oily charm of a coiled rattlesnake. Oxley and Bowie size each other up with some verbal sparring. When Bowie heads off to investigate Craw Green's deserted cabin, Oxley rants at Sheriff Webber and his men, "I made this town, changed it from an overnight stop for trappers and whiskey traders. Now I've got my money invested here and your job is to protect my investment!"

Henry tells his henchman, massive Jed Hubble, to get rid of Jim Bowie. "Use your hands," he says with deadly menace. Quint Oxley, filled with whiskey and hate, had shot and killed Crawford Green and he doesn't want Bowie to discover this. However, a half-breed named Nekeeta (Peggy McCay) that Jim has befriended, saw the murder and knows where Craw is buried. There is a brutal, dirty fight between Hub and Bowie but Jim prevails. Henry, enraged, shoots and kills his other minion in front of the helpless sheriff and goes out to handle Bowie personally. At first, he offers the square-jawed hero $500 in gold to walk away, then $1,000 and finally $2,000. "No sale," says Jim Bowie and the two engage in a fight of their own. Bowie beats Oxley, who is finished. His dark secret – he killed Green who discovered that HE was a half-breed as well. The show concludes with Brandon hauled off to jail. The 'epitaph' of the show's title is both for Crawford Green and Quint Oxley. The second season premiere of *The Adventures of Jim Bowie* aired on the ABC network on September 6, 1957.

M Squad:

Between a string of Western television show gigs, Henry appeared in modern street clothes on the very first episode of a new show called **M Squad** starring Lee Marvin. This pilot episode entitled *The Golden Look* introduces Lt. Frank Ballinger (Marvin) as a member of a special section of the Chicago Police Department that handles unusual and extreme homicides. Ballinger is tough and cynical, but he loves his Chicago and the people who live there. The series kicks off with a slam-bang opening sequence that shows Bert Fallon (Henry Brandon) and his partner attempting to rob a bank moments AFTER an armored car has left with most of the money. A clerk sets off an alarm and Fallon coldly guns down two tellers as they run out of the bank with no money but lots of witnesses.

Things get worse as Henry runs a red light and has a head-on collision with a man and his young son in the other car. Bert Fallon is the only survivor as he's killed the father, his son and his partner. He bolts from the smashed-up stolen car, blood gushing from a head wound and he brains a bystander with his gun butt. So, in just minutes, Frank Ballinger's first televised case involves Brandon committing vehicular manslaughter, armed robbery, grand theft auto, assault with a deadly weapon and first degree murder!

All the witnesses can talk about are the gold front teeth that Brandon had. A city-wide APB is put out for the man with "the golden look." The scene where the wife of the man in the head-on wreck comes down to identify the bodies of her husband and son is gut-wrenching. The father was driving the lad to his first day of school and his powerful scene is calculated to make the viewing audience HATE the Henry Brandon character. Ballinger figures out that the gold teeth are faked, so he focuses on Bert Fallon's rare AB blood type – which leads him to a freighter at the docks about to leave port. Henry and Lee Marvin engage in a vicious fist fight which results in Fallon's apprehension and the case is closed. **M Squad** premiered on September 20th of 1957.

Wagon Train: (1)

In the fall of 1957, a new Western show premiered on NBC called *Wagon Train* that went on to a long run of eight seasons. The series starred Ward Bond as Major Seth Adams, a character he'd portrayed in the motion picture *Wagonmaster*. His co-star was rugged young Robert Horton as the Scout Flint McCullough. Each week brought stories of dangerous journeys West by the pioneers of the United States, thus affording the storytelling of an anthology show with a regular cast and big name guest stars. Henry Brandon appeared as a guest actor on *Wagon Train* more times than on any other television series – he appeared in six episodes during the first four seasons as five different characters – all of them Indians.

Brandon plays Running Horse on his first *Wagon Train*.

In this first season, he played a renegade Indian called Running Horse on the ninth episode of the series entitled *The Charles Avery Story*. Special Guest Farley Granger was Charles Avery, a cavalry officer escorting an Indian chief's daughter from Washington back to her tribe with an important peace treaty to Chief Black Cloud. The Wagon Train happens by in Nebraska when Henry's renegade braves are attacking the cavalry men posing as Comanche and Major Adams sends McCullough with the dwindling contingent to be sure the treaty gets delivered and signed. Granger's Avery seems to have a chip on his shoulder when it comes to these Indians and the treaty.

Running Horse, who wants control of the tribe and nothing to do with peace, taunts Black Cloud. "Your wisdom has vanished with your strength!" he sneers, but he is ignored. Brandon personally takes charge of his war party, wearing white war paint and attacking the delegation as they get closer to Black Cloud's village. McCullough and company are successful in driving back this assault and have a surprise planned.

When the Indians, led by Henry on horseback, attack again they find just the canopy of the wagon left behind, as the cavalry group have gained precious time on horseback and with the wagon bottom, race to the Indian village and safety. There are quite a few long shots showcasing Henry Brandon's considerable horsemanship. He'd made enough Westerns by 1957 on both the big and small screens to develop some serious riding skills.

After the next assault, there are only five Indians left. Henry attempts to fool the Princess by circling around and claiming he's been sent by Black Cloud to accompany them the rest of the way. His remaining men attack after he is unable to persuade the girl to join him and, working together, Avery, McCullough and the Princess make it safely to the Indian camp: Running Horse rides off in failure, not to be seen again. In a twist we learn that Farley's family had been massacred by Black Cloud fifteen years earlier and this has been a mission of personal revenge for Charles Avery. But he's developed a friendship with the Indian Princess and realizes that peace is more important than revenge. The episode aired on November 13, 1957.

The Restless Gun:

Another popular Western that premiered during the Fall of 1957 was a star vehicle for John Payne called ***The Restless Gun***. Payne plays Vint Bonner, a retired gunfighter having adventures throughout the Southwest. The ninth episode of the first season is called *The New Sheriff* and begins with Bonner discovering a bushwhacked old-timer who was shot in his cabin outside of Harmony. Bonner asks him what happened and the grizzled coot replies, with good humor, "I was gored by a butterfly!" Vint takes the injured cowpoke into Harmony and learns he was shot by Gus Cotton, one of the Cotton Brothers and a member of a gang led by Tracer Givens (Henry Brandon). Gus' brother Roy is running for sheriff of Harmony to gain control of the town for Givens. Roy visits Bonner while he's in a bath tub and warns him to leave town before the election, causing the reluctant hero Vint Bonner to stay. ***The Restless Gun*** is a terrific vehicle for John Payne, with solid, funny scripts and a light attitude closer to ***Maverick*** than to ***Lawman***.

When the election seems to be going toward opponent Ernie Schroeder, the Cotton Brothers ride out to get their boss Tracer Givens. Ernie only gets 7 votes to Cotton's 33 – however Vint Bonner is elected Sheriff with 61 votes, just in time to hear that Schroeder was gunned down by Givens and the Cottons. Sheriff Bonner's first job is to amble over to the Harmony Saloon and take on all three desperados! In the saloon, we finally meet Tracer Givens, dressed in black from head to toe. During an exciting climactic shootout in a darkened saloon, Henry has a maniacal glee in his eyes with every gunshot! But they are no match for Bonner, who gives Brandon a solid death scene as he slides slowly down a wall, firing off a rogue shot while he perishes. *The New Sheriff* aired on November 11th, 1957 on NBC.

Suspicion

Henry Brandon shows off his versatility in an interesting role on ***Suspicion***, a one-hour anthology series produced by Alfred Hitchcock (but unrelated to his classic Cary Grant-Ingrid Bergman film of the same name). The episode of the mystery/drama show is called *The Flight* and stars Audie Murphy as Gordon, a pilot who works in a small airport. He's hired by slimy Colonel Palidano (Brandon) and Miguel (Everett Sloane) to fly a 'patient' to Bermuda for a cool $3,000. Henry plays the ethnic part with a Spanish accent and a thin mustache. They leave just after midnight and the 'sick' man seems drugged. Their final destination is the Republic of Puerto Colombo, an island South of Cuba.

When they land, a hearse arrives to transport the 'patient' and Henry ominously explains, "In this country, an ambulance attracts attention, a hearse goes unnoticed!" Nice place. When the old man regains consciousness briefly, he implores Murphy to bring a ring to Washington D.C., but then Palidano knocks Gordon unconscious with his gun butt.

A week passes and it seems that Gordon is something of a prisoner on this tropical, mink-lined prison. Puerto Colombo turns out to be a dictatorship and the "patient" is Señor Bartogas, the Editor of a Spanish-language newspaper that published articles speaking out against Palidano's boss. Henry, in full military uniform, takes Gordon to a sanatorium to see that all is well with Bartogas, but the man seems brainwashed and each one of his fingers is bandaged. Bartogas has been brutally tortured to sway his editorial convictions. The Puerto Colombo underground snatches Gordon, who joins them to extricate Bartogas and escape. He gets the opportunity to return the earlier favor by smashing his gun butt against Brandon's head, knocking him unconscious during the escape attempt. Later, Murphy guns down the bloody-faced Palidano as they make their getaway. *The Flight* plays like a neat little banana-noir picture with Henry Brandon as a key antagonist, lying with every breath and playing another exciting death scene. It was broadcast on November 11, 1957.

Have Gun – Will Travel

This was a wildly popular half-hour Western show that began a healthy run in 1957 and made a star out of Richard Boone as Paladin, the urbane gunslinger for hire. The 14th episode of the first season was called *The Yuma Treasure* and featured Henry Brandon as Chief Gerada of the Maricopa tribe. He plays the role with a quiet, restrained conviction and in Gerada's piercing eyes are echoes of Scar from *The Searchers*. Much of the picturesque episode was filmed at the Iverson Ranch in Chatsworth, California. Paladin is hired to deal with the Maricopa by Major Wilson of the U.S. Cavalry, a disgruntled and disillusioned officer who turns out to be the gold-hungry villain of the piece.

As the compelling Chief Gerada in *Have Gun Will Travel*.

Chief Gerada with Paladin (Richard Boone) in *Have Gun Will Travel*.

The episode was written by Gene Roddenberry, a few years before he created *Star Trek*. Double crossed by Wilson, Paladin finds himself in as precarious a situation as he'd ever faced, striped to the waist and staked to the ground to die in the blazing sun by the unforgiving Maricopa tribe. He escapes thanks to his well-trained horse and finally earns the respect of Chief Gerada in a relationship that foreshadows Roddenberry's future plotlines of humans and Klingons fighting in space... then developing respect and even admiration for the other. Henry Brandon holds his own on screen with the larger-than-life Paladin and the two have several powerful scenes together. The episode was broadcast on December 14, 1957.

Tombstone Territory:

This popular television program ran for three seasons, the first two on ABC and the third in syndication. The show starred Pat Conway as ultra-tough Sheriff Clay Hollister and Richard Eastham as both the Editor of *The Tombstone Epitaph* and the show's narrator. Henry Brandon appeared in an episode toward the end of the first season called *The Outcasts* as hateful cowboy Lige Crown, who has a ranch five miles outside of Tombstone. (He wears a big black walrus mustache that would look more appropriate in a slaptick comedy with Snub Pollard).

Brandon sports the phoniest mustache this side of *Tombstone Territory*.

A group of religious Amish-type families attempt to settle on neighboring land, which angers the intolerant Crown. He threatens them with violence if they don't leave because, "…you ain't my choice for neighbors!" Their leader, Elder Ransom, explains they just want a small portion of land to live on peacefully and Henry murderously intones, "If you're not gone by tomorrow, you'll get a small portion – six feet long and six feet deep!" These are the type of lines that Brandon infuses with menace so effortlessly.

The prejudice for these gentle outsiders is shared by most of the townfolk, and when Elder Ransom comes to fetch the doctor to examine his pregnant wife, Lige Crown strikes him. Sheriff Hollister intervenes and the two trade blows in the muddy street. Hollister smashes Henry several times in the face, knocking him down but not quite knocking that big black mustache off. Crown is beaten but not out and threatens the Sheriff to come out and visit him on his ranch some time, where things will be different. He then riles up the men in a local saloon into an angry mob, complete with tar and feathers, all heading toward a tense confrontation.

Mrs. Ransom is about to give birth and a few of the Tombstone women folk ride out to help, including future Jerry Lewis co-star Kathleen Freeman as Mrs. Woolsey. When the mob arrives, they are shocked to find their wives there for a stand-off! Brandon whines, "They ain't our kinda folks!" to which tough Mrs. Woolsey remarks, "Well, there ain't nothin' so special about YOU, Lige Crown!" She completely diffuses the situation as Crown rides off, defeated and dejected, at least begrudgingly accepting of these new outcast neighbors. It's a juicy part for top-billed guest star Henry Brandon although Kathleen Freeman steals the show. *The Outcasts* was broadcast on April 23, 1958.

Thirty years after this episode aired, both Henry Brandon and Kathleen Freeman were guests at special Sons of the Desert event aboard The Queen Mary in Long Beach, California. It was October 29th, 1988 and the 18th anniversary of the Way Out West Tent, the Los Angeles 'chapter' of the Sons. During the program, Henry was seated next to this book's co-author Bill Cassara. When Kathleen Freeman was introduced and brought up to speak to the 150+ attendees, she proposed a toast to Henry Brandon, "the greatest character actor in America!" Bill said that Henry was incredibly touched by this and the crowd roared in agreement with a heavy round of applause.

The Bob Hope Show:
Way back in November of 1933, as producer Hal Roach purchased the rights to make a film version of *Babes In Toyland* for Laurel & Hardy, the first production of Jerome Kern's new musical comedy *Roberta* made a Broadway star of Bob Hope and he never forgot this important career stepping stone. When the movie version was made a few years later, it starred Irene Dunne, Fred Astaire and Ginger Rogers… but no Bob Hope.

Nearly twenty-five years later, Bob decided to revisit *Roberta* as his first television show of the 1958-59 season in the form of a live 90-minute special broadcast in color from the NBC studios in Burbank. Here Hope returned to the breakout role that led to radio, motion pictures, television and iconic stature as one of the great entertainers of the 20th century.

In *Roberta* he plays Huckleberry Haines, the wise-cracking leader of an American band in Paris supported by Howard Keel and Anna Maria Alberghetti.

Henry Brandon (working with Hope again after film roles in *The Paleface* and *Casanova's Big Night*) plays Ladislaw, a deposed Russian prince, now a doorman, who is thought to be a rival for the heroine's affections but turns out to be her cousin. This first TV presentation of *Roberta* was broadcast on September 19, 1958. Sadly, no kinescope of this version of *Roberta* exists, even in the Hope family film archives.

Wagon Train: (2)
Henry's second appearance on **Wagon Train** toward the end of the second season was a significant one. *The Swift Cloud Story* opens with a bang… quite a few of them. The wagon train to California is being savagely attacked by a group of outcast Indians and renegades led by ruthless Cadol (Lee Papell). They are at odds with a tribe of Chiricauhua Apaches led by the great Chief Fire Cloud (Henry Brandon) and the wagon train is caught right in the middle of it. They ward off two attacks by Cadol, only to be threatened by Fire Cloud, who needs their food and supplies. Ward Bond approaches the

tribe carrying a white flag, but is attacked, captured and brought before Fire Cloud, attired in full-feathered regalia. Henry looks imposing and magnificent, fearsome and proud, revealing yet again why John Ford cast him as the blue-eyed Chief Scar a few years earlier.

Swift Cloud (Rafael Campos) is the son of the Chief and he's lame, a great shame to Fire Cloud, who knows he'll never ascend to lead his people with this affliction. Major Adams negotiates with Fire Cloud to bring his son to a doctor in California to fix the leg for safe passage.

Ward Bond's intense scenes with Henry are dramatically lit and the two actors virtually light off sparks of emotion together. Swift Cloud joins the wagon train and although it takes time, Swift Cloud begins to fit in and even makes a teenaged friend in Tommy. Cadol has been trailing the wagon train and wants the lame boy, which leads to Swift Cloud risking his life by surrendering to the renegade to save his new friends. Tommy steals a horse to rescue Swift Cloud, but is easily captured, followed by Swift Cloud's dramatic escape and return for their journey to California.

The following season **Wagon Train** would present a direct sequel to this episode with "Dr. Swift Cloud" in which Henry Brandon reprises his role as Chief Fire Cloud. *The Swift Cloud Story* aired on NBC on April 8, 1959.

Lawman: (1)

Another of Henry's many Western television gigs were two 1959 Second Season episodes of **Lawman** which starred John Russell as Marshall Dan Troop and Peter Brown as his young deputy Johnny McKay. Brandon played both a white man and an Indian in a pair of stories; the first of which is called *The Last Man*, the fifth episode of **Lawman's** sophomore season.

Torn Cloud, the chief of the Sioux nation is meeting with representatives of the Cavalry for peace talks in Laramie. Henry plays a grizzled old cowboy with a scraggly white beard and long Custer-type locks. In the opening scene he watches from afar and has no dialogue, but conveys burning emotion aflame in his eyes. Later, Henry – who has been revealed as Many

Horses, the white half-brother of Torn Cloud – walks among the town folk unnoticed as he's shaved his beard but still sports those striking long white locks. He tries to stab a Cavalry officer after an emotional scene about finding his young child murdered in his Sioux camp after a battle. Troup and McKay take Many Horses into custody and, in a long sequence with Peter Brown, tries to explain to the naïve deputy why he remained with the Sioux and killed white men in battle. Henry talks about how free they were, about the wind and the trees and rain with such conviction that he earns McKay's respect, if not understanding.

After a clever escape from his jail cell, Many Horses steals some dynamite to sabotage the peace talks but Torn Cloud lances his brother in the stomach before he can blow up the delegation. This shows the prejudiced soldiers just how earnest the Sioux are for peace. As Henry's Torn Cloud rides off to die, his brooding, proud, intense "end of an era" performance dominates the episode.

Henry was the top billed guest performer in *The Last Man* in a cast which included Robert Clarke (*The Hideous Sun Demon* himself). It aired on November 1, 1959.

Lawman: (2)

The ***Lawman*** producers must have been impressed with Henry Brandon's powerful performance since they brought him back just a few months later at the beginning of 1960. His second episode is called *To Capture the West* and features Warren Stevens as a superb Western artist. Henry plays "Tall Horse," his loyal powerful Indian sidekick. Unlike the ***Have Gun – Will Travel*** episode they shared, this time he and Stevens are on the same side.

We see many of the paintings that the artist has done, including a new one of beautiful blonde barkeep Miss Lily (Peggie Castle) that moves her to tears.

An outlaw gang is after Stevens and they catch up with him in Troop's Laramie for a climactic shootout. While the gun play is ably handed by

Troop and McKay, the incredibly strong Tall Horse (we saw him upend a massive wagon single-handed earlier) delivers justice against the gang leader who shot and killed his friend by crushing him to death with his arms. As he carries the limp body of Warren Stevens off into the sunset, Tall Horse proclaims, glancing at his artistic legacy "He'll never die. He'll live… forever." Brandon delivers these lines in stark close-up with subtle yet powerful emotion. This second and final *Lawman* appearance aired on February 7, 1960.

The Texan:

This was a mildly successful series running for two seasons and featuring Rory Calhoun as Bill Langley, a Civil War vet traveling through Texas having adventures. The last episode of the first season was called *The Man Hater* and features The Texan running across a beautiful blonde in big trouble. She's Elizabeth Blake (Lori Nelson), and is on the run from Henry Brandon's "Lightning" Crowley, who has sent his henchmen to bring her back. Rather than an original score, the music used is from the Capitol Stock Library, the same tunes used in the early Hanna-Barbera cartoons.

We see Longley pummeling the two henchmen and preventing Elizabeth's abduction. She accepts the assistance reluctantly, as she is the "man hater" of the title, a woman who mistrusts and hates all men.

A third minion arrives named Pete and he tries to ambush The Texan and is about to finish him when Miss Blake kills him with her revolver. The duo head into town to face off with The Boss – quick draw "Lightning" Crowley.

Henry has this town in a grip of fear, spouting B-Western dialogue like "I give the orders around here!" He has the girl arrested on a false charge of stealing a horse and wagon, sneering boldly into Longley's face. The Texan, whose arm was wounded by Pete, shifts his holster around to draw left-handed against Crowley. He warns him to leave town, but Brandon thinks he can outdraw the wounded gunfighter. "Lightning" is wrong and he bites the dust on the saloon floor.

The simple story concludes with Crowley's minions leaving town and the Man Hater revising her opinion about men… or, at least, one man in particular. After a passionate kiss, The Texan heads off into the sunset and a second season. *The Man Hater* aired on June 15th, 1959.

Medea:

A new series entitled **The Play of the Week** kicked off on October 12, 1959 with a broadcast of the compelling live drama *Medea* starring Judith Anderson and Henry Brandon.

This was a special presentation adapted for the television audiences across America and it was highly anticipated. Though Judith Anderson and Henry performed the stage version on and off for the previous ten years, the play was never accessible to those that did not live in the big cities. The viewers of late 1959 and through the mid-1960's had the chance to watch a filmed version right at home on their 19-inch TV screens. The one hour and forty minute version was cut down in scale and grandeur, but what it lost from the stage was gained by free access by the rolling camera. This allowed contrasting black and white images, close up shots and crisp editing,

Each of the five acts were introduced by crude titles and the sound of a kettle drum with ancient beats likened to a galley slave ship. There was only one set; the imagination took over as Judith Anderson's *Medea* filled the screen with her full range of emotions.

This was "Greek Tragedy" in every sense and it was not sanitized for family viewing. It was a highly anticipated achievement to air this drama with such notable leads. Henry Brandon upheld his role as the legendary "Jason" (of the Argonauts) who also showed his talents in reaction to all of Medea's cycle of moods.

Medea, his former wife and mother of their sons, was seemingly cast aside for Jason's new love interest. Jason explains his rationale:

When Brandon first portrayed the stage role of Jason in *Medea*, he used a make-up application to give himself a traditional Greek profile. Collection of Rick Greene.

Some little things that I on my side have done for you ought to be in the books too: as, for example, that I carried you out of the dirt and superstition of Asiatic Colchis into the rational sunlight of Greece, and the marble music of the Greek temples: is that no benefit? And I have brought you to meet the first minds of our time, and to speak as an equal with the great heroes and the rulers of cities: Is that no benefit? And now—this grievous thing that you hate me for, that I have married Creon's daughter. Do you think I did it like a boy or a woman, out of blind passion? I did it to achieve power here, and I'd have used that power to protect you and our sons, but your jealous madness has muddled everything.

In the last act Medea is surrounded by her two preadolescent sons. Having no wrath like a scorned Medea, vengeance fills her every pore. She kills her children (behind closed doors) just as Jason tries to rescue them. Medea's words are an abomination: *"I have done it because I loathed you more than I loved them."* It is a shocking, chilling proclamation that destroys Jason.

As depressing as this whole infanticide theme is played out, it was hailed by critics as a crowning achievement for television. It was hoped there would be more high-brow entertainment forthcoming as opposed to the slapstick *violence* of the Three Stooges* poking at each other.

Anderson was bestowed an Emmy award for her wailing, vengeful and all engrossing performance. It was well deserved. As for Henry, he looked the part of a Greek god come to life from a coin. He performed his role fiercely and unyielding until his desolate moments of ruin, he demonstrated the latter by collapsing on one knee and clutching his abdomen rocking back and forth. Henry conveyed this *internal* pain and mental suffering and convinces us that it is much more intense than any physical hurt. As Jason, Henry achieved a strong character for the star to play against without overshadowing the star. It was precisely the reason Anderson chose Henry over any other male actor to perform Medea with her intermittently from 1948-

---

* The old "Three Stooges" Columbia comedies were released to television during this year

1965. It is fortunate this definitive theatrical performance was captured on film as it continues to dazzle and impress sixty years later.

(See *Medea* in the "Theater Credits" for more information about the plot synopsis)

Wagon Train: (3)

In the first of Henry Brandon's three appearances on **Wagon Train's** third season, he again portrays a savage war-paint covered Indian, this time Black Panther, the nephew of Chief White Cloud of the Sioux. The episode is called *The Martha Barham Story* and guest stars Ann Blyth as Martha Barham, daughter of Major Barham and one-third of a love-triangle that includes Robert Horton's Flint McCoulough from the Wagon Train and Wade Forrest, who serves under Major Barham.

This is fully a Flint episode as Ward Bond doesn't even appear until the final few minutes in the bumper. Flint and his friend from childhood, Curly Horse of the Sioux, arrive at Barham's fort with grave news about both the Sioux and Cheyenne, mortal enemies, teaming up to war against the white man, who continue to slaughter their buffalo and deprive them of meat. Wade, who is engaged to Martha, is on patrol with his men. They are attacked by Black Panther, who kill everyone except an injured Wade and one man who rides back to the Fort.

Flint, who has been romancing Martha Barham to no avail, is sent with Curly to rescue his wounded rival. While they are out, Henry's braves sneak in and slaughter everyone at the Fort, except a hiding Martha. Her father, Major Barham, is killed. When Flint arrives in the morning, he finds and rescues her while a Cheyenne party arrives to loot the desecrated Fort. However, they are easily captured by the Sioux and Black Panther brings them back to his village.

Martha, Flint and Wade face a horrifying future – the men will be burned alive and Martha will become the unwilling bride of the leering, depraved Black Panther. Henry's expressions of lust for Martha Barham are fearsome to behold. Curly Horse, who appears to have regressed into the savage ways of his people, is shaming. He sneaks Flint a knife and advises him how to escape the circle of fire trap, then has horses and Martha awaiting them in the event they manage to make it after a harrowing walk across the burning embers. Martha realizes she was wrong to hate Flint, that he and Curly have saved her and her fiancé.

The show ends with their arrival at the Wagon Train and safety and the trio has a *Casablanca* moment as Flint gives up Martha for Wade in a noble speech that would make Bogie proud. Meanwhile, Black Panther discovers Curly's betrayal and he is killed by the tribe. This story about love and friendship is both moving and exciting – a superb **Wagon Train** episode. The Martha Barham Story aired on November 11, 1959.

The Deputy:

Another short-lived Western series that Henry landed a significant guest role on was **The Deputy**, a show created by, of all people, Norman "*All in the Family*" Lear. The premise of the show had Henry Fonda's Chief Marshall Fry trying to recruit young Clay McCord as his deputy. Fry was there to do all the heavy lifting (gun fights, narrow escapes, chases) so Fonda could continue his film career but still draw viewers to the small screen. In fact, in *The Big Four*, Fonda only appears in the opening and closing wraparounds, denying fans a reunion of the hero and villain of *Trail of the Lonesome Pine* some twenty-four years later.

Taking place in the early 1880's in Arizona territory, Marshall Fry tells Clay about a new super-gang of crooks which includes Ike Clanton, Billy the Kid and Henry Brandon's Johnny Ringo.

They pull big jobs, well planned – bank and train and stage robberies. Clay goes undercover, posing as a big city rube who claims to be a trick shooter. He easily locates The Big Four and Henry challenges the would-be Deputy to a shooting match, the winner to get a twenty dollar gold piece. Johnny Ringo goes first and hits four out of his five targets. Then McCord shoots and hits six out of six, prompting the gang to knock him out and take him to their cabin hideout – exactly where he wanted to go!

The supporting cast includes George Kennedy as Tex, the gang's simpleton helper, and screen veteran Wallace Ford toward the very end of his career as Sheriff Herc of Silver City. Brandon plays his stock Western cowboy baddie, but his part is the most prominent of the Big Four and he is top billed among the guest cast.

At first the gang offers McCord full partnership, then they discover his ruse and tie him up in their burning cabin. Clay easily escapes and helps prevent the Four from gunning down Sheriff Herc and his posse, taking down Ringo, Ike Clanton and Billy the Kid and rewriting Western history for the purposes of the narrative. A fun and entertaining episode, *The Big Four* aired on November 14th, 1959.

The Lawless Years:

This was a "Roaring '20's" gangster-noir show that ran for a few seasons on NBC and featured Henry Brandon in a showy role on a second season episode called *The Joe Angelo Story*.

Henry plays a street-level mob torpedo named Mendy Hymer who extorts truckers to pay protection money to his Chief Nick Sarecki (Ed Platt - a few years away from playing another famous Chief – for Maxwell Smart's Agent 86 on **Get Smart**). James Gregory plays Barney Ruditsky of the New York Police Department's Gangster Squad and he's been after Sarecki's gang for years.

The episode opens with Mendy having trucker Joe Angelo severely beaten while he keeps amused playing with a mechanical monkey toy – a gift Joe was going to bring his wheelchair bound son. Hymer and his muscle Bugs visit Angelo in the hospital to be sure he keeps quiet and they run into Ruditsky there. Hymer witnesses the stubborn Joe Angelo again refuse to "join" Sarecki's club and announces he is giving up the trucking racket to open a small candy store.

In *The Lawless Years* with Ed Platt.

In the hospital hallway, Gregory and Brandon clash and the sparks fly as Barney accuses Hymer of being nothing but a punk. Henry explodes, "You don't need to treat me like a punk. I'm right up next to The Big Man!" Henry plays Mendy Hymer with a gutter level New York street accent and his unparalleled sneer. He spends the entire half hour talking about being the "big man" he never can be.

Joe opens that candy store, but when the heat is on, Sarecki has Hymer send the eight people who could finger him out of town on "vacations." Joe refuses to go and, later that night, Mendy Hymer exceeds orders and guns him down in cold blood. His horrified son sees it happen and the next day, helps James Gregory in a scheme to trick Platt into giving up Mendy to save his own neck.

As the gang is rounded up, Mendy Hymer gripes about getting out of there because "I got a date with a horse at Belmont." Barney wryly asks, "What's the matter with girls?" and Brandon is not amused. The plan works, the gangsters turn on each other and both Nick Sarecki and Mendy Hymer get the electric chair for the murder of Joe Angelo.

Henry dominates the entire show with a terrific performance as the dirty killer with delusions of grandeur that lead to his downfall and execution. *The Joe Angelo Story* was broadcast on November 19, 1959.

Wagon Train: (4)

On the night *before* the night before Christmas, 1959, **Wagon Train** aired a stirring and deeply moving Christmas episode, albeit a violent one. Called *The St. Nicholas Story*, the episode featured a white haired and bearded gent named John Reid engaging the children of the wagon train by making decorations, stringing popcorn and practicing carols for Christmas on the trail. However, the Ute Indian tribe led by Chief Henry Brandon (in full headdress) and regalia has other ideas. They attack, and Reid takes an arrow in the shoulder while others are killed. Jimmy Sherman, a little five-year-old boy, wanders off in the aftermath of the savage attack, and encounters a little five-year-old Indian child, Little Eagle, who is the Ute Chief's son.

The two innocents spend the day playing, building a rock fort, and even catching and cooking prey for dinner, thanks to the Indian child's training. Meanwhile, the Chief is angered that he lost five braves and twenty wounded in the initial skirmish while only three white men were buried. He vows, in a voice laden with deadly menace, to slaughter the remaining white men, including Ward Bond's Major Adams. "Today the wagon train will move down the mountain," Henry chillingly says, "We will meet them at the foot of the mountain. It will be *easier* there!"

It doesn't look like it will be a very merry Christmas for the Wagon Train. John Reid, his unused Santa suit hanging nearby in his cabin, asks Major Adams to keep his promise to the children of St. Nick's appearance in the wilderness and promptly dies on cue. The two lost children continue to play and fall asleep side by side. Brandon is not only the Chief, but a concerned parent. Before the final attack, Brandon and Bond both seek out their missing children while a recently widowed woman gives birth to her child back at camp.

Henry and Ward meet in a tense scene over the five-year olds. Major Adams holds Little Eagle hostage, bartering for the safe passage of his people, but Henry doesn't trust him, citing a previous encounter with white men that left him grieving. He says to the Major, "Knowledge is an ancient sorrow in my bones. You bring death here!" Major Adams, who admits that both sides have legitimate reasons for mistrust, but knows that peace must begin with a gesture. He drops his gun and hands the sleeping Little Eagle over to his father. Brandon says, "I promise nothing beyond this moment." but "this moment" is a start for possible peace with the Ute tribe.

The episode concludes with a visit from Santa on Christmas Day, with Ward Bond humorously playing the part and scaring all the children! Then the Indians come, led by Brandon. They come not to make war and Chief Henry, magnificent and commanding, comes to embrace this "first moment" and clasps hands with Adams. A child is born, the peace pipe is smoked and there is peace on Earth, goodwill to all men.

The *very* moving episode fades out to the strains of children singing "Silent Night." *The St. Nicholas Story* aired on December 23, 1959.

1960s

The Rebel:

As the 1950's transitioned to the 1960's, Western television roles for Henry Brandon continued to make up a good fifty per cent of his jobs beginning with an offbeat show called **The Rebel**. Crisp, tough scripts about a former Confederate Army soldier named Johnny Yuma, played to tough-as-nails perfection by Nick Adams.

Midway through the First Season, Henry featured prominently in an episode called *Gold Seeker*, which begins with Yuma escorting a prisoner back to stand trial and avert a war with the Apache. The Man, who had spent three years among the Indians with Chief Running Wolf's daughter, is biding his time in order to steal their gold. Yuma had come across the couple as he was making his gold run and as his "wife" Destarte discovers the stolen gold, a gun tussle occurred that had the Man killing her and wounding Johnny, but he quickly gets the upper hand. The Apache catch up with the men and at first believe their brother as he spins falsehoods about Johnny killing Destarte. Both men tell their tales to Chief Running Wolf as Henry, with long graying hair and a scar on his left cheek, listens, his sharp gaze piercing for the truth.

As Apache Chief Running Wolf in *The Rebel*.

The tense standoff ends when Johnny punches The Man into a river bed, revealing more stolen gold that had been sewn into his coat. Henry delivers brutal and swift Apache justice to his "son" and Johnny is rewarded with his freedom.

The Rebel stands out from the glut of video Westerns with sharp writing, great direction and even better actors. Henry dominates the episode, bringing here the very real sense of menace that John Ford knew he would bring to *The Searchers* a few years earlier. Authentic and compelling, the episode is simply terrific. It aired on January 17, 1960. Bookended by Johnny Cash singing *The Rebel* during the credits, this series is as good as Western television gets.

Bronco: (1)

Another well-crafted Western from the Warner Brothers stable of programs, ***Bronco*** stars Ty Hardin as Bronco Lane, a post-Civil War adventurer traversing Texas in search of wrongs to right: he is a general do-gooder of deeds that need doing. Late in the show's second season, Henry Brandon appeared in a pair of episodes as two different Indians.

Brandon in another wig and another bandana as Yellow Moon in *Bronco*.

The first episode was called *Legacy of Twisted Creek* and opens with a murdered Indian Agent from the town of Big Fork. He was killed by a renegade Apache named Char and Bronco is tasked with crossing some difficult and dangerous terrain to find him, capture him and bring him back for trial. Chief Long Shadow (Richard Hale) remembers the bloody massacre at Twisted Creek and seeks to avoid further conflict by cooperating with Bronco, but there is a contingent within the Apache, led by Yellow Moon (Henry Brandon), who simmers with anger and hatred; he favors war with the white man. When Bronco meets Yellow Moon for first time, he remarks that he'll have to remember that name. "You will not need to remember it," sneers Henry, "You will hear it again."

Bronco knows ambitious Indians like this and explains there is one in every tribe – someone who speaks like a Chief, but knows the job is already taken. As Bronco hits the trail after Char, Yellow Moon sends two of his young bucks to follow them and kill them both, in hopes of reigniting hostilities with the white men. What follows after Bronco captures Char include many of the elements of a good B-Western: attempted murder, quicksand, a poisonous cottonmouth attack, corrupt Texans, renegade Indians, a cowardly sheriff and a broken cavalry officer in search of redemption.

Henry plays Yellow Moon with typical ease, hatred and contempt searing from his eyes. The climactic clash between the cavalry troops and the renegade Indians ends with Bronco chasing down Yellow Moon, pulling him off a moving horse and stabbing him in the stomach. Henry Brandon and Ty Hardin are clearly – and impressively – performing their own stunts in this sequence. This tale of redemption aired on April 19, 1960 and was quickly followed by a second ***Bronco*** assignment for Brandon.

Shotgun Slade:

This was another usual Western to kick off the 1960 season. The premise of the show seemed more influenced by the recent smash hit ***Peter Gunn*** than ***Wagon Train*** or ***Lawman***. Slade was a Denver-based Old West freelance detective who first-person narrates each episode like Mike Hammer and is backed by a Mancini-style jazz theme rather than more traditional Western music. In fact, all of the background score, by the prolific Gerald Fried, is in the jazzy *Gunn* mode making for a unique Western television experience.

Scott Brady plays Shotgun as a winking, lusty horn-dog, again more like a street-smart noir private eye than a square-jawed Old West lawman.

Henry appeared in a first season episode called *The Fabulous Fiddle* which saw Slade hired to safeguard a priceless Stradivarius belonging to vaudevillian Professor Maximillian. Brandon plays traveling show sharp shooter Trigg Bronson who is sweet on one of the Professor's two gorgeous nieces who also work in the troupe. As jealous Bronson obnoxiously pokes Shotgun Slade with his finger, Slade grabs and twists Henry's finger, remarking, "One more poke and you're going to be the only nine-fingered sharp shooter in vaudeville!" As Slade ambles off, Trigg mutters "Now there's a fellow I would like to shoot my initials in!"

The easily distracted Slade, lusting after everything in black-seamed stockings, is easily knocked out by a falling sandbag in a second attempt to purloin the violin. One of the nieces invites Slade to her hotel room and seduces him while, in a third attempt, Henry steals the fiddle through an open window. Slade springs into action and corners Trigg after a chase and a furious fist fight. But Henry uses the Strad as a shield, threatening "You pull that trigger and it's goodbye fiddle!" But Slade shoots out a chandelier above Brandon's head, gets the fiddle back and just past the midpoint of the show, Henry is put into jail and sits out the rest of the mystery. It turns out the Professor himself was behind the scheme to have the violin destroyed to collect $10,000, thereby defrauding the insurance company. Shotgun Slade figures it all out and foils the plan. *The Fabulous Fiddle* aired in syndication beginning in May of 1960.

Wagon Train 5:

Now we examine that most extreme of rarities in the Henry Brandon pantheon of performances – the sequel episode of **Wagon Train** in which Henry once again portrays Chief Fire Cloud, father of Swift Cloud. In looking back (and forward) in Henry's long film and television careers, one can think of only one other character that he was given the opportunity to portray a second time – that of Barnaby in both *Babes In Toyland* and *The Our Gang Follies Of 1938*. This pair of Hal Roach comedies aside, Henry's portrayal of Fire Cloud is the only example of playing the same role in a sequel that one can find in the Brandon filmography, so it merits some special attention.

Dr. Swift Cloud comes late in **Wagon Train's** third season, a continuation of the adventures of Swift from *The Swift Cloud Story* in **Wagon Train's** second season which aired thirteen months previously. That episode ended with proud Chief Fire Cloud entrusting his lame son Swift Cloud to white doctors in California to be operated on and, hopefully, cured. In the four years that have passed (story-wise), Swift *has* been cured and has been studying both medicine and the ways of the white man.

In the meantime, Fire Cloud, believing his son has perished, has been attacking every wagon train coming through, and the new episode begins with just such an attack. Ward Bond manages to fend them off, knowing they'll return in the morning to finish them off when Swift reappears and offers to go talk to his father and reveal that he is not only alive but cured of his lameness. But the tribe has killed some of the settlers and they are out for Indian blood. That's when Ward Bond tells them the story of Fire Cloud and his son Swift, enabling the producers to save a few bucks by running more than fifteen minutes of clips from the previous show. When Swift arrives back at the tribe's encampment, he discovers Chief Fire Cloud on his death bed. These scenes showcasing Henry's very different Fire Cloud – weak and dying – and seeing his son again are very moving and powerful, thanks to Brandon's acting skill.

Swift immediately clashes with the tribe's rattle-shaking medicine man.

He can cure his father using the medical knowledge he has gotten from the white man. Fire Cloud has a leg infected from a bullet and it needs to be amputated. If Swift had been able to carry this plan out, it would have ironically made his father 'lame' as his son had been in the earlier episode. However, he is prevented from doing so by the medicine man and Chief Fire Cloud dies. Even though Henry is only in this one new sequence, it feels like he's been in the show much more due to the flashback clips including ALL of his scenes from the original episode. His death causes many complications for both Swift and the Wagon Train but a new era of understanding between these Indians and the white man is achieved by the episode's end and Fire Cloud's legacy lives on in his son. *Dr. Swift Cloud* was broadcast on May 25, 1960.

Bronco 2:

Brandon's second appearance in the second season of **Bronco** came in a tense story called *Winter Kill*. "Pop" Ben Owens (guest star Edgar Buchanan of **Petticoat Junction** fame) is about to be hanged, accused of murdering the son of Mrs. Crowley (Virginia Gregg). Marshall Matt Sample and Bronco arrive to prevent this and bring Pop into the town of Denison for trial. Among the lynch mob is Chato (Henry Brandon), a redskin friend of the Crowley mining family.

Henry has dark braided hair but is otherwise dressed like a cowboy. The Marshall tells them, "That man hangs, you all hang!" When Mrs. Crowley persists in her claims that Pop shot her son in the back, Marshall Sample tells them, "Then he'll hang by a Government rope."

After they leave with Owens, Mrs. Crowley asks the miners that work for her to accompany her to kill the Marshall and lynch Pop. Chato refuses to participate, telling a moving story about another lynching… his own brother, who was innocent but this was discovered too late. He remains with the group, but won't engage in gunplay with Bronco and the posse.

Later, the Marshall is killed and Bronco promises to get Pop to Denison.

The two factions survive a horrific winter storm and end up in climactic gunfight in which the truth is revealed... Crowley's own brother shot him in the back out of jealousy, wanting control of the family mine. When he tries to escape on horseback, Mrs. Crowley aims at her only remaining son. But a shot rings out... and it's Chato, who kills the murdering weasel to save his Mother from having to. "There will be no charge against (Chato)," promises Bronco. Pop goes free and Mrs. Crowley gives herself up to face charges of killing the Marshall.

A typically solid Warner Brothers Television Production Western with Henry contributing mightily if meagerly as his scenes are mainly in the first and third acts. The somber *Winter Kill"* was broadcast on May 31, 1960.

Gunsmoke: (1)

The first of Henry's pair of appearances on the long-running adult Western drama **Gunsmoke** came at the end of the fifth season on a brisk half-hour called *The Deserter*.

Brandon plays Major Robert Honeyman at Fort Dodge, who asks for Marshall Matt Dillon (James Arness) to help in the apprehension of a renegade cavalry corporal who stole a payroll. Henry's Major is a gray-at-the-temples tough and honest officer who sets the stage for the tense story that follows. **Gunsmoke** on television was every bit as good as the original vivid radio series which had starring William Conrad. It's a shame Henry's first episode offered such a brief (but important) good-guy role. It aired on CBS on June 4th of 1960.

Gunsmoke: (2)

The following year, Henry's second **Gunsmoke** brought a substantially more rewarding part although it only offered a bit more screen time. The sixth season show was called *Stolen Horses* and the plot featured Dillon and Chester trailing a pair of murderous horse thieves through Indian country.

Henry plays Chief Quick Knife with long striking gray untethered hair and a dusty cowboy hat. He looks at Matt Dillon with mistrust and hatred simmering in his gaze, but comes to respect him before the half hour is over. When Dillon asks which direction the killers went, Quick Knife replies, "White man dead does not bring sorrow to Indian." He isn't inclined to help until Dillon points out that when they catch him, he'll hang, making TWO dead white men. Henry smiles grimly and points out the direction of the thieves.

In the closing minutes, after one of the thieves is dead and they've killed an innocent rancher, Dillon again is summoned to an audience with Chief Quick Knife. Henry tells him that they have the man he is looking for, that he stole the horse of a young brave and then killed him. He then chillingly tells the Marshall that the Mother will decide if Dillon can take him back to hang. When Matt goes into her tent, he discovers that Indian justice has prevailed and there is no one to take back to Dodge. "I wouldn't want to die like that!" is all Dillon can say, conjuring up some terrible images of what that Indian mother did to her child's murderer. Matt tells Henry that he doesn't agree with his methods, but he respects his ways; the men ride off, the job done.

Powerful stuff told in vivid images and cinematic music, **Gunsmoke** is as impactful as Western television gets and Henry was fortunate to work on two very different episodes. *Stolen Horses* aired on April 8, 1961.

Maverick:

In 1960 Henry finally appeared on *Maverick*, but one season *after* James Garner had left the show in a widely publicized contract dispute. Henry's fourth season episode featured Brett and Bart's cousin Beau Maverick played by a pre-Simon Templar Roger Moore and was entitled *A Bullet For The Teacher*.

The episode opens with a celebratory glass of champagne being shared by new gambling saloon co-owners Beau Maverick and Rand Storm (Henry Brandon), who seems awfully happy to have lost half interest in his twenty-year business in a poker game to Maverick. Henry plays the part broadly with a twinkle in his eye, especially when it comes to Flo Baker, the sultry new entertainer he's hired to sing there. As he skulks up to her room, we know she's no good by the way the camera lingers on her black-stockinged legs. Rand forces himself on the feisty Ms. Baker, who pulls a gun and shoots him in the belly. Henry then gets to play another fine death scene, stumbling down a stairway into Beau's arms. Maverick, as usual, is blamed for the murder and spends the rest of the show trying to clear himself and find the girl.

Another staircase death scene, with Roger Moore in *Maverick*.

For ***Maverick*** fans, it's par for the course but for Brandon fans, he's frustratingly knocked off just six minutes into this hour-long episode. It aired on October 30 of 1960.

77 Sunset Strip:
This was the first of two appearances on the popular Warner Bros. adventure series **77 *Sunset Strip*** for Henry Brandon. *Trouble in the Middle East* came in the show's third season and takes place in a small, fictional Middle Eastern

country in the throes of revolution. The series starred Efrem Zimbalist Jr., Roger Smith, Edward Burns and Richard Long as private investigators, but this stand-alone episode only features Smith as Jeff Spencer, a hapless American traveler trapped in the middle of a violent overseas conflict.

The action kicks off at the Hotel Europa as Jeff awakens to find the facility and the streets outside seemingly deserted. When gunfire drives him back into the safety of the lobby, he finds the cowering hotel clerk, who informs him that his country is at war – the rebels who oppose undue taxation vs. the army of el Presidente. First, the leader of the rebels Kassite (Mario Alcalde) arrives and befriends Spencer, then he is driven away by the coming of the army forces.

Henry Brandon pulls up, exiting a limousine in full military dress, looking like The Man in charge. The revolutionists flee as Brandon, playing Darius, arrives at the Hotel Europa and commands, "Get all of your guests and staff up here in the lobby. I would question them!" He may be a Middle East General, but his manner is pure Gestapo.

The adventure/drama is played with a light, humorous touch, fully and artfully embraced by Henry Brandon. When informed that the hotel's chef has fled to join the rebels, Darius remarks with genuine regret, "There are very few men who can make wild goat taste other than what it is!" Brandon plays the part *very* seriously, but knowing this pompous, powerful man is quite a comic figure, shifts from formal and imperious to flirtatious (interviewing the sole female guest) back to self-important with swift, consummate skill.

Darius interrogates the hotel guests one by one with this undercurrent of humor. When he gets to Jeff Spencer and reviews his passport, he sees that his profession is that of private investigator. Darius asks, "You're a private... eye?" Brandon pauses between the words "private" and "eye" but on the second word, uses his crop to pull down on the lower lid of his right eye. It's a very funny touch, humorizing and humanizing this fearsome authority figure.

Intrigued by the private... eye, Darius issues a command that Spencer will accompany him to their headquarters for questioning. The two leave in Darius' not-so-bulletproof car as rebel's fire upon them from the rooftops.

President Theriot (Paul Dubov) meets Jeff and has a job for him – get his beautiful daughter Ophir out of the country as he's fearful for her safety. As Theriot literally makes himself a target for the rebels, Darius drives Jeff and Ophir toward the airport, but they are cut off by blocked streets. Faced with capture and certain death, Darius does what any sensible Middle Eastern General might do… switches sides for self-preservation! Firing two shots into the air, he brings the enemy to them. When Ophir accuses him of being a traitor, Darius wisely responds, "I cannot be a traitor to a government that no longer exists!"

A surprising new leader arises to take control of this little nation, but not before Jeff gets to belt Darius for his weasely side-switching… twice. Oil's well that ends well in *this* Middle East as Henry Brandon effortlessly steals this **77 Sunset Strip** episode with his sly undercurrent of comedy and masterful character touches. It aired on November 11, 1960.

Wagon Train: (6)

Henry's sixth and final role on **Wagon Train** came in the middle of their fourth season in an episode entitled *The Patience Miller Story*. The narrative stars fiery Rhonda Fleming as Patience Miller, a Quaker widow who assumes responsibility for her husband's duties as a Missionary in Indian country, caught in the middle of a conflict between the Arapaho and the Comanche. Most of the plot revolves around her developing respect and eventual friendship with Arapaho Chief North Star (Michael Ansara) and the complications that ensue when a Comanche brave kills his son Evening Star.

With an Indian war imminent, Quaker Miller bravely enters the Comanche encampment to meet with Chief Dark Eagle (Henry Brandon) and bring home his captive son. Brandon only appears in two short but important scenes as Dark Eagle, who goes to North Star to apologize for the death of his son and to make peace.

The day job was a "thank you" from the **Wagon Train** producers for Henry's superlative work on the series over the past four years. The episode aired on January 11, 1961.

Whispering Smith:

This was a one-season Western that aired in 1961 starring Medal of Honor recipient Audie Murphy as the title character, a railroad detective affectionately referred to as "Smitty" by the town folk of Denver.

In *This Mortal Coil*, Henry Brandon plays a full-bearded, bespectacled businessman-type named Rex Denton, who is strangled by an intruder in his home not one minute into the story! Why hire a character actor of his caliber, fully costumed, made-up and knocked off without a single line spoken, not even a grunt!

All is well for Brandon buffs, as he does come back quite startlingly in the climactic "play" staged by Smitty to reveal the killer, Denton's brother Claude. Henry plays a dual role, the reveal being that he is Mr. Hamilton, a traveling ham actor with florid thespian intonation, who is made up to look like the murdered Rex Denton.

In the final scene, Henry finally has some dialogue, comparing the plot twist to one of Shakespeare's as he boards the outbound stage to bring culture to the old West. It's also nice to see Brandon and Audie Murphy together again after their solid work on an episode of *Suspense* four years earlier. *This Mortal Coil* aired in the summer of 1961 on July 24th.

Adventures in Paradise:

This one-hour adventure series from 20th Century Fox Television ran for three seasons and starred Gardner McKay as Adam Troy, Captain of the schooner Tiki III. Henry had minor roles on two 1961 episodes from two seasons.

In a late second season episode entitled *Angel of Death* he portrayed an Islander called Kahuna. In the third season in an episode called, *The Assassins* he played an island chief named Totani. The story begins with Troy leaving Tahiti and heading to Samoa.

He's asked to transport beautiful guest star Madlyn Rhue, convicted of manslaughter, although it was in self-defense. The ship also contains a bomb in a suitcase, presumably to bump off Rhue. After the bomb is discovered and disposed of, the Tiki III heads for the nearest island, which happens to be ruled over by swarthy Chief Totani. Henry is bare-chested, deeply-tanned and wears a necklace of exotic sea shells. He also is deeply distrustful and wants nothing to do with the white people, but reluctantly allows them to remain overnight until the police arrive the next day.

When a plane lands on the remote island, Troy believes it contains assassins there to finish the job on Madlyn's character Sherry. He asks for protection from Totani, who has his men scour the island for the hit men. When one of his natives is killed, he banishes the members of the Tiki III from his island-- and also vanishes from the rest of the episode.

The assassins, it turns out, are after Captain Troy, not Sherry, to prevent him from testifying in an upcoming trial. *The Assassins* aired on November 11th, 1961.

Interlude

By this time, Henry's lucrative television career had far surpassed his motion picture career in both number of jobs and monetary compensation. During the years of 1959 – 1961, he was constantly busy with TV work, known throughout the industry as a hard-working, prepared character actor who could essay any type of role. In each of these three years, he appeared in about a dozen program apiece, but that all ground to a halt when, in early 1962, he leapt at the chance to return to his native Germany to play the part of Colonel Kabar in MGM's fantasy adventure *Captain Sindbad*.

That winter was particularly brutal in Europe, and although Henry left Munich as soon as shooting was completed, he remained overseas for nearly eighteen months. "It was SO cold!" Henry told a group of Laurel and Hardy buffs in Detroit in 1982, "I wanted to get out of Germany as fast as I could! 1962 was the coldest winter (there) since they'd been recorded! I stayed (out of the United States) a year and a half."

During this period, he landed a job for Walt Disney Productions, which hadn't used him since he'd modeled and performed the part of Captain Hook on reference film for the Disney animators when *Peter Pan* was in production in the early 1950's.

The Ballad of Hector, The Stowaway Dog was a two-part episode for the 10th season of ***Walt Disney Presents the Wonderful World of Color***. "Hector's" tale was filmed in Portugal in 1963 and aired exactly one month before Beatlemania exploded in America, in February of 1964.

Taking that *Captain Sindbad* job was a costly decision, as it effectively derailed his domestic career. When Brandon returned to America in late 1963, his agent spread the exciting news around town that his client was again available for both film and television productions. But Henry only appeared on one other theatrical production in the Sixties (1969's stinker *The Search for the Evil One*). While he was able to revive his stateside video career, he never again enjoyed the abundance of work that he'd seen in the late 1950's and early '60's.

Walt Disney Presents the Wonderful World of Color:

Much of Henry Brandon's performing career on television consists of solid, well-acted guest roles that deliver what his reputation promises: another Western cad or Scar-type Indian chief, another murderous gangster or seasoned military man. But once in a while, Henry delivers a performance on the tube that is a surprise and a revelation, such as his 1951 ***Family Theatre*** role on *Hill Number One* was and this delightful riot of a part on ***Walt Disney Presents***.

The Ballad of Hector, The Stowaway Dog is a two part slapstick adventure on ***The Wonderful World of Color*** and Henry Brandon, as a grungy French roustabout for a broken down traveling circus, has a substantial role as this unnamed comic heavy. Henry only appears in the first of the two parts.

He is especially slovenly in the production, unshaven, drunk, a wet stump of a stogie jammed in the corner of his mouth and holes in his wardrobe. Brandon works for a fifth-rate traveling circus enroute to Lisbon on board the steamer where Hector serves. Hector is a bright sea dog who is owned by the First Mate, has the run of the ship and is beloved by the crew… except for the cat-loving Captain.

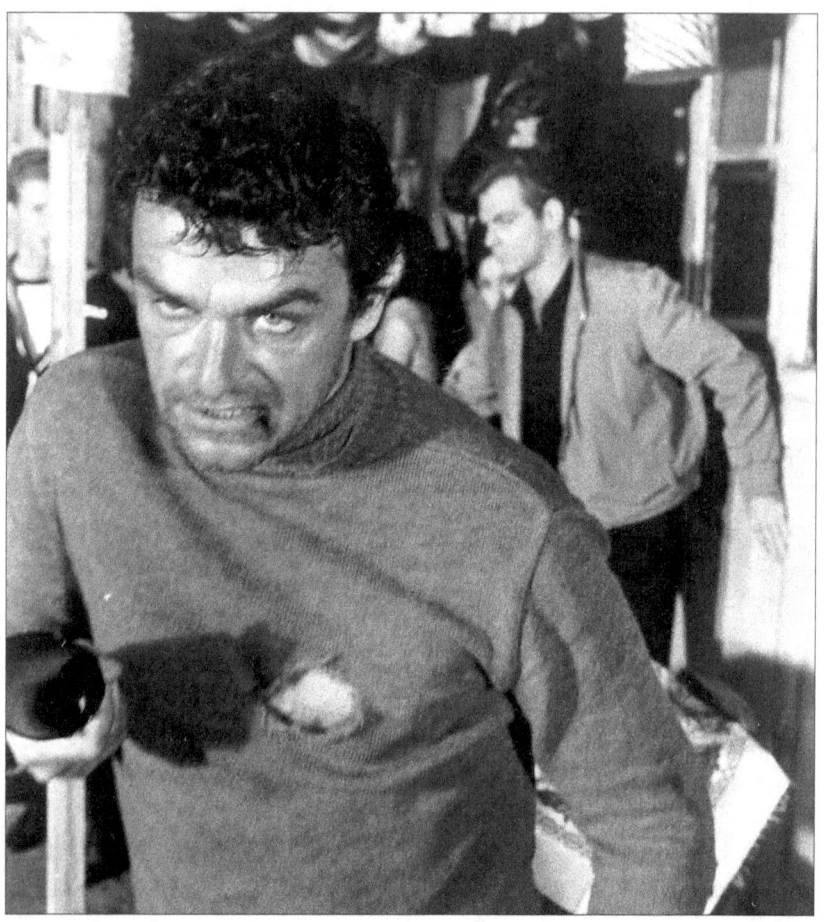

Henry is fighting mad as a circus roustabout in *The Ballad of Hector, The Stowaway Dog.* © Walt Disney Productions. Collection of Rick Greene.

Brandon is one of a pair of ethically-challenged minions who do the dirty work for the circus owner, and this includes dog-napping. Early on, Henry is supposed to be feeding the circus animals in their cages, but he is more interested in teasing a chimp and a leopard. Not a smart move.

The leopard escapes on board the confined craft and Henry plays it broadly, his face askew with cowardly terror. In fact, he is such a coward that when he finally *does* get away from the snarling beast after keeping it at bay with chair, Brandon runs out of the cabin and jumps right off the ship! Henry actually acts with the real jungle cat in several shots, foreshadowing his work with tigers in *When the North Wind Blows* a dozen years later.

The boat docks in Portugal and Henry is charged with creating a disturbance so they can steal Hector for their circus. In town, our roustabout plays even the little touches with expertise, as he plods down a pebbled Lisbon road while street dancers parade by, throwing confetti on him. He brushes it off with such a scowl of irritated contempt, but beautifully funny. Henry uses everything he had learned at The Hal Roach Studios in the 1930's to nail take after take with broad and hilarious expressions. At one point, during the dognapping, he is hit on the head with a flower pot and his cross-eyed takem would do Ben Turpin proud!

Yet there is another moment where Henry pretends to trip over Hector's owner and engages in a fight while his partner steals away with the dog. Brandon takes a bottle and smashes it, brandishing the broken glass as a very deadly weapon with murderous glee in his eyes. The genuine menace in this sequence is startling and expertly played.

Sadly, seeing *The Ballad of Hector* isn't easily accessible as the film was never released on VHS, laser disc or DVD and was last run back in the 1980's on The Disney Channel. It's well worth seeking out.

The two-part episode was later edited into a theatrical feature released overseas as *The Million Dollar Collar* in 1967. Henry's half of the story first aired on Sunday, January 5, 1964.

F-Troop:

Henry was pressed into duty as a "Chief Scar"-type of Indian again for the pilot episode of the popular sitcom *F-Troop*, which was a cross between The Three Stooges and Sgt. Bilko in the old West. *F-Troop's* inspiration also comes from *War Arrow*, a 1953 Universal International release that features Henry Brandon in a rare protagonist role. The elements of the fort with inept management, the pacifist Indians and the dangerous Indians are all present in *War Arrow*, burlesqued in *F-Troop*.

This first episode is called *Scourge of the West* and is set up in the closing months of the Civil War. Narrator William Conrad explains that pollen in the air causes clumsy Quartermaster Captain Wilton Parmenter (Ken Berry) to have a sneezing attack. Union troops mistake his "Ker-CHOW!" sneeze for orders to "Charge!" and they follow him NOT to pick up General Grant's laundry but into battle and unwittingly end the war! The result is a big reputation and Captain Parmenter is sent to Fort Courage to whip into shape the F-Troop, run like a con game by Sergeant Morgan O'Rourke (Forrest Tucker) and Corporal Randolph Agarn (Larry Storch). "Clumsy Parmenter" is in way over his head, and in between slapstick, sight-gags and rousing canned laughter, O'Rourke and Agarn find themselves having to fool the soon-to-arrive Inspector General into thinking they have a crack fighting unit.

They convince the local peaceful Indian tribe to stage a mock attack the following day. Edward Everett Horton does an amusing cameo as the tribe's medicine man Running Chicken and Larry Storch shows them how to do a war dance in a funny, loose-limbed exhibition. But the war dance attracts the attention of a rival tribe, the Shug Indians run by fully-feathered chief Henry Brandon. While everyone else in the cast plays it broad for maximum buffoonery, Henry is chillingly sincere in his desire to spill the white man's blood! "Shugs attack!" Brandon exclaims, "We kill many paleface!" But during the next day's fierce battle, when the Shug Chief overhears that they are up against Parmenter, he shouts "Captain Parmenter! *The Scourge of the West*! Run!" and they beat a hasty retreat.

Ken Berry is the unlikely hero. The Inspector General is suitably impressed and *F-Troop* is off and running for two seasons. This first season was filmed in black and white and premiered on September 14, 1965.

Combat! (1)

One day after Henry's appearance on the premiere episode of *F-Troop* he had his first role (of two) on the popular WWII baby-boomer show *Combat!* Filmed in gritty black and white until its final season, Combat premiered in 1962 and starred Vic Morrow as Sgt. Saunders and Rick Jason as Lt. Hanley. Both of Henry's *Combat* roles saw him playing Nazi officers.

The third season kicked off with an episode entitled *Mountain Man*. The simple plot involves Saunders and Hanley enlisting the aid of a bitter Frenchman named Perrault to guide them through snowy mountains so they can mark a trail for American troops to bring supplies and reinforcements to the Allies.

Henry plays an unnamed German Lieutenant commanding some Nazis in a frigid bunker at the peak of the mountain. He captures the Allies and begins grilling Saunders to find out how many troops comprise the coming American soldiers. Of course, Saunders won't talk, so instead of torture, he merely tosses them all down in a cold storage locker hoping the frigid temperatures will loosen their tongues. It's fun to watch Henry screaming in his native German at the stone-faced Americans.

They escape, of course, through a convenient hole in the back wall of the bunker. Can the Allies get away on foot and escape Germans on skis? Will they be able to warn the approaching forces and prevent an ambush? These are the simple questions that it takes an entire hour to answer. Henry, however is absent from the climactic chase as well as the story's resolution. *Mountain Man* aired on September 15th, 1964.

Branded:
After his long successful run as **The Rifleman**, Chuck Connors returned to Western television in two seasons of **Branded** as Jason McCord, unfairly "branded" as the cowardly sole survivor of the Battle at Bitter Creek. Henry appears as an extra in a second season episode called "Fill No Glass for Me, Part One."

The show opens with McCord arriving at a Mexican Cantina. Sitting at a table is a scruffily-bearded Brandon, drinking a beer with a cowboy buddy. He looks up when McCord orders some wine and two glasses, but does and says nothing. McCord soon leaves and the balance of the two-part episode is told in flashback.

Might Henry have had a larger part that was cut out? It's possible: his character is listed in the end credits with the name of Cleve. Hopefully that beer he was drinking was real, because Henry didn't get much else out of **Branded**. The episode aired on November 7, 1965.

Daniel Boone:
This was a very popular mid-1960's series starring Fess "Davy Crockett" Parker with Ed Ames as his half-Indian/half-British sidekick Mingo. The show ran for six seasons on NBC.

Henry Brandon shows up in the second season in an episode called *The Deserter* which aired on January 20, 1966. Henry plays gruff Lije Moody, leader of a backwoods posse of bounty hunters who are after two deserters from the Continental Army. One of the fugitives is played by a wildly miscast Dick Sargent as half-breed Indian Reuben Stone. Daniel Boone is mistaken as the second deserter by Simon Harman, amusingly portrayed by Slim Pickens. Most of the first half of the hour long episode concerns Harman's efforts to bring his two prisoners back to rendezvous with the gang while Boone's friends Mingo and Jerico (Robert Logan) are tracking them.

Daniel pretty easily manipulates this none-too-swift gang until his friends arrive for the climactic fist fight. Henry and Slim's performances steal the episode from the regulars as the thick, greedy partners who turn on each other while Boone never breaks a sweat.

It's fun to watch Henry play "stupid bad." Moody is not the sharpest arrow in the quiver and Brandon's perpetual dense expression is a hoot.

Laredo:

In 1965, a special 90-minute episode of the popular series *The Virginian* served as a back-door pilot for a new Western adventure show to be called **Laredo** whose premise was an update of the *Gunga Din* concept. Take the quarreling, hard-drinking, brawling trio played by Cary Grant, Victor McLaughlin and Douglas Fairbanks, Jr. and translate them into Texas Rangers based in Laredo and you've got something special.

Playing Quadada on *Laredo* in a truly terrible wig.

The new trio is portrayed by gravel-voiced Neville Brand as Reese, handsome Peter Brown (fresh from three seasons on **Lawman**) as Chad and William Smith as Joe and their rollicking energy assured *Laredo* would be high-octane entertainment.

Toward the end of the first season, Henry Brandon joined in on the fun in an episode called *Miracle at Massacre Mission*, but it was an atypical story. The first season was a massive 30 episodes of an hour-long show, which meant that toward the end of production, they were running behind schedule. Two scripts were written to be filmed simultaneously, splitting up the trio for most of the two shows to help get back on track. As a result, the scene-stealing Reese was only in the beginning ten minutes of *Massacre* and then went off to shoot his concurrent story. Therefore, it was a diluted **Laredo** episode for Henry to appear in, but it gave him quite the opportunity to do some scene-stealing of his own and he took full advantage of it.

The story has Rangers Chad and Joe accompanying two Nuns to reopen a deserted Mission in the middle of Comanche territory. The Nuns, who have gone on ahead against orders, are captured by the Comanche but when Chad and Joe arrive to "rescue" them, they are smoking a peace pipe with the tribe, and getting along fine. For a change, Henry isn't the Chief, but a very talkative Medicine Man called Quahada, right-hand Indian to Red Cloud. Quahada urges the tribe to put the Ranger duo to death while the Nuns attempt to save their rescuers. Brandon chants and glowers and shakes his totem, chewing the scenery with pickles & relish. The Nuns trick the Indians by knocking Quahada out with chloroform, and then reviving him magically. It's nice to see Henry Brandon and Peter Brown reunited for at least a few lines of dialogue given their moving scene in the 1959 **Lawman** episode *The Last Man*.

Things go well for a time as the Sisters begin holding Sunday services even attended by Henry's Quahada. The real villains are The Ford Gang, white men masquerading as Indians and responsible for a string of raids being blamed on the Comanche. They arrive at the Mission, where they've been burying their loot. An exciting gun battle between the Rangers and the Nuns with the Ford Gang culminates with the Comanche arriving to turn the tide (thus the 'miracle' of the title). Quahada even admits that not all white men are bad in the heartwarming coda.

It's so refreshing to see Henry Brandon grinning with the good guys at the end as they drink potent Comanche beer together. Brandon is excellent in this hour long episode playing a Comanche with a character arc. It aired on March 3, 1966.

The Outer Limits:

Each week when the monotones of Vic Perrin advised us that "There is nothing wrong with your television sets…" an entire generation of kids knew they'd be enjoying a full hour of crisp black and white science fiction and a guaranteed creature on *The Outer Limits*. While Henry's appearances in science fiction and fantasy films were limited to a just a few key examples (*War Of The Worlds, The Land Unknown*), he was hired to bring his military conviction to the role of General Crawford on *The Chameleon*, one of the final episodes of *The Outer Limits* first (and best) season broadcast in April of 1964.

Brandon as General Crawford in *The Outer Limits*.

Lunch break on *The Outer Limits* has Henry (far left) dining with Aliens.

A flying saucer full of bulb-headed aliens has landed in a canyon and Crawford's first instincts are to blast it into oblivion. But intelligence suggests there is combustible weaponry on board so former Agent Mace (Robert Duvall) is recruited to be genetically engineered into one of the creatures and infiltrate the ship. "We don't know who they are, what they want or why there are here!" exclaims General Crawford, who reluctantly goes along with the wild plan.

For a change, Brandon is one of the good guys and he's in the entire hour, from the first shot to the last, undergoing a change of heart during the finale and allowing the aliens to depart unmolested with Mace on board.

In fact, Brandon remembered:

> I played an Air Force general. I was technically the heavy because the picture was slanted toward the green men being benign beings to whom we earthlings were hostile without reason. I was the man who ordered they be attacked.

Honey West:

This series featured Anne Francis as a stylish jet-set detective, a kind of female Peter Gunn with a pet ocelot named Bruce.

The fourth episode entitled *A Matter of Wife and Death* aired on October 8, 1965 and had Henry as Alexander Sebastian, a key suspect of sending death threats to his ex-wife Maggie. Playing it just short of over-the-top, an early scene saw Brandon, happy to learn his ex-business partner was dead, grinning ghoulishly at midnight over his grave. Midway through the episode a mysterious frogman enters Sebastian's home through the bay doors and fires a spear gun into Henry's stomach, killing him instantly. It turns out Maggie was sending herself the death threats to steal one million dollars in smuggled diamonds her no-good ex had collected for her.

Get Smart: (1)

Henry appeared several times on a series inspired by Bondmania in the 1960's, the Mel Brooks/Buck Henry-created comedy **Get Smart**. The first of Henry's two appearances on **Get Smart** was in just the third episode of the show called *School Days* and broadcast on October 10th of 1965. *School Days* is a spoof of the S.P.E.C.T.R.E. training camp in *From Russia with Love* (the second 007 film) which sees Maxwell Smart (Don Adams) going undercover as a student at a CONTROL spy school to unmask a K.A.O.S. infiltrator. Max is assisted by the perky Agent 99 (Barbara Feldon) and Fang the Dog. Henry plays Zukor, one of three European trainees, all of whom are suspected of being the infiltrator.

Brandon, sporting a neatly groomed black beard, gets to show off his timing and comedic chops with some funny glances of exasperation at Smart's ineptness. Gags include riffs on the Robert Shaw wristwatch strangling wire in *From Russia with Love* and the "Oddjob" razor-tipped hat from the most recent Bond film, *Goldfinger*. In one scene Henry neatly decapitates a dummy a-la Oddjob and Max's attempt sends the dangerous derby soaring over the roof and breaking a neighbor's window! The episode includes some of the earliest uses of the "Would you believe…?" and "…and loving it!" gags.

During the climax, Henry is revealed to be a true CONTROL trainee but in his second *Get Smart* role, he plays an actual evil K.A.O.S. agent.

Get Smart: (2)

Indeed, in *Pheasant Under Glass* from *Get Smart's* 5th and final season, Henry portrays Belasco, the head agent at the K.A.O.S. Summer Headquarters in New Jersey (although he plays it with a German accent rather than New Yawkish) who has kidnapped Professor Pheasant and imprisoned him in a glass booth. Pheasant under glass… get it?

This premiere episode (Directed by Don Adams) of the 5th season aired on September 26th, 1969 and Maxwell Smart & Agent 99 are now married and she's pregnant. The gags are getting stale but they try to freshen things up with a timely moon landing opening gag.

Max is to pose as a pianist who accompanies a CONTROL agent who sings opera and will hit a high note and shatter the glass prison containing Pheasant, so he undergoes plastic surgery to hide his identity. Several examples of botched plastic surgeries have cameos by Martin Landau and Phyllis Diller with Don Adams' voice as finally Max just wears a false nose and mustache for the mission.

During the opera concert, Henry again has an opportunity to show off his rare comedic side with many incredulous looks of frustration at Smart's piano playing antics. "There is something strange going on around here!"

Belasco exclaims as Maxwell Smart's nose falls off onto the piano keys and he replaces it accidently with an orange slice. *Medea* this ain't.

The script doesn't serve Henry well as his off screen apprehension is merely referenced by The Chief (Edward Platt) in favor of more climactic breaking glass gags.

Mister Ed:

A few weeks before Henry's first **Get Smart** appearance he initiated his foray into Bondian comic spy shenanigans with a Sixth (and final) Season job on **Mister Ed**.

German spy Derek (Brandon) plots against the USA on *Mister Ed*.

The season began with a September episode which had talking horse Mister Ed and his pal Wilbur (Alan Young) getting involved in and solving a spy caper and the third episode, called *Coldfinger* is a sequel of sorts. Ed volunteers Wilbur (via a phone call to the Chief) to solve a second case and locate a stolen ultra-miniature short-wave radio. The culprits are German spies Kosh and Derek (Henry Brandon), holed up in a Chinese restaurant trying to sell the radio to the highest bidder.

Kosh (Oscar Beregi) and Derek and *Mister Ed* himself, of course, of course.

Mister Ed (who refers to himself as Oat-Oat-Seven) sniffs a black glove which leads them to The Flaming Dragon. There, Wilbur poses as a politically incorrect Chinese waiter right out of Jerry Lewis and with Ed's help, locates the missing radio and escapes from Derek and Kosh, who exclaims "When they start sending horses, maybe it's time to get out of the spy business!" Henry plays it fairly straight, using a German accent and wondering in disbelief why that horse is always around.

The whole half-hour goes down smoothly (unlike the radio, which Mister Ed swallows) with Alan Young, a consummate pro, particularly funny. *Coldfinger* (also called "Ed Sniffs out a Cold Clue") aired on September 26, 1965.

Combat: (2)

This series shifted to color in its fifth season when Henry Brandon appeared on his second episode called "*A Child's Game.*" Right off the bat you can tell there won't be too much plot in this episode and that it's called *Combat!* for a reason. The violence is almost mind-numbing as things begin in a fierce three and a half minute battle in a village on the European street section of the Universal back lot – a familiar street where twenty years earlier the likes of Sherlock Holmes, the Wolf Man and the Frankenstein Monster roamed.

On this sunny 1966 day, everything is blowing up and being shot to hell as Vic Morrow's Sgt. Saunders leads his men to commandeer the village and then head out to take a nearby farm house. The deserted farm house is being held by a group of very young German soldiers and when the Americans arrive, the fighting starts again.

Henry's delirious death scene on his second *Combat!* appearance.

Two of the teenaged German's are captured as one of the American's remarks, "They're kids… they're nothing but kids!" We are literally sixteen minutes into the hour-long episode of non-stop violence before there is any meaningful dialogue exchanged between the Combat team and the captured German prisoners. The Americans argue about their ability to capture the scared remaining German kids alive or if they'll have to kill them to take the farm house as ordered. Then everyone starts shooting again. Thirty-one minutes in and thousands and thousands of rounds of ammunition have been expended with just a leg wound to show for it when our side decides to lob in some hand grenades close… but not too close, to scare them into surrendering.

The explosions attract a trio of older, experienced German soldiers led by Henry Brandon, who join in the battle. Henry wounds Sgt. Saunders and accidentally kills one of the German kid prisoners. As he makes his way to the farm house, the other two adult Germans are killed and Henry mortally wounded. He crawls, bleeding through his belly, into the house. Morrow lets the remaining German boy loose to return and convince his troop to give up and save their lives, but the kid can't do it. Once he's back in the farm house, the remaining boys arm themselves and prepare to die. But Henry rears up on his knees in some mighty impressive death throes, sweaty, filthy, grunting and dying. He's riveting in this brief role and his horrific death convinces the German teenagers to lay down their arms, one by one, and surrender to the Allied forces.

Henry's delirious, goggle-eyed death on the dusty farm house floorboards is the highlight of the hour. *A Child's Game* aired on ABC on October 18, 1966.

The Virginian

This was a very popular show, running nine seasons on NBC (only **Gunsmoke** and **Bonanza** ran longer) and offered Henry Brandon a juicy role at about the midpoint of the run.

The episode was called *Yesterday's Timepiece* and, like all episodes, ran 90 minutes long. Having to produce a feature film every week, the producers would focus each week on a different cast member, beginning and ending each episode with the ensemble but following the plot of that specific actor for most of the episode.

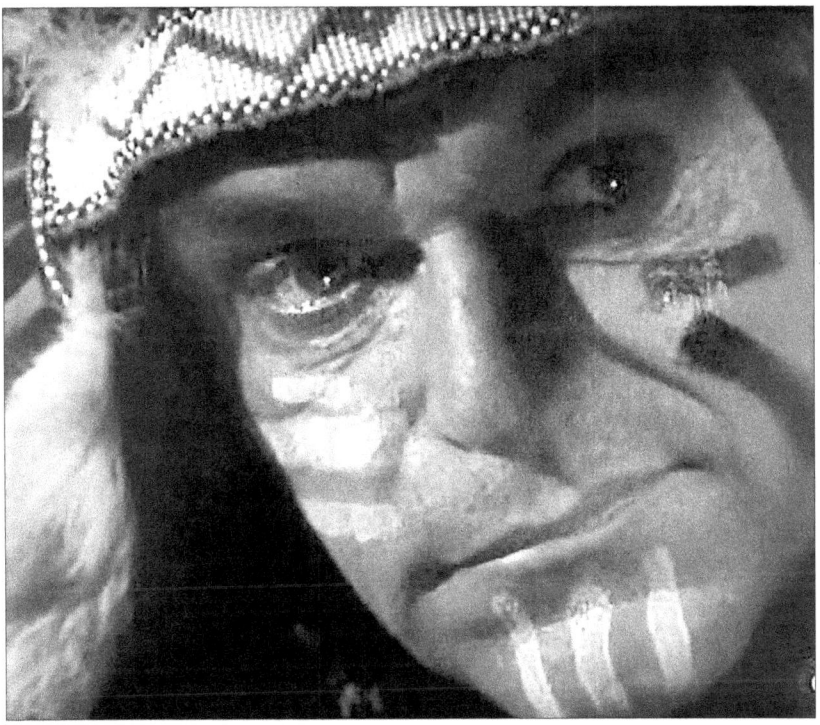

Henry in a dream sequence in *The Virginian*.

Yesterday's Timepiece dealt with Stacey Granger and his powerful reaction to a pocket watch he buys from the delightful Andy Devine, guesting as a traveling peddler. The watch inspires a series of nightmares that always have the same imagery... two young children in peril, sounds of an Indian attack, the watch and the leering, terrifying face of a war-paint covered Indian chief, a man we will come to learn is Swift Wolf (Henry Brandon). For his whole life, Stacey remembers this as the face of the murderer of his parents sixteen years earlier, also as the person who stole the watch.

He takes a leave of absence from the ranch to follow the trail of buyers and traders of the watch, hoping it will lead him back to Swift Wolf and justice for his parents. After a series of adventures in several states of the Union, Stacey's journey for truth finally takes him to Texas and a Comanche Indian reservation. There, he encounters an old, bent Indian fixing a fence and asks where he might find Chief Swift Wolf. Henry straightens up and reveals that HE is Swift Wolf, now with grizzled long gray hair and an old brown hat. Swift Wolf is not the fierce savage of Stacey's nightmares and worse, he refuses to talk about the past.

But Stacey has come too far on this journey to give up and he pushes and pushes the old man, until sparks fly and the story comes. Swift Wolf remembers the raid well. They were out for horses, not scalps. He didn't kill Granger's parents, they were merely wounded. He remembers the little blonde boy, standing over his unconscious parents, protecting them from the warriors. Swift Wolf let them all live to honor the young child's bravery.

That night, Stacey has the same dream but with more details, including the image of one of the murderer's wrist with a long scar on it. He races back to the Comanche reservation in the dead of night for a second confrontation with Swift Wolf, and to examine his wrists. Stacey finally remembers it was NOT Swift Wolf who killed his parents, it was a renegade white man! The trail leads to Houston and final justice.

The two well-played scenes between Stacey Granger and Swift Wolf bristle with emotions and are easily the highlight of the long episode. While it's great to see such stalwart guest stars as Devine, Stu Irwin and the great Pat O'Brien, it's disappointing that Henry Brandon isn't given guest star billing with his peers, especially considering the focus on the Swift Wolf character and his importance to the plot.

Yesterday's Timepiece was the 17th episode in ***The Virginian's*** fifth season and aired on January 18th, 1967.

Mr. Terrific:

In the wake of the **Batman** craze that swept the nation in 1966, there were two super hero spoof shows that hit the airwaves in '67: **Captain Nice** on NBC and ***Mr. Terrific*** on CBS. Both were one season shows, although both are remembered fondly by the Baby Boomers who embraced them. And one of them, *Mr. Terrific*, gave Henry Brandon one of his best villain roles EVER on the small screen.

The episode is called *Harley and The Killer* and the funny script gave ALL the featured players opportunities to shine. Harley Trent is the second banana character played by comic actor Paul Smith, usually relegated to a few funny reaction lines to his Bureau of Secret Projects boss Barton Reed. In *Harley and The Killer* Paul's character is front and center, as a certain Herman Von Brock (Henry Brandon, of course) has escaped from the penitentiary vowing deadly revenge on the man who sent him there for murdering his wife. That man is Harley, who is quickly offered unwanted protection in the form of nebbish Stanley Beamish (Stephen Strimpell).

Stanley is the only man on Earth who Power Pills work on to turn him into Mr. Terrific, a Superman type of character who flies, has super strength and who turns purple when he takes a ten minute Power Pill. Gruff, bearded Von Brock is described as a knife thrower from the circus and a "bad actor!" Henry plays him with a heavy German accent and a murderous gleam in his eye. He kidnaps Harley despite Stanley's best efforts and straps him to a circular Wheel of Death, going about the task of knifing him with a jaunty glee and a spring in his step. "Haircut, Mr. Trent?" Von Brock asks, throwing knives closer and closer to Harley's head.

Brandon is a joy to watch here, chewing up the scenery and casting a palpable feeling of comic menace over the entire half-hour. Mr. Terrific ultimately wins the day and straps the apprehended Herman Von Brock to his own Wheel of Death as Henry spends the last minute of the show spinning around and around and around... a good sport to be sure. *Harley and The Killer* came right in the middle of *Mr. Terrific's* run and aired on March 20 of 1967.

Shortly after *Mr. Terrific* was cancelled, four episodes were cobbled together into a "made for TV" movie called *The Pill Caper*. Henry's episode was one of the four selected.

About twenty years later, at the 1986 Sons of the Desert convention in

Philadelphia, Laurel and Hardy buff Rob Falcone asked Henry about his ***Mr. Terrific*** episode during a Q&A panel. "He told us about how he ad-libbed an old German song he'd learned in his youth while he was throwing knives at Paul Smith in the show's climax." Henry said the director (Arthur Lubin) "loved it, but the guys in legal went nuts trying to find out who owned (the copyright for) the song. I guess they cleared it up, because it stayed in."

Custer:

Henry Brandon made his last appearance in a television Western on an episode of a short-lived series called ***Custer*** that ran only 17 episodes in the Fall of 1967. His episode was entitled *Breakout* and begins as a TV-lite version of John Ford's *Stagecoach*.

An ensemble of characters board a coach – the crusty driver, the beautiful mysterious woman, the single-minded sheriff and his unhinged prisoner named Uvalde and a newsman who longs to write novels of the West named Ned Trimble (played by guest star Ray Walston.) Custer (Wayne Maunder), who has been busted to Lt. Colonel at the time of this series, joins the stagecoach as they attempt to avoid attack by Chief Fire Cloud (Henry Brandon.)

The early outdoor scenes and some of Henry's riding scenes were shot at the Fox Ranch at Malibu Creek State Park where, in just four short years, these same hills would double for Korea in the long-running ***M*A*S*H*** series. The stagecoach travelers make it to a Stage Relay Station but find the station master dead and two outlaws there to break out their prisoner pal, Uvalde. One of the killers is killed himself by an arrow as the group realizes they are surrounded and trapped by Fire Cloud's braves. Ray Walston gives the drama what little interest it has as ***Custer*** is a typical bland Sixties action series with an uncharismatic lead actor in Wayne Maunder.

On the second day of captivity, Custer goes out with a white flag to see if it's him that Fire Cloud is after. Henry finally makes an appearance nearly thirty minutes in and he easily dominates the proceedings. The Chief calls Custer "Yellow Hair" and tells him it's the convict Uvalde he's after… Uvalde has killed his only son. Custer tells Henry that Uvalde is headed for the gallows to pay for his crimes, which infuriates Fire Cloud. "To hang without pain?" he seethes. "To be dead in the blink of an eye, without time to scream for mercy!"

Brandon literally blasts into the episode with his fiery acting chops at full force. Custer refuses to turn over the condemned man and Fire Cloud tells him that they will all die. This is far from the same Fire Cloud from two episodes of **Wagon Train's** second and third seasons nearly ten years earlier. This Fire Cloud is a fearsome red devil, ready to massacre every white person in the Relay Station. That evening, awaiting the final attack, Custer sneaks out and strangles a white stunt man pretending to be an Indian and clears the way for everyone to sneak off while he prepares a diversion.

He drives the otherwise empty Stagecoach in the opposite direction and, predictably, Fire Cloud and his tribe follow. When Henry doubles back to the Relay Station, furious at being deceived, he discovers the Ray Walston character has remained behind, hoping to write the legend of the great Fire Cloud. Brandon, in one of the most savage medium shots of his career – brutally kills him with an Indian lance.

The tribe catches up with the remaining Stagecoach inhabitants to discover that Custer had to kill the tricky Uvalde and he lies dead in the dirt. Fire Cloud lets out a bloodcurdling scream and rides off. As Henry Brandon gallops away, he takes all the good acting in this episode with him.

Breakout aired on ABC on November 11th, 1967. It was one of the last episodes to air even though more were produced, due to outcry from Native Americans and it was slaughtered in the ratings by **Lost in Space** and **The Virginian.**

Mission: Impossible:

Henry shows up in the final moments of a fourth season episode of **Mission: Impossible** called *The Brothers* which aired on December 14, 1969. This was the first season without Martin Landau and Barbara Bain and instead featured Leonard Nimoy, fresh off of three seasons as Mr. Spock on the original **Star Trek.**

As Farid in *Mission Impossible*.

The mission concerns rescuing a kidnapped King of a fictional Arab nation who controls critical U.S. oil interests. Henry plays Farid, the colorfully-robed leader of the Sheiks who are present for the climactic reveal of the rescued King. As usual, Brandon brings the necessary gravitas to his brief but important role.

1970's

The Night Gallery:
This was host Rod Serling's three-season horror anthology successor to *The Twilight Zone* and Henry Brandon shows up in one of the last episodes of the final season.

The story is called *The Doll of Death*, a kind of voodoo soap opera and features the impending wedding of free-spirited Sheila to the ironically named Brandon (Barry Atwater). The wedding is crashed by brutish, handsome Rafael (Alejandro Rey) who easily steals away the bride-to-be. Henry portrays Colonel Vereker, an indignant wedding guest. He is only in the first scene but has several lines and brings some intensity to the proceedings before it turns into a voodoo death doll of vengeance story. It aired on May 20, 1973

Kolchak- The Night Stalker:

Henry was in the 14th episode of the series, entitled *The Trevi Collection* and was broadcasted on January 24, 1975.

Kolchak The Night Stalker saw Brandon portray the leader of a coven of witches.

Darren McGavin plays frumpy Carl Kolchak to bumbling, exasperated perfection, a low-income newspaper reporter who always stumbles across the stories involving zombies, vampires, werewolves and other assorted monsters. Madame Trevi (played by real-life friend of Henry's Nina Foch) is launching a new fashion line and is suspected of using witchcraft to eliminate an industrial spy with murderous mannequins. But high fashion model Madeleine (Lara Parker, fresh from playing Angelique on **Dark Shadows**) is the actual Black Witch. Hers is a deliciously high-pitched performance.

Like his **Night Gallery** appearance, Henry is only in a single scene in *The Trevi Collection* but makes the most of it, playing the bug-eyed leader of a coven of witches. Kolchak infiltrates the gathering for intelligence on witchcraft and ends up on the run while Henry is bedeviled by a haunted, floating pencil. Only a great actor could sell such silly stuff, which Henry Brandon certainly accomplished.

Bud and Lou:

This downbeat 1978 TV-movie starring Harvey Korman and Buddy Hackett that was loosely based (*very* loosely) on the lives and careers of the great Bud Abbott and Lou Costello using a biography by Bob Thomas as source material.

Wooden performances and a largely fictional, maudlin script suck the joy from the Abbott & Costello story and their classic routines, mercifully few of which are recreated here. When Korman and Hackett re-do "Who's On First", the whole routine feels wrong, the timing beats are off and this most-famous pinnacle of their career is rendered as painfully unfunny.

The whole movie is dark and lethargic and presents both Bud and Lou as nasty, crude and vindictive personalities. Henry Brandon completists thankfully don't have to slog through this whole mess to see his very brief bit as Bernie, the cigar-chomping stage manager at Minsky's Burlesque where the Boys perform their stage debut as a team.

To give you some idea of the importance of the role, Henry is listed in the closing credits after Stripper #1 and Stripper #2. This fiasco was broadcast on November 15, 1978 and Harvey Korman spent the rest of his life apologizing for it.

1980's

In the last decade of Henry Brandon's long career, he made startlingly few television appearances and still fewer film roles. This was when he was "rediscovered" and embraced by the movie buff community and spent most of his time appearing at conventions, meetings, panels, talk shows and events discussing his life's work in addition to acting in plays and revivals.

A few roles did come, including a few days' work on films like the Mel Brooks comedy remake of *To Be or Not to Be* in 1983, the television reunion movie of the cast of **Little House on the Prairie** and his performance in the Grade Z clunker *Wizards of the Lost Kingdom II* in 1989.

Evita Peron:

This non-musical TV movie retelling of the story of Evita, who rises from abused actress to ambitious political paramour to ultimate power as First Lady in 1930's & 40's Argentina, features Henry Brandon in a pair of scenes from the first half of the picture.

Brandon portrays General Ramirez, one of the successors of Presidents of Argentina. In his first sequence he seizes power and makes a compelling radio address to his new nation, proudly donning the Presidential sash. Brandon is regal, assured and seasoned, playing South American as easily as he does German, Indian, British or Polynesian.

Later, as Faye Dunaway's Evita sleeps her way to the top, the number two man in the Ramirez government makes a back door deal with Nazi Germany. He stages a coup, marching into the Presidential office and ousting President Ramirez in a humiliating sequence. Ramirez has declared war on Germany, but Peron has none of that and he kicks Brandon out. "What about my clothes?" whines the beaten Ramirez, who is told his things will be sent to him. He is forced to turn over the sash as he slinks out of the office and out of the movie. **Evita Peron** was broadcast on February 23, 1981 on NBC.

Little House on the Prairie- Look Back To Yesterday:

Television "reunion" films were very popular in the 1980's, bringing together original cast members of such shows as *The Man From U.N.C.L.E., Maverick, Gunsmoke, The Wild, Wild West, Cannon, Get Smart* and others. Michael Landon offered up a role for Henry Brandon in the reunion of the *Little House on the Prairie* cast in 1983's *Look Back to Yesterday*. This was the first film of four that kept the cast together after their nine-season run ended on NBC just the year before.

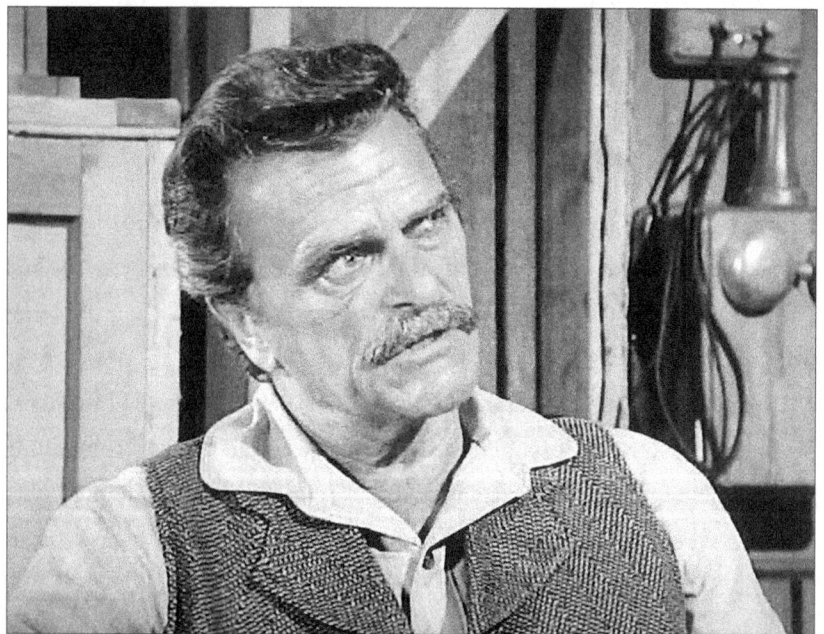

Otis Wagner in *Little House On the Prairie*.

Look Back to Yesterday concerns the return of Michael Landon's character Charles Ingalls to Walnut Grove, where the series took place. (Landon had left the show during its ninth and final season). The town is in something of a recession due to most of their farming output out-priced by the larger firms back East. The story is really nothing more than an extended episode and the acting is broad, theatrical and cutesy.

Henry plays a business man named Otis Wagner in a pair of short scenes, both played with Landon, who convinces Wagner to accept the produce from Walnut Grove if he can combine the efforts of the town into one co-op of farmers to compete with the larger, more modern organizations. Henry, showing compassion as well as business acumen, agrees.

How refreshing it is, at this late stage in his career, to see Brandon effortlessly playing a tough but fair business man – and a *good* man. He could have been such an effective regular on a series like this if given the chance. It's also nice to see him billed as one of the telefilms guest stars in the opening credits. *Look Back to Yesterday* aired on December 12, 1983.

E/R

After a long career that began with his star turn with Stan Laurel and Oliver Hardy in *Babes In Toyland* and included fun roles with the Little Rascals, Bob Hope, Danny Kaye, Dean Martin & Jerry Lewis and Mel Brooks and equally funny parts on television's **Mister Ed, Get Smart, Mr. Terrific** and **F-Troop**, Henry's final comedic role came in October of 1984 on a CBS show called *E/R*.

No, not THAT *ER*, the Chicago-based drama created by Michael Crichton and starring George Clooney, Noah Wyle and Anthony Edwards: THIS *E/R* is a forgotten Chicago-based sitcom that ran two seasons and – ironically – *also* featured a very young George Clooney. It also starred Elliott Gould. Henry appeared on the seventh episode called *Say It Ain't So* as Mr. Pavlic, which aired in November of 1984.

Murder, She Wrote

Henry Brandon's final job as a guest star on a television series came on a 3rd Season episode of the popular Angela Lansbury show **Murder, She Wrote** in a 1987 story entitled *Crossed Up*. Lansbury played an Agatha Christie-type mystery writer Jessica Fletcher who solves real crimes as well as writes novels about them (a premise that would be borrowed by the gender-shifting *Castle* a decade later) for a whopping twelve seasons on CBS.

As both murderer and victim Abel Gorcey in *Murder She Wrote*.

Crossed Up is a kind of cross itself – a combination of the classic *Sorry Wrong Number* and Hitchcock's *Rear Window* as Jessica is bedridden with a bad back and overhears a crossed-wire phone conversation. Hit-man Henry Brandon's full-bearded gruff Abel Gorcey is being hired to murder someone in Cabot Cove that very evening.

No one believes her (of course) and her warnings are ignored by Police Chief Tom Bosley as the product of an overactive imagination suffering from cabin fever. Henry "kills" time in a local diner, awaiting darkness and trying to remain inconspicuous, but he's noticed by both a waitress and Jessica's nephew, who remembers his van with the New York license plate.

The next morning a millionaire lumber magnate is discovered dead, the murder Jessica Fletcher had warned them would occur. Via some bedside sleuthing, Fletcher quickly identifies the killer as Abel Gorcey and just as rapidly, the sheriff's men locate and surround a remote cabin where Gorcey is hiding out. And, just as rapidly again, Henry Brandon's television career comes to an inglorious end as Gorcey is found dead behind the cabin, apparently the victim of a drunken fall.

Members of lumber magnate's family now become the prime suspects of killing the killer as the predictable mystery unfolds without Henry Brandon and the missed opportunity of a psychotic Gorcey stalking bedridden Jessica Fletcher in a blinding rainstorm never happens.

This unlucky thirteenth episode of **Murder, She Wrote's** third season aired on the CBS network on February 1, 1987. As parts in motion pictures and on television grew sparse for Henry Brandon - he only appeared on two TV shows, two television movies and two theatrical films in the entire 1980s – he returned to the theatre and his stage roots and found a *new* outlet for performing… portraying Henry Brandon, Actor, at gatherings of young film buffs for classic comedy, westerns and sci-fi/serial lovers. Not content to merely reminisce, sign autographs or answer questions, Henry brought his "A" Game to these appearances, turning them into performance art and endearing himself to new generations of movie fans around the world.

Henry Brandon mimes some villainous mustache twirling at the England 1984 Sons of the Desert convention. Photo by Marcia Opal.

CHAPTER SEVENTEEN
Film Fandom

BY THE LATE 1970's, Henry Brandon's film and television careers were winding down. In 1979, he appeared in the sleazy *Hollywood Knight* (aka *Hard Knocks*) leaving only two more feature appearances ahead of him. On the small screen, Henry did a bit role in the ***Bud & Lou*** television movie with just three more small supporting roles in the 80's. But as these decades-long big and small screen careers came to a close, another door opened. And Henry found himself in the very role he never thought would come to pass. He was a Star.

Henry Brandon was discovered and embraced by three very different communities of film fandom: the comedy buffs, the Western aficionados and the cliffhanger serial/sci-fi fans. And, at first, each of these groups were surprised – often shocked – to discover that the man who played their beloved Barnaby in *Babes In Toyland* also worked with John Wayne in *The Searchers*, or that the devilish Dr. Fu Manchu and bearded Dr. Hunter from *The Land Unknown* had also performed with Laurel & Hardy, Bob Hope, Martin & Lewis and Danny Kaye!

Film fandom exploded from the nostalgia boom of the late Sixties and early Seventies into organized groups of like-minded fans who gathered to celebrate and enjoy the classic movies from the Golden Age. At these dinners and festivals and conventions, the surviving performers were invited to speak, to sign stills, to be interviewed on panels, photographed for fanzines and to be treated like they were Chaplin or Bogart or Hitchcock. Many of them went from being forgotten to being celebrated and worshiped. The decaying egos of these aging actors and actresses and writers and technicians were hit with a shot of adrenalin at these festivals and fetes. And Henry Brandon was able to reinvent himself as The Man We Loved to Hate… with an accent on the love.

Because Henry's five-decade long career had showcased his astounding versatility in a wide variety of genres, he was "rediscovered" by not just one, but by three or four different groups of fans, which kept him extremely busy attending events on a weekly basis for the final fifteen years of his life.

The Sons of the Desert

The Sons of The Desert, the international Laurel and Hardy organization founded in 1965 in New York City by John McCabe, was probably his favorite fandom group. Where the Western fans might have a banquet once or twice a year, the Sons always had something going on. With more than one hundred "tents" (chapters) internationally, Henry was much in demand due to his appearances with Stan Laurel and Oliver Hardy as well as Our Gang. He traveled to tent meetings, banquets and conventions in dozens of cities across the country and several international meetings as well.

Way Out West Tent First Annual Banquet

It all began at the first annual Way Out West Tent Banquet in the Fall of 1971, Henry's initial appearance at a Sons of the Desert event. The Way Out West Tent was known as "The Tent of the Stars" and routinely had a roster of former Hal Roach Studios alumni appearing at their get-togethers including silent comedienne Anita Garvin, musical director (and composer of the Ku-Ku Song) T. Marvin Hatley, Little Rascals Spanky McFarland, Darla Hood, Buckwheat Thomas, Gordon 'Porky' Lee, Butch Bond and Dorothy Deborba, behind the scenes craftsman Roy Seawright, film editor Richard Currier and, at any number of special events, The Boss Hal Roach himself, who lived to be a feisty and frisky 100 years old.

Henry receives an award at Hollywood '80, the second Sons convention. Photo by Marcia Opal.

This first Way Out West Tent banquet was not only Henry's first appearance before the Laurel and Hardy buffs he would soon consider "family," but it was also the first time Hal Roach and Marvin Hatley attended a Sons function. It was also the only time the great supporting comic Billy Gilbert (voice of Sneezy for Disney's *Snow White*) was at a Sons function. The banquet was held at The Odyssey, a banquet hall and restaurant overlooking the San Fernando Valley in Granada Hills, California.

Henry and Dorothy DeBorba at Detroit '82. Photo by Marcia Opal.

This first banquet didn't go so well for Henry Brandon. He told, for the first time to an eager audience, the famous *Babes in Toyland* behind the scenes story of Stan instructing everyone what they were going to do in the next scene, standing up to say, "Alright, let's shoot it!" and Henry naively asking, "Aren't we going to rehearse?" to which Stan spat back, "Do you want to *spoil* it?" Henry would go on to tell that classic remembrance dozens of times to Sons all over the world, but this first time, he followed it with "Stan Laurel was the biggest son of a bitch I ever met!" The audience, who naturally, worshipped Stan Laurel-Comedy Genius, was aghast. Thirteen years later, Brandon recounted this memory for co-author Rick Greene, adding, "I thought they were going to lynch me!"

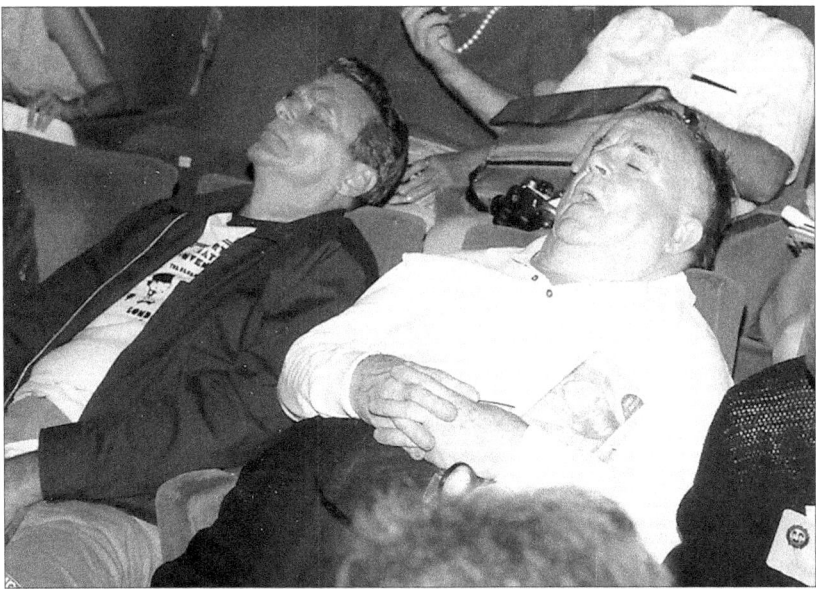

Henry and Stan Laurel's valet Jimmy Murphy nap before a London screening in 1984. Photo by Rick Greene.

What Henry meant was that Stan's comment, while in keeping with a motion picture artist and comedy craftsman, was the antithesis of how a theater professional would work. Henry Brandon actually got along great with both Laurel and Hardy and thought the world of them as men and as comedy giants. But that "Do you want to *spoil* it?" comment certainly rankled at the time. Henry's S.O.B. commentary effectively got him *uninvited* back for another eight years.

Long-time Way Out West Tent Grand Sheik Bob Satterfield joined the organization as a thirteen year old shortly after this first Banquet and toward the end of the decade found himself running the Tent. He tried and tried to get Henry Brandon back, but got nothing but resistance. Brandon was the guy who called Stan Laurel an S.O.B. in front of a hundred fans! But time passed and Satterfield got Brandon on the guest list for the annual Banquet eight years later.

Henry's triumphant return to The Sons of the Desert occurred on

October 6th, 1979. This was the night that co-author Greene met Henry Brandon for the first time at the 9th Annual Sons of the Desert Banquet & Bash of the Way Out West Tent. The event was held at the Hollywood Roosevelt Hotel, in the same room as the site of the very first Academy Awards ceremony in 1927. Sons came in from San Diego and San Francisco, as far away as London, to attend this now annual star-studded celebration of all things Laurel and Hardy. In addition to Henry Brandon, also present this evening was Hal Roach, Trudy Marshall, Lois Laurel, Lucille Hardy Price and the *Swiss Miss* herself, Della Lind.

The Philly '86 *Babes in Toyland* reunion of Barnaby, Mother Goose and Tom Tom. Photo by Rick Greene.

Henry told his "Aren't we going to rehearse?" story, without the S.O.B. comment, and he told his Hal Roach hiring him for *Babes* story, where Roach made the comment, "You aren't that old son of a bitch I saw on stage last night?" but that was okay. Henry killed it that night, which led to Way

Out West Tent board members, with short memories, asking why on earth it took so long to get the amazing Henry Brandon to one of their events. All Bob Satterfield could do was give an "Oliver Hardy sigh," glad that once again Brandon was a Sons A-Lister.

Hollywood '80

His gig at the 9th Annual Way Out West Banquet led to Henry being invited, one year later, to his first Sons Convention, the fabled Hollywood '80 gathering of nearly 500 Sons from all over the world. This five-day celebration is still looked back upon as one of the very greatest of the Sons bi-annual conventions.

Henry (with Lois Laurel Hawes) goofs off for the camera in '86. Photo by Kevin Mulligan.

The second international convention of the Sons, Hollywood '80 was held from July 30 through August 3, 1980 at the Los Angeles Hilton. The convention featured tours of Laurel and Hardy filming locations, a massive Our Gang Reunion, a live pie-fight covered by the television show *Real People*, a back-lot tour and banquets loaded with celebrities. The stars at

Hollywood '80 included Hal Roach, Lois Laurel, Lucille Hardy Price, Anita Garvin, Della Lind, T. Marvin Hatley, Spanky, Buckwheat, Porky, Woim, Butch, Dorothy, Joe, Sunshine Sammy and dozens more.

Also in attendance was Henry Brandon who was soaking in the "boos and hisses" when he was introduced, loving the outbursts as much as the applause. Henry Brandon was a smash again, repeating his Hal Roach Studios stories to this larger audience. He also reunited with Spanky MacFarland at this convention, seeing him for first time since they worked together in *Trail of the Lonesome Pine* and *Our Gang Follies of 1938*.

There was an informal courtesy hosted bar that was set up before the festivities. Spanky just happened to be behind the bar mixing his own cocktail when up stepped Henry. Thinking Spanky the evening's bartender, Henry ordered his drink. Spanky immediately recognized the actor but kept his cool. He went to work and produced Henry's drink. Unceremoniously, Henry turned slightly and downed the spirits. The *bartender* asked, "How is it?" Before Henry could answer, Spanky announced, "I put poison in it." As Henry turned to face him, Spanky raised his voice and said, "You killed me in *Trail of the Lonesome Pine* and I just got you back." They hit it off as adults immediately and one could always find Spanky and Barnaby hanging out together at the various bars at meetings and conventions from Hollywood '80 onward.

Sons Conventions in England/Valley Forge/St. Paul

After Hollywood '80, Henry went on to attend the next four consecutive Sons of The Desert conventions: Detroit in 1982, London/Ulverston in 1984, Valley Forge in 1986 and finally St. Paul in 1988. Bob Satterfield recalls an amusing incident that took place at the Detroit conclave (that he later recounted at Henry's memorial service). Each convention usually featured side trips and both pre and post-convention activities. In Detroit, there was a bus trip up into Canada for a day, which Henry Brandon attended.

Spanky McFarland and Henry at the bar in 1988. Brandon was growing his beard for *Wizards of The Lost Kingdom II*. Photo by Rick Greene.

Bob Satterfield:

After a long day of sightseeing, the bus was stopped at the border by customs officials who asked for confirmation by a show of hands that everyone on board was a U.S. citizen and was born in the United States. Everyone, anxious to get back over the border and to the hotel, raised their hands… except one. "Nope!" said Henry, "Berlin!" This caused the officers to remove our vicious villain of vintage cinema from the vehicle to check him out, accompanied by the groans of the tired L&H buffs. After some discussion, they seemed satisfied… until they asked if 'Brandon' was his real name. "Nope," Henry confirmed, "Kleinbach!" During these Cold War days, they had to check out this Kleinbach character, causing a further thirty-minute delay. When they were finally convinced that Henry was not a threat to the United States of America, he reboarded the bus and sat next to Bob Satterfield, who again was able to do his Oliver Hardy impression saying, "You *had* to say "Berlin," didn't you!" This earned him a hearty Brandon belly-laugh.

Brandon at the mic in St. Paul '88. Photo by Rick Greene.

In 1984 Henry trekked to London and Ulverston (Stan Laurel's birthplace) for an epic Sons of the Desert Convention that ran from July 29 through August 6. The first half of the event was in London and the last half up in the Lake District, where Ulverston is located. Longtime Son and author Irv Hyatt remembers a barroom laugh that reflects Henry's lifetime love of spirits:

> At the England '84 convention I had the pleasure of spending quite a bit of time with Jimmy Murphy. Henry also enjoyed Jimmy's company. In the Ulverston Grand Hotel, the bar opened at 10:30 AM. Jimmy and I went down, and I asked him "Want a

pint, Lad?" which was an ongoing joke that we both used to indicate who was buying. As I went up to the bar, Henry Brandon came in. I asked if he wanted a beer. He looked at me with a shocked expression and in his best "Christmas present in the middle of July?" voice he said, "Are you kidding? It's 10:30 in the morning!" After a short pause, he followed that question with "I'll have a triple-Vodka."

One of the highlights of the 1988 Son's convention was a public viewing of Laurel & Hardy and Our Gang films at the World Theater in St. Paul, Minnesota (courtesy of Tracy Tolzmann). That little rascal, Spanky McFarland, set up some of the film fare to include *Our Gang Follies of '38*. Spanky then introduced Henry to the appreciative audience who gave the two a long standing ovation. Henry took the opportunity to inform the crowd that he "killed" little Spanky in the film, *Trail of the Lonesome Pine*.

Bill Cassara shares the following St. Paul 1988 memories of that night:

> The highlight of one evening was a film festival featuring Laurel & Hardy, the Our Gang kids and Henry Brandon. Sharry Han, the Grand Sheik of the Jitterbugs Tent in Las Vegas, had the foresight to rent a car which provided us with instant transportation to the 900-seat theatre. Since Henry Brandon's room was next to mine at the hotel, we asked Henry if he would like to be driven to the show, as opposed to riding in one of the busses that were provided. Before you could say "air conditioned ride," Henry joined us to our destination.
>
> As part of the film festival, a local television celebrity introduced each Our Gang alumni and showed film clips of their careers. Little did the audience realize, but Spanky MacFarland insisted on introducing Henry Brandon to the crowd. Spanky wanted to introduce Henry because he admired him as an actor and for his

ability to last 50-plus years in the film business. Spanky was very familiar with Henry as an "Actor's actor." Henry

Our Gang Follies of 1938, which featured Henry in his "Old Barnaby" role, was screened to the appreciative audience. Just before exiting the stage, Spanky announced: "Henry and I are going to finish our story telling in private." After the film festival, it was time to head back. Henry asked, "Is it okay if we take Spanky along with us?" Henry suggested we go back to his room to talk, where he could offer a bottle of vodka to share. Also invited to Henry's room was good friend, Alex Bartosh. During the course of the evening, Sharry and I just looked at each other as if to say, "Can you believe we're sitting here listening to Henry and Spanky?"

Before you knew it, hours had passed. I don't know if it was the vodka or the unthreatening atmosphere, but Spanky became completely relaxed and sincerely enjoyed the time with Henry. In fact, it seemed as though he relied on Henry to fill in details that Spanky, the child actor, either forgot, or was never exposed to. Spanky wanted to take advantage of the opportunity to ask Henry questions about people they had both appeared in films with. Questions that Spanky had been asked over the years and had been expected to answer, but couldn't, because he may have been only five years old at the time of filming.

Spanky asked Henry, "What was Henry Fonda like?" Henry told stories that displayed his instant recall. As Spanky listened attentively, Henry told about Henry Fonda, Fred MacMurray and others during the early stages of their careers in films. Henry told of advice and direction he gave to big name actors who took advantage of Henry's experience on contract negotiations and screen image.

Spanky shared with us that he is always asked if he was influenced by Oliver Hardy when he was a little actor. Spanky usually denied it in public, but handily confirmed to it to Henry. "Of course Oliver Hardy was influential to me in my mannerisms, I had the best role model there was."

Henry told of stories of Spanky on the Roach set and how he hated his studio teacher and especially how Spanky would recoil at little old ladies who would coo over him. Henry said Spanky had a "salty mouth" even as a small child. He would shock his elder female admirers with: "Ah, you old ladies give me a pain in the ass."

Henry's instant recall of events that occurred fifty years ago was amazing, especially considering how many different films and actors he had come into contact with. The man was a living book of cinema history.

Sadly, St. Paul was the last of Henry Brandon's five consecutive Sons of the Desert conventions. The 1990 Clearwater, Florida gathering was held just five months after Henry died, leaving a gaping hole in their guest roster as saddened Sons shared their fond memories of spending time with Henry Brandon, with love and hisses.

Schnitzelbank

At each convention, Henry had his time in the spotlight, retelling his handful of Laurel and Hardy/*Babes in Toyland* stories, sitting on celebrities' panels where he was asked about other films and television shows from throughout his long career, and socializing with hundreds of adoring comedy buffs. After a few years of this, even though he enjoyed meeting new fans and performing his recollections with the artistry of a great storyteller, Henry had to come up with something to keep these appearances fresh... for himself *and* the audiences. And in the mid-1980's, he came up with something spectacular.

Growing up in the United States, Henry's family kept their Germanic roots and heritage alive by speaking in German and recounting stories and songs from the Old Country. One such song that Henry had great fondness for was the Schnitzelbank Song, a short rhyming children's sing-along with humorous verses that build on each other and lead to a sentimental chorus. This traditional folk song was always sung as a group effort, with the leader asking questions of his audience, who answers in sing-song good spirits. Henry had performed the Schnitzelbank during the Olio after each performance of *The Drunkard* in the 1930s for hundreds of audiences.

Brandon in mid-performance of his Schnitzelbank at a San Diego banquet. Photo by Rick Greene.

Henry wrote a Laurel and Hardy version of the Schnitzelbank, incorporating mentions of Ollie (Dicker Dummkopf) and Stan (Doffer Dummkopf), of James Finlayson, Charlie Hall, Mae Busch, Hal Roach and Lois and Tony Hawes mixed with "Fuss Ball", Motor Coaches and a 'Sexy Tush" to rhyme with "Busch." Artist Tony Hawes created a massive five foot by five foot illustrated backdrop that traveled with Henry with fully painted cartoons of each of the sing-song items so that Henry could lead his audiences while pointing at each image with his baton. We would sing each verse in answer to Henry's question, ending with a heartfelt "Ei du schoene, ei du schoene, ei du schoene, schnitzelbank!"

Brandon would assume the accent and eccentric characteristics of an old German musical professor, as always playing the part to the hilt, rolling his 'R's with gusto and thrilled to be sharing something of his childhood while entertaining us. He found a way to take center stage and give an entertaining performance without having to pull out his old chestnut Stan Laurel/Hal Roach stories.

Way Out West Tent [W.O.W.] Meetings & Banquets

While the bi-annual Sons of the Desert conventions were and still remain the centerpiece activity of the organization, Henry Brandon also appeared at dozens and dozens of more traditional monthly meetings, banquets and special events in between the international conventions.

Since he lived in Hollywood, one would most often find Henry Brandon at Way Out West Tent meetings. From 1979 onwards, he rarely missed their annual Banquets in the Fall, but he also popped in to the normal monthly gatherings in North Hollywood at the Mayflower Club. Grand Sheik Bob Satterfield explained that while most of the Laurel and Hardy related celebrities needed to be specially invited and arranged for, Henry Brandon often attended W.O.W. meetings by just walking in the door. He never needed special treatment... if he was in town and available, he was there.

There were many meetings of the W.O.W. Tent throughout the 1980's that did focus on Henry, including a number of Christmas celebrations built around *Babes in Toyland* screenings. December 1981 was the first of these *Babes* Holiday gatherings, held at the Golden Valley Auditorium in Van Nuys, California.

At the Way Out West Banquet 1979, co-author Greene (with Elliot Becker) meets Henry for the first time.

Another special Christmas meeting was planned for W.O.W.'s 1984 meeting featuring a proposed *Babes in Toyland* reunion. This was to be when Henry Brandon and co-star Felix Knight had their first meeting since 1934 on the set, but Felix rarely traveled West and this reunion had to wait a few years until the Valley Forge convention of 1986. However, Henry was there, which is all that was needed to make a memorable Way Out West Tent holiday event, this time held at the famous Masquer's Club in the heart of Hollywood. Henry was a long-time member of the Masquers and would feature in some of their unusual non-Laurel & Hardy related cinema celebrations later in the 80's.

A Way Out West Tent Stan Laurel Birthday Party held on June 11th of 1985 was covered in a *Los Angeles Times* article by James Bacon noting the attendance of Lois Laurel Hawes, Marvin Hatley, with Tony Caruso and Henry Brandon lumped together as the "heavys" of the films, Mabel Langdon, the ingénue of *Bonnie Scotland* June Lang and the team of Chuck McCann and Jim MacGeorge, who were famous for, among other things, their spot-on Laurel and Hardy impressions for television commercials.

Henry Brandon with John Duff on the Queen Mary for a 1987 Way Out West Tent Banquet. Photo by Rick Greene.

At the March 1986 meeting of W.O.W. held at The Mayflower Club in North Hollywood, Henry Brandon took the stage to offer a eulogy for Ben Price, Lucille Hardy Price's second husband and a beloved member of the Sons of the Desert family. Henry's heartfelt salute to Ben left not a single eye dry in that packed house.

Henry Brandon and Stan Laurel's birthday were celebrated at the W.O.W. Tent's June 9th 1987 meeting with two large cakes. Amongst the revelers were Billy Benedict from the Dead End Kids and Frank "Junior" Coghlan, both of whom appeared in the Republic serial *The Adventures of Captain Marvel*.

Way Out West Tent meeting with Henry reuniting with two of the Three Little Pigs – Payne Johnson and Little Angelo Rossito. Photo courtesy of Bob Satterfield.

This serial, along with Henry's *Drums of Fu Manchu*, are often cited as the two finest serials of all-time. Also attending for the first of many times was Peggy Lynch (Margaret Kerry) who famously was filmed by Disney Studios – as was Henry Brandon – performing *Peter Pan* sequences on camera for the animators to study. Margaret was Tinker Bell to Henry's Captain Hook. They also both appeared in the Hal Roach two-reeler *Our Gang Follies Of 1938*.

December 8th of 1987 saw another W. O.W. *Babes in Toyland* themed holiday meeting called "Henry Brandon Night." In addition to the annual *Babes* screening, a chapter of *Drums of Fu Manchu* was also unreeled to the delight of the audience.

Henry recreates a *Drums of Fu Manchu* pose at a San Diego banquet. Photo by Rick Greene.

Henry was always among the invited guest roster for the W.O.W. annual banquets each Fall. After his triumphant return to these banquets in 1979, he attended the October 30, 1982 edition, which was the 12th Annual Banquet. This was the biggest gathering of L&H celebrities since Hollywood '80 and included editor Richard Currier, costumer Jay Dare, Dorothy 'Echo' DeBorba, Edith Fellows, Marvin Hatley, Lois and Tony Hawes, William Janney from *Bonnie Scotland*, Walter Woolf King from *Swiss Miss*, Harry Langdon's widow Mabel, Sunshine Sammy Morrison, Lucille Hardy Price,

Hal Roach, Anita Garvin and author Jack Scagnetti. Those were the days when it almost seemed that the guest stars outnumbered the audience!

Henry Brandon and co-author Bill Cassara in 1986 at a Way Out West Tent Police Academy Banquet circa 1987.

The following year saw the W.O.W. Tent's 13th Annual Banquet, this time held at The Sportsman's Lodge in Studio City. Many of the same celebrities from the previous year were asked back, this time including Producer Joe Rock, Eddie Quillan, Edith Fellows, the infamous mistress of W.C. Fields, Carlotta Monti and widow of stalwart Roach cameraman Art Lloyd, the delightful Venice Lloyd.

Henry joined a tremendous list of guests for a very special event aboard The Queen Mary in Long Beach for the Way Out West Tent's 14th Annual Banquet on October 28, 1984. Joining Henry on board the famous ship were his dear friend and co-star Anthony Caruso along with the usual list of Laurel and Hardy royalty. The dinner was held in the glamorous Queen's Salon dining room, where both Laurel and Hardy spent many evening on their various Atlantic crossings in the 1940's and '50's. The evening was such a smash that it virtually assured Way Out West would return to the Queen for a future banquet.

The Midnight Patrol was the "cops and robbers" theme for the 1986 banquet of Way Out West, with attendees encouraged to dress up as criminals and their molls, or lawmen. Henry Brandon was there on Saturday, October 25th, along with Tony Caruso, Dorothy DeBorba, William Janney, Trudy Marshall, Sunshine Sammy Morrison, Eddie Quillan and Hank Worden.

The 1987 Banquet of W.O.W. was held on September 13th at the Valley Hilton in Sherman Oaks and featured another stellar roster of stars including Henry Brandon joined by Hal Roach, Iris Adrian, Norma Drew from *Chickens Come Home*, Buster Keaton's widow Eleanor and ten alumni of the Our Gang for a 65th anniversary reunion.

W.O.W. returned to the Queen Mary for the October 29th, 1988 banquet with Henry Brandon among the list of honored passengers. This was the spectacular evening in which Bill Cassara was seated next to Henry when Kathleen Freeman turned her introduction into a full-on Henry Brandon tribute, moving the actor to near-tears.

The Saps At Sea Tent

Henry also attended meetings and events for the other West-Coast based chapters including several holiday banquets of the San Diego Saps At Sea Tent. Henry appeared at both the 9th and 11th Annual Holiday Banquets, held at Torrey Pines in 1986 and San Diego's famous Balboa Park in 1988. At the second of Henry's two Saps Banquet appearances, he performed his Schnitzelbank Song.

At the Torrey Pines event, Sap Elliot Becker sat next to Henry during the screenings, which included *The Our Gang Follies Of 1938*. Elliot was surprised when Henry mentioned that he hadn't seen the film in a number of years and as they watched together he whispered in admiration "Aren't those children wonderful!" He also seemed to appreciate being acknowledged for his non-Barnaby roles at Sons events, so gladly posed for a photograph holding an 8x10 glossy from *Drums of Fu Manchu* that future Saps Grand Sheik John Field brought for him to sign, recreating the sinister image in the still down to his evil raised eyebrow.

Henry takes the stage during the Saps Catalina Event. Photo by Rick Greene.

Another All-Star Saps At Sea event – possibly the biggest gala that Tent ever put on – was the Saps Catalina Cruise on May 17th, 1986. Members from four local Tents participated, with Way Out West, Unaccustomed As We Are and Call of the Cuckoos Tent members joining the Saps for a gorgeous day on Catalina Island. The centerpiece of the day was a 35mm screening at the Avalon Theater of several Laurel and Hardy shorts including two silent films with live organ accompaniment. Lois and Tony Hawes and Henry Brandon joined the festivities and welcomed the attendees on stage at the Avalon, Henry giving a particularly heartfelt appreciation for being asked to come.

More than 125 Sons made the boat ride from San Pedro to Catalina and back, giving the event a one-day convention atmosphere. Tony and Lois were so enamored with Catalina that day that they planned two additional Laurel and Hardy cruises back a few years later as part of their informal Our Relations Tent.

The Midnight Patrol Tent

Bill Cassara remembers the Midnight Patrol Tent banquets that Henry traveled up to Northern California for in the mid-1980's:

> Henry came to our annual banquets in 1986, 1987 and 1988. Our tent hosted many celebrities over the years who were all willing to drive that 400 miles from Los Angeles to Monterey and experience the California First Theater. It was very dear to see Henry reunited with Connie Palms who was by then blind.
>
> At one of our banquets Henry told our group the story of his fight he got into while production of *Babes in Toyland* was halted during Stan's injury. Interestingly, Henry described it thusly: "Stannie **faked** the injury so he could get his way with Roach." As production ceased Henry celebrated this "paid vacation" with his friends at a restaurant/bar in Los Angeles (recounted elsewhere in this book) when a fight broke out between his friends and the waiters. Henry said, "They called the "fuzz" and I *hate* the fuzz." Then he looked directly at me off to the side (everyone there knew I was in law enforcement), and the comment elicited a great laugh.
>
> At the conclusion of our 1988 version, Henry, Tony Hawes and Anthony Caruso and I all went out to dinner at Clint Eastwood's "Hog's Breath Inn." There was a brief moment when Henry turned to me and asked: "Do you know what put Carmel on the map?" I had no idea, he told me it was when Aimee Semple McPherson [the evangelist], who was allegedly kidnapped in 1926 and reappeared five weeks later in Mexico. According to Henry, "They found her shacking up with her radio man in Carmel." He then gave a "Barnaby" sadistic laugh about it.

Other Sons of the Desert Meetings

Tony Hawes founded a chapter of The Sons called, appropriately enough, the Our Relations Tent, as his wife Lois was Stan Laurel's daughter. Since most of the members of this tent also belonged to Way Out West, and the visiting celebrities were the same core group – which included Henry Brandon – Our Relations really felt like the San Fernando Valley-West branch of Way Out West. Tony ran a series of fun themed evenings, most of which Henry attended.

For April Fools weekend of 1984, shortly before the Masquer's Clubhouse was torn down in Hollywood, Tony Hawes held a series of four Our Relations/Masquers screenings through the weekend focusing on rare films and documentaries with Lois Laurel and Henry Brandon there for all of them, along with Lucille Hardy Price, Marvin Hatley, Jim MacGeorge, Anita Garvin, Vivian Blaine and Dorothy Granger. Tony was a larger than life impresario who was hard to resist so Henry happily was trotted out each evening, getting the expected Barnaby "boos" and playing it up to the delight of the packed houses on Sycamore Avenue in Hollywood.

At all of his 1988 and 1989 Sons Tent and Convention appearances, Henry performed the Schnitzelbank – even doing it on live television! His 1988 appearances included a Christmas In July event in San Francisco with The Call of the Cuckoos Tent, the July St. Paul convention and the San Diego Saps Holiday banquet.

Another of the San Francisco Cuckoo's Grand Sheiks – Gary Cohen – recalls an unusually sensitive Henry Brandon during the 1988 St. Paul convention and how he was able to step in and smooth out some hurt feelings:

> After the Piano Wrecking Event (Sons took swings at a real piano with sledge hammers – watched with genuine amusement by Henry Brandon in the sweltering Summer heat), we had some time to get ready for the evening dinner banquet. Something was troubling Henry and he mentioned it to me. He said he had brought along the lederhosen that Stan Laurel had worn in *Swiss Miss*, given

to him by Lois Laurel. He also brought the giant yellow banner he had hand painted that he used to perform the Schnitzelbank Song. However, nobody from the convention host tent had asked him to perform. I said, "I'm sure they would love for you to perform it. It would be a highlight of the convention. I'm sure of it! They are probably so busy it may have been an oversight. Let me see what I can do." Henry was unsure and said he would probably just stay in his room for the evening. I said, "No, you can't do that. Too many people would miss you and I know they will love the song! Just remember how it went in San Francisco?"

Henry and I worked up a brief routine for his introduction. I went to a couple of people in the Blockheads and told them of the mix-up, that Henry wanted to perform the song but he felt maybe the convention did not want it. They said absolutely they wanted Henry onstage to do the Schnitzelbank Song. I asked them to have host Tracy Tolzmann introduce me and I'll introduce Henry. I went back to Henry's room, picked up the lederhosen and handed them to him. "Get dressed; we are going to do the Schnitzelbank Song!" This memory of what *almost* did not happen – then what did – and the overwhelming ovation that Henry received that evening is one happy moment I will not forget."

Henry Brandon never slowed down. His last full year of life, 1989, saw him attending a full slate of Sons of the Desert meetings and banquets including many W.O.W. Tent meetings, a second Saps At Sea Tent holiday banquet and a very special Blotto Tent tribute.

It was called "An Evening with Henry Brandon" and hosted by Phil and Phyllis McCoy at their Blotto tent in Santa Clara. Henry traveled up to Northern California for the salute on March 18, 1989. A marvelous souvenir program was produced with a cover sketch of Henry in his roles from *Babes in Toyland, Drums of Fu Manchu* and *The Land Unknown*. The sketch was surrounded by the names of all of the motion pictures he had appeared in. Inside was the title of the event, "An Evening with Henry Brandon" followed by the sub-heading "Honoring America's <u>Best</u> Character Actor." A full color photograph of Henry looking dapper in a dress tuxedo was inserted into the program. He signed quite of few of these throughout that special evening. Music that night was supplied by The Monterey Bay Classic Jazz Band, of which most of whom were tent members.

W. C. Fields Festival

Henry Brandon never made a film with W. C. Fields, but there is a connection which resulted in his participation in a weekend celebration in the late 1980s.

The location of the W. C. Fields 1940 comedy classic *The Bank Dick* was Lompoc, California, because Fields found the name of the town funny although, the movie was shot on the Universal back lot. The city of Lompoc, however, is very proud of the cinematic connection. For this reason, a 1987 W. C. Fields Film Festival was planned to take place in Lompoc and one of the important events there was a revival of *The Drunkard* starring, naturally, Henry Brandon.

Henry served as an off-screen advisor during the filming of Paramount's *The Old Fashioned Way*, which featured many of his thespian co-stars who recreated their *Drunkard* stage roles in a sequence involving the play. Henry couldn't do likewise since Fields himself played the part of Cribbs on screen, but the connection to the great comedian facilitated the show's revival during the festival.

Produced by Tony Hawes with the full support of the Lompoc Chamber Of Commerce, the festival was held on October 16-18, 1987. It featured a showcase of vintage automobiles, a three-day Fields film festival, a memorabilia museum and dealers' room, a golf tournament, several all-star banquets that included Fields' co-star Gloria Jean and many Fields family members, as well as a staging of *The Drunkard* with Henry Brandon for a mere ten bucks! There were two performances, a Saturday evening show and a Sunday matinee at The Lompoc Theatre.

With Gloria Jean and Una Merkel at the W.C. Fields event in Lompoc.

Both of this book's co-authors were in attendance and report that seeing Brandon take the stage in his most famous theatrical role was a thrill. Henry played Lawyer Cribbs just a shade under over-the-top and gave a larger-than-life performance that stole the show. Granted, the audience was full of visiting Sons of the Desert and other comedy buffs, pre-disposed to adore just about anything Henry Brandon might do. However, he didn't coast through with a stale performance; Henry gave it his all, with verve, with gusto and had that audience right in the palm of his sinister hands. The standing ovation he received at the end was well-deserved as he beamed out at us, our Barnaby, showing us what Hal Roach saw that started this whole life-long journey. It was, literally, an honor to witness.

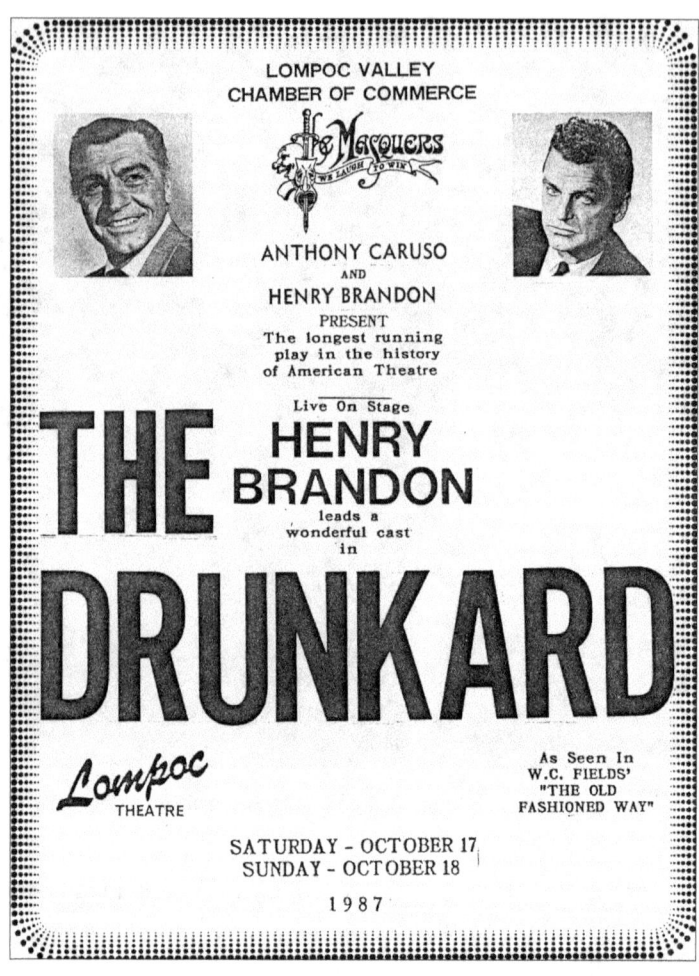

Drunkard revival in Lompoc. Collection of Tony Hawes.

The Memphis Film Festival

There is a massive community of Western film fans who hold a variety of event gatherings to this day, chief among them The Lone Pine Festival (held since 1990) and the Memphis Film Festival (held since 1972), both of which are still flourishing in the 21st Century. Back in the 20th Century, Henry Brandon was a special guest in Memphis at their 11th annual fest.

The 1983 Memphis Film Festival had a Western flair during their August 3 – 6 weekend event, headlining a "Five-Star John Ford Reunion" with Ben Johnson, Harry Carey Jr., John Agar, John Russell and Henry Brandon comprising the panel. Also featured was the Lone Ranger himself, Clayton Moore. Other guests included Beverly Garland, Susan Oliver and Henry's pal Anthony Caruso.

Rounding out the Western theme were appearances by a number of Henry's friends and co-workers including Iron Eyes Cody, Jock Mahoney, Victor French, Sunset Carson, Eddie Dean and Lash Larue. An astounding 200 films were shown over the four days including Buster Keaton's *Go West*, some Tom Mix films and the usual dealers' room and a memorabilia exhibition.

Masquers Club Events

During the 80's, Tony Hawes revitalized the venerable Masquers Club, an ancient Hollywood private club similar to The Friars. The Masquers had lost their longtime headquarters building in Hollywood and most of their archives moved to The Variety Arts in Los Angeles and to The Magic Castle, also in Hollywood. Henry Brandon was a long-time member of The Masquers, and due to his Laurel & Hardy connection with Tony, was invited to attend a number of all-star type film events to raise funds for the organization.

A tribute evening for Virginia O'Brien was held at The Variety Arts Center in Los Angeles on Sunday, June 8th, 1986 with invitations extended to Henry Brandon, Cesar Romero, Sybil Brand, Kathryn Grayson, Alan Young, Virginia Mayo, Herb Jeffries, Joe Baker, June Lang, Betty Garrett, Shirley Jones, Bob Crosby, Iron Eyes Cody, Rose Hobart, William Campbell and The Nicholas Brothers. The celebrities gently roasted Virginia in The Roof Garden Restaurant and then enjoyed dinner and dancing.

One of the biggest of the Masquers theme nights was Gangsters and Their Molls: A Roaring Twenties Dinner and Dance held in The Blossom

Room of the Hollywood Roosevelt Hotel on Monday, September 12th, 1988. Tony Hawes and Tony Caruso produced the event, which featured period music by Art Deco and His Society Orchestra and quite the roster of film personalities. In addition to Henry Brandon, guests included William Campbell, Mae Clarke, Virginia Christine, Steve Drexel, Fritz Feld, Coleen Gray, Marc Lawrence, Mike Mazurki, Cesar Romero, Penny Singleton, Mamie Van Doren, Joe Vitale and Marie Windsor. When Henry was introduced, his resume of crime thrillers was listed.

Sons Remember Henry Brandon:

Kathy Luhman:

I remember the contrast between the character Barnaby and the man, Henry. I watched *Babes in Toyland* as a kid and was afraid of Silas Barnaby! When I met him, he was a little shy but a gentleman. He was the opposite of what I thought of him as a child. When we first met him, we were in awe of him. He never saw himself that way. He loved cats… and had *three* of his own!"

Gary Cohen:

One evening, Henry and I were walking down the street going to dinner. As we crossed the street, we passed in front of a car that had stopped for the light. The driver leaned out his window and said, "Hey, aren't you a movie star?" Henry turned and without missing a beat answered, "I'm not a movie star, I'm an actor!"

Paul Kantus:

I remember him telling about starring in the film, *When the North Wind Blows* and how the film company furnished very expensive "waterproof" boots flown in at no small expense to the location shooting in the snow in a Canadian winter. The boots lasted about a week in the slush and snow.

Becky Gray:

Although I'd met Henry briefly once before, I didn't get to know him until the 1984 convention in England. Since we were often on busses for hours at a time, all you had to do was sit near Henry and ask questions. Henry was in a theater company in WWII, playing in *The Drunkard*. He told me that on V-Day, his ship was anchored off the coast of Italy. They could hear jubilant celebrations from the shore, but they had to stay on the ship. Henry said they cried—not because the war was over, but because they couldn't join the parties.

Ron Stephenson:

Henry was especially happy when I'd start talking about serials especially the Fu Manchu serial he starred in. He hadn't see Fu Manchu for many years. We showed an episode at our "Christmas in July Banquet" in 1988. In England, everyone asked about *Babes in Toyland,* but I asked him about the four serials he was in. Henry thought he'd throw me a curve. Henry was the villain in the serial, *Secret Agent X-9*. He asked me who played the hero. I answered, "Scott Kolk." He did a double take because I knew the answer. Neither one of us had ever heard of him before or after that. Henry also told us that when Spanky was an adult, Henry reminded him of a story from their past. During the shooting of *Trail Of The Lonesome Pine*, an older woman came up to little Spanky and started making a big fuss over him. She started telling him, "Aren't you the cutest little thing!" Spanky looked up at her and told her, "You women give me a pain in the ass!" Henry said that Spanky didn't remember saying that.

Henry was one of the nicest, most accessible actors I have met. I screened chapter four of *Drums of Fu Manchu*, where the hero is put under a pendulum device, similar from the Poe story. Henry did his "Fu" voice, "Are you ready for your circumcision Mr. Parker?"

Henry told me that his agent got him the role of the henchman in *Buck Rogers* and he asked why not the part of the lead heavy. His agent told him; "The lead heavy works for one day, the henchman works three weeks, which part did you say you wanted?"

Steve Runyan:

I hosted a dinner in his honor at San Francisco's Stanford Court Hotel (Christmas in July 1988). Henry was our special guest of honor and he did his famous "Schnitzelbank" 1988). When he changed into his costume (worn by Stan in *Swiss Miss*), he asked me to hol hold his wallet. When I later gave it back to him, I said in front of a number of hold his wallet. When I later gave it back to him, I said, in front of a number of members, "Here's your wallet, I lifted it from you earlier." A number of eyebrows were raised.

Jack Roth:

The last time Henry was in New York City, the executive board members of our founding tent, of which I was a member, were taking him out to dinner. I was to leave work and meet them at the restaurant. At the last minute, one of our employees played hooky and I had to work his hours. Was I disappointed I couldn't see Henry. About a half hour before we closed the store, the phone rings…and it's Henry on the phone! He called to tell me how disappointed he was that we couldn't see each other. We chatted, and before he hung up, he wished me well until we saw each other again. That was the last time I talked to Henry because he passed away not too much longer afterwards. One of those "not meant to be" moments. I was terribly shocked by his passing but I still remember all the wonderful conversations we had at our conventions and other functions. God Bless Henry, he was a very special and gracious human being.

Rebecca Kane:

I went to the 1986 convention in Philadelphia not knowing anyone and the first night Vince Giordano and his Nighthawks were lighting up the place playing LeRoy Shield's music and others from the 1920s and '30's. A man walk up to me and asked if I'd like to dance the Charleston with him. I didn't realize it until later that the man was Henry Brandon. I excused myself because I didn't dance.

James Wiley II:

During the 1982 Detroit convention, my wife Kris and I were sitting alone at a four seat table for lunch at Greek Town. Henry saw us and along with Anita Garvin, they asked us if they could join us for lunch. We all talked through the meal and became lifetime friends. That's the kind of person Henry Brandon was.

Gary Cohen:

I was a guest on KUSF radio in 1983 and put in a call to Henry Brandon. He commented on his friendship with Charlotte Henry* and how she would have Saturday afternoon parties. He described the huge set taking up two entire sound stages. Henry said the set was painted in primary colors and he recalled how it was breathtaking to walk onto the set. He said they used live alligators in the Bo Peep scene where she gets off the raft and "the alligators smelled horribly."

Roger Gordon:

Henry Brandon was contacted long before the July 1986 convention took place and agreed to attend. He was a most positive person and liked everything about the Sons of the Desert. He arrived one day before the convention and was met at the airport. After getting into his hotel room he agreed to appear before the Cinekyds. This was a non-profit organization that helped children make video films in Willow Grove, Pennsylvania. They were preparing a live presentation for the upcoming convention loosely based on the motion picture film *Babes in Toyland*. They were to lip-sync the words directly from the film sound track. To everyone's knowledge this had never been done before. When Henry arrived at the campus the children were *awed*. Imagine a real movie star in their midst. The children, all high-school age, were recreating the film live, to be presented on the final night of the

---

* Bo-Peep from the film *Babes in Toyland*

convention at the Sheraton Hotel in Valley Forge, Pennsylvania. The leading characters were to be played by two adults, Joe Rooney as Stan, and Mike Spack as Ollie.

As Henry watched the rehearsal, he could not resist stopping the action and giving instruction about how lines were to be delivered and actions were to be taken. The kids were thrilled and took to his instruction with enthusiasm. He also had time to talk to the kids about how movies were made in Hollywood and answered a never ending amount of questions. Henry seemed thrilled to be with them.

The next day was the convention and three days later, the night of the banquet. Henry could not contain his excitement. After seeing the children play the wedding scene, he decided to recreate the wedding scene himself, live following the Cinekyds performance. He had gotten Tony Hawes, the husband of Lois Laurel, to play the minister and recruited Joe Rooney to again put on the wedding dress. Tracy Tolzmann was to play Ollie. The cast had rehearsed in Henry's room for a day along with some encouragement from a cool bottle of vodka. How did the hastily prepared scene work out? The audience loved it. Henry was exhilarated and toasted the success of the evening. From then on Henry was the star of the convention. When it concluded, he didn't wish to leave.

Del Kempster:

In 1988 the *Helpmates* tent of the Sons of the Desert organized a trip to our International Convention in St. Paul/Minneapolis, I was part of that group. After a great convention we all travelled down to Hollywood for the second part of our holiday. When we reached LAX we even had Tony Hawes and Lois Laurel Hawes there to greet us. Well, on one of our days Tony and Lois had tickets for the Ringling Brothers and Barnum & Bailey Circus. They were attending with Cassidy (Lois' grand-daughter) and Henry Brandon. Two of us from our group were also invited to join them, Jack Stevenson and myself. The tickets had been given to Lois by some of the clowns who worked there and they had even started a tent of their own. So, we all had a nice day out at the circus.

As part of the show, three members of the audience were picked to go and sit in the middle of the arena. It was pre-planned that that they would pick Lois, Cassidy and Henry. They got a tremendous cheer as they were introduced. They then brought out some real mean looking alligators that walked round our trio, but then they just sat there. Poor Cassidy was terrified while Lois held her tight to reassure her. Henry just looked in disdain at the beasts.

Afterwards Henry told me he was not a bit afraid, because he had worked with carnivorous animals many times before and the trick is to feed them well before bringing them out to show them to the public because after a meal they are always really docile. However, just as they were about to return to their seats in the audience, he stared down and realized one of his testicles was hanging out of the short trousers he was wearing. So it was just a matter of luck that, hungry or not, one of the gators did not decide to help himself to a tasty little snack!

CHAPTER EIGHTEEN
Final Curtain

This penultimate chapter of Henry Brandon King of the Bogeymen is structured a bit different from the rest of the book. It's the most personal, intimate and emotional chapter and since most of the memories are first hand memories and stories from the authors, we thought we'd present them that way. So, you'll read Henry Brandon stories from Bill Cassara, Rick Greene and **"For the Love of Henry"** blog group founder, Lisa Ballantyne told in the first person. Because now, inevitably, it is time to ring down the curtain…

Rick Greene:
I first met Henry Brandon on October 6, 1979 at the 9th Annual Way Out West Tent banquet at Hollywood Roosevelt Hotel. It was his second Sons of the Desert event, after a long hiatus due to his ill-advised Laurel-bashing comment at the 1st Annual Banquet eight years earlier. This night, Henry was in top form. It was the first time I heard his stories about how Hal Roach discovered him in *The Drunkard* and hired him for *Babes In Toyland*, how he asked Stan Laurel "Aren't we going to rehearse?" and how he returned to the studio four years later to film the *Our Gang Follies Of 1938*.

In the coming years, I would hear these stories countless times at Sons meetings, banquets and conventions across the country and overseas, but this sparkling Hollywood night, I was enchanted by Henry's ability to draw his audience into these reminiscences, using his acting skills to almost make us feel as if we were there, too. I met Henry at his banquet table and had him sign my *Laurel & Hardy* book by John McCabe, Al Kilgore and Richard W. Bann, which he did in between puffs of his cigarette. He signed the *Babes in Toyland* page, near a photograph of himself as Silas Barnaby, simply 'Henry Brandon' with no endearment.

Intra-Tent Journal #45 from 1985. Courtesy of Rick Greene & The Sons of the Desert Archives.

That would change as in the coming years; I assumed the editorial responsibilities for *The Intra-Tent Journal*, the international publication of The Sons of the Desert, in 1982. As such, I was in constant contact with the celebrities of our Laurel and Hardy world, obtaining rare photographs and background stories to share with our readers. I became very close with Lucille Hardy Price, Lois Laurel Hawes, Anita Garvin, Marvin Hatley and many others… but none more so than Henry Brandon.

Bill Cassara:

I first met Henry in 1984. It was arranged that I pick him up at the train station in San Jose to drive him to Gary Cohen's "Call of the Cuckoos" tent meeting that evening in San Francisco. He was so down to earth, friendly and much younger looking than I could ever imagine. We exchanged pleasantries and I was anxious to ask him about his film career, but I didn't want to pounce on him. I asked politely if he was married; he took a thoughtful few seconds, bowed his head and said, "Oh…a long time ago." Henry asked what I did for a living and I answered that I was a "Cop" in Monterey County. He was amused by this.

As we were driving out of town I pointed in an unspecific direction and said; "My father grew up in San Jose and he told me that the Red Light District was over there." I expected a reaction and I got one. Henry said, "Well, your father and I have something in common, *we both got our first piece of ass in San Jose.*" It was an ice-breaking moment.

I drove him up north on the El Camino Real that connected all the towns between San Jose and San Francisco. It took longer than the freeways and I was thankful for that. I asked Henry if I could buy him lunch, and pulled up to an old restaurant named "Dinah's Shack." It was an institution going back to the 1920's. Henry absolutely lit-up; he said, "I haven't been in here since my college days at Stanford." After lunch, we stopped in Palo Alto to pick up his brother, Hugo and proceeded to The City. Both brothers were dressed in sport coats and ties, and were very professional looking. As they were greeted by the knowledgeable tent members, I was setting up my newfangled video camera and tripod to record what Henry was to say. Henry answered questions from the audience after a screening of *Babes in Toyland* and a chapter from his *Drums of Fu Manchu* series. The rudimentary recording of highlights of that meeting has since been posted on YouTube.

I sent him a copy of a newspaper that was reproduced from 1936 celebrating the reopening of California's First Theater built in 1850 in Monterey. I thought it would peak Henry's interest because the actors were to perform "The Drunkard." There was a producer named that didn't have any meaning to me, but it sure did for Henry. The name front and center was "Galt Bell." Henry informed me that it was this same person who had hired Henry for the role of Lawyer Cribbs in *The Drunkard* in Los Angeles. Mr. Bell had his roots in Monterey and had married a local girl, Connie Palms (who was in the original play with Henry).

Henry wrote me a wonderful letter telling me about Connie, that she was "the youngest old lady he ever met." He also said, "She buried five husbands, so look out!" Included with the letter was a photograph of himself as Indian Chief Scar from *The Searchers*. In the communication he said, "Here Bill, it's one of my favorites." It was inscribed; "To Bill with my gratitude."

Rick Greene:

I'm not sure why I gravitated toward Henry and developed a bond and a relationship just a little closer than the other stars. But we became close and spent quite a bit of time together throughout the 1980's. Each Christmas I'd get a holiday card from Henry, usually signed: "Love, Barnaby" or "All my best, dear Rick, Barnaby." I still have them all. After one weekend visit to the "Call of the Cuckoos Tent" up in San Francisco, Henry wrote a thoughtful card that read:

The weekend in S.F. was great. Gary (Cohen) has a fine bright group of L&H buffs. I enjoyed the whole thing. Had a good visit with my brother in Palo Alto and with three Stanford fraternity brothers I haven't seen in years.

I really enjoyed being with you the previous weekend. Love, Barnaby.

Another card arrived one spring from Henry that was – of all things – a Happy Passover card! The inscription read, "Dear Ones, I'm thinking of you with great affection, Happy Passover. See you on the 28th at the Variety Arts. Love, Barnaby."

He truly loved being our 'Barnaby' and played that role to the hilt, endearing himself to hundreds of Laurel and Hardy fans over the years. As the **Intra-Tent Journal** Editor, I decided that I would do a special Henry Brandon issue and, for the first time, was invited over to his home on North Spaulding Drive in Hollywood in February of 1985 to sift through his memorabilia in search of photos for my newsletter. Henry had a large brown box brimming to the top with vintage 8x10 glossies, lobby cards, pressbooks and behind the scenes photos that I sorted through, looking for *Babes in Toyland* material. None of it was organized, it was just haphazardly tossed into the box, but he had treasures from throughout his long career and I found a half-dozen or so photos I wanted to use. He let me take whatever I wanted and the issue came out great.

It was **ITJ** issue number 45 from the spring of 1985 (the ITJ was, and still is, a quarterly publication) and featured the same half-Henry/half-Barnaby photograph that adorns the cover of this book. Inside I published three other rare photos, including one of Henry fully made up as Squire Cribbs in *The Drunkard* to show how similar the make-up was to Barnaby. Another photo was an early make-up test at the Roach Studios as they searched for the right look for their lead villain. Henry was delighted with the issue and to be featured on the cover. It is one of my favorite covers from the eight years of issues that I edited.

In Henry's box, when I returned his borrowed photographs, was a VHS tape of his *Drums of Fu Manchu* serial. I asked about it and he told me, "Some fan sent it to me when I told him I didn't have a copy. Do you want to borrow it?" I was thrilled as I had never seen *Drums* at that point and was very anxious to. Henry gave me the tape and, even though it was a dupe with poor sound, I had my first screening of his incredible performance as Dr.

Fu Manchu. When I brought the tape back, he wanted my full review of the chapter-play, which I raved about much to his twinkling-eyed delight. He then talked about the making of the film, his co-stars, the directors, the film's success, the fact that a sequel was never made due to pressure from the War Department and how theatre owners hated him for years due to the scores of little children urinating on the seats out of their fear for Fu! I was astounded at his recall of people and places from decades past. Henry Brandon was ALWAYS present in the moment, observing and living a full, rewarding life.

During those first visits to Henry's home in February and March of 1985, he introduced me to his roommate, Mark Herron. Mark, of course, was Henry's long-time partner. When I arrived for that initial visit, Mark very politely excused himself from the living room, allowing Henry to visit with us privately. As he exited the room, Henry leaned in to me and whispered conspiratorially, "You know, he was married to Judy Garland!" I *didn't* know, but later learned that indeed Mark Herron was Ms. Garland's fourth husband (of five), coming together in 1964 and getting briefly married in 1965. The odd marriage didn't last, with the couple splitting up seventeen months later, after which he quietly returned to Henry, picking up where they left off.

Henry was a very private person when it came to his personal life. Whether he was straight, gay or bi-sexual was not discussed openly. This was more a product of the times in which we lived than a desire for secrecy. He seemed content with who he was and, in these later years when surrounded by much younger friends from the world of fandom, he was candid when asked questions on any topic. Most of us respected his desire for privacy so… we didn't ask. He made a few casual mentions of being married "a long time ago," with a hint of sadness perhaps, or regret. When he'd make these comments, he'd quickly shift to happier topics, embracing the present *and* the future.

Henry was a guest of the Saps At Sea Tent of San Diego, the Sons Tent that I was the Grand Sheik of during the 80's, three times. First, at our Saps Go to Catalina cruise in 1986 and then twice at our Holiday Banquets for

Babes in Toyland celebrations. Poor Henry had to sit through dozens and dozens of screenings of *Babes in Toyland* over the years, and he never complained (unless it would get a laugh) and he never left the room. He was trouper in every respect

Bill Cassara:

Over the years Henry and I exchanged many letters, postcards and phone calls. There was one day he sent me a simple envelope and it had his name-badge from his Sons convention in England. He signed his name over it and it became a precious token of our friendship. I remember a time when he told me that he was in Italy doing voice-overs for some "Sword and Sandal" films after he finished *Captain Sindbad*. When he came back home later in 1963, he had heard that the Hal Roach Studios had closed. He drove over there and confirmed it was true, Henry admitted it drove him to tears that day.

Rick Greene:

The first time he came down for a Saps Holiday Banquet, we stayed overnight in San Diego and drove back on Sunday. I picked Henry up at his home and we spent three delightful hours going down and three coming back the next day, chatting in the car about anything and everything. That Saturday night after the Banquet, we stayed at my Father's townhouse in Pacific Beach. Henry never demanded a fancy hotel room, he never demanded anything… he was happy to go with the flow, and he enjoyed new experiences and meeting new people.

Now, my father David Greene was not a Laurel and Hardy fan and didn't really understand my devotion to The Boys or my involvement in The Sons of the Desert. It was something he tolerated, knowing it brought me great pleasure and purpose but scratching his head over the whole thing. That is, until the day I brought Scar from *The Searchers* into his home to spend the night.

I'd never seen my father star-struck before, but he was with Henry Brandon. I just told him I was bringing the guy who played Barnaby in

Babes In Toyland to spend the night in his guest room (I took the couch that weekend) he said, "Fine, whatever." But when we walked in and I introduced them, David Greene's eyes lit up and he said, "You were Scar! You worked with John Wayne! You were in The Searchers!" Henry laughed and said, "Yes, that was me."

My Father *worshipped* John Wayne above ALL other actors, like most of our fathers did. Growing up, our family went to see every new Wayne picture in the 1970's as they came out. And now, one of the Duke's co-stars *was in his living room!* Dad was giddy and started peppering Henry with questions about John Wayne. Henry was not only patient with my goofball Dad, he seemed to enjoy talking about making *The Searchers*, about the other John Wayne pictures he appeared in and that afternoon and during brunch the next morning, my father never let up! It was a blast to watch and listen to the two of them.

Dad asked Henry what John Wayne was like on set and Henry replied:

> He kept to himself most of the time. Remember, he was a big star back then, the biggest star in all of Hollywood, so he was quite busy with his agent and reading other scripts and the business of being John Wayne. So he didn't mingle much with the cast. But I do recall one time that really struck me as an example of the man he was. We made that picture in Monument Valley and we were trucked from the lodge where we all stayed down to the filming location each day. It was a long bouncing truck ride but most of us were so tired at the end of a long shooting day, we didn't mind.
>
> One evening, I was still in my Scar make-up and costume, just dog-tired wanting to get back to my room and collapse. I walked over to the flatbed truck but it was nearly full. And sitting there on the end, with all the grips and extras and bit-players, was John Wayne, waiting for the ride back to the lodge. He could have demanded a limo or a special car, but not Duke. He was sitting there, right with

the crew, like any normal person. He saw me dragging up, hoping for a spot and he shouted, "C'mon Henry!" and reached out a hand to pull me up onto the flatbed. We bounced back to the lodge together. I never forgot that. He was a good man.

My Father was just *delighted* by this story and I remember saying to him, "What do you think about my Sons of the Desert involvement now?" That morning, he thought it was pretty damn cool.

February 1990

Henry had just finished several performances of a Christmas pantomime show put on by Tony Hawes for the Masquers in January of 1990 at The Mayflower Club in North Hollywood. There was not a hint of illness or any health complaints; Henry had many friends and plenty more to see and do. He was scheduled to participate in the Stan Laurel 100th birthday anniversary at Catalina Island that spring. Henry was active until the end. That end came when he was 77 years old, on February 16, 1990.

The day before, Henry Brandon's last day of life was not much different from the days and weeks and months that had preceded it. He was busy and bustling with energy and productivity on that fateful winter's Wednesday.

While Israel attacked troops at their border near Egypt and the Soviet military occupation of Afghanistan came to an end, Henry Brandon had done a costume check for a forthcoming film role and stopped by a local University to consult with some students studying acting, offering advice and encouragement. He had an appointment in the studio to record some commercial voice-overs, which he did, then he went grocery shopping and had his car washed. After all this activity, which would have tired a thirty-year old, much less a man of seventy-seven, Henry decided to cut back the trees in the backyard garden! After this, he went to bed, at which time he suffered a fatal heart attack during the night.

These last-day events from Henry's schedule were related by his partner Mark Herron to Marcus Maier, a fan who visited with him a few months later. Mark told him, "Henry worked himself to death, but it was his time." While his passing was a shock to those fans and family who knew him as a youthful force of nature, photographs of Henry from his final months show a man whose age had at long last caught up with him, a man who looked... tired.

Word came quickly that Henry passed away peacefully in his sleep at his home; 1033 North Spaulding Ave. in West Hollywood. By February 21 of that year, Henry's agent, Gary Butcher wrote a press release of his career highlights and it was picked up by the Associated Press wire services. Henry's picture and obituary were printed in thousands of newspapers, large and small across the country.

According to his Death Certificate, Henry succumbed to a heart attack [myocardial infarction] complicated by hypertension cardiac disease. He was pronounced dead at Cedars-Sinai Medical Center in Los Angeles at 39 minutes after the hour of midnight.

Henry's remains were released to his sister; Marie Philips of Glendale, California. She listed Henry's marital status as "divorced." Henry preceded his older sister and brother in death. He was cremated and his ashes were scattered in unknown directions.

The news of Henry's sudden death spread quickly through the fan community and many in The Sons of the Desert went into mourning. Henry had planned to attend the upcoming 7th International Convention of the Sons of the Desert in Clearwater, Florida that July.

Bill Cassara:

Thinking about Henry missing the Clearwater convention after attending the previous five conventions, brought to mind a touching – now tragic - moment I witnessed at the 1988 convention and shared during the Memorial service. A young boy took a photo of Henry in St. Paul and immediately afterwards Henry quietly walked up to him and said, "Now when you get that picture developed, bring it with you to the 1990 convention and I'll sign it for you." I told the crowd; "and now Henry won't be able to ..."

This moment of high emotion was one of many that choked up his friends and co-stars less than six weeks later at a very special event.

Henry Brandon Memorial

There were no public ceremonies by his family, but friend Tony Hawes decided to "give Henry a good sendoff" by rounding up his personal friends for a celebration of life service at the Mayflower Club. Many members of the Masquers and Sons of the Desert attended on March 11, 1990.

Preceding the memorial, music from *Babes in Toyland* was played to set the mood. The esteemed Master of Ceremonies; **Tony Hawes** welcomed everyone and introduced **Donald Randolph**, who read "The Masquer's Oath." Following this was the introduction of television personality; Tom Hatten who gave forth fond memories of some of Henry's films. A newly discovered trailer for "Babes" was projected on the screen; this was a brand new experience for the audience who gasped at the revelation.

The Harlequin (President) of the Masquers, **Anthony Caruso** spoke of what Henry meant to the organization, his friends and peers. They had many shared experiences in show business over the years.

Hawes then introduced Henry's acting friends to come to the podium to speak, they were:

William Lanteau—acting peer and friend

Ryan O'Neal--Talked about his father's (Charles O'Neal) friendship with Henry. Charles signed the Naturalization papers for Henry to officially become an American Citizen (in 1938) and produced Henry in *The Road to Rome* and *Family Portrait*. O'Neal shared that his drive to become an actor was based on early conversations with Henry Brandon at their family home.

Patrick Wayne-- John Wayne's son who worked with Henry in *The Searchers* (he played the young 2nd Lieutenant).

Hank Worden – Another old character actor who worked with Henry in *The Searchers* (as Mose Harper).

Mark Herron—Henry's roommate

Don Porter—acting peer and friend, appeared with Henry in the stage productions in

Summer stock theater in Monterey (1941)

Sons of the Desert representatives followed to the podium, they were:

Orson Bean-- representing the founding tent of New York

Rick Greene-- representing the Saps at Sea tent

Bill Cassara--representing the Midnight Patrol tent

Randy Skretvedt--representing the Unaccustomed As We Are tent

Bob Satterfield –representing the Way Out West/45 Minutes From Hollywood tent

The touching tribute was ended with the Masquers sign off:

The door marked "Exit"
As actor leave the stage-
Leaves not to darkness
But to a brighter age-
The age eternal
Where they who went before-
Will call us gladly-
As we pass the door.

For the occasion, Tony Hawes drew a fascinating portrait of Henry in his Barnaby character. The framed image was almost as big as a door. What to do with it was the question. The decision was made to donate it to the collection of the McCoy's in Santa Clara, California. This was the same home that the Sons of the Desert hosted a tribute to Henry March 18, 1989 with Henry and his brother, Hugo in attendance.

The *Los Angeles Times* published an article written by Zan Thompson describing the Masquers ceremony and reminisced about her dear friend, Henry. It is reprinted here in its entirety from March 18, 1990.

> I worked with Henry Brandon in a melodrama called *The Drunkard* which ran for 27 years at the Theatre Mart in Los Angles. Henry was 21 then, had attended Stanford and Occidental, and played the villain in the show. He was a tall, long-legged, green eyed young man, and a superb actor and steadfast friend.
>
> Henry had been with *The Drunkard* for two and one-half years when he began to get motion picture work. He left the theater, but not the cast. We were close, proud of the show, crazy for our director, Galt Bell and delighted with our success. From a standing start, we had suddenly become quite grand. Our theater was the place to go to entertain out-of-town guests.
>
> Henry's memorial featured a number of actors who had known Henry and treasured his friendship. One of these was Don Porter, a distinguished actor in theater and television, who reminisced about sharing an apartment with Henry and Blackie O'Neal, father of Ryan O'Neal.
>
> I lived with the gentlemen for about a month one time when I was 18 and between apartments. They were delighted to have me because I could make meat loaf out of a small amount of ground meat and boxes of breakfast flakes. Henry said to me, "Zan come the revolution, you'll be perfectly safe in spite of your Tory background. No one would harm anyone who can make meat loaf like this."
>
> I was as safe when I was asleep on the studio couch in the dining room after doing the show as I was during the day when I was a student at Mount St. Mary's College. Don, Henry and Blackie

were upstairs and the stairs creaked, so if one of them had stepped on the second step, the other two would have sprung from their beds to dissuade him.

Henry was totally protective of me. He drove off a tall, rich, Texas boy who drove a Packard convertible by telling him, "Leave her alone, she's off-limits," Henry did nothing for my social life. Henry appeared in dozens of motion pictures, but his love was the theater. He was an "actor's actor," as someone said at the memorial.

Notably, he played Jason opposite Dame Judith Anderson in "Medea." No one could stride on wearing the shin plates, breastplate, and regalia of an ancient warrior and take stage like Henry.

When I was living with the gentlemen, I had a date with a dull boy with lots of money to go to a party his parents were having. I stuffed a napkin with smoked oysters and all manner of tasties that weren't included in our meat loaf menus.

When my date drove up in front of that flat, there was a light on in Henry's front bedroom. I said, "Mother always waits up for me." The boy saw me to the door and when I opened it, Henry called in a rusty voice, "Did you have a good time, dear?"

I never saw that boy again. I just said he was rich, I didn't say he was stupid. Henry, Don and Blackie loved the treats. Henry was an actor and a gentleman, a superb cook and a good friend."

Tribute

Six months after Henry's memorial service in Southern California, Bill Cassara arranged for another tribute up in Monterey.

Bill Cassara:
On September 15, 1990, our Monterey Midnight Patrol tent arranged a special tribute to Henry Brandon at the California First Theater in this city. The "Troupers of the Golden West" were putting on a performance of *The Drunkard* and it was arranged for the entire cast of the play to come back out on stage for a curtain call and to accept a present. It was a specially matted and framed still of Henry in his Barnaby role. A list of his films were included; the artifact was honorably placed on the wall and was admired by Sons who attended a screening at this same venue during the Edgar Kennedy Celebration in Monterey in 1997.

Legacy

Henry Brandon has been gone for nearly thirty years, yet his legacy lives on. In this digital age, there are movie buff blogs and groups on Facebook for just about any entertainment industry personality or genre one can imagine. Henry is mentioned often in Classic Western and B-Western group posts, especially when *The Searchers* is the topic. He comes up with regularity in science-fiction and serial groups when members weigh in on *Buck Rogers, The Land Unknown, The Outer Limits* and *Kolchak: The Night Stalker*. Classic comedy groups and Sons of the Desert members offer up their opinions and memories when Henry's films with Laurel and Hardy, Our Gang, Martin and Lewis, Bob Hope and Danny Kaye are covered.

However, until very recently, Henry Brandon never had his own website or Facebook group, dedicated specifically to his long entertainment industry career. That changed in early 2017 when Lisa Ballantyne founded the **For the Love of Henry** group on Facebook which specifically led to *this* book being written!

Like many of the Baby Boomer generation, Lisa's first exposure at age five or six to Henry Brandon was during television screenings of *March Of The Wooden Soldiers* and being terrified by Barnaby and his Bogeymen.

Years later, she was part of the Los Angeles music industry on the production side: It was life in the fast lane. She remembers a party that would have quite an impact on her.

Lisa Ballantyne:

There are always music industry events being put on by various labels and producers. In the mid-1980's, I was invited by a friend in the casting industry to a party one night. He was hoping to break into the modeling industry, so attended lots of events to get his name out there. We walked into a crowded, noisy room and there was Henry, taller than everyone in the room. We looked at each other and smiled, but I did not realize who he was. It was later that my friend told me it was Henry Brandon. I did not get to speak to him that night as he seemed to be engaged in conversation with someone else.

I was taken aback at how handsome he was. I had not yet seen *The Searchers* or any of his films, as those American Westerns seemed to throw Native people into one big stereotyped category, so I generally avoided them. That night, I didn't actually connect Henry with old Barnaby who had made me squirm in fear on the couch! But I do remember that a song was playing when we made eye contact, Roberta Flack's *The First Time Ever I Saw Your Face* which, in hindsight, was remarkably appropriate.

Rick Greene:

Later, Lisa saw *The Searchers* and, as a Native American, she decided to learn more about this compelling actor who was clearly *not* a member of the Tribe, but portrayed this role of Scar with such respect and power. She discovered that Henry Brandon was so much more than the roles he played and felt a real connection that had begun with that chance eye-contact and went beyond the screen. It was an unspoken connection that led to a dream, followed by real life connections with Bill and myself.

Lisa Ballantyne:

Sometimes, dreams do come true. However, the dream that led to founding **"For the Love of Henry"** and reaching out to Rick Greene and Bill Cassara belonged to Henry Brandon. One night, while half-asleep, I heard Henry say, "Please don't let them forget me." My response was, "What should I do?" Henry told me that I'd figure it out.

When I was fully awake, I didn't quite know what to think of this experience at first. Time passed, many months, and I kept thinking about what Henry told me that night. Yes, it was a dream… but it was so much more. I began to research who might have known Henry and began reaching out to the names that my sourcing had uncovered. After months of sending emails and texts to people I didn't know with no response, things looked bleak.

I founded a Facebook group called **"For the Love of Henry"** hoping to attract people who knew him or people who admired his film and television work. The group had one member for the longest time – myself. Then, one day I came across a name, one of the names on the front cover of this book… Rick Greene. I messaged him expecting no response, but lo and behold, he answered me saying he'd been a close personal friend of Henry's. I told him about the Facebook page, that we had only one member. Over the course of the next twenty-four hours, Rick changed all that.

Rick Greene:

Lisa reached out to me in February of 2017 and told me she'd founded a Facebook group called **"For the Love of Henry,"** asked me if I'd join it and share some of my Henry Brandon memories. Life was hectic at that time, but something resonated in Lisa's plea. I had been pretty close with Henry through the Sons of the Desert but hadn't thought about him much lately. I asked Lisa how many members were in her group and was surprised to hear that she was the only member! I told her that I'd have one hundred members in her group within twenty-four hours and dropped everything and got to work. I reached out to dozens of members of the Sons and other film buff friends and made good on my promise. Suddenly "**FTLOH**" was a vibrant, exciting place where his many fans posted photos and shared thoughts and personal memories. That's when Lisa planted the idea of this book.

Lisa Ballantyne:

To say that nothing has been the same since Rick's vow to swell the **FTLOH** membership to one hundred plus members is an understatement. The wonderful people I have met as a result of this dream is almost indescribable. When Bill Cassara came into the picture, I lucked out once again! Another amazing author in his own right, I suggested to both Rick and Bill that Henry's story needed to be told in print.

Rick Greene:

I'll never forget Lisa suggesting to me, "You should write a book on Henry!" My first response was, "No, I can't write a book about Henry Brandon, but I'll definitely buy that book and read it!" She didn't push me, but seemed to know something that I didn't know and had to discover for myself. Lisa Ballantyne is like that and I've found her gentle, knowing ways to be quite motivating.

It didn't take long. I kept thinking that maybe I *could* write a book about Henry. He certainly deserved one and there was virtually nothing in print on his career. I thought that my friend Bill Cassara would be a better choice but maybe I could be involved. I knew I didn't want to do it alone, so I reached out to Bill to broach Lisa's crazy idea. It turned out she'd planted the same seeds with him and he had been thinking about calling *me* to discuss it! We quickly came to the conclusion that it needed to happen and it needed to be us… and that Henry would have been *delighted* that it was us.

Lisa Ballantyne:

Henry Brandon was a true talent. Not only was he handsome and dashing, but his quick wit and devastating smile made him a successful working actor. He could cock an eyebrow up and give you a sinister glare in such a unique way. He performed many times as an American Indian. Looking back into history, we must be careful not to fault the individual when the social norms of those times would not be acceptable today. Most producers of that era would not allow Native American actors to play major Native characters.

Instead, they were played by actors such as Iron Eyes Cody and Michael Ansara, among others. While they themselves were not Native, they looked the part which was good enough for Hollywood. As Native people ourselves, we can say that Henry, unlike other white actors, did not make a career of this and had true respect for Native people. When an actor got a paying part, they needed to accept it or risk missing out on other roles, or worse, suspension.

If an actor of the stature of Marlon Brando couldn't change Hollywood at the Oscars when he turned down his award in protest of the treatment of Native Americans in the cinema, we could not hold Henry to such a standard. In an interview with television legend Joe Franklin, Henry said when asked about his Native roles, "Haven't we taken away enough from these people? They should be able to take their roles back!"

Henry Brandon:

I always got along wonderfully with the native Indians. There was never any resentment. In those days, most of them had no pretensions toward acting. They were content to work as extras, but almost none of them had any theatrical training of any kind. There were no feelings of competition or envy or anything. Now they've developed quite a few good Indian actors through workshops, and I'm no longer able to play those parts. I don't resent it at all. I think it's only fair that they should play their own parts. It should have happened much earlier. I know that whenever I worked with a (Native actor) and he was given a line to say, I would always go off in a corner somewhere and coach him, help him with his lines. They were always very grateful and wonderful. My relationship with them was always great.

Last Encounters: "An Evening with Henry Brandon" Tribute

Bill Cassara:

The last time I saw Henry was at a special tribute to him on March 18, 1989 at the residence of Phil and Phyllis McCoy in Santa Clara, California. Henry was surrounded by friends, family and admirers. He sincerely enjoyed this special night, music was provided by the Monterey Bay Classic Jazz Band to set the tone. Grand Sheik Phil McCoy and I emceed the events of the evening that included film, toasts, cocktails and an on-stage interview with Henry. Members from four different Tents were present along with Henry's brother, Hugo. As part of the festivities there were huge baskets that were passed around containing "Oh Henry" candy bars. Standing on the stage Henry told us of his just completed movie he was in, *Wizards of the Lost Kingdom II*; He said sarcastically, "I didn't even know there was a *Wizards of the Lost Kingdom I.*" Henry warned us it wasn't a very good film but admitted, "At least I got to do my evil laugh."

Remembering a story that Henry had told me, I informed the crowd that Henry has always wanted to play the part of Abraham Lincoln. He certainly had the stature and face for it. After sharing this, I presented him with a stove-pipe hat, which he promptly displayed and posed in a Lincoln-like manner. If Henry was chosen to portray *Young Mr. Lincoln* in the 1939 film, and made a big box-office star, then I might not have had the opportunity to meet and get to know him.

My last contact with Henry was by phone in October of 1989. He knew I was attending the World Series in San Francisco when a devastating earthquake broke out. It took 18 hours to get home from the choked roadways to Monterey and the next day he called to see if I was alright. It was sure good to hear from him. He died unexpectedly only four months later, shortly after I had received an annual Christmas and Happy New Year card from him.

When I think back on Henry Brandon, I saw a very learned man who was near double my age. Henry didn't know it, but he was sort of a father figure to me. It never occurred to me to do an in depth question and answer period with him because, at the time, I didn't know that much about his other film, television or stage works. Besides, I cherished his friendship more than his celebrity. It always amused me that when Henry had an audience; he would say things just to get a reaction, and he never took himself seriously. I was highly entertained to watch some fans circle around Henry as if they were terrified of him. I just smiled.

There was that time when Henry was a guest on the *Joe Franklin Show*; the host brought up the Sons of the Desert organization and mocked the society as "Laurel and Hardy worshippers" expecting Henry to jump in. Henry changed his entire tone, "I know them, and they're friends of mine." Henry was many things to many people, but the virtues of loyalty, patience and generosity were paramount.

Last Encounters: *Talk of the Town*

Rick Greene:
At the beginning of 1989, I was contacted by the Guest Coordinator for a cable television show on Simmons Cable in Long Beach, California called *Talk of The Town*. The Producer Ron Petke was a massive Laurel and Hardy fan, as was the host of the show John Craig. They invited me to come on as a guest and talk about The Sons of the Desert and *The Intra-Tent Journal*, our quarterly publication.

I appeared on their March 22, 1989 episode which went very well.

Afterwards, Petke told me of his idea to found a new Sons of the Desert tent that would hold occasional meetings *on live television* with a studio audience. He asked if I knew Henry Brandon and if I could get him as a guest, and I answered in the affirmative to both questions. A charter meeting was planned for that Summer at which time I would return along with Henry for a very special live television event – the first broadcast meeting of a Sons Tent!

Henry on *Talk of the Town* in June of 1989.

On the afternoon of June 28th, 1989, I drove over to Henry's home in Hollywood to await a stretch limo that would whisk us through the Los Angeles rush hour traffic to Long Beach. As Henry and I sat in his den, waiting for our ride, we shared a private moment together. My seven-year marriage had ended just weeks earlier and Henry had heard about it through the Sons of the Desert gossip mill. He was very close to both myself and my now 'ex' and he was struggling with the news. He saw that I was in a great deal of personal trauma and, reached over and put his hand supportively on my sagging shoulder. "She'll come back," he said, hopefully. But, knowing better, I told him, "No, Henry. She won't." He saw the finality in my eyes, nodded his head and said simply, "I'm sorry." It was painful for him too, and I deeply appreciated the gesture. It actually helped me to focus, shake it off and put on a good show a few hours later in the studio.

Talk of the Town **with Henry, Rick Greene and host John Craig. Collection of Rick Greene.**

Our long black stretch limo arrived and we were both surprised at the enormity of it! We left Hollywood for Long Beach, talking about the show, what we'd discuss, if we'd be on together and thanks to the carpool lane, we arrived about an hour later. The first meeting of the *We Faw Down* Tent was underway, with Grand Sheik Ron Petke calling the meeting to order and leading the Sons song with a studio audience of about thirty brand new Sons Of the Desert. Then host and Vice Sheik John Craig took over, first chatting with me about the ITJ, how large the Sons organization was, how Laurel and Hardy first teamed up and other brisk subjects during my twelve-minute interview. The second segment began with Craig introducing Henry Brandon, who touched on a variety of career highlights including *The Drunkard, Babes*

In Toyland, The Searchers, John Ford's perversity, the 1934 bar fight and arrest, *Trail Of The Lonesome Pine* (Henry noted, "I was pretty evil in that!") and more.

Craig commented, as the camera lingered on Henry's tanned, weathered features, "People look at this face of yours and they know they've seen it before!" Henry announced that he had played an American Indian at least thirty-five times on screen. John Craig then showed the entire *Babes in Toyland* wedding scene and had an inspired idea. It was time to cut away to a commercial and he asked Henry if he would ask the viewers to remain with us – as Silas Barnaby!

Henry quickly shifted into vicious-villain-of-vintage-cinema mode, looked directly into the camera and intoned, "Please don't go away! We'll be right back! We have more amusement and fun and FROLIC here!" Then, as if to deflate his own ego, added wryly, "How hammy can you get!" It was marvelous.

Next up was a phone conversation with Hal Roach that was quite lengthy. The show then ended with Henry, dressed in his red and white Laurel and Hardy shirt and olive *Swiss Miss* lederhosen, doing a performance of his Schnitzelbank song. He introduced himself with a twinkle in his eye as Dr. Schmutz and, rolling those 'r's outrageously, led the whole group in the song with his usual colorful backdrop and baton. The audience joined in enthusiastically.

The hour-long show was a great success with the promise of future installments on Simmons Cable, but Henry and I had made our first and last appearance together at the "We Faw Down Tent." I would see Henry a few more times in the following seven months, at several Way Out West Tent meetings and I saw him in the Christmas pantomime at The Mayflower Club in January of 1990, however this was the last real one-on-one time I would have with him.

By the time we boarded our limo for the return trip to Hollywood, it was dark in Los Angeles, the twinkling lights of the port of Long Beach and

The Queen Mary our backdrop. We fell into the plush back seat of the sleek, black car, stretching our legs out wide in front of us, slumping down and enjoying the sheer luxury of being ferried around like movie stars. As the car eased onto the 405 freeway, traffic was light and we didn't speak for a long while. I heard the quiet hum of the car's engine, the whoosh of passing cars and I smiled silently in the dark. I was in a limo with my dear friend Henry Brandon, being chauffeured back to his home on Spaulding Drive in West Hollywood after a successful show and – in spite of my personal troubles – all felt right with the world.

After about twenty minutes of relaxed silence in the limousine, Henry finally spoke, saying simply, "This is livin'!" I smiled a bit broader and replied, "Yes, it is." They were the last truly connected personal moments I'd get to share with him.

Minutes later, in front of his house, we bid each other goodnight. "That was fun," I commented, to which Henry replied, "Yes, it was." He bent over slightly to give me a hug, a kiss on the cheek and added, "Good night, dear one." I smiled again. "Good night, Barnaby!" I replied and he chuckled, turned and disappeared into the darkness, exit, stage left.

I got into my Honda Accord for the drive back to Encino, reflecting on how very lucky I was to have a friend in Henry Brandon, King of the Bogeymen, Actor of a Hundred Personas, celebrated performer on stage, screen and television. And most *definitely* that elusive label that he both longed for and denied… a Movie Star.

Film Editor Rick Brandon with Tommy Kirk and Annette Funicello on the Disney lot. Collection of Rick Brandon.

CHAPTER NINETEEN
Epilogue: Evelyn Brandon & Henry Richard Brandon

HENRY BRANDON WAS A private person when it came to details of his personal life. Once in a while, late at night when he had imbibed a drink or two, he would make an offhand comment about being married "a long time ago" and that "it didn't work out," but not much more than that. He never mentioned her name and certainly didn't reveal that he and his wife had a son. He did not like to talk about the period when his family was torn apart, and rightly so. Who was Henry Brandon's wife, and what of their son? What happened to him?

Dolores Brandon made a career in show business until the last five years of her life when she worked as a prescriptionist for Southwest Optical Co. in the Los Angeles area. Her obituary said she appeared for about ten years with the late Dante, the Magician as a stage assistant, was a member of the Ladies Comedy Club of Hollywood and she was born in Camden, New Jersey.[*]

Dolores died on August 9, 1959 when she was only forty-two years old, a victim of lung cancer and heart failure. Her mother (Evelyn Asken) survived her as well as her son, Henry Richard Brandon. The family home was 5640 Franklin Ave. in Hollywood. She is buried at the Hollywood Cemetery.[†]

---

[*] *Los Angeles Times* August 10, 1959
[†] Ibid

Henry and Dolores' son, Henry Richard Brandon was known as "Rick." He is retired from the film industry as a film cutter and magazine editor and lives in Las Vegas. Family dynamics and Henry's service commitments 1941-1946 created the unfortunate circumstances where father and son did not emotionally bond together in those very essential early years. They were estranged but there were no animosities.

Rick went to Hollywood High which he described as a "professional school" where many show business children were immersed in the culture and acquaintances. He learned his trade, but it was behind the camera. He often ran into his father at the various studios they worked and they were always pleasantly professional with each other. Rick told co-author Bill Cassara, "Many actors came up to me and told me they 'killed' my father in movie scenes.[*] Another fond memory Rick had of his father was when he went to see him perform as Jason in *Medea* in Los Angeles [October 1965]. "It was magnificent."

Regarding his father, Rick shared: "He had a great career, had money and good friends. He got to do what he wanted."[†]

---

[*] Phone interview with Rick Brandon on September 30, 2017
[†] Ibid.

CHAPTER TWENTY
Stage Synopsis/Theater Credits

EVER SINCE HIGH SCHOOL, Henry showed an aptitude for acting on the stage. Performing in front of an audience was an exhilarating experience and something he sought out the rest of his life. Henry considered himself an *actor* first and never a film star.

There was a big push in the early 1930's to find stage actors who could translate their talents on the screen; a lot came from Broadway, a few from vaudeville and some started in bit parts and progressed up the ladder. That was the plan, but any actor who "made it" will tell you that talent is only part of the equation; the X-factor is "being in the right place at the right time." Henry verified this in later years and attributed *The Drunkard* as that lucky break.

Though Henry expanded into films in 1934 (*Babes in Toyland*) and 1935 (*Metropolitan Nocturne*), he knew his bread and butter was his role as Squire Cribbs. It also equated to a consistent salary every payday. If Henry was going to make it in films he had to go to casting calls and make himself available for location shoots.

Finally an opportunity presented itself: after 132 consecutive stage performances (spanning a year and a half) as Squire Cribbs in *The Drunkard*, Henry landed an important role in *Trail of the Lonesome Pine*. The fact it was shot on location in the San Bernardino Mountains necessitated an extended stay in the make-shift camp for the actors.

Henry now had his foot in the door for filmmaking, but he was always drawn back to the theater and the audience reaction. In films he was often the heavy, but in plays he frequently played the love interest.

Queen Victoria

This local production was based on the success of the play *Victoria Regina* that was packing them in on Broadway concurrently. It took place from 1837 through 1897 during the reign of England's Queen. The sets were authentically reflective of the Victorian era and the costumes lavish. Doris Lloyd had the title role and Henry (Kleinbach) performed as Prince Albert. The *San Bernardino County Sun* reviewed the play on April 1, 1936:

> Dramatically depicted are the familiar scenes with her Prince Consort, her submissive and wholly adoring devotion to him, the famous conferences with Disraeli, the high point in her Diamond Jubilee address, and a thoroughly human chronicle of events in the life of the Queen.

A follow up story about the play was written by the same newspaper on April 15, 1936:

> Pages of history that turn slowly in reading are flashed vividly and indelibly over the footlights in the present production of *Queen Victoria* does much to tear the veil of superstition that has hung about the head of the famous queen. The tight-willed little lady of Britain's crown, whose sanctities and repressions were to give an age a name, offered up to the world of the theater one of the most vitally moving plays in its history.

The *Hollywood Reporter* weighed in on April 8, 1936:

> Doris Lloyd does her downright best by the title role as her German husband, Henry Kleinbach, once the menace of *The Drunkard* gives a performance that is dashing. The sets depict

Victorian grandeur with regal charm of the period. Occasionally tears start triumphantly to the eyes and none of us but enjoys a good cry now and then.

In the seven episodes covering 60 years of her reign, Victoria is shown as a wife. She interrupts discussions of state by lamenting over three grey hairs in her husband's beard.

Troilus and Cressida

Shakespeare's play of the Trojan War was performed at the Pasadena Community Playhouse from June 15-August 1, 1936. Patricia Walsh and Henry Kleinbach were in the name roles. The play officially opened the Midsummer Drama Festival at this venue. The *Los Angeles Express* described the first night:

> The drama, "Troilus and Cressida" deals with the private ding of Paris and Helen which brought the avenging tents of the Greeks for so many years outside the walls of Troy and resulted in the dragging of Hector's body around the city and the eventual death of his slayer, Achilles. .Plenty of two box office sure-shots—sex and fighting—is in this play and in the treatment of the loves of the Trojans and the Greeks, especially the doings of Pandarus, few punches have been pulled.

The Los Angeles Times chimed in on June 19, 1936:

> These plays at Pasadena take you back to the time when "sweet Will" and his players presented plays in the Globe, with practically no scenery, where coarse jokes and the antics of fools were the chief reliance's for laughs. These plays evoke the rugged ancestry of present-day stage and screen.

> The people of Pasadena may well be proud of their community playhouse, which is dedicated to preserving the artistic traditions

and cultural influences of the stage. It is no idle dream which they cherish, to make Pasadena a name to ring with Malvern in England, and Salzburg in Austria.

Electra

The Greek mythology character of Princess Electra was the daughter of a king and queen. She had a brother, Orestes, who plot and kill their mother and stepfather for revenge for the murder of the siblings' father. Disney this is not.

These Greek tragedies were a specialty of Henry, as he played in various types of these roles over the years. This one was staged at the Greek Theater in Berkeley, California on Sept. 18, 1937, as Henry Kleinbach he was the male lead character as Orestes. The female lead was Blanche Yurka, an actress with success from New York.

The performance was a "warm-up" before bringing the production to a bigger audience and venue a few days later. On Sept. 21st Henry reprised his role at the Philharmonic Auditorium in Los Angeles. As usual, Henry was mentioned only in that he was the actor "remembered as Henry Kleinbach" the villain of *The Drunkard*. Henry had since changed his professional and personal surname to "Brandon."

Lady Precious Stream

Henry had an important role in this "Chinese drama" that was performed at the famed Curran Theater in San Francisco. His part was "Wei, the Tiger General." The play was allegedly a 2,000 year old fable.

The plot was described by the *San Francisco Chronicle* on Jan. 4, 1938:

> Lady Precious Stream is the youngest, the most beautiful and most spirited of His Excellency's three daughters. She rejects the wealthy suitors approved by her father and defies parental authority by marrying the gardener.

In poverty she waits for her husband in a cave for 18 years while he is away at the wars. The gardener eventually makes good, becomes king of the Western Regions and returns to lead his loving wife back in triumph to her haughty family.

Each player was draped in authentic Chinese attire and interestingly, introduced themselves to the audience. Most surprisingly, the play apparently did not take itself too seriously; the *Chronicle* describes the action as "engaging foolery." For instance, the property men had set a table that served as a rock, a whip as a horse, a framework of cloth as a walled fortress. During the scenes the prop men would unceremoniously rearrange the sets. The prop men took a bow at the end and got the biggest applause, and they even received mention in the paper by name.

Boudoir

Famed French playwright Jacques Deval wrote and directed this play that opened on Feb. 7, 1941 on Broadway at the John Golden Theatre. The setting took place in the boudoir of Cora Ambershell's house on Madison Avenue in New York City in 1882 with the leading lady (Devul's wife) having her portrait painted in her boudoir. Mostly unclothed she talks to her coachman, butler and friends. Henry Brandon played Enrico Palfieri, the love interest. It ran for only eleven performances in the 800- seat theater. *Boudoir* was killed by the drama critic Arthur Pollock of the *Brooklyn Daily Eagle*: The play has the appearance of not having been directed at all.

The Road to Rome

No, this isn't a Bob Hope-Bing Crosby movie title; it's a three-act play that was adapted in 1929 and performed on Broadway. It takes place in a courtyard in the house of Fabius Maximus (a Roman dictator) in 216 B.C. and Hannibal's headquarters in a temple three miles east of Rome. It depicts the two camps just before the Battle of Cannae.

Henry Brandon was engaged in summer stock theater in Monterey, California in 1941. His good friend, Charles O'Neal (better known as "Blackie)* was the producer. O'Neal had the blessings of S.F.B. Morse who as President of Pebble Beach Co. authorized the conversion of a clubhouse to a playhouse in the world class Del Monte Hotel.

The purpose of building a theater was so Army personnel (who were stationed at Fort Ord a couple of sand dunes over), could be entertained. This was the period just before America entered the war that was blazing in Europe.

The season opened May 19th for *Road to Rome*. It was described as a "hilarious satire."[†] Henry Brandon, Douglas Wood and Helen Gahagan[‡] headed the cast. *The Los Angeles Times* heralded the inauguration of the first real professional summer stock at this venue and further added:

> Though the Hotel Del Monte has donated a handsome club building on the estate for the theater, all casting will be done here in Hollywood. Del Monte was chosen because of its proximity to several Army camps and the stars are taking moderate salaries in order that the soldiers may have high-class entertainment.

A Family Portrait

This religious presentation was also performed at Hotel Del Monte June 23, 1941. A play in four acts it takes place in the "House in Nazareth, the Wine Shop in Capernaum, the House in Nazareth, the street in Jerusalem and the House in Jerusalem."

The original play debuted on Broadway in 1939 starring Judith Anderson

---

* Blackie O'Neal was quite the playwright in his day. Acting was in his blood; Ryan O'Neal was his son and Tatum O'Neal his granddaughter.
† *San Francisco Chronicle* March 24, 1941
‡ Helen Gahagan was a formable Broadway actress and was married to Melvyn Douglas

as "Mary mother of Jesus." Anderson had just scored in the Hitchcock film *Rebecca* and made a memorable evil character as Mrs. Danvers. Who better to reprise the role in Monterey than Judith Anderson? She was a hot property and a prestigious one at that.

The sophisticated *San Francisco Chronicle* theater critic reviewed the play after opening night:

> Words are pitifully inadequate when it comes to describing a performance like this or the effect it has upon an audience. When you have said Miss Anderson's exalted portrayal of Mary is acting at its very greatest, you have spoken a plain truth; and yet you have said nothing. One can only accept art as wonderful as this humbly and be grateful for it.

Special mention was made of Henry Brandon, who "plays with great sincerity as the eager young disciple whose name is revealed, in a shattering curtain-line, as Judas Iscariot. In a side note, the critic mentioned, "It is hard to see why the Roman administrator for first-century Nazareth should dress like an officer from Fort Ord."

Tower Beyond Tragedy

Robinson Jeffers was a well-known poet and playwright who lived in Carmel at his Tor House. He was known mostly as a poet, but had penned *Tower Beyond Tragedy*, a narrative poem in epic form that explores the story and psyche of Orestes (Henry Brandon) after the death of Agamemnon. The poem was adapted into a play of the same title. It was a Greek legend of Clytemnestra, who murdered her husband and was in turn murdered by her children, Electra and Orestes. The star was the renowned Judith Anderson of stage and screen. Henry Brandon as Orestes, plays her son.

This "Major event" as described by the *San Francisco Chronicle* (July 2, 1941) "receives its first professional production at the Forest Theater in Carmel." The Forest Theater was built in 1910 as an outdoor stage, perfect for the production of *Tower Beyond Tragedy*. A V.I.P. audience turned out, to include its author to take in this drama. *A Family Portrait* and *Tower Beyond Tragedy* were the start of many professional associations between Judith Anderson and Henry Brandon.

Macbeth

Henry Brandon's close personal and professional association with Judith Anderson paid dividends; he was selected by Maurice Evans to play the important role of "Ross" in William Shakespeare's *Macbeth*…on **Broadway!**

Evans lived, ate and drank Shakespeare and was the foremost dramatic actor of Shakespeare plays both in England and the New York stages. To many audiences, Maurice Evans *was* Macbeth.

Judith Anderson was selected by Evans to portray Lady Macbeth based on her performance in the same role in 1937 opposite Lawrence Olivier in London. Both Evans and Anderson were at the top of their game and garnered respect and adulation in their dramatic portrayals.

For Henry Brandon this was a progression of his acting skills and reputation; he was always busy in his thespian pursuits, but working on Broadway with "Gods of the stage" as Evans and Anderson was the zenith of his career. He was a *legitimate* actor.

Macbeth was written in 1603 as a tragedy that resulted from greed; there were encounters with witches, haunting dreams and murder. Evans' portrayal of Macbeth mesmerized the audiences; he kills for political gain but suffers from ghostly appearances.

Lady Macbeth promotes her husband's evil deeds, but she cracks under the pressure. She sleepwalks at night; her eyes are vacant, her nightgown flows and her movements float eerily. Death is on her hands.

Henry's "Ross" character was important in the play. It is because of Ross that Macbeth realizes the witches' prophecies (as a future King) are coming true. Ross is at first a confidant and supporter, even while witnessing Macbeth in murderous acts. By Act 4, Ross turns against Macbeth

Macbeth on Broadway was a box office smash; it played 131 continuous performances from November 11 of 1941 to February 28th 1942. The critics raved and the audiences adored this well-known play; it was the actors, music and sets that made such an impactful experience. Flowers were thrown at their feet.

Plans were made immediately to take *Macbeth* on a road tour of major eastern and Mid-West cities. Tickets were sold in advance by mail order securing a profitable venture. Some of the cast was supplemented for the road, but Henry was a fixture. The stars of the show created quite a stir when coming into respective cities; here was high class entertainment and *Broadway* was coming to them. The troupe took in 14 different cities ending the run on May 22, 1942 at Columbus' Hartman Theater.

After the run of *Macbeth*, Henry Brandon and Judith Anderson returned to the Monterey Peninsula in California for the Warner Bros. filming of *Edge of Night*. Henry went into the service December 23, 1942 and was honorably discharged March 11, 1946

Button Your Lip June 14, 1943 46th St. Theater, Aug. 2-Sept.4, 1943 Martin Beck Theater New York City (Ryan)

Under the auspices of the United States Army, a special regiment of soldiers performed on Broadway a series of five comedy skits/dramas to raise money for the relief fund. Henry is credited as an actor in this named title. The whole Army show featured those who had some kind of show business experience before the war. Of note, Sgt. Arthur O'Connell was the director. The highlight of the show featured an on stage "walk-on" of a pinup girl who comes to give one of the soldiers a kiss. Some of the participants were: Joan Blondell, Carole Landis, Glenda Farrwell and Gypsy Rose Lee.

Ramona

It was the *San Francisco Chronicle* March 24, 1946 that announced:

The original villain of *The Drunkard* at the Theatre Mart, formerly known as Henry Kleinbach, now is out of the service and is to be the Alessandro in the forthcoming production of *Ramona* outdoor pageant staged at Hemet, Ca. Henry Kleinbach now is Henry Brandon.

The City of Hemet is nuzzled at the foot of Mt. San Jacinto in Riverside County, California. Since the 1920's the community put on an outdoor play *Ramona* in their natural amphitheater. Some 300 citizens of the area put on the production. It is still an annual event.

The play was adapted from a novel of the same name (published in 1884) and took place circa 1848. The story was of Ramona, a woman of mixed race (Scottish and Native American) who balks over her arranged marriage. Ramona falls in love with Alessandro, a Native American and they elope and start their new life together.

This was a unique engagement for Henry in many ways; he was back in the States after an absence of almost four years. He was recruited for the role by none other than actor Victor Jory, who had performed the role since the 1920s. The natural bowl can seat up to 2,000 people and embrace the 300 local non-professionals that augment the play.

Henry was invited back for the 1947 version; it was directed by Victor Jory and his wife, Jean Inness. Henry's professional performance added much to the prestige of the pageantry.

Rosalie Sept. 7-22, 1946 Greek Theater Los Angeles, California

Henry was listed as a supporting player for this well-known musical with George Gershwin and Cole Porter songs. The plot was similar to the movie version filmed a few years earlier. The stars listed in the *Los Angeles Times* were Lee Dixon, Jack Norton, and Judy Clark.

Macbeth Nov. 28-Dec 29, 1946 El Patio Theater Los Angeles, California. (MacDuff)

This time Henry played the role of "Lord MacDuff," a nobleman from Scotland. It was an important role; MacDuff slays Macbeth in the final act. Henry was listed as a supporting player for this well-known musical with George Gershwin and Cole Porter songs. The plot was similar to the movie version filmed a few years earlier. The *Los Angeles Times* noted: "MacDuff is in good hands, with Henry Brandon enacting the role of Macbeth's chief adversary."

Three Musketeers June 17, 1947 Philharmonic Auditorium Los Angeles, California. (Count de Rochefort)

This was a fun one; it's a musical and comedy version of the famous historical novel set in Paris 1625-1628. It was adapted to the stage by Morrie Ryskind,* who lampooned the adventures of the three swordsmen, one of which was Henry Calvin.† Henry played the heavy with comic flair as "Count De Rochefort." With Henry's sword skills on display it must have been quite a sight to see him in a duel with Calvin and his mates. The play was repeated in San Francisco July 7-13, 1947.

Dark of the Moon Sept. 28, 1947 Coronet Theater Los Angeles, Ca. (Marvin Hudgens)

This was a "Pelican Production" with music, it centered on a "Witch Boy" who wishes to become human after falling in love with a beautiful girl. This was originally a staged play on Broadway in 1945 and produced by the Shubert Bros. This local production was highlighted by folk singer and writer "Pete Seeger who appeared as a musical interlocutor, introducing

---

* Ryskind was a very successful theatrical and screenwriter most closely associated with the Marx Bros. biggest hits.

† Best known as "Sgt. Garcia" in Walt Disney's television series *Zorro*

each scene with a verse of: *The Ballad of Barbara Allen.*'" Stage and screen star Jane Darwell played "Ma Allen" and Henry played a character named "Marvin Hudgins. The setting was in the Appalachian Mountains.

Story of a Soldier May 21-30, 1948 Nordhoff Auditorium Ojai, California. (The Soldier)

As part of the Ojai Festival (Ventura County, Ca.) this version features a returning G.I. Joe (Henry Brandon) who sells his fiddle to the devil for riches and the promise of love. If this sounds like the premise of Faust, you're right. Albert Goldberg of the *Los Angeles Times* wrote:

> It is difficult to classify *The Story of a Soldier*, but whether it be considered a ballet, drama, or a combination of the two, it makes for excellent entertainment. Henry Brandon made a handsome soldier and enlisted the requisite sympathy for the role. Even the touch of Hamlet, he now and then brought to the part was not amiss.[†]

Medea Sept. 10, 1948 Lobero Theater, Santa Barbara, California. (Jason)

Judith Anderson as Medea had starred on Broadway for 214 performances. It prompted a nationwide tour starting at the Santa Barbara venue. Henry Brandon played her leading man as Jason; King of the Argonauts.[‡] The title of the play was adapted by Robinson Jeffers from the Greek tragedy written by Euripides.[§] *Medea* tells of a timeless love turned to hatred.

---

[*]   *Los Angeles Times* Sept. 28, 1947
[†]   *Los Angeles Times* May 22, 1948
[‡]   In the Broadway production it was John Gielgud
[§]   A Greek playwright of 400 B.C.

Judith Anderson and Henry Brandon in *Medea* circa 1949.

Opposite Miss Anderson is Henry Brandon as Jason, the hero who faithlessness drives Medea to her swift and terrible revenge. This will be Mr. Brandon's fourth appearance with Miss Anderson, the others being in *Family Portrait*, The *Tower Beyond Tragedy* on the West Coast and in the moving picture, *Edge of Darkness*.[*]

---

[*] *Omaha World-Herald* Sept. 5, 1948

In this savage duel between a man and a woman who have loved, Henry Brandon as Jason is physically oaken-strong, his profile straight and Greek.* Brandon gives a good portrayal as "Jason;" his is a passive role, but he makes it strong enough for the star to play against.†

Anderson and Brandon as Medea and Jason. Collection of Rick Greene.

---

*   *Detroit Free Press* Feb. 1, 1949

†   *Democrat and Chronicle* (Rochester, New York) March 5, 1949

Henry and Anderson teamed up to perform this play in many cities during 1948-1949. The two would team up for many revivals over the years to include Broadway and television.* (*See Henry Brandon Television Credits*).

Twelfth Night Oct. 3-11 through Nov. 12, 1949 Empire Theater New York City, June 14, 1965 University of California at Los Angeles, California. (Orsino)

This famous Shakespeare play (here presented in two acts) was yet another Broadway production in which Henry performed. This time it was as Orsino the Duke of Illyria, a lovesick bachelor. There is a famous line to this character: "If music be the food of love, play on."

Taming of the Shrew July 14, 1953 Pasadena Playhouse (Petruchio)

Another Shakespeare play, this time at Henry's old haunt, the Pasadena Playhouse. Here he was a homegrown "star" in a triumphant return. Henry played the character of "Petruchio," a gentleman from Verona who seeks a wealthy woman to marry. He finds such a woman, but the drawback is she is a shrew. Petruchio doesn't care about this as long as her dowry is ample enough. He is often boisterous, eccentric and sometimes drunk.

The Los Angeles Times reported: "Petruchio, using an old device, simply adapts Katharine's noisy and raucous tactics and outdoes her. Henry Brandon cut a fine figure as the swashbuckling Petruchio, not only dominating the fair Katharine but every scene."

---

*   As an interesting side-note; actor Bruce Gordon (known to Baby Boomers as "Frank Nitti" in the "Untouchables" television series 1959-1962) was a regular in the play through the years, he was Aegeus "King of Athens."

Lady's Not for Burning Feb. 21-28, 1957 Carnegie Hall Playhouse NY. City (Mendip)

Henry Brandon in the lead male role in an engagement at Carnegie Hall! This romantic, dark comedy was set in the Middle Ages. Henry's character was Thomas Mendip, a role that John Gielgud made famous in London and on Broadway. The plot has to do with a beautiful woman who is accused of being a witch; the townspeople accuse her of many incidents of sorcery. Mendip is a recently discharged soldier who is cynical and demands to be hung for crimes he didn't commit; the mayor refuses. The prose is a nod to Shakespeare:

> Mendip: "I've never seen a world so festering with damnation. I have left rings of beer on every alehouse table from the salt sea coast across half a dozen counties, but each time I thought I was on the way to a faintly festive hiccup, the sight of the damn world sobered me up again. Where is the Mayor? I've business with His Worship".
>
> Clerk: "Where have you come from?"
>
> Mendip: "Straight from the alehouse. Damnation's pretty active there this afternoon, licking her lips over gossip of murder and witchcraft. There's mischief brewing for someone. Where's the Mayor?"

Henry also played this role three years earlier at the Ivar Theater in Hollywood in 1954. The *Los Angeles Times* praised his performance: "Brandon read his longer speeches with genuine feeling—notably the bitter recital of Mendip's paid debt to mankind and his shuddering admission of the weight of nocturnal events."

> Mendip: "I have been cast adrift on a raft of melancholy. The night-wind passed me, like a sail across a blind man's eye…"

Bell, Book and Candle July 6, 1958 Laguna Playhouse Laguna Beach, California. (Henderson)
Henry again was cast in the male lead at this lighthearted fantasy about a witch loving a mortal and putting a spell on him. This version was an adaptation of the original play on Broadway, and performed months before the movie version was released. Henry's character was Shepherd "Shep" Henderson, a New Yorker. This is the role Jimmy Stewart played in the film version.

Once More with Feeling Jan. 9-17, 1960 Palm Springs Playhouse Palm Springs, California. (Fabian)
This was another play from a Broadway adaptation. Just as in Henry's film performance in *Metropolitan Nocturne*, he plays the male lead as a musical genius. As Victor Fabian he is a symphony conductor who woos his harpist girlfriend (Jan Clayton).* Fritz Feld played a supporting role.

The *Los Angeles Times* reviewed the play:

> A farce, almost bedroom slapstick. Music, love and artistic egotism are the ingredients of the tale. Jan Clayton and Henry Brandon bring skill and style to their leading roles. As the long-suffering harpist, so cynical and yet so vulnerable, Miss Clayton is especially adroit with the tricky, finely honed lines.
>
> Mr. Brandon, the harassed genius who must nightly render *The Stars and Stripes* for a rich benefactress to keep his job and his podium, is altogether impressive.

In the Broadway version, Joseph Cotton played the conductor and Yul Brynner played it in the film version that was released later that year.

---

* Jan Clayton is known to "Baby-Boomers" as Ellie Miller in the original "Lassie" series for television.

Girl of the Golden West July 8-17 1960 Farnsworth Park Altadena, California. (Jack Rance- Sheriff)

The play is from a classic story of an innocent girl who comes to a tough mining town in early California, and gets a job in the town saloon. Instead of being the "heavy" in this one, Henry Brandon played the Sheriff of the town. There was a film musical version of this title shot in 1938 starring Jeanette MacDonald and Nelson Eddy. The Sheriff character was played by Walter Pidgeon.

Days of the Dancing May 11, 1961 Beverly Hills Playhouse Beverly Hills, California. (Opera star)

This was a new play by James Bridges. The setting is Venice Beach in Southern California and the action concerns a woman who has an obsession with the bottle and engages with sundry love affairs. She was once a great lady and the discoverer of a famous operatic basso, the current object of her affections.[*] Henry Brandon "looks and acts the part of the opera star to perfection."[†]

Missouri Legend Dec. 2, 1965 Masquers Club, Los Angeles, California. (Jessie James)

Henry was a longtime member of the Masquers Club which occasionally made films and produced plays open to the public. One such production was a 1965 performance of *Missouri Legend*. Henry starred as Jesse James. This version of the play had music added, unlike the original Broadway play which debuted in 1938. *The Los Angeles Times* eagerly noted:

> The Masquers, actors themselves who hate to throw a play to the wolves by careless casting, waited until they could get Henry Brandon to play Jesse James before opening "*Missouri Legend*."[‡]

---

[*] *Los Angeles Times* May 17, 1960
[†] Ibid
[‡] *Los Angeles Times* Nov. 27, 1965

Brandon had notably portrayed Jesse James to cinematic perfection in the motion picture *Hell's Crossroads* less than ten years earlier.

Life and Death of King John April 3, 1966 Pierce College Los Angeles, California.

A Shakespeare play over the current crown of England, Henry Brandon was listed as head of the cast of twenty-four. It was a benefit performance for the school.

Bus Stop Oct. 5-17, 1980 Beverly Dinner Playhouse New Orleans, Louisiana. (Dr. Lyman)

Henry Brandon found himself as an important character in this dinner theater adaption of an original Broadway play (and loosely based on a film of the same name). His part was as Dr. Gerald Lyman, a philosophy professor who is charming but has an alcohol problem. The setting is a bus stop outside of Kansas City during a snowstorm; a group of passengers find refuge during a snowstorm in a diner.

Henry was 68 when he took on this play; the demands included physical dexterity and stumbling about. Fortunately a reporter from the local paper sought out Henry to interview; it is one of the few in existence discussing his approach to stage roles.

> This marks Henry Brandon's first brush with *Bus Stop* and the role of Dr. Lyman, yet he brings an uncanny accuracy to the sorrowful character. The actor reports that this is also his first time playing a drunk, but he does so with much authenticity that he had the opening night audience gasping at the character's fumbling moves.
>
> "Those moments are dangerous," Brandon suggests, "because the audience doesn't know if you're really stumbling or if it's part of the character. I've put in a few more gestures early on, so now

they're better prepared. A few people have asked me after the show what I drink during the performance, and a few have even accused me of being drunk on stage. You can't drink and act; that would be fatal. I save my drinking for after the performance."*

The Drunkard July 9 – Sept. 9th, 1983 Masquers Club, Los Angeles, California. (Squire Cribbs)

Another revival of the melodramatic temperance play that made Henry famous, this time for the Masquers at their Hollywood clubhouse. His good friend, actor Anthony Caruso was the director.

Arsenic and Old Lace April 5, 1985 Burt Reynolds Jupiter Theatre Jupiter, Florida. (Mortimer)

This is a very celebrated title made famous from the Broadway play and filmed version. Henry's character is Jonathan Brewster, an escaped killer. It was the same part that Boris Karloff created for the stage.

The Drunkard Oct. 17, 1987 Lompoc Theater Lompoc, California. (Squire Cribbs)

This was Henry's last traditional stage performance and it was fitting he ended it as Squire Cribbs. The occasion was part of the festivities of the W.C. Fields Festival at the comedian's favorite city of Lompoc. At the age of 75 Henry had vitality in his role and he cherished the persona he created. The hisses and boos from the audience were right on cue; and the two authors of this book were witnesses that fine day.

---

*   *New Orleans Times* Oct. 5, 1980

Henry Brandon Stageography:

Dance of Death May 7, 1931 Little Theater Stanford University
The Inspector General July 13, 1931 Stanford University
Berkeley Square Jan. 7-16, 1932 Pasadena Playhouse
When Knighthood Was in Flower March 3-12 1932 Pasadena Playhouse
Peter Gynt Aug. 6, 1932 Pasadena Playhouse
Everyman Sept. 1932 Occidental College, Los Angeles, Ca. (Everyman)
The Drunkard July 6, 1933-35 Theatre Mart, Hollywood, Ca. (Squire Cribbs)
Queen Victoria April 7-18, 1936 Pasadena Playhouse (Prince Albert)
Troilus and Cressida June 15-Aug. 1, 1936 Pasadena Playhouse (Troilus)
Electra Sept. 18, 1937 Greek Theater Berkeley, Ca. (Orestes)
Electra Sept. 21, 1937 Philharmonic Auditorium Los Angeles, Ca. (Orestes)
Lady Precious Stream Jan. 3, 1938 Curran Theater San Francisco (General Wei)
Boudoir Feb. 7, 1941 John Golden Theatre (Broadway) New York City
Road to Rome May 19, 1941 Del Monte Theater Monterey, Ca.
Family Portrait June 23-27, 1941 Del Monte Theater Monterey, Ca. (Judas)
The Tower Beyond Tragedy July 3-4, 1941 Forrest Theater, Carmel (Orestes)
Macbeth Nov. 2, 1941 Colonial Theater Boston, Mass. (Ross)
Macbeth Nov. 11, 1941-Feb. 28, 1942 National Theater New York City (Ross)
Macbeth March 7, 1942 Bushnell Theater Hartford, Conn. (Ross)
Macbeth March 9-9, 1942 Locust St. Theater Philadelphia, Pa. (Ross)
Macbeth March 16-23, 1942 Ford Theater Baltimore, Ma. (Ross)
Macbeth March 30, 1942 Nixon Theater Pittsburg, Pa. (Ross)
Macbeth April 1-6, Cass Theater Detroit, Mi. (Ross)
Macbeth April 14-15, 1942 English's Theater Indianapolis, Indiana (Ross)
Macbeth April 16-18, 1942 Taft Theater Cincinnati, Oh. (Ross)
Macbeth April 21, 1942 American Theater St. Louis, Missouri (Ross)
Macbeth April 27, 1942 Erlanger Theater Chicago, Ill (Ross)
Macbeth May 12-13, 1942 Lyceum Theater Minneapolis, Minn.(Ross)
Macbeth May 16, 1942 (unk.) Theater Milwaukee, Wisconsin (Ross)
Macbeth May 18-22, 1942 Hartman Theater Columbus, Oh (Ross)
Button Your Lip June 14, 1943 46th St. Theater New York City (Ryan)

Button Your Lip Aug. 2-Sept.4, 1943 Martin Beck Theater New York City (Ryan)

Ramona April 27-28, May 4-5, May 11- 12 1946 Ramona Bowl Hemet, Ca. (Alessandro)

Rosalie Sept. 7-22, 1946 Greek Theater Los Angeles, Ca.

Macbeth Nov. 29-Dec 29, 1946 El Patio Theater Los Angeles (MacDuff)

Ramona April 19, 1947 Ramona Bowl, Hemet, Ca.(Alessandro)

Three Musketeers July 7-13, 1947 Curran Theater San Francisco, Ca. (Count de Rochefort)

Three Musketeers June 17, 1947 Philharmonic Auditorium Los Angeles, Ca. Count de Rochefort

Dark of the Moon Sept. 28, 1947 Coronet Theater Los Angeles, Ca. (Marvin Hudgens)

Story of a Soldier May 21-29, 1948 Nordhoff Auditorium Ojai, Ca. (The Soldier)

Medea Sept. 10, 1948 Lobero Theater, Santa Barbara, Ca. (Jason)

Medea Sept. 6-25 1948 Geary Theater, San Francisco, Ca. (Jason)

Medea Sept. 27- Oct.10, 1948 Biltmore Theater Los Angeles, Ca. (Jason)

Medea Oct. 18, 1948 Russ Auditorium, San Diego, Ca. (Jason)

Medea Oct. 21-22, 1948 White Theater Fresno, Ca. (Jason)

Medea Oct. 25, 1948 Mayfair Theatre, Portland, Ore. (Jason)

Medea Oct. 31, 1948 Metropolitan, Seattle, WA. (Jason)

Medea Nov. 9, 1948 Capital Theater, Salt Lake, Utah (Jason)

Medea Nov. 11, 1948 KRNT Radio Theater, Des Moines, Iowa (Jason)

Medea Nov. 15, 1948 American Theater St. Louis, Mo (Jason)

Medea Nov. 22, 1948 Blackstone Theater Chicago, Ill. (Jason)

Medea Jan. 19-22, 1949 Lyceum Theater Minneapolis, Minnesota (Jason)

Medea Jan 25-26, 1949 Hartman Theater Columbus, Ohio (Jason)

Medea Jan. 31-Feb. 7, 1949 Cass Theater, Detroit, Michigan (Jason)

Medea Feb. 14-20, 1949 Cox Theater, Cincinnati, Oh. (Jason)

Medea Feb. 21-29 1949 Hanna Theater Cleveland, Ohio (Jason)

Medea March 1-2, 1949 Empire Theater, Syracuse, New York (Jason)

Medea March 3, 1949 Strand Theater Ithaca, New York (Jason)

Medea March 4-5, 1949 Auditorium, Rochester, N.Y. (Jason)

Medea March 7-8, 1949 Nixon Theater, Pittsburgh, PA.. (Jason)

Medea March 14, 1949 Forrest Theater, Philadelphia, PA.(Jason)

Medea March 21-26, 1949 Ford Theater, Baltimore, Maryland (Jason)

Medea March 29, 1949 Lyric Theater, Allentown, PA (Jason)

Medea March 30, 1949 Trenton War Memorial Theater Trenton, New Jersey (Jason)

Medea April 1-2, 1949 Playhouse, Wilmington, Delaware (Jason)

Medea April 4, 1949 Bushnell Memorial Theater, Hartford, Conn. (Jason)

Medea April 11-26, 1949 Shubert Theater Boston, Ma (Jason)

Medea May 2-15, 1949 City Center, New York (after a 37 week transcontinental tour)

Medea May 16, 1949 Memorial Gymnasium Univ. of Virginia Charlottesville, Virg. (Jason)

Medea May 18, 1949 National Sylvan Theater, Washington D. C. (Jason)

Medea June 27-July 3, 1949 Dillingham Hall, Honolulu, Hawaii

Twelfth Night Oct. 3-11 through Nov. 12, 1949 Empire Theater New York City (Orsino)

Medea May 31, 1952 Nordhoff Auditorium Ojai, Ca. (Jason)

Taming of the Shrew July 9-14, 1953 Pasadena Playhouse (Petruchio)

The Lady's Not for Burning July 13-Aug. 8, 1954 Ivar Theatre (Hollywood) (Thomas Mendip)

The Lady's Not for Burning Feb. 21-28, 1957 Carnegie Hall Playhouse New York City

Medea 1958 Russ Auditorium San Diego, Ca. (Jason)

Bell Book and Candle July 8-13, 1958 Laguna Playhouse Laguna Beach, Ca. Shep Henderson

Once More with Feeling Jan. 9-17, 1960 Palm Springs Playhouse Palm Springs, Ca. (Conductor)

Girl of the Golden West July 8-17 1960 Farnsworth Park Altadena, Ca. (Jack Rance- Sheriff)

Days of the Dancing May 11, 1961 Beverly Hills Playhouse Beverly Hills, Ca.(Opera star)

Much Ado About Nothing April 26, 1964 San Diego, Ca. Old Globe Theater (Benedict)

Twelfth Night June 14, 1965 U.C.L.A. Los Angeles, Ca.

Medea Oct.12-24, 1965 Valley Music Theater, Woodland Hills, Ca. (Jason)

Missouri Legend Dec. 2, 1965 Masquers Club, Los Angeles, Ca. (Jessie James)

Life and Death of King John April 3, 1966 Pierce College Los Angeles, Ca.

Bus Stop Oct. 5-17, 1980 Beverly Dinner Playhouse New Orleans, Lo. (Dr. Lyman)

The Drunkard July 9 – Sept. 9, 1983 Masquers Club, Los Angeles, Ca. (Squire

Cribbs)

Arsenic and Old Lace April 5, 1985 Burt Reynolds Jupiter Theatre Jupiter, Fl. (Mortimer)

The Drunkard Oct. 17, 1987 Lompoc Theater Lompoc, Ca. (Squire Cribbs)

*As Henry Kleinbach

Bibliography

Books:
Stanford University Quad Yearbook 1929-1931

Eymann, Scott/Duncan, Paul. *John Ford: The Searcher* (2008) Taschen Pg. 156

Maltin, Leonard/Bann, Richard. *Our Gang: The Life and Times of the Little Rascals* Crown Publishers, New York (1977)

Frankel, Glenn. *The Searchers: The Making of an American Legend* Bloomsbury, New York (2013)

Jordan, Richard Tyler. *But Darling, I'm Your Auntie Mame! The Amazing History of the World's Favorite Madcap Aunt* Capra Press 1968

Nollen, Scott Allen. *Three Bad Men: John Ford, John Wayne, Ward Bond*, McFarland (2013) Pg. 258

Skretvedt, Randy. *Laurel and Hardy the Magic Behind the Movies,* Bonadventure Press Irvine, Ca. (2016)

Press books:
(1939) RKO - *Marshal of Mesa City*

(1940) Republic-*Drums of Fu Manchu*

(1957) Universal International Showman Manual- *The Land Unknown*

(1974) Premiere Releasing Organization-*The Manhandlers*

(1974) Sun International Productions, Inc. - *When the North Wind Blows*

Newspapers:
San Francisco Chronicle May 7, 1931

San Francisco Chronicle July 13, 1931

San Mateo Times July 14, 1931

Hollywood Citizen News Dec. 4, 1933

Los Angeles Times February 14, 1934

Los Angeles Times June 13, 1934

Los Angeles Times July 23, 1934

Los Angeles Times August 18, 1934

San Bernardino County Sun August 19, 1934

Los Angeles Times Jan. 16, 1936

Augusta Chronicle January 29, 1936

State (Columbia, South Carolina) Dec. 27, 1936

San Bernardino County Sun April 1, 1936:

Hollywood Reporter April 8, 1936:

San Diego Union May 17, 1936

Pittsburgh Post-Gazette May 28, 1936

Los Angeles Times June 19, 1936:

Los Angeles Express June 15, 1936

San Francisco Chronicle Jan. 4, 1938

Brooklyn Daily Eagle Feb. 7, 1941

San Francisco Chronicle March 24, 1941

San Francisco Chronicle July 2, 1941

San Bernardino County Sun April 11, 1946

Los Angeles Times Sept. 7-22, 1946

Los Angeles Times Sept. 28, 1947

Los Angeles Times May 22, 1948

Omaha World-Herald Sept. 5, 1948

Detroit Free Press Feb. 1, 1949

Democrat and Chronicle (Rochester, N.Y.) March 5, 1949

Los Angeles Times July 14, 1953

News-Press (Fort Myers, Florida) March 21, 1957

Los Angeles Times Jan. 9, 1960

Los Angeles Times May 17, 1960

Los Angeles Times Nov. 27, 1965

New Orleans Times Oct. 5, 1980

Los Angeles Times March 18, 1990

Daily Mirror July 19, 2008

Magazines:
Picturegoer Weekly Dec. 22, 1934 "Behind the Scenes of *Babes in Toyland* "
Those Enduring Matinee Idols 1972-73 #20 "Henry Brandon, Fu Manchu"
Cinemacabre #6, Summer 1984
Starlog Magazine #114 January 1987
Cliffhanger magazine #15 1991

Public Records:
Kroonland Vessel Passenger Listings-1912
United States Census: 1920/1930/1940
Henry Brandon Military (National Archives)
Brandon versus Brandon Divorce Decree #B307444
Henry Brandon Death Certificate #39019008723

Hal Roach Payroll Records
August 7-November 3, 1934 (Courtesy University of Southern California)

The Films of Henry Brandon

This is the most complete filmography for Henry Brandon, compiled from multiple sources and includes his every known motion picture appearance. Following the title of the movie we've listed the name of the character Henry portrayed in parenthesis. In his first six films, he is credited as Henry Kleinbach. Beginning with *Garden Of Allah*, he is credited as Henry Brandon. However, many of these appearances are uncredited roles.

1932
Sign Of The Cross (Coliseum Spectator) uncredited
D: Cecil B. DeMille **C:** Fredric March, Claudette Colbert, Elissa Landi, Charles Laughton **P:** Cecil B. DeMille Released by Paramount Pictures
Henry's first appearance on film was as an extra in this DeMille epic

1934
Babes in Toyland (Barnaby) **D:** Gus Meins, Charley Rogers **C:** Stan Laurel, Oliver Hardy, Charlotte Henry, Felix Knight, Virginia Karns, Florence Roberts **P:** Hal Roach Released by Metro-Goldwyn-Mayer

1935
Metropolitan Nocturne (The young composer)
D: Leigh Jason **P:** Lee S. Marcus
This RKO Radio short subject is not known to exist, although the script survives.

1936
Trail of the Lonesome Pine (Wade Falin)
D: Henry Hathaway **C:** Sylvia Sidney, Fred MacMurray, Henry Fonda, George 'Spanky' McFarland **P:** Walter Wanger Released by Paramount Pictures

This is the first feature length motion picture filmed on location and released in three-strip Technicolor.

The Preview Murder Mystery (The Bat Man)
D: Robert Florey **C:** Reginald Denny, Frances Drake, Gail Patrick **P:** Edward F. Cline Released by Paramount Pictures

Big Brown Eyes (Don Butler)
D: Raoul Walsh **C:** Cary Grant, Joan Bennett, Walter Pidgeon **P:** Walter Wanger Released by Paramount Pictures

Garden Of Allah (Hadj)
D: Richard Boleslawski **C:** Marlene Dietrich, Charles Boyer, Tilly Losch **P:** David O. Selznick Released by United Artists
This is another early three-strip Technicolor film.

Killer At Large (Mr. Zero)
D: David Selman **C:** Mary Brian, Russell Hardie, George McKay, Lon Chaney Jr. **P:** Columbia Pictures

1937
Black Legion (Joe Dombrowski)
D: Archie Mayo **C:** Humphrey Bogart, Ann Sheridan, Dick Foran **P:** Jack L. Warner Released by Warner Bros.

Jungle Jim (The Cobra)
D: Ford Beebe, Clifford Smith **C:** Grant Withers, Betty Jane Rhodes, Raymond Hatton **P:** Ben Koenig Released by Universal Pictures
This is a twelve-chapter serial

Secret Agent X-9 (Blackstone)
D: Ford Beebe, Clifford Smith **C:** Scott Kolk, Jean Rogers, David Oliver, Lon Chaney Jr. **P:** Ben Koenig Released by Universal Pictures
This is a twelve-chapter serial

I Promise To Pay (Fancyface)
D: D. Ross Lederman **C:** Chester Morris, Leo Carillo, Helen Mack, Thomas Mitchell **P:** Myles Connolly Released by Columbia Pictures Corporation

Carnival in Paris (Louis)
D: Wilhelm Thiele **C:** Ann Rutherford, Harry Burns **P:** Metro-Goldwyn-Mayer
This is two-reel musical short subject

Island Captives (Dick Bannister)
D: Paul Kerschner **C:** Edward J. Nugent, Joan Barclay **P:** Stephen Tabor Released by Falcon Pictures Corporation

Last Train From Madrid (Radio Announcer)
D: James P. Hogan **C:** Dorothy Lamour, Lew Ayres, Gilbert Roland, Lionell Atwill, Anthony Quinn **P:** George M. Arthur Released by Paramount Pictures

West Bound Limited (Joe Forbes)
D: Ford Beebe **C:** Lyle Talbot, Polly Rowles, Frank Reicher **P:** Ben Koenig Released by Universal Pictures

Conquest (Staff Officer)
D: Clarence Brown, Gustav Machaty **C:** Greta Garbo, Charles Boyer, Reginald Owen **P:** Bernard H. Hyman Released by Metro-Goldwyn-Mayer

Our Gang Follies Of 1938 (Barnaby)
D: Gordon Douglas **C:** George 'Spanky' McFarland, Carl 'Alfalfa' Switzer, Darla Hood **P:** Hal Roach. Released by Metro-Goldwyn-Mayer
This is the final two-reel comedy produced at The Hal Roach Studios

Wells Fargo (Larry)
D: Frank Lloyd **C:** Joel McCrea, Bob Burns, Frances Dee, Lloyd Nolan **P:** Frank Lloyd Released by Paramount Pictures

1938

I Met My Love Again (Bruno The Painter)
D: Joshua Logan, Arthur Ripley **C:** Joan Bennett, Henry Fonda, Louise Platt
P: Walter Wanger Released by United Artists

Three Comrades (Valentin)
D: Frank Borzage **C:** Robert Taylor, Margaret Sullavan, Franchot Tone **P:** Joseph L. Mankiewicz Released by Metro-Goldwyn-Mayer

Spawn of the North (Davis)
D: Henry Hathaway **C:** George Raft, Henry Fonda, Dorothy Lamour **P:** Albert Lewin Released by Paramount Pictures

If I Were King (Soldier)
D: Frank Lloyd **C:** Ronald Colman, Basil Rathbone, Frances Dee **P:** Frank Lloyd Released by Paramount Pictures

The Last Express (Pinky)
D: Otis Garrett **C:** Kent Taylor, Dorothea Kent, Greta Granstedt **P:** Irving Starr Released by Universal Pictures
This is a Crime Club production

The Last Warning (Willie The Creep)
D: Albert S. Rogell **C:** Preston Foster, Frank Jenks, Joyce Compton **P:** Irving Starr Released by Universal Pictures, a "Crime Club" production

1939

Pirates of the Skies (Jake Austin)
D: Joseph A. McDonough **C:** Kent Taylor, Rochelle Hudson, Regis Toomey **P:** Barney A. Sarecky Released by Universal Pictures

Buck Rogers (Captain Laska)
D: Ford Beebe, Saul. A. Goodkind **C:** Buster Crabbe, Constance Moore, Jackie Moran **P:** Barney A. Sarecky Released by Universal Pictures
This is a twelve-chapter serial

Beau Geste (Renouf)
D: William A. Wellman **C:** Gary Cooper, Ray Milland, Robert Preston **P:** William A. Wellman Released by Paramount Pictures

Conspiracy (Carlson)
D: Lew Landers **C:** Allan Lane, Linda Hayes, Robert Barrat **P:** Lee S. Marcus Released by RKO Radio Pictures

Nurse Edith Cavell (Lt. Schultz)
D: Herbert Wilcox **C:** Anna Neagle, Edna May Oliver, George Sanders **P:** Herbert Wilcox Released by RKO Radio Pictures

The Marshal of Mesa City (Duke Allison)
D: David Howard **C:** George O'Brien, Virginia Vale, Leon Ames **P:** Bert Gilvoy Released by RKO Radio Pictures

1940

Drums of Fu Manchu (Dr. Fu Manchu)
D: John English, William Witney **C:** William Royle, Robert Kellard **P:** Hiram S. Brown Jr. Released by Republic Pictures
This is a fifteen-chapter serial

Half a Sinner (Handsome)
D: Al Christie **C:** Heather Angel, John 'Dusty' King, Constance Collier **P:** Al Christie Released by Universal Pictures

Ski Patrol (Jan Sikorsky)
D: Lew Landers **C:** Philip Dorn, Luli Deste, Stanley Fields **P:** Warren Douglas Released by Universal Studios

Florian (Groom)
D: Edwin L. Marin **C:** Robert Young, Helen Gilbert, Charles Coburn, Lee Bowman **P:** Winfield R. Sheehan Released by Metro-Goldwyn-Mayer

The Ranger and The Lady (General Augustus Larue)
D: Joseph Kane **C:** Roy Rogers, George 'Gabby' Hayes, Julie Bishop **P:** Joseph Kane Released by Republic Pictures

Doomed To Die (Attorney Victor Martin)
D: William Nigh **C:** Boris Karloff, Marjorie Reynolds, Grant Withers **P:** Paul Malvern Released by Monogram Pictures. This is an entry in the 'Mr. Wong' mystery series.

Under Texas Skies (Tom Blackton)
D: George Sherman **C:** Robert Livingston, Bob Steele, Rufe Davis **P:** Harry Grey. Released by Republic Pictures. This is an entry in the popular 'Three Mesquiteers' film series.

Dark Streets of Cairo (Hussien)
D: Leslie Kardos **C:** Sigrid Gurie, Ralph Byrd, Eddie Quillan, George Zucco **P:** Joseph Gershenson Released by Universal Pictures

Son of Monte Cristo (Lt. Schultz)
D: Rowland V. Lee **C:** Louis Hayward, Joan Bennett, George Sanders, Clayton Moore **P:** Rowland V. Lee Released by United Artists

1941

Underground (Joseph)
D: Vincent Sherman **C:** Jeffrey Lynn, Philip Dorn, Kaaren Verne **P:** Jack L. Warner Released by Warner Bros.

Ghost Treasure (Mariano Arguello)
D: Will Jason **C:** Carey Wilson, Roman Bohnen **P:** Metro-Goldwyn-Mayer This MGM one-reel short was part of the *Carey Wilson Miniatures* series and was the final short subject that Henry Brandon appeared in.

Two in a Taxi (Professor)
D: Robert Florey **C:** Anita Louise, Russell Hayden, Noah Beery Jr **P:** Irving Briskin Released by Columbia Pictures

Shepherd of the Hills (Bald Knobber)
D: Henry Hathaway **C:** John Wayne, Betty Field, Harry Carey **P:** Jack Moss Released by Paramount Pictures

Hurricane Smith (Sam Carson)
D: Bernard Vorhaus **C:** Ray Middleton, Jane Wyatt, Harry Davenport **P:** Jack Moss Released by Republic Pictures

Bad Man of Deadwood (Ted Carver)
D: Joseph Kane **C:** Roy Rogers, George 'Gabby' Hayes, Carol Adams **P:** Joseph Kane Released by Republic Pictures

The Corsican Brothers (Marquis de Raveneau)
D: Gregory Ratoff **C:** Douglas Fairbanks, Jr., Ruth Warrick, Akim Tamiroff **P:** Edward Small Released by United Artists

1942
Night In New Orleans (Croupier)
D: William Clemens **C:** Preston Foster, Patricia Morrison, Albert Decker **P:** Sol C. Siegel Released by Paramount Pictures

1943
Edge of Darkness (Major Ruck)
D: Lewis Milestone **C:** Errol Flynn, Ann Sheridan, Walter Houston, Judith Anderson **P:** Henry Blanke. Released by Warner Bros.

1947
Northwest Outpost (Chinese Junk Captain)
D: Allan Dwan **C:** Nelson Eddy, Ilona Massey, Joseph Schildkraut, Elsa Lanchester **P:** Allan Dwan. Released by Republic Pictures

1948
Old Los Angeles (Larry Stockton)
D: Joseph Kane **C:** Bill Elliott, John Carroll, Catherine McLeod, Andy Devine **P:** Joseph Kane. Released by Republic Pictures

Canon City (Freeman)
D: Crane Wilbur **C:** Scott Brady, Jeff Corey, Whit Bissell **P:** Bryan Foy Released by Eagle Lion Films

Hollow Triumph (Big Boy)
D: Steve Sekely **C:** Paul Henreid, Joan Bennett, Eduard Franz **P:** Paul Henreid Released by Eagle Lion Films

Joan Of Arc (Captain Giles de Rais)
D: Victor Fleming **C:** Ingrid Bergman, Jose Ferrer, Francis L. Sullivan **P:** Walter Wanger Released by RKO Radio Pictures

The Paleface (Wapato Medicine Man)
D: Norman Z. McLeod **C:** Bob Hope, Jane Russell, Robert Armstrong **P:** Robert L. Welch Released by Paramount Pictures

Wake of the Red Witch (Kurinua)
D: Edward Ludwig **C:** John Wayne, Gail Russell, Gig Young **P:** Edmund Grainger Released by Republic Pictures

1949

The Fighting O'Flynn (Lt. Carpe)
D: Arthur Pierson **C:** Douglas Fairbanks, Jr., Helena Carter, Richard Greene **P:** Douglas Fairbanks, Jr. Released by Universal International

Tarzan's Magic Fountain (Siko)
D: Lee Sholem **C:** Lex Barker, Brenda Joyce, Albert Dekker **P:** Sol Lesser Released by RKO Radio Pictures

1951

Cattle Drive (Jim Currie)
D: Kurt Neumann **C:** Joel McCrea, Dean Stockwell, Chill Wills **P:** Aaron Rosenberg Released by Universal International

The Golden Horde *(Juchi)*
D: George Sherman **C:** Ann Blyth, David Farrar, George MacReady **P:** Robert Arthur, Howard Christie Released by Universal International

Flame of Araby (Malik)
D: Charles Lamont **C:** Maureen O'Hara, Jeff Chandler, Maxwell Reed **P:** Leonard Goldstein Released by Universal International

1952

Harem Girl (Hassan Ali)
D: Edward Bernds **C:** Joan Davis, Peggie Castle, Arthur Blake **P:** Wallace MacDonald Released by Columbia Pictures

Scarlet Angel (Pierre)
D: Sidney Salkow **C:** Rock Hudson, Yvonne De Carlo, Richard Denning **P:** Leonard Goldstein Released by Universal International

Wagons West (Clay Cook)

D: Ford Beebe **C:** Rod Cameron, Noah Beery Jr., Peggie Castle **P:** Vincent M. Fennelly Released by Monogram Pictures

Hurricane Smith (Sam)

D: Jerry Hopper **C:** Yvonne De Carlo, John Ireland, James Craig **P:** Nat Holt Released by Paramount Pictures

1953

War of the Worlds (Cop At Crash Site)

D: Byron Haskin **C:** Gene Barry, Ann Robinson, Les Treymayne **P:** George Pal Released by Paramount Pictures

Scared Stiff (Pierre)

D: George Marshall **C:** Dean Martin, Jerry Lewis, Lizabeth Scott, Carmen Miranda, Dorothy Malone **P:** Hal Wallis Released by Paramount Pictures

Pony Express (Joe Cooper)

D: Jerry Hopper **C:** Charlton Heston, Rhonda Fleming, Jan Sterling, Forrest Tucker **P:** Nat Holt Released by Paramount Pictures

Raiders of the Seven Seas (Captain Goiti)

D: Sidney Salkow **C:** John Payne, Donna Reed, Gerald Mohr, Lon Chaney Jr., Anthony Caruso **P:** Sidney Salkow Released by United Artists

Tarzan and the She-Devil (M'Tara)

D: Kurt Neumann **C:** Lex Barker, Joyce Mackenzie, Raymond Burr, Tom Conway **P:** Sol Lesser Released by RKO Radio Pictures

The Caddy (Mr. Preen)

D: Norman Taurog **C:** Dean Martin, Jerry Lewis, Donna Reed, Barbara Bates, Fred Clark **P:** Paul Jones Released by Paramount Pictures

War Arrow (Maygro)
D: George Sherman **C:** Maureen O'Hara, Jeff Chandler, John McIntire **P:** John W. Rogers Released by Universal International

1954
Knock On Wood (Second Trenchcoat Man)
D: Melvin Frank, Norman Panama **C:** Danny Kaye, Mai Zetterling, Torin Thatcher **P:** Melvin Frank Released by Paramount Pictures

Casanova's Big Night (Captain Rugello)
D: Norman Z. McLeod **C:** Bob Hope, Joan Fontaine, Audrey Dalton, Basil Rathbone, John Carradine, Lon Chaney Jr. **P:** Paul Jones Released by Paramount Pictures

Vera Cruz (Captain Danette)
D: Robert Aldrich **C:** Gary Cooper, Burt Lancaster, Cesar Romero, Denise Darcel **P:** James Hill Released by United Artists

1955
Lady Godiva of Coventry (Bejac)
D: Arthur Lubin **C:** Maureen O'Hara, George Nader, Victor McLaglen **P:** Robert Arthur Relased by Universal International

1956
Silent Fear (Cliff Sutton)
D: Edward L. Cahn **C:** Andrea King, Peter Adams **P:** Edward L. Cahn Released by Gibraltar Motion Picture Distributors

Comanche (Black Cloud)
D: George Sherman **C:** Dana Andrews, Kent Smith, Nestor Paiva **P:** Carl Krueger Released by United Artists

The Searchers (Chief Scar)
D: John Ford **C:** John Wayne, Jeffrey Hunter, Vera Miles, Ward Bond, Natalie Wood, Harry Carey Jr. **P:** John Ford Released by Warner Bros.

Bandido (Gunther)
D: Richard Fleischer **C:** Robert Mitchum, Ursula Thiess, Gilbert Roland **P:** Robert L. Jacks Released by United Artists

The Ten Commandments (Commander Of The Hosts)
D: Cecil B. DeMille **C:** Charlton Heston, Yul Brynner, Anne Baxter, Edward G. Robinson, Yvonne De Carlo **P:** Cecil B. DeMille Released by Paramount Pictures

1957

Hell's Crossroads (Jesse James)
D: Franklin Adreon **C:** Stephen McNally, Peggie Castle, Robert Vaughn **P:** Rudy Ralston Released by Republic Pictures

The Land Unknown (Dr. Carl Hunter)
D: Virgil W. Vogel **C:** Jock Mahoney, Shirley Patterson, William Reynolds **P:** William Alland Released by Universal International

The Life, Loves and Adventures of Omar Khayyam (Commander)
D: William Dieterle **C:** Cornel Wilde, Michael Rennie, Debra Paget **P:** Frank Freeman Jr. Released by Paramount Pictures

1958

The Buccaneer (British Major)
D: Anthony Quinn **C:** Yul Brynner, Claire Bloom, Charles Boyer, Charlton Heston **P:** Cecil B. DeMille Released by Paramount Pictures

Auntie Mame (Acacius Page)
D: Morton DaCosta **C:** Rosalind Russell, Forrest Tucker, Coral Browne **P:** Morton DaCosta Released by Warner Bros.

1959
Okefenokee (Joe Kalhari)
D: Roul Haig **C:** Peter Coe, Peggy Maley **P:** Aaron A. Danches Released by Film Service Distributing Corp.

The Big Fisherman (Menicus)
D: Frank Borzage **C:** John Saxon, Howard Keel, Susan Kohner **P:** Centurion Films

1961
Two Rode Together (Chief Quanah Parker)
D: John Ford **C:** James Stewart, Richard Widmark, Shirley Jones, Andy Devine **P:** John Ford Released by Columbia Pictures

1963
Captain Sindbad (Colonel Kabar)
D: Byron Haskin **C:** Guy Williams, Heidi Bruhl, Pedro Armendariz **P:** King Brothers Productions Released by Metro-Goldwyn-Mayer

1967
The Search for the Evil One (Martin Borman)
D: Joseph Kane **C:** Lee Patterson, Lisa Pera **P:** E. Stanley Williamson Released by Ambassador Films

1973
Gentle Savage (Holy Man)
D: Sean MacGregor **C:** William Smith, Gene Evans, Joe Flynn **P:** Redwine International

So Long, Blue Boy (Buck)
D: Gerald Gordon **C:** Arthur Franz, Richard Gates, Neile Adams **P:** Maryon Productions

1974
When the North Wind Blows (Avakum)
D: Stewart Raffill **C:** Herbert Nelson, Dan Haggarty **P:** Joseph and Stewart Raffill Released by Sun Classic Pictures

The Manhandlers (Carlo)
D: Lee Madden **C:** Carla Burgess, Judith Brown, Rosalind Miles **P:** Ed Carlin and Gil Lasky Distributed by Premiere Releasing Organization

1976
Assault on Precinct 13 (Chaney)
D: John Carpenter **C:** Austin Stoker, Darwin Joston, Laurie Zimmer **P:** J. S. Kaplan Released by CKK Corporation

1977
Run For the Roses (Jeff)
D: Henry Levin **C:** Vera Miles, Stuart Whitman, Sam Groom **P:** Pan American Films

Mission to Glory: A True Story (Father Canion)
D: Ken Kenney **C:** Richard Egan, Ricardo Montalban, John Ireland, Joseph Campanella, Cesar Romero, Keenan Wynn, Rory Calhoun, Anthony Caruso, Aldo Ray, Victor Jory **P:** Key International Pictures

1979
Hollywood Knight aka **Hard Knocks/Mid-Knight Rider (Curley)**
D: David Worth **C:** Michael Christian, Donna Wilkes, Keenan Wynn, John Crawford, Mark Herron **P:** Michael Christian Released by Artaxerxes Productions

1983
To Be or Not To Be (Nazi Officer)
D: Alan Johnson **C:** Mel Brooks, Anne Bancroft, Ronny Graham, Christopher Lloyd, Tim Matheson, Jose Ferrer, Jack Riley **P:** Brooksfilms, Released by Twentieth Century Fox

1989
Wizards of the Lost Kingdom II (Zarz)
D: Charles B. Griffith **C:** David Carradine, Mel Welles, Robert Jayne **P:** Reid Shane Released by New Classics

Henry Brandon's – 12 Greatest Film Roles:
1. *Babes In Toyland* – Silas Barnaby
2. *Drums Of Fu Manchu* – Dr. Fu Manchu
3. *The Searchers* – Scar
4. *When The North Wind Blows* – Avakum
5. *Edge Of Darkness* – Major Ruck
6. *Hell's Crossroads* – Jesse James
7. *The Land Unknown* – Dr. Carl Hunter
8. *The Marshal Of Mesa City* – Duke Allison
9. *Three Comrades* – Valentin
10. *Jungle Jim* – The Cobra
11. *Vera Cruz* – Capt. Danette
12. *Black Legion* – Joe Dombrowski

Television Appearances of Henry Brandon

This chronological listing of Henry's television appearances rivals in quantity his number of film appearances and is as complete as possible. Compiling a definitive list of video roles is a challenging proposition as the authors discovered nearly a dozen additions to this list while writing this book. There will almost certainly be new discoveries in the coming years of Brandon television shows to add, but we believe this is the most definitive such listing as of the publication of this book.

We list the name of the show, the title of the episode, the role Henry played, the season and episode number and finally the date the show first aired. We were able to locate and review nearly sixty of these episodes in the Television chapter.

1949

The Clock
Wrong Woman Mad
Guest Star
Season 1, Episode 18
9/14/49

Suspense
The Case of Lady Sannox
(Dr. Douglas Stone)
Season 2, Episode 17
12/27/49

1950

Lights Out
The Riverman
Guest Star
Season 2, Episode 17
1/2/50

1951

Family Theatre
Hill Number One
(Cassius Longinus)
Season 1, Episode 1
3/25/51

1952

Gruen Guild Theatre
Counterplot
Guest Star
Season 2, Episode 6
6/5/52

Gruen Guild Theatre
Out of the Dark
Guest Star
Season 2, Episode 14
8/26/52

Cavalcade of America
Poor Richard
Guest Star
Season 1, Episode 1
10/1/52

The Schaefer Century Theatre
Portfolio Twelve
Guest Star
Season 1, Episode 12
10/5/52

Biff Baker USA
Koblen
Guest Star
Season 1, Episode 1
11/6/52

1953

Hollywood Opening Night
The Shepard Touch
Guest Star
Season 2, Episode 18
2/2/53

1954

Rocky Jones, Space Ranger
Pirates of Prah
(Rinkman)
Season 1, Episodes 11, 12 & 13
5/4/54 – 5/6/54

1955

Stories of the Century
"Nate Champion
(Nate Champion)
Season 2, Episode 7
2/6/55

Soldiers of Fortune
The Greatest Beast
(Ki Yang)
Season 1, Episode 5
2/20/55

1956

Broken Arrow
Passage Deferred
(Judd Buckley)
Season 1, Episode 5
10/30/56

1957

Robert Montgomery Presents Your Lucky Strike Theatre
Victoria Regina
Guest Star
Season 8, Episode 30
4/8/57

The Adventures of Jim Bowie
Epitaph for an Indian
(Quint Oxley)
Season 2, Episode 1
9/6/57

M-Squad
The Golden Look
(Bert Fallon)
Season 1, Episode 1
9/20/57

Wagon Train
The Charles Avery Story
(Running Horse)
Season 1, Episode 9
11/13/57

Suspicion
The Flight
(Colonel Palidano)
Season 1, Episode 9
11/25/57

Matinee Theatre
Out of My Darkness
Guest Star
Season 3, Episode 35
12/3/57

Have Gun-Will Travel
The Yuma Treasure
(Chief Gerada)
Season 1, Episode 14
12/14/57

1958

Tombstone Territory
The Outcasts
(Brother Simon Webb)
Season 1, Episode 28
4/23/58

Decision
The Tall Man
(Frank Dawson)
Season 1, Episode 4
7/27/58

The Bob Hope Show
Roberta
(Ladislaw)
90 Minute Special
9/19/58

Westinghouse Desilu Playhouse
The Case for Dr. Mudd
(Williams)
Season 1, Episode 3
10/20/58

1959

Wagon Train
The Swift Cloud Story
(Fire Cloud)
Season 2, Episode 27
4/8/59

The Texan
The Man Hater
(Crowley)
Season 1, Episode 37
6/15/59

The Play of the Week
Medea
(Jason)
Season 1, Episode 1
10/12/59

Bourbon Street Beat
Woman in the River
(Gator Joe)
Season 1, Episode 4
10/26/59

Lawman
The Last Man
(Joshua Haney)
Season 2, Episode 5
11/1/59

Wagon Train
The Martha Barham Story
(Black Panther)
Season 3, Episode 6
11/4/59

The Deputy
The Big Four
(Johnny Ringo)
Season 1, Episode 10
11/14/59

The Lawless Years
The Joe Angelo Story
(Mendy Hymer)
Season 2, Episode 6
11/19/59

Wagon Train
The St. Nicholas Story
(Ute Indian Chief)
Season 3, Episode 12
12/23/59

Zane Grey Theater
The Ghost
(Whit Ransome)
Season 4, Episode 13
12/31/59

1960
Lock Up
A Reputation
(Johnny Kelso)
Season 1, Episode 16
1/9/60

The Rebel
Gold Seeker
(Running Wolf)
Season 1, Episode 15
1/17/60

The Loretta Young Show
Mrs. Minton
(John Buckley)
Season 7, Episode 17
1/24/60

Lawman
To Capture the West
(Tall Horse)
Season 2, Episode 18
2/7/60

General Electric Theater
The Story of Judith
(Anchior)
Season 8, Episode 22
2/28/60

Bronco
Legacy of Twisted Creek
(Yellow Moon)
Season 2, Episode 16
4/19/60

Shotgun Slade
The Fabulous Fiddle
(Trigg Bronson)
Season 1, Episode 29
5/6/60

Wagon Train
Dr. Swift McCloud
(Chief Fire Cloud)
Season 3, Episode 33
5/25/60

Bronco
Winter Kill
(Chato)
Season 2, Episode 19
5/31/60

Gunsmoke
The Deserter
(Major)
Season 5, Episode 38
6/4/60

Maverick
A Bullet for the Teacher
(Rand Storm)
Season 4, Episode 7
10/30/60

77 Sunset Strip
Trouble in the Middle East
(Darius)
Season 3, Episode 9
11/11/60

1961
Adventures in Paradise
Angel of Death
(Kahuna)
Season 2, Episode 21
3/6/61

Gunsmoke
Stolen Horses
(Chief Quick Knife)
Season 6, Episode 29
4/8/61

Gunslinger
The Death of Yellow Singer
(Two Bows)
Season 1, Episode 11
5/11/61

Tallahassee 7000
The Hostage" and "Best Laid Plans
(Otto)
Season 1, Episodes 16 and 17
5/14/61 and 5/21/61

Whispering Smith
This Mortal Coil
(Rex Denton/Mr. Hamilton)
Season 1, Episode 12
7/24/61

The Bob Cummings Show
Fifi
Guest Star
Season 1, Episode 8
11/23/61

Adventures in Paradise
The Assassins
(Totani)
Season 3, Episode 9
11/26/61

Follow the Sun
The Girl from the Brandenburg Gate
(Mosley)
Season 1, Episode 16
12/31/61

1962

77 Sunset Strip
Diplomatic Caper
(Benin)
Season 4, Episode 19
1/26/62

1964

Walt Disney's Wonderful World of Color
The Ballad of Hector, the Stowaway Dog
(Circus Roustabout)
Season 10, Episode 12
1/5/64

Temple Houston
The Gun That Swept the West
Guest Star
Season 1, Episode 23
3/5/64

Grindl
Grindl: Girl Wac
(German Major)
Season 1, Episode 25
3/15/64

The Outer Limits
The Chameleon
(General Crawford)
Season 1, Episode 31
4/27/64

Combat!
Mountain Man
(German Officer)
Season 3, Episode 1
9/15/64

1965

F Troop
Scourge of the West
(Shug Indian Chief)
Season 1, Episode 1
9/14/65

Mister Ed
Ed Sniffs Out a Cold Clue or Coldfinger
(Derek)
Season 6, Episode 3
9/26/65

Get Smart
School Days
(Zukor)
Season 1, Episode 3
10/2/65

Honey West
A Matter of Wife and Death
(Alexander Sebastian)
Season 1, Episode 4
10/8/65

Branded
Fill No Glass for Me, Part One
(Cleve)
Season 2, Episode 8
11/7/65

1966

Daniel Boone
The Deserter
(Lije Moody)
Season 2, Episode 18
1/20/66

Laredo
Miracle at Massacre Mission
(Quahada)
Season 1, Episode 23
3/3/66

Combat!
A Child's Game
(Hans)
Season 5, Episode 6
10/18/66

1967

The Virginian
Yesterday's Timepiece
(Swift Wolf)
Season 5, Episode 17
1/18/67

Mr. Terrific
Harley and the Killer
(Herman J. Von Brock)
Season 1, Episode 10
3/20/67

Custer
Breakout
(Fire Cloud)
Season 1, Episode 8
11/1/67

1969

Get Smart
Pheasant Under Glass
(Belasco)
Season 5, Episode 1
9/26/69

Mission: Impossible
The Brothers (Farid)
Season 4, Episode 11
12/14/69

1970
Omnibus
Ian Fleming: Creator of the James Bond Myth
Guest Star
Season 4, Episode 1
1/4/70

1972
O'Hara, U. S. Treasury
Operation: Lady Luck
(Ham Jason)
Season 1, Episode 15
1/14/72

1973
Night Gallery
The Doll of Death"
(Vereker)
Season 3, Episode 15
5/20/73

1975
Kolchak: The Night Stalker
The Trevi Collection
(The Man)
Season 1, Episode 14
1/24/75

The Rookies
The Voice of Thunder
(Doug Shore)
Season 4, Episode 14
12/9/75

1978
Bud and Lou
(Bernie)
TV Movie
11/15/78

1981
Evita Peron
(General Ramirez)
TV Movie
2/23/81

1983
Little House on the Prairie
Look Back to Yesterday"
(Otis Wagner)
TV Movie
12/12/83

1984
E/R
Say It Ain't So
(Mr. Pavlic)
Season 1, Episode 7
10/16/84

Murder, She Wrote
Crossed Up
(Abel Gorcey)
Season 3, Episode 13
2/1/87

Index

Abbott & Costello 246, 380
Adams, Don 367-368
Adams, Nick 343
Adventures In Paradise 355-356
Adventures Of Jim Bowie 321-322
Adrian, Iris 407
Ahn, Philson 140-141
American Film Institute, The 72
Ames, Leon 144
Anderson, Dame Judith 77, 208, 335-338, 436, 456-459, 462-465
Andrews, Dana 167, 170
Angel, Heather 104
Ankers, Evelyn 257
Ansara, Michael 354, 441
Armendariz, Pedro 276,
Arness, James 350
Arsenic And Old Lace 470
Assault On Precinct 13 290-291, 491
Atwill, Lionel 21, 189,
Auntie Mame 188, 210-213, 490
Avery, Tol 249

Babes In Toyland 1, 2, 4, 5, 22-32, 62, 86, 120, 126, 215, 301, 331, 348, 383, 387, 390, 399, 402, 404, 409, 411, 416-417, 419, 423, 426-427, 429, 433, 445, 451, 478
Bad Man Of Deadwood 149, 151-153, 484
Ballantyne, Lisa 423, 438-441
Bandido! 206-207, 489
Bann, Richard W. 23, 30, 147, 424
Barber of Seville, The 87, 88
Barclay, Joan 225
Barker, Lex 256-257, 261
Barnum, P. T. 13, 15
Barry, Gene 267-268
Barrymore, John 192
Bartosh, Alex 398
Bavaria Studios 276
Bean, Orson 434
Beau Geste 193-194, 482
Becker, Elliot 402, 407
Beckett, Scotty 316
Beebe, Ford 163
Beery, Noah Jr. 244
Bell, Gault 13, 16, 18,
Bennett, Joan 101, 187, 241

Beregi, Oscar 370
Bergman, Ingrid 198
Berkeley Square 12
Berry, Ken 360
Big Brown Eyes 101-103, 479
Big Fisherman, The 213-214, 490
Black Legion 186, 221-223, 479
Blaine, Vivian 410
Bletcher, Billy 24,
Blue, Monte 130-132
Blyth, Ann 261
Bob Hope Show, The 331
Bogart, Humphrey 186, 221-223, 311, 339, 387
Bolton, Whitney 82
Bond, Ward 196, 199, 311, 323, 331, 338, 342-343, 348
Boone, Richard 311, 327-328
Borgnine, Ernest 201
Borzage, Frank 191
Bosley, Tom 384
Boudoir 455
Boyer, Charles 185-186
Brady, Scott 245, 347
Branded 362
Brandon, Dolores (Comely) 74, 75, 76, 79, 449-450
Brandon, Henry Richard (Rick) 74, 75, 76, 79, 222, 448-450
Brass Rail, The 29,
Brenner, Yul 208, 210
Brent, Evelyn 120, 121,
Bride Of Frankenstein, The 124, 127, 134,
Bromberg, J. Edward 156
Bronco 345-346, 349-350
Bronson, Charles 201

Brooks, Mel 101, 367, 381, 383
Brown, Peter 332, 363
Buccaneer, The 209-210, 489
Buck Rogers 119, 133-141, 163, 417, 437, 481
Bud And Lou 380, 387
Burgess, Kara 288
Burr, Raymond 260-261
Bus Stop 469-470
Byrd, Ralph 240

Caddy, The 113-115, 487
Call Of The Cuckoos Tent 408, 410, 425-426
Cameron, Rod 161
Cannon, Vince 288
Canon City 245-246, 485
Canutt, Yakima 141
Captain Sindbad 276-280, 296, 356-357, 429, 490
Carpenter, John 290
Carroll, John 157
Carnival In Paris 90, 158, 480
Carradine, David 295-296, 298-299
Carradine, John 185, 208
Carter, Helena 200
Caruso, Anthony 180, 275-276, 403, 406-407, 409, 414-416, 433
Casanova's Big Night 116-117, 331, 488
Casey, Jack 22
Cass, Peggy 212
Cassara, Bill 68, 72, 297, 307, 309, 330, 397-399, 406-407, 409, 423, 425-426, 429, 432-434, 437, 439-440, 442-443
Castle, Peggie 109, 162, 173, 333
Cattle Drive 158-160, 486

Cinemacabre Magazine 80, 119, 317
Chandler, Jeff 164, 166, 264
Chaney, Lon 26
Chaney, Lon Jr. 126-127, 132, 218-219, 263-264, 273-274, 276
Chapin, Michael 161
Chase, Charley 24, 25,
Chatterton, Tom 49,
Christian, Michael 293
Christie, Al 103
Clark, Fred 211
Clooney, George 383
Cody, Iron-Eyes 65, 108, 415, 441
Coe, Peter 282
Cohen, Gary 18, 410-411, 416, 419, 425-426
Collins, Jim 26
Columbia Studios 109, 125, 133, 217, 223, 243
Comanche 65, 167-171, 488
Combat! 360-361, 371-372
Conquest 186-187, 480
Conried, Hans 94,
Conspiracy 234, 482
Cooper, Gary 193, 201, 205
Corman, Roger 295
Corrado, Geno 86, 87
Corsican Brothers, The 200, 251-252, 484
Crabbe, Buster 133, 138, 141
Craig, John 66, 443, 445-446
Cristal, Linda 168, 175, 178
Currier, Richard 388, 405
Custer 376-377

Dance Of Death 10
Daniel Boone 362
Daniell, Henry 21,

Dante The Magician 74, 76, 449
Dantine, Helmut 77
Dare, Jay 405
Dark Of The Moon 461
Dark Streets Of Cairo 239-241, 483
Davidson, Max 24
Davis, Rufe 154
Davis, Joan 101, 109-
Days Of The Dancing 468
De Carlo, Yvonne 208, 249-250, 265
DeBorba, Dorothy 388, 390, 394, 405, 407
DeMille, Cecil B 18, 182, 208-210
Denny, Reginald 215
Deputy, The 339-340
Devine, Andy 158, 175, 373-374
Dietrich, Marlene 185
Disney, Walt 38,
Donlevy, Brian 193
Doomed To Die 236-238, 483
Dorn, Philip 242
Dracula 54, 120, 234, 268
Drake, Francis 215
Drew, Norma 407
Drums Of Fu Manchu 24, 44-62, 119, 141, 185, 197, 301, 319, 404-405, 407, 411, 417, 426-427, 482
Drunkard, The 13-20, 25, 29-31, 81, 96, 98, 101, 181, 313, 400, 412-414, 417, 423, 426-427, 435, 437, 445, 451, 459, 470
Dugan, Tom 106
Duff, John 403-404
Dunaway, Faye 381
Duvall, Robert 311, 366

Eagle-Lion Films 245, 247
Eastwood, Clint 409
Eddy, Nelson 197
Edge Of Darkness 74, 80-83, 484
Elam, Jack 201
Electra 454
Elliot, Wild Bill 157-158
E/R 383
Ethridge, Samuel 14
Evita Peron 381
Eyeman, Scott 66
Fairbanks, Douglas Jr. 199, 251-252, 363
Falcone, Rob 376
Family Portrait, A 456-457
Family Theatre 213, 314-315, 357
Farrar, David 261
Federal Theatre Project 73
Feg Murray's Seein' Stars 17
Feldon, Barbara 367
Fellows, Edith 406
Ferrer, Jose 199
Feuer, Cy 51,
Field, John 407
Fields, W. C. 16, 18, 107, 406, 412
Fighting O'Flynn, The 199-201, 486
Film Daily, The 62
Finegan, Richard 104, 129, 131, 135-136, 138, 140-141, 172, 174, 185, 212, 218-219, 228-230, 232, 239, 249-250
Finlayson, James 24, 186, 400
Flame Of Araby 164, 263-264, 486
Flash Gordon 46, 120, 124, 127, 133-135, 315,
Fleming, Rhonda 163
Fleming, Victor 198
Florian 195-196, 482

Flynn, Errol 77, 78,
Flynn, Joe 287
Foch, Nina 208
Fonda, Henry 183-184, 187, 192, 339, 398
Fontaine, Joan 116
Foran, Dick 223
Ford, John 65, 67, 175-176, 179-180, 311, 332, 345
Ford, Wallace 126-127
For The Love Of Henry 438-440
Foster, Preston 231, 244
Francis, Anne 367
Frankel, Glenn 67, 72
Frankenstein 54, 120, 123, 234, 268
Franklin, Gloria 49,
Franklin, Joe 441, 443
Freeman, Kathleen 330, 407
Frye, Dwight 54, 234
F-Troop 312, 317, 360-361, 383
Fu Manchu Strikes Back 61

Garbo, Greta 186-187, 189
Garden Of Allah, The 73, 185-186, 240, 479
Garland, Judy 428
Garvin, Anita 388, 394, 406, 410, 425
Gentle Savage 287-288, 301, 490
Get Smart 367-369, 382-383
Ghost Treasure 93, 94, 483
Gilbert, Billy 390
Girl Of The Golden West 468
Golden Horde, The 261-263, 486
Gordon, Roger 1, 419-420
Gordon, Ruth 77
Gould, Elliott 383
Granger, Dorothy 410

Granger, Farley 324
Grant, Cary 101-103, 363
Grapewin, Charley 189
Gray, Becky 417
Greene, David 429-431
Greene, Rick 33, 34, 44, 50, 52, 53, 55, 105, 110, 113-114, 182, 197, 216, 253, 258, 269, 305, 315, 318, 358, 390-392, 395-396, 400, 402-405, 408, 423-431, 434, 438-440, 443-447
Gregory, James 340
Grenier, Larry 29, 31
Gunsmoke 317, 350-351, 372, 382

Haas, Hugo 197
Hackett, Buddy 380
Haggarty, Dan 305
Haig, Sid 298-299
Hal Roach Studios 5, 25, 26, 29, 85, 101, 111, 134, 186, 316, 359, 388, 394, 429
Half A Sinner 103-106, 482
Han, Sharry 397-398
Hardy Price, Lucille 392, 394, 403, 405, 410, 425
Harem Girl 109-111, 486
Hardin, Ty 345
Hardsuk, Betty 11
Hassan, Jammel 185
Hatley, Marvin 135, 388-389, 394, 403, 405, 410, 425
Hatton, Raymond 121,
Have Gun – Will Travel 317, 327
Hawes, Tony 3, 17, 400-401, 405, 408-410, 412, 414-416, 420, 430, 433-434

Hayden, Russell 243
Hayes, Annette 177
Hayes, Gabby 149, 151, 169
Hayes, Linda 234
Hell's Crossroads 171-175, 469, 489
Henreid, Paul 247
Henry, Charlotte 33, 419
Herbert, Victor 37, 42
Herron, Mark 292, 428, 432, 434
Heston, Charlton 163, 164, 208, 210
Hollow Triumph 247-248, 485
Hollywood Knights/Hard Knocks 292, 387, 492
Hollywood '80 393-394
Honey West 367
Hood, Darla 85, 89, 388
Hope, Bob 64, 65, 101, 108-109, 111, 115-117, 331, 383, 387, 437
Horton, Edward Everett 360
Horton, Robert 323, 338
Hudson, Rochelle 232-233
Hudson, Rock 249-250
Hull, Henry 189
Hunter, Jeffrey 68,
Hurricane Smith (1941) 156, 484
Hurricane Smith (1952) 265-266, 487
Huston, Walter 77
Hyatt, Irv 396-397

I Met My Love Again 187-189, 481
Inspector General, The 10
Intra-Tent Journal, The 423-424, 427, 443
I Promise To Pay 223-225, 480
Ireland, John 265
Island Captives 186, 225-226, 480
Iverson Ranch 56, 153, 155, 173, 327,

Jean, Gloria 412-413
Jenks, Frank 231
Joan Of Arc 198-199, 485
Johnson, Payne 404
Jones, Shirley 175, 178
Joyce, Brenda 256
Jungle Jim 118-127, 134, 163, 186, 256, 479

Kane, Becky 4, 6, 418
Kantus, Paul 416
Karloff, Boris 18, 45, 46, 47, 62, 236-238
Karns, Virginia 4, 392
Kaye, Danny 101, 115, 383, 387, 437
Keaton, Buster 108, 407, 415
Keaton, Eleanor 407
Kellard, Robert 56,
Kelly, Patsy 24, 25
Kempster, Del 262, 420-421
Kennedy, Edgar 24, 212
Kennedy, George 340
Kerry, Margaret 404
Kibbee, Guy 189
King, John 105,
Killer At Large 217-221, 479
Kleinbach, Hildagard 7,
Kleinbach, Hugo 6, 65, 73, 434
Kleinbach, Hugo O. 7, 8, 10,
Kleinbach, Maria 7,
Knight, Felix 1, 4, 392, 402
Knock On Wood – 115-116, 488
Kolchak The Night Stalker 379-380, 437
Kolk, Scott 129, 417
Korman, Harvey 380

Lady Godiva Of Coventry 164, 263-265, 488
Lady Precious Stream 454-455
Lady's Not For Burning 466
Lamour, Dorothy 192
Lancaster, Burt 201, 203, 205
Land Unknown, The 209, 268-273, 365, 387, 411, 437, 489
Landon, Michael 382-383
Lane, Allan 234
Langdon, Harry 24,
Langdon, Mabel 403, 405
Lansbury, Angela 383
Laredo 363-365
Last Train From Madrid, The 192, 480
Last Warning, The 231
Laurel And Hardy 1, 2, 4, 24-28, 32, 34-43, 107-108, 149, 356, 383, 387-388, 390, 392, 397, 399-404, 408, 415, 437
Laurel Hawes, Lois 1, 392-394, 400, 403, 405, 408, 410, 420, 425
Lawless Years, The 340-342
Lawman 162, 173, 312, 317, 325, 332-333, 346, 363-364
Lee, Christopher 62
Lee, Porky 85, 88, 388, 394
Lee, Rowland V. 241
LeMay, Alan 66
Lesser, Sol 256, 260
Lewis, Jerry 111-115, 330, 370
Life, Loves And Adventures Of Omar Khayyam, The 209, 489
Life Of Emile Zola, The 98
Lind, Della 392, 394
Little House On The Prairie 381-383
Littlefield, Lucien 232-233

Livingston, Robert 154
Lloyd, Frank 143
Lloyd, Harold 24,
Lloyd, Venice 406
Lom, Herbert 214
Los Angeles Times 19, 25, 31, 402, 435, 460-462, 468
Love, Montagu 242
Lucas, George 58,
Luhman (Lubman), Kathy 416
Lugosi, Bela 238
Lux Radio Theatre, The 98

Macbeth 458-459, 461
Mack, Helen 223
MacMurray, Fred 183-184
Mahoney, Jock 268-270
Maier, Marcus 82, 295, 431
Main, Marjorie 196
Malone, Dorothy 111, 112
Manhandlers, The 288-289, 294, 301, 491
Marion, Ruth 14, 16
Marriage Of Nannette 8
Marshal, Alan 187
Marshall, George 111
Marshall, Trudy 392
Marshal Of Mesa City, The 144-149, 482
Martin & Lewis 101, 111-114, 116, 383, 387, 437
Martin, Dean 111-114
Marvin, Lee 322
Marx, Groucho 16,
Mask Of Fu Manchu, The 45
Masquer's Club 402, 410, 415-416, 430, 470
Massey, Ilona 198

Massey, Raymond 209
Mathis, Jack 44
Maverick 317, 325, 351-352, 382
Mazurki, Mike 170, 416
McCabe, John 1, 388, 424
McCarey, Leo 27
McCarey, Raymond 27, 28
McCoy, Phil and Phyllis 411, 442
McCrea, Joel 143, 158, 186
McFarland, Spanky 85, 87-90, 183, 388, 394-395, 397-398
McGavin, Darren 379
McGee, Corliss 28
McIntire, John 166
McNally, Stephen 171
Medea 335-338, 369, 436, 450, 462-465
Meins, Gus 34,
Memphis Film Festival, The 414-415
Metropolitan Nocturne 91, 451, 478
MGM Studios 90, 120, 186, 189, 195, 256, 276
Mickey Mouse 41,
Middleton, Charles 46
Middleton, Ray 156
Midnight Patrol Tent, The 30, 43, 409, 437
Miles, Vera 69, 291-292
Milland, Ray 193
Mission: Impossible 377-378
Mission To Glory: A True Story 180, 301, 491
Missouri Legend 468-469
Mitchell, Thomas 21, 224
Mitchum, Robert 206-207
Mohr, Gerald 274-275
Monogram Studios 161, 163, 236-238
Montalban, Ricardo 180

Monterey Bay Classic Jazz Band, The 412
Montgomery, Robert 96-98
Monument Valley 68, 72, 430
Moore, Clayton 241, 415
Moore, Constance 136,
Moore, Michael 164
Moore, Roger 351
Morris, Bert 31
Morris, Chester 223, 225
Morrison, Patricia 244
Morrison, Sunshine Sammy 394, 405, 407
Morrow, Vic 361, 371
Motion Picture Daily, The 62,
Mr. Ed 369-370, 383
Mr. Terrific 240, 312, 374-376, 383
M-Squad 322-323
Mulligan, Kevin 393
Muni, Paul 98-99
Murder, She Wrote 312, 383-385
Murphy, Audie 326, 355
Murphy, Jimmy 391, 396
My Little Chickadee 108

Nader, George 265
Neale, Anna 194
Nelson, Lori 334
Neumann, Kurt 158
Night Gallery 312, 379-380
Night In New Orleans 244-245, 484
Nimoy, Leonard 311, 377
Nolan, Jeanette 178
Nolan, Lloyd 102, 103
Nollen, Scott 84
Northwest Outpost 197-198, 485
Nugent, Eddie 225
Nurse Edith Cavell 194-195, 482

O'Brien, George 144, 147
O'Hara, Maureen 164, 263-265
Okenenokee 209, 281-285, 490
Old Los Angeles 157-158, 485
Oliver, Edna May 195
Once More With Feeling 466
O'Neal, Blackie 433, 435-436, 456
O'Neal, Ryan 433, 435
Opal, Marcia 3, 386, 389-390,
Our Gang 24, 85, 90, 388, 393, 397, 437
Our Gang Follies Of 1938 32, 85-90, 186, 348, 394, 397-398, 404, 407, 423, 480
Our Relations Tent 408, 410
Outer Limits, The 365-367, 437

Paget, Debra 209
Paiva, Nestor 169
Pal, George 267
Palms, Connie 409, 426
Paleface, The 64, 65, 107-108, 331, 485
Panama, Norman & Frank, Melvin 115
Paramount Studios 26, 143, 192-193, 196, 209, 215, 261, 265
Parker, Fess 362
Parker, Lara 380
Parker, Jean 132,
Pasadena Playhouse, The 12, 28, 453
Payne, John 273, 325
Payne, Sally 152
Peter Gynt 12
Peter Pan 94, 404
Petke, Ron 443-445
Pickens, Slim 362
Pidgeon, Walter 101,
Pirates Of The Skies 232-234, 481
Pitts, Zasu 195

Platt, Ed 340-341, 369
Preston, Robert 193
Preview Murder Mystery, The 215-216, 479
Price, Ben 403
Price, Vincent 116, 208
Pony Express 163-164, 487

Queen Victoria 452
Quillan, Eddie 240
Quinn, Anthony 209

Raffill, Stewart 303
Raft, George 192
Raiders Of The Lost Ark 58
Raiders Of The Seven Seas 218, 273, 487
Rains, Claude 21
Ramona 84, 459-460
Ranger And The Lady, The 149-151, 483
Rathbone, Basil 116, 185
Ratterman, George 29, 31
Raymond, Alex 120, 126
Real People 393
Reap The Wild Wind 256
Rebel, The 343-345
Reed, Donna 114, 273-274
Reicher, Frank 227-228
Rennie, Michael 209
Republic Studios 45, 46, 47, 55, 62, 91, 119, 141, 149, 154, 156-157, 171, 173, 197, 253-254, 265, 317
Restless Gun, The 325
Reynolds, Marjorie 237
Rhodes, Betty Jane 120
RKO 144, 149, 194, 234
Roach, Hal 5, 24-29, 31, 43, 126, 135, 331, 388-389, 392, 394, 400, 404, 406-407, 409, 413, 446
Road To Rome, The 455-456
Roberts, Florence 33,
Rocky Jones, Space Ranger 315-317
Robinson, Ann 267
Roddenberry, Gene 328
Rogers, Charlie 28,
Rogers, Jean 127, 133
Rogers, Roy 149-153
Rogers, Will 18, 24
Rohmer, Sax 45, 46, 47,
Roland, Gilbert 206
Rolfe, William 47,
Romero, Cesar 180, 201-202, 415-416
Rooney, Joe 4, 420
Rosalie 460
Rossito, Little Angelo 404
Roth, Jack 418
Rowles, Polly 212, 227-228, 230
Royle, William 47, 53
Run For The Roses 291-292, 491
Runyan, Steve 418
Russell, Jane 108,
Russell, John 319, 332, 415
Russell, Gail 256
Russell, Rosalind 210
Rutherford, Ann 90

Salter, Hans 236, 239, 241
San Diego Union 73
San Francisco Chronicle 10
Sanchez, Gali 68
Sanders, George 21, 195, 241
Saps At Sea Tent 405, 407-408, 410-411, 428-429
Satterfield, Bob 391, 393-396, 401, 404, 434

Saxon, John 213
Scared Stiff 111-113, 487
Scarlet Angel, The 249, 486
Schnitzelbank 18, 399-401, 407, 410, 418
Scott, Zachary 206
Search For The Evil One 285-287, 289, 301, 357, 490
Searchers, The 22, 23, 24, 62, 63-72, 167, 176-177, 180, 301, 311, 327, 387, 426, 429-430, 437-438, 446, 489
Secret Agent X-9 119, 126-133, 163, 186, 218, 417, 479
Sellers, Peter 62
Sennett, Mack 24,
Selznick International Pictures 185, 257
Serling, Rod 378
Shakespeare, William 9, 47, 63, 315, 458, 465
Sharpe, David 140-141
Shepard Of The Hills 65, 196, 484
Sheridan, Ann 77, 78, 80
Sherman, George 164
Shield, LeRoy 135, 418
Shobe, Preston 13
Shotgun Slade 346-347
Sidermann, Morris 52
Sitka, Emil 111
Skretvedt, Randy 28, 29, 31, 36, 434,
Ski Patrol 235-236, 482
Smith, Paul 375-376
Smith, Kent 167
Smith, Shawn 268
Soldiers Of Fortune 319-321
Son Of Frankenstein 236, 241
Son Of Monte Cristo, The 241-242, 483

Sons Of The Desert 1, 26, 30, 90, 238, 300, 330, 375, 386, 388-411, 413, 424-425, 430, 432, 443-445
Spawn Of The North 192-193, 481
Spielberg, Steven 58
Stagecoach 65, 176, 376
Stanford University 8, 9, 10, 11
Star Trek 135, 261, 316, 328
Starlog Magazine 8, 57, 96, 120, 134, 256, 273
Steel, Tom 140
Steele, Robert 154
Stedman, Eric 46, 51, 320
Stephenson, Ron 417
Stevens, Warren 333-334,
Stewart, Jimmy 175, 177, 311
Stockwell, Dean 158
Storch, Larry 360
Stories Of The Century 317-318
Story Of A Soldier 462
Strimpell, Stephen 375
Sugarman, Abe 73
Sullavan, Margaret 189
Sumac, Yma 209
Suspense 311-314
Suspicion 325-326
Switzer, Alfalfa 85, 87-90,

Talbot, Lyle 227, 229-231
Talk Of The Town 29, 66, 443-444
Taming Of The Shrew 465
Tamiroff, Akim 251
Tarzan And The She-Devil 260-261, 487
Tarzan The Ape Man 120, 256
Tarzan's Magic Fountain 256-260, 486
Taylor, Kent 232
Taylor, Robert 189, 191

Ten Commandments, The 208, 213, 489
Texan, The 334-335
Thatcher, Torin 115
Theatre Mart 13, 18, 19, 25, 27, 435, 459
Thiess, Ursula 206
Thomas, Buckwheat 85, 89, 388, 394
Thompson, Zan 435-436
Three Comrades 189-191, 481
Three Musketeers 461
Todd, Thelma 24, 25
To Be Or Not To Be 301, 381, 492
Tolzmann, Tracy 3, 397, 411, 420
Tombstone Territory 329
Tone, Franchot 189
Tower Beyond Tragedy 457-458
Trail Of The Lonesome Pine 181-184, 196, 215, 251, 339, 394, 397, 417, 446, 451, 478
Troilus And Cressida 453-454
Tucker, Forrest 163-164, 360
Twelfth Night 465
Two In A Taxi 243-244, 484
Two Rode Together 175-180, 490
Tyler Jordan, Richard 212

Under Texas Skies 154-155, 483
Underground 242-243, 483
United Artists 206, 241, 245, 273
Universal Studios – 45, 52, 103, 119-120, 125, 126, 133, 199, 227, 235, 239, 250, 256-257, 261, 268, 273

Vale, Virginia 144
Vasquez Rocks – 136
Vaughn, Robert 171
Vera Cruz 201-206, 488
Vertigo 177

Villain Still Pursues Her, The 96-98
Virginian, The 363, 372-374, 377

Wagon Train 199, 312, 323-324, 331-332, 338-339, 342-343, 346, 348-349, 354, 377
Wagons West 161-163, 293, 487
Wake Of The Red Witch 65, 253-256, 485
Walsh, Raoul 103
Walston, Ray 376
Walt Disney Presents 276
Walt Disney Studios 94, 96, 357
Walt Disney's Wonderful World Of Color 266, 357-359
Wanger, Walter 187
War Arrow 65, 164-167, 263, 360, 488
War Of The Worlds 267-268, 365, 487
Warner Bros 77, 81, 186, 211, 225, 242, 350, 352
Waxman, Franz 124, 127,
Way Out West Tent 388, 401-408, 410-411, 423, 446
Wayne, John 23, 66, 68, 71, 72, 91, 154, 196, 253-254, 311, 387, 430
Wayne, Patrick 434
Weaver, Dennis 165
Weissmuller, Johnny 125, 256
Welles, Orson 267
Wells, Jacqueline 149
Wells Fargo 143, 186, 480
West Bound Limited 163, 212, 227-231, 480
When The North Wind Blows 292, 301-309, 359, 416, 491
Whispering Smith 355
Whitman, Stuart 291

Widmark, Richard 175, 177
Wilde, Cornell 209
Wiley, James II 419
Williams, Guy 276
Williams, Jeffrey 18
Wills, Chill 159
Wilson, Dooley 244
Withers, Grant 120, 121,
Wizards Of The Lost Kingdom II 292, 294-300, 381, 395, 442, 492
Wood, Helen 96, 97
Wood, Lana 68,
Wood, Natalie 70, 176
Woods, William 77

Wooley, Monte 189
Worden, Hank 407, 434
Wyatt, Jane 156
Wynn, Keenan 180, 293-294

Young, Alan 369-370, 415
Young, Gig 254
Young, Robert 189, 195

Zorro's Fighting Legion 46
Zucco, George 21, 189, 238-240

77 Sunset Strip 312, 352-354

About the Authors:

BILL CASSARA IS A retired law enforcement professional whose interest in film comedy is long standing. He founded the Midnight Patrol tent in the Sons of the Desert-Laurel & Hardy appreciation society in 1984 which thrives to this day in Niles, California. He has written three books: *Edgar Kennedy-Master of the Slow Burn* (2005), *Vernon Dent-Stooge Heavy* (2010) and *Ted Healy-Nobody's Stooge* (2014) all published by Bearmanor Media. He lives with his wife, Michelle in Woodland, California.

RICHARD S. GREENE IS also a life-long film comedy buff, having founded the Big Business Tent of Cleveland in 1973, which still is sharing laughs in Ohio. Rick was the Editor of the Sons of the Desert's quarterly publication *The Intra-Tent Journal* for most of the 1980's. He has written two comic-fantasy novels entitled *Boofalo!* (2004) and *'Shroom!* (2007). He lives with his wife, Patty and son Anthony in Santa Clarita, California.

www.ingramcontent.com/pod-product-compliance
Lightning Source LLC
Chambersburg PA
CBHW060311230426
43663CB00009B/1666